The Sandinista Revolution

The New Cold War History

Odd Arne Westad, *editor*

This series focuses on new interpretations of the Cold War era made possible by the opening of Soviet, East European, Chinese, and other archives. Books in the series based on multilingual and multiarchival research incorporate interdisciplinary insights and new conceptual frameworks that place historical scholarship in a broad, international context.

A complete list of books published in the New Cold War History is available at https://uncpress.org/series/new-cold-war-history.

The Sandinista Revolution

A Global Latin American History

· ·

MATEO JARQUÍN

The University of North Carolina Press Chapel Hill

© 2024 The University of North Carolina Press
All rights reserved
Set in Charis by Westchester Publishing Services
Manufactured in the United States of America

Library of Congress Cataloging-in-Publication Data
Names: Jarquín, Mateo, author.
Title: The Sandinista revolution : a global Latin American history /
    Mateo Jarquín.
Other titles: Global Latin American history | New Cold War history.
Description: Chapel Hill : The University of North Carolina Press, [2024] |
    Series: New Cold War history | Includes bibliographical references and
    index.
Identifiers: LCCN 2023048930 | ISBN 9781469678481 (cloth ; alk. paper) |
    ISBN 9781469678498 (pbk. ; alk. paper) | ISBN 9781469678504 (epub) |
    ISBN 9798890887283 (pdf)
Subjects: LCSH: Frente Sandinista de Liberación Nacional—History. |
    World politics—20th century. | Nicaragua—History—Revolution,
    1979—Influence. | Nicaragua—Politics and government—1979–1990. |
    Nicaragua—History—1979–1990. | Latin America—Politics and
    government—1980– | BISAC: HISTORY / Latin America / General |
    POLITICAL SCIENCE / International Relations / General
Classification: LCC F1528 J37 2024 | DDC 972.8505/3—dc23/eng/20231103
    LC record available at https://lccn.loc.gov/2023048930

Cover art by Luca Nicoletti on unsplash.com.

This book will be made open access within three years of publication
thanks to Path to Open, a program developed in partnership between
JSTOR, the American Council of Learned Societies (ACLS), the University
of Michigan Press, and the University of North Carolina Press to bring
about equitable access and impact for the entire scholarly community,
including authors, researchers, libraries, and university presses around
the world. Learn more at https://about.jstor.org/path-to-open/.

For Claudia and Edmundo

Contents

Maps

Preface

Writing the History of the Nicaraguan Revolution

A few years ago—in May 2019, to be exact—I helped organize a conference on the history of the Sandinista Revolution. The meetings, held over three days at Brown University's Watson Institute for International and Public Affairs, deliberately coincided with an anniversary: forty years had passed since the collapse of Nicaragua's Somoza regime.[1] The conference brought together top commanders, ideologues, and policymakers from the left-wing Sandinista National Liberation Front (FSLN) that ruled Nicaragua for a decade after leading the dictatorship's overthrow in 1979. It also convened senior figures from the anti-Sandinista opposition, including the United States–backed Contra insurgency. Never before, faculty organizer Stephen Kinzer noted, had leaders from both sides met to publicly reflect on their involvement in—and responsibility for—the revolutionary conflicts that rocked Nicaragua in the 1970s and '80s.[2] Like similar post–Cold War rendezvous in Hanoi (also sponsored by Brown's Watson Institute) and Havana, former US diplomats also participated.[3] There was also an intergenerational component; representatives from a new generation of Nicaraguan political actors—twenty-something university leaders—bore witness and lent shape to the conversation.

Anybody who attended Nicaragua 1979–1990: The Sandinista Revolution after 40 Years must have been struck by two things. First, Nicaraguans are only beginning to ask—let alone confront—the basic historical questions of the Sandinista Revolution: its origins, its character, its legacies. For the participants looking back upon their early political careers, the panel sessions on various topics—such as the war that wrecked the country in the 1980s, or the great hopes and disappointments that accompanied social reform efforts—seemed like an emotionally exhausting exercise. Second, we very much need answers to those historical questions. Public life in Nicaragua today—its political arrangements, institutions, the way people identify themselves—developed as a result of, or in reaction to, the conflicts engendered by the crisis of the Somoza dictatorship and the subsequent attempt by the Sandinistas to rapidly vanquish poverty and inequality. We live, to paraphrase Mexican intellectuals writing about their own country's contemporary history, in the "shadow" of the Sandinista Revolution.[4] Many attendees spent as much time debating Nicaragua's present as they did relitigating its Cold War past. This was especially true for those from my age cohort; I was born in 1991, when *la revolución* and *la guerra* had already become memories. The revolutionary period's ideological polarization and violence—tens of thousands of Nicaraguans lost their lives from armed conflict in the 1970s and '80s, a monstrous sum in a country its size—makes it hard even today, even for those who did not experience it firsthand, to discuss what took place. But enough time has passed, and sufficient sources have been mined, for the Revolution to become history. This book is an early contribution toward that collective goal.

Four decades ago, Sandinista leaders were something like global celebrities. By virtue of their outsized ambitions and plucky defiance of US hegemony, they had become icons of the late Cold War era. "David and Goliath! Progressive socialist guerrillas, undogmatic and good-looking, too! The world went wild," as journalist Alma Guillermoprieto recently put it.[5]

But many readers will be more familiar with the Nicaraguan drama through American characters like President Ronald Reagan and Lieutenant Coronel Oliver North, who—perceiving a Soviet-sponsored threat in Central America—worked to undermine the FSLN government in Managua (most famously by arming the opposition). Historian Piero Gleijeses has helpfully observed that, unlike paramilitary operations in other countries like Cuba and Angola, this one was known to the American public as it unfolded.[6] Therefore, events in Sandinista Nicaragua prompted passionate arguments among American citizens that unfolded in the US Congress and on university campuses. With the ghost of Vietnam looming large, they debated whether it was necessary to intervene in another impoverished, Third World "hot spot." And as details of the Reagan administration's illegal Contra efforts came to light, a crisis emerged over transparency and accountability at the highest levels of government.

Those debates colored US-based scholarship on the Nicaraguan Revolution in various ways. We see their influence in a stream of publications from the era that analyzed FSLN governance with an eye toward either confirming or debunking Reagan's view that the Sandinistas were fanatical, tyrannical, and incompetent communists who had to be stopped. The political stakes of the 1980s also reveal themselves in the prevailing tendency, at least outside of country specialists, to think of the Sandinista Revolution primarily as a chapter in the history of US foreign relations. This is not always a bad thing. For example, historians approaching from this vantage point have used the Nicaraguan Revolution to look back and explore the broader scope of American hegemony in Latin America, or to look forward and better contextualize twenty-first-century adventures in Iraq and Afghanistan.[7] Additionally, analysts have successfully assessed the motivations and consequences of Reagan's intervention in Nicaragua. This work is indispensable, not only because US citizens deserve to know what their leaders do abroad in their name, but also because American policies—which went beyond the Contra operation to include economic sanctions, diplomatic isolation, and direct sabotage by CIA agents—had a decisive impact on Nicaragua's revolutionary process. Among other things, they constrained the Sandinistas' policymaking and helped fuel the devastating armed conflict mentioned earlier. And when that war came to a conclusion, the resolution of American policy debates was a decisive factor.[8] Political scientist William Leogrande, who wrote the best account of US foreign policy in Central America in the 1980s, is therefore right to say that the fate of the region's inhabitants "depended fundamentally on decisions made in Washington."[9]

However, they did not exclusively depend on decisions made in Washington. US actors were extraordinarily influential, but their decisions overlapped with a panoply of national and—as the present book seeks to demonstrate—international dynamics. Moreover, viewing Nicaraguan politics exclusively through the narrow prism of US foreign policy debates can both deny local agency and create unhelpful terms of reference. To begin creating new histories of the Revolution, new context must be given to old frameworks.

I am grateful to follow scholars who, writing during and after the Revolution, have transcended Reagan-era framings and treated the topic with necessary nuance. Thanks to their research, it is easier than ever to build histories of twentieth-century Nicaragua that Nicaraguans can actually recognize themselves in. For example, we now know much more about the social, cultural, and economic foundations of the Somoza dictatorship.[10] We also have a more sophisticated understanding of both the early FSLN movement and the broader revolutionary coalition it led in 1979.[11] Social scientists have mapped out changes and continuities in Nicaraguan political economy and political culture before and after the revolutionary period.[12] Interestingly, historians have even produced thought-provoking analyses of the Revolution's social and cultural memory in Nicaragua today.[13] I say interesting because, as Michel Gobat noted around the time I began my research, most historiography has not yet tackled the revolutionary period itself, when the Sandinista Front actually ruled the country.[14]

In my research for this book, I strove to center the story on the Nicaraguans who wielded state power between 1979 and 1990: the political and military elite of the Sandinista government, with a special focus on its foreign relations apparatus. This design choice posed several obstacles. For one, Nicaragua lacks a strong and accessible public archives system. To gain an inside perspective on the FSLN leadership, I leveraged personal contacts and found nontraditional sources of documentation, such as the private archives of senior Sandinista officials who had crates of untouched documents collecting dust in their homes. Alejandro Bendaña graciously provided documents from the Sandinistas' Ministry of Foreign Relations, where he served as secretary general. Importantly, the personal papers of Sergio Ramírez (member of the Junta of National Reconstruction, 1979–84; vice president, 1985–90), archived at Princeton University's Firestone Library, complemented FSLN-related materials housed at the now defunct Instituto de Historia de Nicaragua y Centroamérica (IHNCA) at Universidad Centroamericana (UCA).[15] Cuba's Ministry of Foreign Relations Archive was another unexpected repository of internal FSLN government documents. Finally, I consulted countless published memoirs and documentary collections produced by revolutionaries, counterrevolutionaries, and everyone in between. Thanks to the recentness of this historical episode and the relative youth of its protagonists, oral history was a viable research methodology. I conducted on-the-record interviews with members of the FSLN's nine-person National Directorate (the collective, supreme leadership of the Revolution), generals from the Sandinista Popular Army, top diplomats, and numerous figures from the party intelligentsia. MP3s or rough transcripts of these conversations are available upon request. I spoke with many more off the record.

My research also reconfigures the terrain upon which the Sandinista Revolution unfolded. Nicaragua, like all other countries in the Western Hemisphere, does not exist in a vacuum with the United States. Beyond key socialist partners like the Soviet Union and Cuba, state and non-state actors from Europe, Africa, Asia, and the Middle East saw something relevant at play in Central America's Cold War conflicts and involved themselves in ways that shaped the Nicaraguan revolutionary process. The stakes were particularly high in Latin America, where the 1979 Sandinista Revolution represented the first seizure of state power by the armed Left since the Cuban Revolution twenty years earlier. Thus, I also procured archival sources and conducted oral history interviews with leaders in Mexico City, Havana, San José (Costa Rica), and Panama City.

In pursuing this multisite, transnational research, I worked in tandem with other young historians who have been taking the Sandinistas beyond the realm of US–Latin American relations.[16] All of us are influenced by on-going efforts by Latinamericanists to provide a more kaleidoscopic vision of the region's Cold War experience, which themselves form part of a broader wave of "new Cold War histories"—often associated with Odd Arne Westad's *The Global Cold War: Third World Interventions and the Making of Our Times*—that understand twentieth-century international history as being shaped by a global ideological confrontation between capitalism and communism that involved Asian, African, and Middle Eastern leaders as much as Europeans and North Americans.[17] Especially influential to me are histories of Third World revolutions that take the perspective of their leaders and place their dilemmas in international perspective; these include Tanya Harmer's work on Chile's Allende government, Lien-Hang Nguyen on North Vietnam, Matthew Connelly on Algeria's war for independence, and Paul Chamberlin on the Palestine Liberation Organization (PLO).[18] Following these examples, a globalized, international history of the Sandinistas can help us better understand Nicaragua's revolutionary process because events, actors, and conflicts beyond the country were a key variable in determining the possibilities for change inside it. At the same time, this approach frees up space to ask what the Sandinista episode tells us about international politics in the years immediately before and after the Cold War ended.

As scholars revisit the Sandinista Revolution and place it in global perspective, they must think carefully about how to characterize the Nicaraguan actors involved. Specifically, new histories must refuse the temptation to either romanticize or demonize Sandinista leaders. The same goes for their opponents. All revolutions have a Manichaean quality, and contemporary polarization in Nicaragua—where longtime Sandinista leader Daniel Ortega has consolidated a family dictatorship built upon an unforgiving police state—has accentuated this facet in the Revolution's historical memory. For solidarity movement activists who traveled to Nicaragua in the 1980s and deposited great hopes in its revolution, or for those in the Nicaraguan diaspora who fled violence or persecution in that period, this history is understandably sensitive. But the 2019 conference at Brown showed that it is possible to reflect in colors beyond black and white. It is also necessary. Nicaraguans today, the vast majority of whom were born after the Revolution, are poorly served by histories that *uncritically* reproduce the perspective of one segment of society, or that otherwise frame the Revolution and subsequent war as stories of heroes and villains, patriots and traitors, or freedom fighters and thugs. This book tries to avoid these sorts of facile characterizations.

This is not to say, of course, that I am free of predispositions. Both of my parents participated enthusiastically in the Sandinistas' revolutionary project. They were joined by many of their friends and relatives. But they found just as many people they cared for, such as some of their siblings, on the other side—including the Contra. Countless Sandinista guerrillas came from somocista families, and many Contra commanders previously cut their teeth fighting in FSLN columns against Somoza's National Guard. Nicaraguan politics, like those of any country, are complicated. Combined with the geopolitical and ideological stakes of the Cold War, that complexity played out in horrific ways during the 1970s and '80s: the conflict between the Sandinista government and the Contra, like the previous war that ousted Somoza, was fought within communities and families. Mine were ripped apart and, in that sense, I am like many Nicaraguans of my age. Being so close to the tearing of the social fabric—as well as the fraught process of reconciliation that came afterward—shaped how I approach Nicaraguans' revolutionary and counterrevolutionary struggles, as well as the violence they entailed.

One thing that makes me different from most Nicaraguans is that I come from a privileged background in a country marked, both before and after the Revolution, by unacceptable levels of poverty and inequality. My parents held relatively senior posts in the FSLN government. My mother, Claudia Lucía Chamorro, is a daughter of Nicaragua's best-known political family, one that has dominated public life since the founding of the republic. Her father Pedro Joaquín, assassinated by the Somoza dictatorship in 1978, was a central figure in the origins of the revolution that triumphed the following year. My grandmother, Violeta Barrios de Chamorro, was a member of the Revolution's first governing Junta and later became president, defeating her former Sandinista allies in elections in 1990. Members of my family continue to play prominent roles in Nicaraguan politics to this day: as influential journalists, presidential hopefuls, and—more recently— as political prisoners and exiles.[19] Unlike most of my compatriots, then, I can say that those close to me have both suffered at the hands of the state and wielded its power. This, too, is reflected in my research. In approaching the history of the Sandinista Revolution, I mostly focus on the thinking and decision making of national elites. A comprehensive account also requires a bottom-up, grassroots perspective that this one lacks. But the concentration of power that comes with overwhelming social inequality—even in the context of a redistributive, socialist-inspired political project—suggests that decisions made by the FSLN upper echelon are a great place to start writing the history of the revolutionary period.

There are countless other ways that my background informs my scholarship. One worth mentioning is that both of my parents were diplomats and later worked for international organizations, and that I spent much of my childhood living outside Nicaragua. It always struck me as curious that the Sandinistas were so well known abroad—that they had found so much success in revolutionizing the international scene—even though they had clearly struggled to bring about social transformation at home. This is one of the motivating ironies of my research. I am also motivated by a basic commitment to help Nicaraguan civil society confront the country's present—and build its future—by engaging first in spirited debates about its recent past. Starting with the introduction to this book, I begin by arguing that the history of the Sandinista Revolution can only be understood in international context. Doing so, I hope, will reveal a story worth revisiting by many people beyond Nicaragua, because it provides a unique window into the end of the Cold War and the global transition to what came afterward.

Abbreviations

AD	Acción Democrática (Venezuela)
ARDE	Alianza Revolucionaria Democrática
ARENA	Alianza Republicana Nacionalista (El Salvador)
COSEP	Consejo Superior de la Empresa Privada
COSIP	Consejo Superior de la Iniciativa Privada
DRI	Departamento de Relaciones Internacionales
EPS	Ejército Popular Sandinista
FAO	Frente Amplio Opositor
FDN	Fuerza Democrática Nicaragüense
FMLN	Frente Farabundo Martí para la Liberación Nacional
FSLN	Frente Sandinista de Liberación Nacional
GPP	Tendencia Guerra Popular Prolongada
IACHR	Inter-American Commission on Human Rights
M-19	Movimiento 19 de Abril (Colombia)
MDN	Movimiento Democrático Nicaragüense
MPU	Movimiento Pueblo Unido
NAM	Non-Aligned Movement
OAS	Organization of American States
PLO	Palestine Liberation Organization
PRI	Partido Revolucionario Institucional (Mexico)
PSN	Partido Socialista Nicaragüense
SI	Socialist International
SMP	Servicio Militar Patriótico
TP	Tendencia Proletaria
UDEL	Unión Democrática de Liberación Nacional
UNO	Unión Nacional Opositora
URNG	Unidad Revolucionaria Nacional Guatemalteca (Guatemala)

The Sandinista Revolution

Introduction

· ·

A Nicaragua obsession gripped the United States in the 1980s. For one, the unlikely overthrow of the US-backed Somoza dictatorship by left-wing guerrillas electrified progressives. Tens of thousands of Americans—including Bernie Sanders, the young mayor of Burlington, Vermont—traveled in solidarity to the previously obscure Central American country to help the Sandinista National Liberation Front (FSLN) redistribute wealth and transform its society. At the same time, the 1979 Sandinista Revolution alarmed conservatives. President Ronald Reagan told Americans that this "malignancy in Managua" would spread Marxist-Leninist terrorism and bring the Soviet threat to America's "doorstep."[1] The US government thus began funding anti-Sandinista insurgents known as the Contra, as in *contrarrevolucionarios*, helping mire Nicaragua in civil war.

That policy also ignited fiery debates in Washington, which culminated in Reagan's near-impeachment during the Iran-Contra scandal. Throughout, Americans used events in Nicaragua to press their case about their country's foreign affairs and domestic politics. Neoconservative intellectual Robert Kagan—a State Department staffer during the Reagan years—recognized that much of the controversy "was not about Nicaragua at all. It was a battle to define America at home and abroad."[2] A flood of scholarship and reporting on the Sandinistas, often based on US sources and adopting the view from Washington, D.C., was strongly colored by those debates. Unsurprisingly, when the FSLN was voted out of office in 1990 and as the Cold War ended, Nicaragua and its revolution lost their centrality in that conversation. The obsession ended rather swiftly.

In Nicaragua, however, the Sandinista Revolution was harder to leave behind. Only a generation ago, it abruptly raised—and then dashed—colossal hopes for socioeconomic and political renewal, generating devastating conflicts in the process that have fundamentally shaped public life in the country ever since. A narrow focus on US foreign policy, aside from denying local agency, cannot tell us why there was a revolution in Nicaragua, what its leaders hoped to accomplish, or how they set about the messy business of remaking a country.

Moreover, the view from Washington can obscure the Nicaraguan Revolution's global dimensions. It was the last gasp of armed revolution—a historical climax, as FSLN leader Sergio Ramírez noted in his memoir, for an entire generation who admired Lumumba and Guevara, read Fanon's *The Wretched of the Earth*, celebrated decolonization in Asia and Africa, protested in 1968, and believed that socialism held the key to modernity and development. In Western Europe, the Sandinistas' promise to blend Marxism with liberal democratic sensibilities played well to an appetite for a "third road" in Cold War politics; English punk rock band The Clash—led by Joe Strummer, a self-described socialist and anti-imperialist who rejected Soviet-style communism—named their fourth album after Nicaragua's revolutionaries.[3] The Revolution's symbolism was especially pronounced in Latin America. Nicaragua represented the hope, Ramírez added, of "retribution for the lost dreams in Chile [after the fall of the Allende government], and even further back, for the lost dreams of the Spanish Republic, passed down through generations since the 1930s."[4]

After all, it was the first and only time since the Cuban Revolution in 1959 that the armed Left seized power in Latin America. This is the primary context through which historians should understand the Nicaraguan Revolution, more than the oft-studied framework of US intervention in the so-called Third World. *The Sandinista Revolution: A Global Latin American History* provides a narrative account of the Sandinistas' rise and fall that is centered on their government and guided by their Revolution's reverberations in Latin America and across the global Cold War. An international history of the Sandinistas allows me to help answer the following questions: Why was there a social revolution in Nicaragua? What did it mean for Latin American politics in the final years of the Cold War? What risks and opportunities did the global confrontation between capitalism and socialism create for the Sandinistas' political project? And how did global trends otherwise inform Nicaragua's revolutionary process? The answers to these questions are crucial to Nicaraguans. But they also put the history of contemporary Latin America—and of the strange global transitions that accompanied the end of the Cold War—in a new light.

To answer these questions, I sought documentary access to the Revolution's military, political, and foreign policy elite. I probed archives containing documents from the Nicaraguan presidency, Foreign Ministry, and internal Sandinista Front institutions. I also conducted oral history interviews with top Sandinista Front officials, including several cabinet officials, generals, and *comandantes* of the nine-person National Directorate—the

Revolution's collective leadership. Oral histories and written testimonies open a window into decision making and motivations where archival access is spotty at best. And, perhaps more interestingly, they allow us to see how Nicaraguan leaders' very notion of revolution changed over time as the situation on the ground—and the world around them—evolved. Because their Revolution was so enmeshed with international affairs, I also explored archives and conducted interviews in Mexico, Cuba, Panama, and Costa Rica. This multinational source base paints a picture of a global event. US diplomat Jeane Kirkpatrick was not alone in seeing Central America as "the most important place in the world" in the 1980s; actors from around the world, from Peru to Palestine, saw much at stake in Nicaragua and invested in either the defense or destruction of the Sandinista Revolution.[5] This may come as a surprise to Nicaraguans today, who are not accustomed to seeing themselves in international headlines. Back in the 1980s, this small country—among the poorest in the Western Hemisphere—impacted the world in a way that belied its size and strategic importance. This is a story of how, and to what effect, a "small" national politics comes to attain very large, global dimensions.

The conventional view of the Cold War as a conflict between great powers sometimes leads to an underappreciation of small states' own interests, autonomy, and capacity to influence events. This is especially true in the Americas. In a historical context of overwhelming US dominance, Latin American countries are sometimes perceived as passively reacting to the policies and whims of the regional hegemon.[6] By contrast, this book treats the FSLN elite that ruled Nicaragua between 1979 and the 1990s as policymakers and statespersons in their own right, situating them in a global decision-making environment rather than the narrow plane of bilateral relations with Washington. For example, I take seriously the worldview and ideology of the Revolution's core leadership. The insurrectionary coalition they led in 1979 was extraordinarily diverse, and Sandinista militants themselves responded to numerous political goals and symbols, including Christian ones derived from the overlap of leftism with the Liberation Theology current of Catholic doctrine. For its part, the National Directorate was "eclectic" in its worldviews and pragmatic in their application to local conditions.[7] But all of its members believed, as Comandante Humberto Ortega noted, that their purpose was at minimum to "assure that future conditions could mature to allow for socialism."[8] Like contemporaries who led decolonizing revolutions in Asia and Africa, they were nationalists who sought modernity and national liberation in a context of underdevelopment and imperialism. But importantly, the top Sandinistas believed that Marxist-Leninist models of politics and development paved the road to that destination. This did not mean, of course, that they attempted a transition to socialism in Nicaragua—as Carlos Vilas argued, little about revolutionary Nicaragua's nonindustrialized agrarian economy, class structure, or politics approximated a model of "real socialism."[9] Nor did they deem such a thing possible in their lifetimes. But it did mean that, after living through a decades-long dictatorship sustained in part by the country's poverty and inequality, their main priority was to democratize society along social and economic lines by redistributing wealth and expanding access to basic services like health care and education. Self-identifying as a "revolutionary vanguard party," they were skeptical about the role of elections, selective in their respect for human rights and individual liberties, and relatively intolerant of criticism from within and without their movement. "Institutionalized political democracy," Comandante Luis Carrión later wrote, "was not an explicit objective of the Revolution."[10]

The book also identifies the FSLN government's strategic goals and plans to achieve them. Once in power, their principal objective was to shield the revolutionary state against a US-backed counterrevolution or direct intervention by American armed forces. But they did not simply react to a threat emanating from Washington; they anticipated and took steps to manage what they considered an inevitable confrontation. For example, they tried to pursue a long-term strategic partnership with the Soviet Union and socialist camp. US hostility limited Nicaraguan options and often pushed them in that direction, but did not determine this policy preference in the first place. This did not mean that the Sandinistas (let alone Soviet analysts) thought that Nicaragua would vault across the Iron Curtain, or that the Reagan administration's pretext for intervention was founded in a reasonable conclusion that this small Central American country threatened the American way of life. Nor did it mean that the FSLN became directed by Soviet or Cuban interests, even as they became dependent on them for survival. In fact, Nicaraguan leaders were conscious of the limits of reliance on Cuba and the Warsaw Pact, especially as signs of Soviet decline became apparent over the course of the 1980s. They therefore diversified their support portfolio, building ties with national liberation movements across the world—including support for an armed leftist revolution in nearby El Salvador. Simultaneously, they worked hard to develop legitimacy in the eyes of Western European and nonaligned states.

In analyzing the Sandinista Front's pursuit of domestic and foreign policy goals, I pay careful attention to how priorities and cost-benefit analyses changed over time. From the beginning of their insurrection to their final days in power, FSLN leaders made decisions for tactical or circumstantial reasons—such as alliances with non-leftist partners or commitments to alter their program—designed to shore up their political project in the short term. But, in a dynamic identified in retrospect by Sandinista leaders such as Sergio Ramírez and Comandante Jaime Wheelock, these tactical maneuvers often took on a life of their own, becoming difficult to reverse and sometimes permanently supplanting their original, strategic vision for revolutionary change.[11] This feedback loop between tactical and strategic choices helps us understand how the young revolutionary leadership struggled to reckon, not always successfully, with one of their core dilemmas: their being trapped—as Ileana Rodríguez recently put it—between liberal and radical political philosophies, believing they could create social harmony by improvising a mix of both.[12] Their idea of the politically possible also changed, of course, as Nicaraguans reacted to their reform agenda in unexpected ways. All of these dynamics in the Nicaraguan revolutionary process were mediated by the interplay between domestic and international factors—my book's core theme.

In taking Sandinista leaders' perspective, the book inevitably complicates the role that Americans played in the Nicaraguan Revolution. Previous histories of Third World revolutions turned Cold War hot spots—such as those in Guatemala in the 1950s or Vietnam and Chile in the 1960s and 1970s—have achieved similar results.[13] In Nicaragua, US policymakers were extraordinarily influential, but never enjoyed the level of control they would have liked. For example, FSLN leaders and their international allies knew well that US president Jimmy Carter did not command the allied Somoza regime, and they manipulated this fact to their advantage. Once in power, they initially judged the Contra—and most anti-government activity, in general—as the work of US agents and exiled remnants of Somoza's National Guard; over time, however, they came to the more nuanced view that the insurgency also had local roots, and that it unfolded in ways that defense and intelligence officials in Washington had not anticipated. By recontextualizing US involvement, we better account for an outcome that saw no clear winners and losers. While US intervention succeeded in creating conditions that undermined FSLN popularity ahead of its defeat in the 1990 elections, the FSLN government survived rather long given the circumstances. Reagan administration hard-liners did not succeed in forcing the Sandinista

Front's military defeat, turning it into an international pariah, or erasing it from Nicaragua's political landscape. This was the case because, contrary to what many might think, American leaders routinely fail to determine outcomes even when they enjoy staggering resource advantages.[14] Another reason was that US foreign policy, as indispensable as it is for Latin American and world politics, was not the only game in town; state and non-state actors from Latin America, Europe, Asia, and Africa also shaped outcomes.

I chose to focus this analysis on the years between 1977 and 1990, the period in which the Sandinistas ruled Nicaragua, and the years immediately preceding the fall of the old regime. It was their seizure of state power that made them unique among Latin American peers in the Cuban Revolution-era armed Left, who otherwise failed to do the same. In fact, the Sandinista Front was far less known than peer organizations until it struck its surprising 1979 victory. This was also what made Nicaragua's revolutionaries relevant in international affairs. By taking and then consolidating state power in the face of foreign intervention, they—among other things—helped intensify struggles for and against revolutionary change in the Americas and set up a crisis in US–Latin American relations. Importantly, this all happened at a time when the face of Latin American politics was changing rapidly. The life span of the Nicaraguan Revolution, waged by socialist revolutionaries against an anti-communist dictator, coincided with a different sort of transformation in the region: the Third Wave of democratization, which saw most Latin American countries transition from military dictatorships toward civilian, democratically elected rule.

This book is organized according to three "phases" of the Sandinista period, which will be familiar to scholars and students of revolutions. Each phase—insurrection and state breakdown, consolidation in power, and civil war—posed unique dilemmas for the revolutionary leadership. The choices they made forged the Revolution's political outcome in the final years of the 1980s, the focus of the book's fourth section and conclusion. My central argument is as follows: At every stage, and in many ways—such as its ideology, the way it organized its political economy, its rise to power in the first place, and surprising outcome in the form of a transition to electoral democracy—the Sandinista Revolution was shaped by how it fit within a global picture. Being so thoroughly internationalized, the Nicaraguan Revolution—like the Mexican and Cuban revolutions before it—helped set the agenda in hemispheric politics: it influenced revolutionary-counterrevolutionary struggles and created terms of reference for debates on sovereignty and democracy at a time when most Latin American countries underwent a watershed political change toward liberal-democratic governance. Globally, the rise and fall of the Sandinistas sheds light on many dynamics that accompanied the Cold War's end. These include the abrupt aggravation and then easing of superpower tensions, the collapse of world communism as an alternative to capitalism, the replacement of bipolarity with multipolarity in international affairs, and the rapid adoption of liberal democracy in areas of the world with little or no prior experience with that form of government.

Part 1 revisits the origins of the 1979 Sandinista Revolution. At least since the publication that year of Theda Skocpol's *States and Social Revolutions*, scholars have increasingly emphasized how international pressures have historically combined with national state characteristics and class dynamics to determine the crisis and collapse of ancien régimes.[15] In Nicaragua, where myriad groups had unsuccessfully tried to topple a family dictatorship for four decades, the FSLN jumped through an opening created by a favorable international context. The Sandinista Revolution could not have succeeded without the confluence of regional actors who worked with Nicaraguan revolutionaries to unseat Somoza and put a significant transformation of society on the agenda.

Chapter 1 surveys the foundations of the Somoza dictatorship and describes how it began to crumble in the 1970s. During this period, various short- and long-term developments in Nicaraguan society created the potential for a broad-based revolutionary coalition that would bridge the gap between working- and middle-class opposition to the regime, while also leveraging the discontent of elite interest groups that had historically collaborated with the dictatorship. At this crucial junction, a faction of the Sandinista Front conspired with a transnational network of allies—such as Colombian writer Gabriel García Márquez and Costa Rican ex-president Pepe Figueres—to make armed, socialist-led revolution viable. By mid-1978, Nicaragua, which previously had seemed like an island of stability, was alive with Sandinista-led insurrection. The situation alarmed Cold War realists like US national security adviser Zbigniew Brzezinski, who suggested buttressing the Somoza regime, a longtime gendarme of US anti-communism in the Caribbean Basin. However, these strategic concerns clashed with President Jimmy Carter's emphasis on human rights as part of his administration's foreign policy agenda. As with the Iranian government of Shah Mohammad Reza Pahlavi, Washington waffled in its support for the old regime, leading the ousted Anastasio Somoza Debayle to decry a "sordid betrayal." In his view, the "nation was truly delivered into the hands of the Marxist enemy by President Jimmy Carter."

But as chapter 2 demonstrates, changes in US foreign policy did not determine a revolutionary outcome. While Somoza was losing the support of his main benefactor, the FSLN was winning key battles abroad. Indeed, the outgoing dictator himself noted that "in this treachery, [Carter's] most active accomplices were Venezuela, Panama, Costa Rica, and Cuba."[16] In fact, these Latin American countries (he should have added Mexico, the ruling party of which played an essential role) were no mere accomplices; they were intellectual and material authors of his replacement by a Sandinista-led revolutionary coalition, an outcome Carter's advisers clearly sought to avert. An ideologically diverse coalition of leaders, including unlikely allies like Fidel Castro and Venezuela's Carlos Andrés Pérez, came together under the shared objective of eliminating Somoza and challenging unilateral US policy in the hemisphere. This transnational fellowship armed the Sandinista Front, helped broker unity among its disparate factions, and waged a diplomatic war to block foreign attempts to save Somoza's regime. Consequently, the FSLN-led provisional government was recognized by most Latin American governments well before Sandinista columns were near Managua. As Somoza Debayle notes in his memoir, this foreign policy defeat made his ouster a fait accompli; this was a "diplomatic revolution" if there ever was one.[17] Notably, the Sandinistas' foreign sponsors used their support to "buy stock" in the FSLN, in the words of Panamanian military leader Omar Torrijos, shaping the creation of a popular front that saw armed leftist radicals join forces with moderate allies under a revolutionary program for "a mixed economy, political pluralism, and non-alignment in international affairs."

New questions instantly emerged after Somoza's ouster on July 19, 1979: Who in the revolutionary coalition would wield real power? What reforms and laws would the government pass? What would be the government's international orientation in the heated Cold War context? Because Somoza's overthrow had been a regional effort, the new regime's consolidation—the focus of part 2—was inevitably followed with interest by foreign governments. Sandinista leaders, for their part, pondered how their plans—such as agrarian reform, ambitious social welfare projects, and the institutionalization of participatory democracy—would reverberate not only in Moscow and Washington but also in the capitals of the Global South and the halls of international organizations like the United Nations.

Chapter 3 shows how the FSLN, emboldened by its military victory and empowered by significant popular support, seized control of the state and moved the agenda toward the more radical goal of fundamentally remaking the structure of Nicaraguan society, down to the creation of a utopian "New Man" and "New Woman" imbued with revolutionary values. The Sandinistas' moderate political allies were marginalized and the class groups they represented saw their interests severely challenged by the government's redistributive economic policies. The revolution's early consolidation did not resolve its identity crisis as a political project caught between liberal and socialist impulses. But it did create the political alignments that would polarize society through the rest of the decade: the broad, anti-Somoza coalition from 1979 had collapsed by 1982 and a new Sandinista-anti-Sandinista divide emerged in its place. The radicalization of the Revolution, which owed primarily to the ideological and strategic consensus of the FSLN's nine-man National Directorate, worried some of its European and Latin American friends. But many heads of government and intellectuals held out hope that Nicaragua could chart a new path that would combine the most appealing attributes of the Cuban and Mexican revolutions, advancing both social justice and individual political freedoms.

The most contentious issue in the Revolution's early years was Sandinista foreign policy, the subject of chapter 4. The international environment posed grave dangers, including incipient US efforts to undermine and perhaps overthrow the revolutionary government. But the global confrontation between socialism and capitalism also created unique opportunities for support—from the Soviet bloc, national liberation movements in Asia and Africa, and even many democracies in Europe and Latin America—that allowed the Sandinista government to withstand threats from enemies at home and abroad. In navigating this environment, the Nicaraguan Foreign Ministry and FSLN Department of International Relations (DRI) pursued a dual-track policy of nonalignment on the one hand, and relative alignment with Cuba and the Warsaw Pact on the other. Not unlike Castro's rise to power, the Sandinistas' ascent had a convulsive effect on the region, which witnessed a spike in both insurgent and counterinsurgent violence in the 1970s and 1980s. For Central American guerrillas in particular, the war slogan became "Nicaragua ayer, El Salvador hoy, Guatemala mañana." Fearing this prophecy might come true, right-wing forces from as far as Argentina and Chile mobilized to shore up anti-communist dictatorships on the isthmus. Other political forces in the middle—such as centrist Latin American governments, Western European democracies, and the parties of the Socialist International (SI)—worked in and around Nicaragua to prevent the Revolution from becoming the locus of inflamed East–West tensions.

By 1982 the stage was set for the transnational, multilayered war explored in part 3. Tens of thousands of Nicaraguans would die—a toll comparable to, if not worse than, that claimed by the 1979 struggle against Somoza—in the fighting between the Sandinista Popular Army and the US-backed Contra.[18] Due to the United States' primary role in arming and training the Contra insurgency, analysts have long debated whether the armed conflict is best characterized as a civil war or a war of foreign aggression.

Chapter 5 argues that this creates a false binary. In retrospect, senior Sandinista Popular Army officials describe fighting against a military threat that was both internal and external in nature. The local dimensions (such as the opposition of former elite allies, or discontent among parts of the rural population with the Sandinista Front's reforms and governing style) and the external dimensions fed back into one another in a tragic loop. The global Cold War created mortal danger for the Sandinista government because, absent guns and money from Washington, the Contra could not have developed the way that it did. But it also extended lifelines in the form of financing, equipment, and military advice from Cuba, the Soviet Union, Eastern European Warsaw Pact states, and left-leaning nationalist governments such as those of Libya and Algeria. Internationalist militants from foreign national liberation movements pitched in as well. The war effort consumed the revolutionary government, derailing ambitious policy efforts in the realms of education, health care, and economic growth. But, notably, it was not defeated. Instead, a stalemate emerged by 1985: neither could the Contra seize significant territory from which its political leaders could declare a provisional government, nor could the Sandinistas rout them.

The FSLN fought for more than just territorial control. Its government waged another war common to revolutionary regimes: one for legitimacy in the eyes of other states. The Nicaraguan Question—my term for international debates over the Sandinista government's compatibility with the inter-American system—is the subject of chapter 6. In justifying its paramilitary operations in Nicaragua, the Reagan administration implied that the Sandinsita government—along with ongoing leftist insurgencies elsewhere in Central America—lacked legitimacy due to its Marxist leanings, ties to the Soviet bloc, and alleged totalitarianism. The FSLN's diplomatic counterattack dovetailed with international trends that cut against Washington's narrative. Most Western European states, which had benefited from the superpower détente of the previous decade, argued that Reagan's intervention was recklessly destabilizing world affairs. They believed US hostility, moreover, would push Nicaragua further into the arms of the Eastern

Bloc. European governments created diplomatic cover for the growing chorus of Latin American governments that, in reaction to the threat that US intervention posed to their shared interests, created a multilateral peace framework—the Contadora process—premised on nonintervention and respect for national sovereignty. As anti-communist dictatorships collapsed and gave way to democratic regimes, opposition to the Contra program increased. Though the so-called Contadora process failed to end Central America's armed conflicts, this rare exercise in Latin American autonomy had important consequences. Chief among them were the isolation of the United States' Central America policy in the international arena, and the relative legitimization of Managua's left-wing government.

These battles on the international front were just as important as local military conditions in explaining how a "second Cuba" survived an assault led by the United States and supported by Nicaragua's Central American neighbors. This is one of the outcomes explored in part 4. Because Soviet support had limits—Moscow, especially under the reformist premiership of Mikhail Gorbachev, was uninterested in assuming major commitments with the Nicaraguans and unwilling to provoke Washington over them—the Sandinistas' Western European and Latin American backers became increasingly vital over the course of their decade in power. The Nicaraguan Revolution went in new directions as a result. As they participated in negotiated settlements to save their project, Sandinista leaders found themselves drifting toward positions and policies they had not anticipated.

In chapter 7, I analyze the peace agreements that gradually put an end to the war between the Sandinista Popular Army and the Contra. Three main factors contributed to peace. First, a changing superpower context—decreasing support for Reagan's Contra policy in the US Congress, combined with Soviet withdrawal from competition over the Third World—made it harder for either belligerent to see through plans for a military victory. Second, Central American politics also shifted in the 1980s. Elections in Costa Rica and Guatemala brought about governments that reversed their countries' support for the Contra program and promoted a peace framework similar to the earlier Contadora process. Third, the *desgaste* ("wearing out") of the revolutionary process, as Sandinistas leaders often put it, forced the Nicaraguan government to assume a more flexible posture in negotiations. As their popularity declined alongside economic collapse and the carnage of war, FSLN leaders found that the only way to save their Revolution was to make significant concessions to their foes. The resultant Central American Peace Accords, signed by the region's presidents at Esquipulas,

Guatemala, in August 1987, sought to end interrelated civil wars in their countries by swearing off superpower intervention in their affairs and creating political transitions wherein all involved parties could advance their agendas through electoral competition rather than armed violence. In signing, the FSLN reversed its prior refusal to modify its internal system of government in order to satisfy foreign interests. But in return, Sandinista leaders helped deal a significant blow to US military aid to the Contra. And crucially, they won a battle that revolutionary regimes often lose: one for legitimacy in the eyes of neighbors, who increasingly treated Sandinista leaders as legitimate equals and took steps to integrate their own armed left-wing groups into mainstream politics.

Chapter 8 shows how Nicaragua's revolutionary process evolved in the context of those international agreements. Between 1987 and 1989, Sandinista leaders liberalized Nicaragua's political system, made concessions to the civilian opposition, and met face-to-face with Contra leaders to negotiate a cease-fire. They also reformed the electoral system in anticipation of national elections. The government had previously taken some steps to institutionalize a system of pluralistic political competition, notably by holding elections in 1984 where the US-backed opposition opted not to participate. But the 1990 elections would see the future of the Sandinista government meaningfully on the ballot and at stake for the first time. In the economic sphere, the Sandinistas moved away from central planning and deepened privatizing reforms. On the foreign plane, they toned down support for El Salvador's Frente Farabundo Martí para la Liberación Nacional (FMLN) and came to terms with its right-wing government as well as that of Honduras, which had hosted most of the Contra. The FSLN's entire international support network—Western European and Latin American governments, but also Cuba and the Soviet Union—encouraged these dramatic steps, in no small part because they undermined the position of US president George H. W. Bush, whose administration was generally ambivalent about the Esquipulas framework. As a result, the Revolution hewed closer than ever before to the 1979 promise of nonalignment, a mixed economy, and political pluralism. And, as historian Rafael Rojas recently observed, Sandinista reforms codified important differences between the Nicaraguan and Cuban revolutions. There were dissimilarities from the start, but with the implementation of the 1987 Constitution—which made no reference to a vanguard party, and formally enshrined both representative institutions and ideological pluralism—the Nicaraguans broke the paradigm of Latin

American revolutionary thinking established by the Cubans' socialist project, which itself had supplanted that of the Mexican Revolution.[19]

The decisions made by the FSLN's upper echelon also collided with international trends to determine the Revolution's paradoxical final act. The Sandinista Front was ousted from power in 1990, albeit not by US marines or proxy "freedom fighters," but by Nicaraguan voters in free elections. And as Sergio Ramírez—a member of the revolutionary Junta (1979–84) and vice president (1985–90)—explained, the Sandinistas had not changed Nicaragua in the way they had set out: "The revolution did not bring justice for the oppressed as had been hoped; nor did it manage to create wealth and development. Instead, its greatest benefit was democracy, sealed in 1990 with the acknowledgment of electoral defeat. As a paradox of history, this is its most obvious legacy, although it was not its most passionate objective."[20]

In the conclusion, I explore President Daniel Ortega's unexpected defeat at the polls, which owed to the interplay between shifting political alignments inside Nicaragua and the effects of external intervention led by the United States. I also expand on Ramírez's retrospective analysis, putting it in international perspective. Given that poverty remained widespread and social hierarchies were largely unaltered, Guatemalan sociologist Edelberto Torres Rivas—one of the foremost analysts of Central America's revolutionary upheavals—was justified in calling it a "revolution without revolutionary changes."[21] This assessment, however, comes from a relatively specific vision of what constitutes revolutionary change, and reflects crushed expectations for Central America's revolutionary struggles (Torres Rivas, like many other scholars of the era, was an important activist in his own right). The unquestionable continuities should not obscure the fact that both Nicaragua and Latin America changed in other ways between 1979 and 1990. The Sandinistas' rise and fall was not only the story of the prospects for socialist transformation in Latin America; it was also one of collapsing military dictatorships across the continent and their fraught, often contradictory, replacement by liberal democracies. In fact, many Sandinista commanders have in retrospect concluded that toppling the Somoza dictatorship, and then handing over power peacefully in a democratic transition, were the two most revolutionary acts they ever committed. They thus foreshadowed Hugo Chávez and other leaders of the so-called Pink Tide, who in the twenty-first century made promises of social transformation, albeit within the confines of electoral competition and representative institutions rather than armed struggle. As the face of Latin American politics changed in the 1980s and through the post–Cold War era, so did the way that Latin American countries related to the United States and to one another: the collective reaction to US intervention set up renewed efforts at multilateralism and regional integration in the 1990s and 2000s.

In the conclusion I also fast-forward and briefly survey the equally paradoxical afterlife of the Sandinista Revolution. In 2006, the FSLN—by then hegemonized by Daniel Ortega, and shorn of most of the revolutionary elite from the 1980s—returned to the presidency through elections. The Ortega-era FSLN mostly abandoned redistributive politics and incorporated a newfound emphasis on conservative Christian social values, but still retained much of its revolutionary rhetoric, as well as its suspicion of US influence. Ortega has also redrawn Nicaragua's political landscape, and in doing so constructed a repressive dynastic dictatorship—he co-governs with his wife, Vice President Rosario Murillo—eerily similar to the one the Sandinistas helped overthrow four decades ago. The Sandinista Revolution therefore lives on, albeit in a mutated form that constitutes a bizarre mix of changes and continuities. Many in Nicaraguan civil society, looking back in dismay, wonder how the transition to liberal democracy and market economics degenerated into another personalist dictatorship. The international picture, again, is important: the rise of the Ortega dictatorship happened in a regional context of democratic backsliding, stagnant socioeconomic progress, and collapsing multilateral institutions, even as market-driven economies and global integration remained the norm. A close look at the fall of the Revolution and the end of Latin America's Cold War reveals the highly contingent nature of those transitions: the only thing certain was that nothing was certain.

Much the same can be said about global politics. Many twenty-first-century challenges—such as the declining quality of democracy worldwide, the realignment of alliances and international frameworks in place since the Second World War, and persistent inter- and intrastate armed conflict—demand new histories of that misunderstood inflection point in world history. The end of the Cold War, a group of historians and political scientists recently argued, did not represent a tabula rasa upon which a new world was created.[22] Nor was the fall of the Sandinista Revolution— and the hopes of socialist transformation it brought down with it—simply an ending, a footnote in a closed chapter of ideological confrontation and superpower conflicts. It was the last revolution of a bygone era, but also the first one of our times.

Part I **Origins, 1933–1979**

·····································

1 The Old Regime and a Transnational Conspiracy

· ·

Nicaragua seemed an unlikely locale for the "second coming" of the Cuban Revolution.[1] In the decade following Castro's rise to power in 1959, the Central American country achieved one of the fastest rates of gross domestic product (GDP) growth in Latin America. This performance saw the Nicaraguan government attain poster child status in the Alliance for Progress, a US foreign aid program designed to combat communism in the hemisphere through nation-building and economic development. Most Cold War–era US presidents did not find it "sufficiently threatened by Communist-inspired insurgency," to borrow the Kennedy administration's language, to merit significant interventions of the kind seen in Guatemala, Brazil, Guyana, and the Dominican Republic.[2] In fact, Nicaragua was so stable that it had done away with disruptive changes in government altogether; a single family had ruled the country uninterrupted since the early 1930s. Even after a 1972 earthquake flattened the capital city of Managua, most analysts thought of the country as an island of stability in an increasingly tumultuous region. The opposite of a "hot spot," in other words.

When Nicaraguans suddenly erupted in rebellion just a few years later, US policymakers were therefore taken aback. Their understanding of Cold War geopolitics tended to be zero-sum. For most, any instance of Third World instability created a vacuum that would inevitably be filled by Soviet communism. Lawmakers in the US Congress suddenly scrambled to understand what had gone awry in this patch of America's "own backyard." At a 1978 hearing of the Senate Foreign Relations Committee, they started by asking diplomats for a brief lesson in Nicaraguan history:

> *Senator John Sparkman:* How long has the Somoza family been in power?
> *Assistant Secretary of State Viron P. Vaky:* It is something like 40 years.
> *Senator Sparkman: How* long?
> *Senator Clifford Case:* How did they get in in the first place?
> *Asst. Secretary Vaky:* I think we helped them get in. His father was installed after the Marines left in the early 1930s.[3]

An old regime's flaws often become evident only in hindsight. Some experts on the subject have called this the "paradox of revolution."[4] In many respects, the Somozas had run a well-oiled machine. To a population exasperated by a generations-long cycle of civil wars and foreign occupations, they offered pacification. At least initially, they cultivated some working-class support by promoting unionization. To the United States government, which had helped install Anastasio Somoza García in the first place, the family promised Nicaragua's enthusiastic Cold War alignment so long as Washington ignored its grisly human rights abuses. Finally, and perhaps most importantly, Nicaragua's traditional capitalist class acquiesced to the Somozas' authoritarian project because it advanced economic policies favorable to their interests. These authoritarian bargains allowed Nicaragua's rulers to create a forty-year equilibrium and accomplish the stunning feat of dynastic succession. Such a thing has rarely been witnessed in Latin American history. The Somozas pulled it off twice.[5]

But in doing so, they quietly set the stage for future upheaval. Working-class Nicaraguans came to resent the state repression bundled in with the *pax somocista*. And once the Somoza estate grew large enough to encroach on its interests, Nicaragua's aristocracy began to rue the power-sharing agreements they had built with the regime. The Somozas also faced a classic "dictator's dilemma." As they expanded the economy and modernized the state, they inadvertently nurtured democratizing impulses. For example, a burgeoning university student sector chafed under the indignities of arbitrary, dynastic rule and rejected the inequalities created by uneven economic development. "There was such a sense of humiliation, frustration, and inequality," recalled Moisés Hassan, a physicist (with a PhD from the North Carolina State University), university professor, and social movement organizer who would go on to play an important role in the Revolution. "If you were traveling and you said you were from Nicaragua, people said, 'Ah, Somoza's hacienda.'" Perhaps it should have been obvious that a violent uprising would flare up in a country where one family viewed the national territory as a private estate and treated its inhabitants like "oxen."[6]

US policymakers had thought that by supporting the Somozas, warts and all, they were actually minimizing the possibility of a bloody conflagration in a traditionally American sphere of influence. Nicaragua's dictatorship was a beneficiary of the Cold War–era national security doctrine, wherein Washington allied with Latin American militaries and conservative elites to combat "internal" communist subversion in the Western Hemisphere at all costs. But in Central America and the Caribbean, similar policies predated the superpower conflict. Because of Central America's strategic importance—the isthmus narrowly bridges the Pacific and Atlantic oceans—and proximity to the Rio Grande, US policymakers had long construed stability there as a national interest. Economic interdependence, best symbolized by the United Fruit Company's dominance in several of its countries, also heightened the stakes. In the early twentieth century, the US government pursued stability by installing collaborative governments, undermining unfriendly ones, and employing military force to take direct control when necessary. Local elites frequently twisted American engagement and dollars to help maintain the social status quo in the poorest and most unequal part of Spanish America.[7] As diplomatic historian Walter LaFeber wrote, the quest for stability backfired. By undermining institutional development and consistently siding with transnational forces opposed to any form of social change, US policy helped embed explosive inequalities that made late twentieth-century revolutions in Guatemala, El Salvador, and Nicaragua "inevitable."[8] Their anti-American flavor was similarly foreordained.

Nevertheless, while the crisis of Nicaragua's old regime may have been foreseeable, the revolutionary outcome was anything but. When Sandinista Front founder Carlos Fonseca Amador was killed in combat in 1976, the Somozas' would-be topplers were broke, isolated from politics, and mired in internecine conflict. FSLN efforts to build Guevara-style, insurrectionary *focos* had failed. Cuba and the USSR had long abandoned what little interest they had in encouraging revolution in Nicaragua. Even when cracks appeared in the dictatorship's foundations in the late 1970s, few expected that Anastasio Somoza Debayle—the original dictator's second son—would resign. None expected left-wing rebels to take power.

This chapter explains how the Sandinistas conspired to put radical revolution on the agenda. In 1977, a faction of the Sandinista Front broke with strategic orthodoxy and sought alliances with "patriotic" elements of the bourgeoisie. Much of that story takes place outside Nicaragua. Crucially, the young guerrilla leadership secretly built a network of allies among notable intellectuals and statesmen around the Caribbean Basin. These foreign benefactors gave them bases, money, and weapons to launch their first major incursions against Somoza's National Guard. Taken together, these domestic and transnational allies helped the Sandinistas transcend their status as fringe extremists. As a result, the armed Left positioned itself to capitalize on discontented popular sectors and wavering elites, convincing both that only the armed struggle—and the promise of radically remaking Nicaraguan society—could defeat the dictatorship.

But they would have to tread lightly. As their Latin American sponsors kindly warned them, one misstep could attract the wrong kind of attention in Washington and kill their revolutionary dreams. Panamanian leader Omar Torrijos therefore urged moderation as the Sandinistas gathered steam in their fight against Somoza. "That's right. Forget radicalisms," he told FSLN conspirator Sergio Ramírez as he lit his usual cigar and listened to audacious plans to unseat a symbol of US imperialism in Latin America: "Careful with the Yankees. You have to play with the leash, but not the monkey."[9]

The Editor and the Manuscript

After winning independence from Spain in the early nineteenth century, Nicaragua succumbed to a cycle of political violence. Rather than building a modern state or constructing a coherent national identity, elite families from the two colonial-era power centers—León and Granada—endlessly tussled for control. North Americans, including business groups competing to build routes for transcontinental travel through the country, tended to inflame their periodic civil wars. A casualty of Manifest Destiny, the country was invaded in the 1850s by soldier of fortune William Walker, a Tennessean who proclaimed himself president, restored slavery, and sought Nicaragua's annexation by the United States until a joint Central American army gave him the boot. Later, US secretary of state Philander Knox, a practitioner of so-called dollar diplomacy, conspired to topple dictator José Santos Zelaya when he ran afoul of American economic and strategic interests. The Wilson administration subsequently turned Nicaragua into a virtual protectorate of the United States. Through military occupation they imposed the humiliating Chamorro-Bryan Treaty, which gave the United States exclusive and perpetual rights to dig an interoceanic canal through the country. The United States having already built one in Panama, there was no chance Nicaragua could benefit from this infringement of national sovereignty.

Like the 1901 Platt Amendment that brought newly independent Cuba under Washington's control, these episodes became synonymous with an informal US empire in Latin America. Unsurprisingly, Nicaragua became a hotbed for anti-imperialist voices like that of poet Rubén Darío, who de-

Central Highlands of Nicaragua

HONDURAS

Tegucigalpa

EL SALVADOR

NORTH CARIBBEAN COAST
AUTONOMOUS REGION

N

JINOTEGA

NUEVA SEGOVIA

Siuna

MADRIZ

ESTELÍ

Estelí   Jinotega

NICARAGUA

Matagalpa

CHINANDEGA   LEÓN   MATAGALPA

Lake
Managua

Corinto

León

BOACO

MANAGUA

SOUTH CARIBBEAN COAST
AUTONOMOUS REGION

CARIBBEAN
SEA

Managua

Masaya

MASAYA   Granada   CHONTALES

Nandaime   GRANADA

CARAZO

RIVAS   Lake
Nicaragua   RÍO
SAN JUAN

PACIFIC
OCEAN

Sapoá

San Juan River

Coco River

0   30   60 mi

0   50   100 km

COSTA RICA

San José

Nicaragua

nounced the United States, for all its modernizing prowess, as godless and barbaric in his famous 1904 *Ode to Roosevelt*. Under the surface, Nicaraguans were actually rather ambivalent about their relationship with US imperialism. When American troops landed on their shores, they usually did so at the behest of national elites seeking an edge against their rivals or looking to "import" the US path to prosperity and modernity. Those members of the oligarchy who opposed intervention, rather than invoking a righteous defense of national sovereignty, sometimes did so because they feared American ideas and presence would threaten the country's social hierarchy or traditional values.[10] The consolidation of Nicaragua's Somoza dictatorship occurred at the intersection of US intervention with local political alignments and social dynamics. Similarly, American imperialism—and the complex responses it engendered in Nicaragua and elsewhere in Latin America—would later backdrop the origins of the Sandinista Revolution.

More immediately, the story begins with the last US occupation of Nicaragua, which took place between 1926 and 1933. After the interventionist excess of the Wilson, Taft, and Roosevelt administrations, the Republican presidents of the 1920s sought to cancel US protectorates in Honduras and the Dominican Republic while winding down military occupations throughout Central American and the Caribbean. Pulling out of Nicaragua proved difficult. Having been occupied since 1912, the country exploded into civil war as soon as the marines withdrew in 1925. The following year, the Coolidge administration sent them back to impose peace between the Liberal and Conservative parties and supervise democratic elections. But one military leader, Augusto César Sandino, saw this pax Americana as an unacceptable violation of Nicaraguan sovereignty. Refusing to play along, he took to Nicaragua's northern highlands and mounted a fierce guerrilla insurgency. By championing the "indo-hispanic race," swearing to redeem the oppressed, and demanding the departure of the "yankee invader," Sandino became an icon to Latin American radicals of various ideological persuasions. And by denouncing collaborationist Nicaraguan elites as *vendepatrias*—sellouts, but with a nationalist twist—he laid the basis for a new form of civic nationalism in Nicaragua based on principled intransigence against foreign interference. In 1933, having failed to destroy Sandino's Army in Defense of the National Sovereignty of Nicaragua, the Hoover administration finally retired the marines. As in Cuba and the Dominican Republic, the US government tried to outsource its quest for stability to local surrogates. Thus, the marines trained professional, nonpartisan security forces before heading home. In their absence, the new "National Guard" would supposedly maintain order by keeping peace between warring factions and overseeing democratic transfers of power.

It did not work quite as intended. Within two years, the freshly anointed chief of that new institution—Anastasio Somoza García—had murdered Sandino in cold blood and usurped the democratically elected president (who happened to be the uncle of the Guard chief's wife). Much like Cuba's Fulgencio Batista and the Dominican Republic's Rafael Trujillo, and with greater success, Somoza forged the desired stability by establishing a dictatorship. It would last over four decades.

Though invested by a foreign power, Somoza García built domestic pillars of support. Seen as a crude, middle-class upstart by much of the country's traditional ruling aristocracy, he used economic success—achieved through monetary reform, expansion of state institutions, and trade policies favorable to the agro-export sector—and power-sharing agreements to co-opt elite families in his own Liberal Party as well as those of the rival Conservative Party.[11] At the same time, his regime implemented a populist strategy to develop working-class support. At one point in the 1940s he even forged a short-lived, tacit alliance with the Partido Socialista Nicaragüense (PSN), implementing labor laws that permitted some unionization by rural and urban workers; Nicaraguan organized labor sometimes saw the regime as an ally against the old landowning and financier class that Somoza had replaced.[12]

Despite the upper crust's growing acquiescence, and although some popular sectors contributed to his authoritarian consolidation, Somoza García was despised by a younger generation of middle-class students and professionals. In April 1954, the National Guard neutralized an armed plot against the regime. Two years later—on September 21, 1956—a twenty-seven-year-old poet named Rigoberto López Pérez infiltrated a party in León and shot the dictator in the chest. Bodyguards killed the assassin on the spot. Somoza, tellingly, died at a US military hospital in the Panama Canal Zone a few days later.

He was immediately succeeded by his oldest son Luis Somoza Debayle, who unleashed an indiscriminate wave of retaliatory repression against regime opponents. Among the dozens of young people rounded up and tortured was Pedro Joaquín Chamorro, the thirty-two-year-old editor of the opposition daily *La Prensa*. The Chamorro family of Granada was among the most important of the country's nineteenth- and early twentieth-century oligarchy, and it had dominated the Conservative Party since its earliest wars with León's Liberal families. But Pedro Joaquín—a Social Christian in political orientation—clashed with his family and the leadership of the Conservatives, who in 1950 signed a pact with the ruling Liberal Party, earning the right to participate in sham elections in exchange for accepting Somoza's autocracy. Already an intransigent opposition journalist, his experience with imprisonment, combined with the elation generated by the Cuban Revolution, pushed him to lead an ill-conceived and unsuccessful armed uprising in May 1959. Its failure, along with the communist and authoritarian turn of Cuba's revolutionary government, persuaded him to abandon the armed struggle. He instead returned to journalism and legal opposition to the dictatorship.[13]

Another young man arrested in the post-assassination roundup was Tomás Borge. Only a few years younger than Chamorro, he was likewise dissatisfied with the Conservative Party's option for anti-Somoza politics. Unlike Chamorro, though, Borge saw Marxist politics as a viable alternative. Like his friend Carlos Fonseca Amador, he joined the aforementioned Nicaraguan Socialist Party (PSN)—the Moscow-line communist organization. At the very beginning of their political careers, they looked to the Soviet Union for inspiration as they imagined Nicaragua's post-Somoza future. Fonseca traveled to the Eastern Bloc in 1958 and wrote a gushing description of life and society in the USSR, complete with a spirited defense of the recent Soviet invasion of Hungary.[14] But communist party membership also proved disappointing. Like many Moscow-line parties in the Global South, the PSN maintained that the conditions for socialism were a long way off in Nicaragua and that gradual, legal, and peaceful struggle—as opposed to armed insurrection—was the appropriate strategy for bringing about social change.

The success of Fidel Castro's Movimiento 26 de Julio sent an entirely different message to Borge, Fonseca, and other young dissidents from the Conservative and Socialist parties. When Cuba's Batista government fell, the prospect of toppling the US-backed Somoza regime suddenly seemed less fantastical. Moreover, the Cuban revolutionaries provided a blueprint for taking and exercising power in Nicaragua that was far more relevant than anything on offer in the Soviet sphere. In the months after Castro and company took control in Havana, Fonseca participated in a revolutionary incursion led by a Honduras-based, Cuban-supported guerrilla column named after Somoza García's assassin, Rigoberto López Pérez.

Though Fonseca was wounded and the operation failed, Nicaragua's armed Left was only getting started. Over the course of spirited debates in Honduras, Venezuela, Costa Rica, and especially Cuba—which had become a hub for Latin American revolutionaries of all orientations (even Chamorro visited Havana in 1959)—young, middle-class radicals (many of them, like Borge and Fonseca, students at the Universidad Nacional Autónoma in León) dreamed up plans for a military organization that would pose a sustained, long-term challenge to the dictatorship. The members of this revolutionary cohort all took inspiration from Sandino's earlier anti-imperialist struggle, which itself had inspired the Cuban 26th of July Movement.[15] Hence the name they eventually settled on: Frente Sandinista de Liberación Nacional (FSLN). The Sandinista Front often dates its founding to a meeting in Tegucigalpa on July 23, 1961. But both Borge and Victor Tirado López—a Mexican Communist Party militant who joined the Nicaraguans in this period—later admitted that nobody knows the exact date or place when the Sandinista Front was constituted.[16]

As Tirado's presence in its leadership suggests, the early FSLN was shaped by engagement with revolutionary movements beyond Nicaraguan borders. Their name bore the obvious inspiration of the Vietnamese and Algerian *fronts de liberación nacional*. But they also forged direct connections. For example, FSLN-affiliated university students, exiled after participating in anti-Somoza operations, connected with leftist parties in Latin America and Western Europe while continuing their studies abroad. Other Sandinistas went as far as the Middle East. In exchange for guerrilla training in Jordan and Lebanon, cadres supported Palestinian national liberation operations; the connection surfaced when Nicaraguan Patricio Argüello died in a failed 1970 airplane hijacking organized by a branch of the Palestine Liberation Organization (PLO).[17] Carlos Fonseca Amador spent time in Guatemala with Luis Turcios Lima—founder of that country's Fuerzas Armadas Rebeldes (FAR)—and trained in North Korea.[18] But Castro's Cuba was the main haven, support base, and training ground.[19]

Throughout most of the 1960s, Sandinista Front leaders sought to schematically reproduce what they believed had worked for the Cubans during the previous decade. FSLN cells carried out targeted assassinations, which they called *ajusticiamientos*, of notorious National Guard commanders and torturers. They also mounted bank heists to finance their budding operations. Most importantly, they worked to implement Che Guevara's foco style of guerrilla warfare: a small vanguard would post up in Nicaragua's mountainous central highlands, launching surgical strikes at National Guard positions in the hope of generating a popular rebellion that would subsequently allow revolutionary forces to challenge the regime head-on. Their efforts at imitation went to such extremes that they drew up a twenty-five-month timetable for their mountain-based struggle, based on the exact amount of time it had taken Castro's men to overthrow Batista from the Sierra Maestra.[20]

They found little success. After early military actions near the Honduran border were easily repelled in 1963, the FSLN refrained from further armed operations and instead focused on developing ties with social movements and left-leaning, anti-Somoza political parties. By 1967, they were ready to go again. But National Guard forces wiped out an entire Sandinista column near the mountain of Pancasán in Nicaragua's central Matagalpa region, resulting in the death of FSLN cofounder Silvio Mayorga. *Foquismo-*inspired operations had failed to deliver any significant blow to Somoza's military. Perhaps more worryingly, Sandinista forces remained isolated from the local populations that, motivated by their own grievances with the dictatorship, might eventually constitute a powerful revolutionary coalition; by Tomás Borge's own admission, the FSLN lacked either minimal infrastructure or a base of support in the mountainous countryside they sought to liberate.[21] During the 1960s and '70s, the KGB—which was critical of the Pancasán operation—completely dismissed the Sandinistas' revolutionary prospects.[22] Cuba increasingly lost faith as well. Revealingly, despite living in Havana for several years, historic leader Carlos Fonseca was never deemed worthy of an interview with Fidel Castro.[23]

The Pancasán catastrophe forced FSLN leaders back to the drawing board. As further setbacks resulted in the killing or arrest of numerous Sandinista cadres, Bayardo Arce—who joined in 1969—recalled that things were so bad that "the best thing for the future of the Revolution was to make the government believe that it had annihilated us."[24] Once again, the Nicaraguan armed Left suspended major military operations; many Sandinista guerrilla chiefs speak of a period of *acumulación de fuerzas en silencio.* According to Mónica Baltodano, another Sandinista guerrilla, the decision to step back and quietly amass strength was the result of a lesson drawn from the movement's military defeats: such operations could not prosper unless the FSLN rooted itself more deeply among the population.[25]

Thus, Sandinista militants redoubled efforts—already underway in the 1960s—to join social movements, unions, and civil society organizations (or help create new ones) in order to expand the FSLN's base of potential recruits and collaborators. For example, the Sandinista Front enhanced its appeal in the student sector, developing a powerful university arm in the Frente Estudiantil Revolucionario (FER). A major factor in the development of the revolutionary Left was its overlap with the growing influence of the Liberation Theology current within global Catholicism. As progressive priests encouraged their faithful to question their social reality, Church communities sometimes began sympathizing with radical opponents to the dictatorship. At the same time, participation in Christian social programs in marginalized neighborhoods helped expose middle- and upper-class Nicaraguans to the social misery experienced by most of the population; for many of them, Catholic activism was a gateway to anti-Somoza politics or even a Marxist analysis of the country's problems. The FSLN's ability to attract members from the traditional bourgeoisie would help set it apart from similar armed Left movements and deeply influenced its prospects down the line. In her memoir, Nicaraguan poet and novelist Gioconda Belli (as in the rest of Central America, revolutionary politics were especially appealing in intellectual circles) wrote of her FSLN militancy: "Being an upper-class woman was an ideal alibi for my subversive endeavors. I knew that I had to keep my position in that world in order to eventually blow it up from the inside."[26] By pausing major military offensives, FSLN leaders also created time and space to further develop a revolutionary doctrine and political program unique to their movement: in 1969 Sandinista leaders laid out their vision for society in their *Programa Histórico*. While the Sandinista Front in the late 1960s and early 1970s broadened its work in the towns and cities, it never stopped sending cadres to the mountainous countryside, which remained the heart and soul of its revolutionary imaginary.

All of these efforts would pay off in the long run. In the short run, however, the regime—led in the 1970s by Anastasio Somoza Debayle (the original dictator's youngest son)—seemed well entrenched. "Tachito" Somoza Debayle had deepened his father's corporatist model, refreshing power-sharing agreements with the pseudo-opposition Conservative Party and expanding the state's social control through a variety of popular organizations and workers' groups. The Somozas' modernization of the economy produced 4.8 percent GDP growth between 1967 and 1977, one of the fastest rates in the hemisphere. Clearly, the regime's collapse at the end of the decade was not immediately caused by a major economic crisis.[27] Economic growth, however, masked problems that made the regime vulnerable. As a report by the Inter-American Commission on Human Rights noted, a boom in the dominant agricultural sector actually worsened rural poverty and displacement as the production of export crops—most importantly, cotton—became increasingly mechanized and modernized. In general, most Nicaraguans did not share in the benefits of an expanding economy; roughly half the population lived in absolute poverty during the 1970s, a fact related to a host of problems including an especially severe crisis of child malnutrition.[28] Additionally, parts of the traditional economic elite were also beginning to grow ambivalent about the economic model. The cotton boom and Nicaragua's participation in the Central American Common Market had required greater state intervention, which put the Somoza family in a better position to participate directly in the country's economic life in the 1950s and '60s. Using its control over institutions and the political process to unfair advantage, the Somoza estate by the 1970s had grown to the point of encroaching upon the economic interests of Nicaragua's most important capital groups.[29] As one political scientist explains, this illicit expansion "violated time-honored elite arrangements which encouraged a close relationship between government and business."[30] Finally, political parties and social movements were met with vicious repression whenever they tried to transcend the Somozas' social contract. In January 1967, for example, National Guard troops massacred hundreds in Managua protesting against rigged elections.

Many of the flaws in the Somozas' authoritarian bargain were exemplified by the government's response to the 1972 earthquake that destroyed much of the capital city, killing thousands and displacing orders of magnitude more. Massive relief and reconstruction aid flowed in from abroad, much of which the ruling family brazenly pilfered. The regime's corruption, combined with its inability to effectively address the natural disaster, undermined its standing in popular opinion. It also made the private sector—which soon after created its own independent organization, the Consejo Superior de la Iniciativa Privada (COSIP)—wonder if its economic interests were still compatible with those of the Somoza clan.

Nonetheless, few in the early and mid-1970s doubted the regime's durability. Most of those problems would only seem obvious in retrospect. Somoza Debayle could project strength, in part, because his political opponents were relatively weak and isolated. The legal struggle embodied by Unión Democrática de Liberación Nacional (UDEL)—the Pedro Joaquín Chamorro-led, pan-opposition alliance of legal parties, which included dissident Liberals and Conservatives as well as the Moscow-line PSN—was stagnant. UDEL struggled to convince traditional parties to swear off power-sharing agreements with Somoza that ultimately legitimized his family's autocracy. According to a close collaborator and biographer, in the first half of the 1970s, "Somoza was stronger than ever, and the civic-democratic opposition seemed increasingly useless." Chamorro felt he was "preaching in the desert; he was seen as annoying, uncomfortable, and intransigent even by his closest friends."[31] Meanwhile, the revolutionary Left was also struggling to go mainstream.[32] In December 1974, the Sandinista Front made a splash when a group of commandos boldly invaded the home of a well-known Somoza ally, taking hostage the aristocratic guests who had arrived for a New Year's party that evening. As a result, they secured the release of several political prisoners, built a piece of revolutionary mythology (Colombian writer Gabriel García Márquez would later write a screenplay about the stunt), and won many new admirers. But this operation, according to guerrilla leader Edén Pastora, was also like "a cry in the desert," because the FSLN "had not yet reached the organic development at the national and international level required to capitalize on its effects."[33] In the middle of the 1970s, neither the armed nor the legal struggle could provide the middle and upper classes with a realistic alternative to the regime. Nor were they sufficiently connected with working masses that could help build a revolutionary coalition from below.

The Sandinista Front also developed major internal problems over the course of the 1970s. Composed of perhaps 250 active members in 1977, the FSLN was far smaller than its left-wing guerrilla counterparts elsewhere in Central America, and certainly no match for the highly trained and well-supplied National Guard.[34] Worse still, by that point the movement had become mired in internecine conflict. The setbacks of the 1960s had inspired productive, albeit difficult debates over the best approach to challenge the dictatorship. Programmatic and tactical disagreements exacerbated—or were exacerbated by—personal rivalries and disciplinary problems in the guerrilla structure.[35] By the time FSLN talisman Carlos Fonseca fell in combat in November 1976 (a day after the death of Eduardo Contreras, another high-ranking figure), internal disputes had matured into three competing *tendencias*, or factions.

One faction, which included surviving founder Tomás Borge, enjoyed the clearest connection to the Sandinista Front's early doctrine and traditional modus operandi. The Guerra Popular Prolongada (GPP) tendency, as it came to be known, still viewed the mountain countryside as the arena where revolutionary forces would develop. They saw in rural peasants the FSLN's main constituency. Though most of its leaders came from towns and cities, the GPP did not believe that Nicaragua's relatively small urban workforce could be the main agent of revolutionary change. At the same time, they revised the early Sandinista strategy in significant ways. Importantly, GPP leaders traded the Cuban experience and Che's foco theory for lessons drawn from the Chinese, Algerian, and Vietnamese revolutions and the associated idea of a prolonged "people's war."[36]

By contrast, the Tendencia Proletaria (TP) took greater influence from orthodox Marxism with more of an Eastern European flavor. As its name would suggest, the Proletarian faction saw wage laborers—not only in cities, but also in those rural areas where agricultural production was relatively industrialized—as the key constituents of the revolutionary coalition. Thus, they advocated for developing the causes of organized labor in Nicaragua.[37]

Military action should wait; as Jaime Wheelock, one of its principal leaders, put it: "We considered it of capital importance to mature the organizational conditions of popular sectors before launching armed offensives."[38]

A third faction thought that the conditions for armed insurrection were as ready as they were ever going to be. The Tendencia Insurreccional (commonly known as the Tercerista tendency) promoted a more voluntarist approach. They saw urban centers and border regions as the principal theater for Somoza's overthrow. Its leaders—most notably the brothers Camilo, Daniel, and Humberto Ortega but also Germán Pomares and the Mexican-born leader Victor Tirado—called for the broadest possible alliance with all anti-Somoza elements in Nicaraguan society, regardless of their class background. Controversially, this also implied Sandinista ties with progressive elements of the bourgeoisie.[39]

The Terceristas—despite the Sandinista Front's fractiousness, and in spite of the dictatorship's outward image of stability—started working in early 1977 to make their "insurrectional thesis" a reality. Its leadership—based in the Costa Rican and Honduran capitals, rather than the Nicaraguan interior—planned an "October Offensive" aimed at two main objectives. First, Sandinista fighters would strike a military blow at the National Guard, shattering Somoza's image of invincibility. A direct hit might also sabotage his ongoing negotiations with the US government, which under the aegis of the Carter administration's human rights–focused foreign policy—and with the support of the pseudo-opposition parties—sought to polish the regime's democratic record without questioning its underlying legitimacy. Second, military success would undermine the peaceful, civic struggle led by Chamorro's UDEL. The Ortega brothers, along with Tercerista leaders Victor Tirado, Germán Pomares, and Edén Pastora, met in San José and drew up a three-pronged strategy—with Northern, Pacific, and Southern Fronts—to seize several National Guard garrisons and thereafter arm local populations for a general uprising. Most importantly, the Southern Front would conquer a large piece of territory along the Costa Rican border in order to establish a provisional government.[40]

In May of that year, writer Sergio Ramírez convened a group of eleven other well-known Nicaraguan citizens in a secret rendezvous at a hotel in San José, Costa Rica. Some were intellectuals like Ramírez, Father Fernando Cardenal, or university administrator Carlos Tünnerman Bernheim; others were wealthy capitalists, technocrats, or professionals. At the meeting Ramírez and Humberto Ortega outlined their insurrectionary plans, which the former described in retrospect as "pretty crazy, and totally blown out of proportion." They also asked each of the men to pledge $100,000 for the October Offensive.[41] At a second meeting in Cuernavaca, Mexico, in July, they decided that these twelve Nicaraguan notables would constitute the Revolutionary Junta that would run and represent the provisional government.[42] The odds of success were less than slim, and when one asked what would happen in the event of defeat, the absence of a "Plan B" quickly became evident.[43] Despite this bleak reality, these mostly older notables decided to risk it all on a group of young, ragtag guerrillas. Some of them, like Jesuit priest Fernando Cardenal, were already committed to some form of socialist renewal. But crucially, the revolutionary agenda they adopted in Cuernavaca was hardly radical. The program emphasized what would become the "three pillars" of the Sandinista Revolution: a mixed economy, nonalignment in international affairs, and a democratic regime with full political liberties.[44] Just as important, as Ramírez remembers, these men assumed a fundamentally moral commitment based on their hatred of Somoza. The children of two members, wealthy businessmen Joaquín Cuadra Chamorro and Emilio Baltodano, were already serving among the FSLN's ranks.[45] The involvement of elite youth in the Sandinista Front—itself the result of a conscious strategy dating back to the 1960s—was essential to the budding alliance between parts of the radical Left and parts of the aristocracy.[46]

Provisional governments mean little without foreign recognition. With this in mind, Ramírez traveled to Bogotá in August to deliver a letter from the Terceristas to Gabriel García Márquez, informing the writer of his group's plans and asking him to persuade Venezuelan president Carlos Andrés Pérez to recognize the Junta once it set foot in Nicaragua. After shredding the Tercerista missive to avoid leaving a paper trail, el Gabo booked a flight to Caracas and promised to inform Ramírez of his mission's outcome. Indeed, just a few days later, Ramírez received a call from the Colombian literary giant, with a coded message signaling Pérez's approval of the Sandinista plans and willingness to support them financially: "The editor," he said, referring to the Venezuelan leader, "is willing to buy the manuscript. And he's also willing to pay some handsome royalties." From September 1977, FSLN allies like poet-minister Ernesto Cardenal and Joaquín Cuadra Chamorro flew to Caracas to secretly meet with Pérez's camp and bring back suitcases filled with monthly payments of $1 million in cash.[47]

Why would Pérez, an anti-communist social democrat, throw his weight behind the FSLN? As later events would demonstrate, his government was committed to Somoza's ouster. Importantly, the Terceristas could argue that, given the GPP and Proletarians' discomfort with building bridges to the bourgeoisie, their faction was the best bet for a moderate, "social democratic" option. The lack of guerrilla or military leaders in the proposed provisional government helped soften its image. Personal connections also helped lubricate the process. Pérez was already acquainted with the proposed president of the Revolutionary Junta—business magnate Felipe Mántica—through a Nicaraguan friend who had lived in Venezuelan exile for decades.[48]

With the money from their bourgeois and Venezuelan benefactors, the Terceristas bought hunting rifles and other small arms from legal gun shops and black-market vendors in San José for the October Offensive. The coordinated attacks, which took place on October 13, were mostly a disaster in military terms. On the Northern Front, Daniel Ortega and Victor Tirado succeeded in establishing a foothold in the mountainous region bordering Honduras.[49] But uprisings in Pacific towns never materialized. Worse still, the National Guard easily repelled Sandinista fighters on the Southern Front, forcing them to retreat back across the border to Costa Rica. The failure, which seemed to validate the GPP's dismissal of the offensive as "adventurism," badly demoralized the Terceristas. To their surprise, however, the twelve members of the provisional government urged them to press forward. Carlos Andrés Pérez reaffirmed his own support to Ernesto Cardenal.

Further encouragement came from Costa Rican ex-president José "Pepe" Figueres. In 1948, Figueres had risen to power with the support of a loose amalgam of regional statesmen (most prominently, Guatemala's Juan José Arévalo) and exiles, including Nicaraguans, sometimes referred to as the "Caribbean Legion." In exchange for their support in toppling a government in San José that happened to enjoy good relations with Somoza García, Figueres assumed a commitment to host Nicaraguan exiles and back efforts to oust their country's dictator.[50] Among other plans, he supported Pedro Joaquín Chamorro's failed 1959 uprising (he also lent support to plots against Trujillo and Batista in the Dominican Republic and Cuba, respectively). For their part, the Somozas and allied governments in the region supported Costa Rican exiles when they invaded their country and tried to depose Figueres. In a concrete linkage to that earlier "Caribbean Cold War," the Costa Rican caudillo literally unearthed hundreds of weapons and crates of ammunition that he had buried on his farm—aptly called La Lucha Sin Fin—at the end of the Costa Rican civil war and provided them to the FSLN's Tercerista faction after their failed offensive.[51] Figueres's friend Carlos Andrés Pérez, who had lived in Costa Rica while exiled by Venezuelan dictator Marcos Pérez Jiménez, helped convince him of the Terceristas' bona fides.

Ditching the provisional government idea for the time being, on October 14, Ramírez and company published a communiqué revealing themselves as El Grupo de los Doce (the Group of Twelve). The Doce stated their intention to return to Nicaragua and promote a broad anti-Somoza front in support of the FSLN's armed struggle. According to the *New York Times*, the appearance among them of priests, conservative aristocrats, wealthy empresarios, and respected intellectuals "provoked disbelief" in the Nicaraguan political class.[52] It also changed the game for the Sandinista Front. No longer in mountainous isolation, one of its factions—as Proletarian tendency leader Jaime Wheelock later put it—had "a broad and politically acceptable national face," something that "credibly prefigured an alternative to the government."[53] At the time, however, the public revelation of this bourgeois support group threatened to deepen the rift between Terceristas and rival factions within the FSLN. In December, a group of GPP sympathizers crashed a UDEL conference in Matagalpa, chanting *"¡UDEL, Los Doce, y Somoza son la misma cosa!"* (UDEL, *los Doce*, and Somoza are all the same!). Upon hearing those chants from the FSLN's far left, Pedro Joaquín Chamorro realized that UDEL and the Terceristas had common ground. Moreover, the backing of the Group of Twelve—which included close friends and family of Chamorro—made the armed path seem more viable and less likely to produce a radical government. Later in December 1977, Chamorro sent Sergio Ramírez a friendly note in which, in a cheeky insinuation of his willingness to join the project, he signed off as "the likely number thirteen." Shortly thereafter, in early January of the new year, Chamorro's surrogates made arrangements for him to secretly meet with Daniel Ortega and Ramírez in Mexico the following month.[54]

That meeting never happened. On January 10, two assassins shot Chamorro through his open car window, in broad daylight on a well-trafficked Managua thoroughfare. Subsequent investigations determined that the intellectual author of the crime was not Somoza Debayle, but rather business associates of his son Anastasio Somoza Portocarrero, known derisively by Nicaraguans as simply *"El Chigüín"* (the Kid). The dictator, pointing to the fact that he had quickly arrested the hitmen, insisted on his innocence. After all, had he so desired, he could have arranged Chamorro's death at any point in the past. But he knew very well that killing a popular journalist and activist—one, notably, from the country's traditional elite—would be an unforced error that might spell disaster for his regime.[55]

The Detonator

Ernesto Cardenal later called Chamorro's assassination the "detonator" that triggered the Revolution.[56] The Somozas had weathered many storms in the past. But this time they proved unable to restore the loyalty of Nicaraguan elites or reclaim streets seized by the angry masses. A previously favorable international context also deteriorated at the worst possible time. After four decades, the regime finally entered unstable equilibrium in 1978.

Scholars widely agree that the assassination of Pedro Joaquín Chamorro finally turned the bourgeoisie against Somoza.[57] As previously mentioned, the dictatorship's mutual understanding with the Nicaraguan private sector was already strained in the 1970s. Nonetheless, pseudo-opposition parties that represented the business elite continued working within the regime's political framework until 1978. While the regime had tortured and murdered countless dissidents, it was not until the elite activist's assassination that COSIP (the federation of chambers of commerce, the maximum expression of elite business interests in Nicaragua) openly called for Somoza's resignation. They backed their demand by gut-punching the economy with a two-week commercial and industrial lock-out launched on January 23. As Lenin would have put it, Chamorro's death convinced the upper classes that it was no longer possible "to live in the old way."[58] Thus, new potential was created for Sandinista leaders to build a revolutionary coalition with powerful elite sectors.

In murdering a popular personality, the dictatorship also engendered the first wide-scale popular rebellion in its four-decade history. In Managua, thousands of mourners accompanied the slain journalist's coffin to its burial place, while others sacked and burned Somoza family businesses. In both the capital and other cities, young men and women attacked National Guard posts with whatever small arms and improvised weapons they could muster. The most notable of these impromptu rebellions took place in the historically Indigenous Monimbó neighborhood of Masaya in the last week of February, where violent rioting spread after National Guardsmen prevented the community from renaming a town square after Chamorro. When normal infantry proved incapable of quelling the unrest after a few days, Somoza ordered a combined tank and helicopter assault. Tercerista leader Camilo Ortega, like many other FSLN fighters who joined the spontaneous popular revolts of early 1978, died alongside dozens of civilians in the attack.[59] Camilo's brother, Humberto, later wrote that Pedro Joaquín's death helped create unity behind the cause of armed struggle: "He became—along with Carlos Fonseca Amador—the other fundamental pillar in the struggle for liberation and democracy under the enveloping mantle of Augusto C. Sandino."[60] A few months later, a CIA report observed that the Chamorro assassination had spurred FSLN recruitment.[61] Meanwhile, Somoza held phony municipal elections in February to demonstrate his popularity.[62]

The speed with which so many Nicaraguan youth collaborated with FSLN fighters, joined in labor strikes, or took up arms suggested that the distance between middle-class revolutionary leaders and mass opposition to the regime was finally closing. FSLN engagement at the bases and with "intermediate organizations" had clearly borne fruit: students, workers, and those toiling in the informal economy all came out in massive numbers in 1978–79.[63] The popular anti-Somoza alliances were not only built from above, however. As historian Jeffrey Gould notes of a long-running agrarian workers' movement in the cotton-producing region of Chinandega, rural Nicaraguans had independently developed nodes of anti-Somoza resistance that, in turn, generated fighters and collaborators for the FSLN. Though rural participation in the 1978–79 insurrection was proportionally low at the national level, the case that Gould studied was nonetheless emblematic of broader, crucial change that had taken place over time: "Workers and campesinos chipped away and finally, together with the Sandinistas, knocked down those political barriers of isolation and silence that for decades had ensured the survival of Somocismo."[64]

The resulting coalition was a very young one, because the vast majority of Nicaraguans on the barricades were less than a quarter century old. It was also a "dual-gender coalition," as Karen Kampwirth termed it, because the number of women combatants as a proportion of the total was high compared to other revolutionary movements around the world.[65] Robert Sierakowski recently argued that working-class Nicaraguans responded not only to the Sandinistas' critique of social inequality and regime repression but also to their more conservative promise to restore law and order and bring about moral renewal after Somoza.[66]

Chamorro's death had fatal implications for the dictatorship on the international scene. Somoza had long held a claim to be, as Panamanian president Aristides Royo described him to a US diplomat, "the most hated man in Latin America . . . Pinochet and Stroessner are almost likeable by comparison."[67] After Chamorro's assassination, Somoza's repressive tactics drew even more attention abroad, a problematic turn of events given the Carter administration's promise to emphasize human rights in US foreign policy.

In his memoir, Somoza blamed that foreign policy shift for undermining his government. Indeed, as former Carter administration officials have explained, this policy made it harder for Somoza to attain the weaponry needed to quash the insurrection. US policy also compelled him to make concessions like lifting a state of siege in October 1977. But the Carter administration, despite its disapproval of the regime's rights record, was not considering pushing Somoza to resign in early 1978. For one thing, the president had promised to break from his predecessors in the Oval Office and avoid intervening so openly in Latin American affairs. He was also restrained by a more traditional, Cold War logic that saw Washington maintain cordial relationships with anti-communist military dictatorships in the Global South; Somoza remained a solid ally in geopolitical terms.

In any event, changes and continuities in US foreign policy only go so far in explaining the fall of Somoza and the rise of the Sandinistas. To be sure, the preference for nonintervention and respect for human rights may have left Washington with "fewer tools to prevent" a left-wing revolutionary outcome in Nicaragua.[68] But State Department officials did not arm Nicaraguans or call on them to rise up against their government; they also actively sought to minimize the possibility that the Sandinista Front would reach power. In fact, US officials often struggled to influence the situation on the ground at all. As Robert Pastor (director of Latin American Affairs on Carter's National Security Council) remembers, "others, marching to different drummers, moved to center stage with the objective of overthrowing Somoza militarily."[69]

One of them was Carlos Andrés Pérez, who was enraged by the slaying of Chamorro, a longtime friend. Chamorro had attended the Venezuelan's inauguration in 1974 and begged his assistance in overthrowing Somoza, but Pérez maintained that Nicaraguans first needed to create conditions for regime change before he could add his support (an intent confirmed by his covert assistance for the Terceristas' 1977 October Offensive). In an interview given after the 1979 Revolution, Pérez said that his friend's assassination made him compromise his earlier position.[70] He started taking a more direct role, which included blocking the sale of his country's plentiful oil to Nicaragua. On January 31—three weeks after the assassination—Pérez sent Carter a letter urging him to pressure Somoza to resign, and refused to meet with the US ambassador to Venezuela until he received a response. According to Pastor, the letter pushed National Security Adviser Zbigniew Brzezinski and other high-ranking officials to see the Nicaraguan crisis as a "political issue" for the first time. Carter responded on February 17, pledging to pressure Somoza on human rights issues but refusing to mention the possibility of regime change.[71] In the coming months, his Venezuelan counterpart voiced agreement but quietly started going his own way. The payments to the Doce had begun months earlier, and according to one Venezuelan government official, Pérez may have ended up spending as much as $100 million to oust Somoza.[72] That support, as illustrated by the earlier Gabriel García Márquez connection, was highly secretive. Ramírez describes Pérez as a "gutsy conspirator" in his own right, who by mid-1978 had left the US ambassador in Caracas with no clue as to the Venezuelan government's involvement with the FSLN.[73]

Venezuela, like the other countries that eventually got involved—Panama, Costa Rica, Cuba, and Mexico—had specific goals and interests at play. In a recent study, Mexican historian Gerardo Sánchez Nateras meticulously detailed their unique motivations, highlighting the diversity and complexity of Latin American foreign policies in the late twentieth century.[74] More importantly, their intentions reveal what each government expected to get in return for assisting the rebels. As Sandinista guerrilla leader Joaquín Cuadra Lacayo recalls with respect to Pérez's support for the Revolution, "there's no such thing as a free lunch."[75]

There were ideological, economic, and strategic dimensions to Pérez's incipient intervention in Nicaragua. A founding member of Venezuela's social democratic Acción Democrática (AD) party, he was imprisoned and exiled for his opposition to the dictatorship of Marcos Pérez Jiménez, an ally of the Somozas. Upon its overthrow, Pérez Jiménez's military regime was succeeded by the democratically elected administration of Carlos Andrés Pérez's mentor, Rómulo Betancourt. In his first address to Venezuela's congress in 1959, Betancourt called for the nonrecognition of Latin American states that had come to power via nondemocratic means. In doing so, he challenged the US national security doctrine, a policy that saw Latin American militaries and conservative elites join forces to keep "internal" communist subversives at bay while Washington managed the "external" Soviet threat. Betancourt's approach also contrasted with Mexico's Estrada Doctrine of nonintervention in other states' internal affairs.

The Betancourt Doctrine, as it came to be known, was a core element of Pérez's first presidency (1974–79). Indeed, Betancourt's understudy took the defense of democracy further. He advocated both nonrecognition of authoritarian regimes in Latin America *and* aggressive action to actively undermine them. This ideological crusade, along with a more general push to increase Venezuelan influence in the Caribbean Basin, was made possible by soaring energy prices in the second half of the 1970s. Oil-rich Venezuela's new assertiveness included backing for Panama's quest to reclaim its canal, and the creation alongside Mexico of the Latin American Economic System (SELA), an early attempt at regional integration on the margins of the US-dominated Organization of American States (OAS). Aside from favorable commodity prices, the global background for Venezuela's expansionism was the cooling of superpower tensions known as détente. This Cold War context was not lost on Sandinista strategists, either. Humberto Ortega recalls how, as the situation on the ground in Nicaragua evolved, Tercerista leaders factored in the potential end of détente between East and West in the late 1970s: "In this context I pointed out the need to take advantage of Carter's human rights policy and support for bourgeois social-democratic forces . . . that situation would not be present for much longer, because crises in Africa and the Arab world were tensing the international political situation. It is for this reason that we proposed the overthrow of the dictatorship in the briefest time frame possible."[76]

Another Venezuelan goal was to contain Castro, who had previously sponsored a leftist insurgency against the Betancourt government, where Pérez served as interior minister.[77] Thus, when weighing the risks and opportunities created by the crisis of the Somoza regime, one of his main instincts was to do everything possible to avoid a "second Cuba" in Nicaragua. In a March 1978 meeting with President Carter in Caracas, he argued that the longer Somoza remained in power, "a very dangerous situation will develop . . . the Sandinistas are growing in power and have the support of all anti-Somoza factions. The situation is like that of Batista."[78] Unlike some US Foreign Service officers, Pérez knew enough about Nicaragua's political landscape to recognize that, if outside actors were to prevent the rise of a decidedly Cuban-oriented government, it was wiser to support moderate elements of the FSLN than to seek a non-leftist alternative to the Sandinistas, which might not even exist. Thus, as fighters on the ground like Victor Hugo Tinoco noted, "the most important [Venezuelan] aid was directed to the factions that they considered most plural and most social-democratic."[79] As Venezuela's involvement deepened in 1978, Pérez increasingly used his support as leverage to push the FSLN toward the Terceristas' more flexible—and ultimately more effective—path to power, as well as to empower moderate elements within that faction itself.[80]

The Venezuelan statesman was joined in this scheming by his friend Omar Torrijos, who had provided safe haven to Sandinistas of various tendencies beginning in 1977, or perhaps even earlier. The Panamanian caudillo was not as different from Somoza as his democratically elected partner in conspiracy from Venezuela. He also had his own reasons for pursuing regime change in Nicaragua. On the one hand, Torrijos—a School of the Americas graduate and lifelong army officer—came to power in a coup and was therefore not opposed to military governments in principle. On the other hand, in a conversation with senior US officials in 1977, Torrijos voiced "extreme displeasure for Somoza's right-wing dictatorship, not because he disliked Somoza (because he didn't) but because he considered it such a feudal country."[81] In fact, Torrijos had a populist-leftist streak that distinguished him from his Nicaraguan counterpart. The Panamanian Revolution, as he and his allies termed it, implemented an agrarian reform and its civilian government—though frankly subordinate to the Panamanian National Guard—featured leftists and communists in important posts. During the 1970s, its government adopted an increasingly assertive and Third Worldist foreign policy, leading to clashes with US-aligned Nicaragua over such issues as Torrijos's attempts to create an OPEC-style cartel of banana-exporting countries (which Somoza helped scuttle) and his reopening of diplomatic relations with Cuba (which Somoza denounced).[82] Most importantly, Somoza did not support the real goal behind Panama's diplomatic offensive in the nonaligned world: its desire to negotiate a handover of its US-owned and -operated interoceanic canal.

Torrijos eventually came to see Nicaragua's national liberation struggle as a key element in Panama's own anti-colonial project to reclaim the waterway. As the window of détente appeared to close, a hostile Somoza government—one connected with the most conservative sectors of the US political system—might threaten diplomatic (and in the worst case scenario, military) efforts to nationalize the canal. As Panamanian diplomat Marcel Salamín, one of Torrijos's closest advisers, explains: "As the confrontation with Somoza sharpened, [Torrijos] suggested that it was vital for Panama to open up democratic space for itself in Central America; because without democratic space, Panama could not truly complete the task of approving and implementing the [Torrijos-Carter] treaties . . . if the negotiations failed, he realized, the Central American-Nicaraguan problem would become a vital one in the strategy to recover the Canal through armed means if the Treaties were rejected in the North American Congress."[83] Torrijos and the Carter administration signed the two Panama Canal Treaties—which arranged the closing of the Panama Canal Zone and the eventual transfer of the canal to Panamanian administration—in September 1977. But the treaties still faced a difficult ratification process in the US Congress in the spring of 1978. After that, Carter would still have to negotiate implementation legislation with lawmakers, providing the project's opponents in Washington with ample opportunity to weaken or altogether frustrate the transfer of canal ownership to the Panamanian government.

In light of that uncertainty, Panamanian leaders saw Somoza's ouster as strategically beneficial—a fact that Sandinista leaders were aware of.[84] Like Pérez, Torrijos carefully supported the Tercerista faction because he believed in their military strategy, but, more importantly, in order to ensure a pluralistic transitional government wherein the Sandinistas would share power with other important political actors.[85] Torrijos worried that the rise of a radical, leftist-dominated government would almost certainly provoke an aggressive response by the United States, giving anti-communist lawmakers more ammunition to tank the Torrijos-Carter treaties. A direct US invasion of Nicaragua would also complicate any Nasser-style backup plan for seizing the canal by force.[86]

Torrijos, who was fond of political allegory, compared Central America to a DC-10 airplane. Overthrowing Somoza would be like taking a screw out of the aircraft in midair.[87] To keep the Central America plane flying, the Sandinistas had to "maintain the right speed." In another transportation metaphor that Salamín recalls, Torrijos explained that "depending on the velocity . . . the whole Central American train could be derailed. If [the FSLN] became too radicalized, the train would be driven toward greater confrontation with the United States."[88] Moreover, he had the canal treaties to worry about. If he made too much noise in Nicaragua, the situation could easily blow up in his face. Throughout the negotiations and ratification process for the Canal Treaty, Torrijos therefore turned the pressure on Nicaragua up or down as the situation demanded. Overall, he struck a successful balance. Throughout 1978–79, Torrijos secretly supported the FSLN and assured his friend Jimmy Carter of the Terceristas' good intentions. For its part, the Carter White House frequently cited Torrijos's involvement as proof that there was a multilateral effort to prevent the revolution from becoming "Castroist and Communist."[89]

The Insurrectional Flame

Like Pérez, Torrijos used his influence to nudge the FSLN toward the strategy he believed would ensure Somoza's ouster, create a sustainable transition, and ward off a disastrous US intervention every step of the way. The crux of that strategy was the Tercerista policy of promoting broad alliances and focusing the action in the cities. Some Sandinistas still opposed these initiatives. But as conditions changed on the ground and popular rebellions exploded across the country, the other factions were drawn like magnets to the "insurrectional" thesis.

In the spring of 1978, leaders from different tendencies attempted unification talks in Panama and other foreign sanctuaries. Embryonic unity efforts allowed for some limited coordination in military operations. It also helped Sandinista leaders harmonize efforts in the nonmilitary sphere: cadres from the different tendencies jointly helped create the Movimiento Pueblo Unido (MPU)—an alliance of Sandinista-led popular organizations including neighborhood associations, women's groups, youth organizations, and unions—that helped articulate and organize the revolutionary coalition being built from below. But it was too soon to mend differences altogether. Some GPP leaders remained critical of the Terceristas' military "adventurism" in the first half of 1978, such as their March 8th assassination of Somoza's army chief of staff. Furthermore, leaders from across the Sandinista Front worried that alliances with bourgeois or moderate forces might distort the cause. Indeed, even Tercerista commanders like Hugo Torres Jiménez found it difficult to "understand, let alone complacently accept, a policy of alliances with the bourgeoisie . . . which we considered complicit in the perpetuation of the dictatorship." But internal doubters like Torres recanted as they began to see the fundamental, immediate contradiction in Nicaragua as not one of class but of "the people against the dictatorship."[90]

The alliance-building strategy took more formal shape with the emergence of organized, anti-Somoza political organizations in the spring of 1978. The late Chamorro's UDEL coalition joined forces with the Movimiento Democrático Nicaragüense (MDN), a pro-business party founded by the young private sector leader Alfonso Robelo. Together, they created the Frente Amplio Opositor (FAO—Broad Opposition Front). Thanks to Doce efforts to "give the Broad Opposition Front a popular face," that newly created FAO subsequently allied with the MPU. By the summer of 1978, in other words, organized support for the FSLN's armed struggle encompassed a remarkably wide range of actors including the private sector, Liberals, Conservatives, communists, socialists, civil society, and grassroots organizations. This popular frontism was an early expression of the "multiclass coalition" that social scientists have identified as the key ingredient that distinguished the successful Nicaraguan Revolution from failed uprisings elsewhere in the Global South.[91] Leaders from all three tendencies have noted that Tercerista control over the most important political connections (domestic and international) was a reason why their faction became ascendant over the others during the crisis of the Somoza dictatorship.[92]

By the middle of 1978, Somoza's armed overthrow was truly on the agenda. As Jaime Wheelock of the Proletarian leadership explained: "The ability, timing, and audacity of the Tercerista tendency in sparking armed actions in the cities opened the path to the insurrection. That, along with the policy of alliances that they put in practice, gave revolutionary forces the appearance of a credible alternative to the government."[93] Somoza Debayle was somewhat slow to keep up. In a conversation with the US ambassador the day after the hit on his army chief of staff in March, Somoza dismissed the opposition as representing a "minority" and claimed that a rebellion within his Liberal Party or National Guard was a more likely threat to his presidency.[94] By late April, however, he began expressing concern that the crisis was no longer being directed by the political opposition, but by "Marxist revolutionaries."[95] It is a testament to the highly contingent nature of the 1979 insurrection that its principal victim did not take the FSLN seriously enough until fifteen months before its climax.

Even when he realized the changing nature of the threat, Somoza did not consider major concessions, let alone resigning. One reason for his confidence was his belief that he still enjoyed backing by the highest authorities in the United States. In July, Somoza secretly met with Pérez for a four-hour meeting on a small island off the coast of Venezuela, where the Nicaraguan leader brandished a letter from Carter that he interpreted as an endorsement of his ambitions to stay in power. By Somoza's own account, Pérez—who hoped to convince his foe to resign voluntarily—responded coldly: "I don't care what Carter says. Our position is firm. You have to go."[96]

Meanwhile, the multiclass coalition was scoring further victories. On July 8, the Doce returned to Managua to help bolster the unity of the broad anti-Somocista front, push the FAO further into the arms of the FSLN, and mobilize the masses in support of a popular insurrection.[97] Somoza's propaganda apparatus attacked this FSLN support group for being out-of-touch millionaires and Costa Rica–based traitors. But their highly choreographed return to Managua—bearing the slogan "the dictatorship is a cadaver, we're here to bury it"—was received by throngs of adoring sympathizers. Further adding to the atmosphere of rebellion was an August 5 statement by the conservative Catholic Church hierarchy calling for Somoza's resignation.[98]

The time was ripe for a major stunt. The Sandinistas called the Nicaraguan congress, which was composed of Somoza's Liberals and representatives from the various puppet parties, la Chanchera (the Pigsty). In the summer of 1978, they made plans to take the National Palace, where the legislature was housed, by force. The main goals of Operation Pigsty were to secure the release of dozens of FSLN prisoners and to trigger a massive insurrectionary response by the population. Tercerista tacticians considered the mission part of a broader strategy of "armed propaganda," a reference to the style of urban guerrilla warfare popularized by Uruguay's Marxist Tupamaro movement, which seized high-profile sites in Montevideo to spectacular public relations effect. On August 22, Edén Pastora led the Ribogerto Lopéz Brigade, named after Somoza Garcia's assassin. Disguised as National Guard troops, the commandos simply strolled into the main chamber. Within three minutes, they had quietly secured the building and taken its occupants hostage. After defending the position from a series of counterattacks by elite National Guard troops, the operation ended in stunning success. Following a mediation by Catholic Cardinal Miguel Obando y Bravo, Somoza agreed to pay a ransom, publish a Tercerista communiqué, and release all FSLN prisoners (from all three factions) and allow them to fly to Panama and Venezuela on a plane sent by Carlos Andrés Pérez.[99]

In a visceral illustration of the FSLN's internal divisions and how those fissures were refracted by the involvement of Latin American leaders, the transportation of the freed prisoners did not go according to plan. As Ramírez explains,

> In a novel twist, symbolic of the new alliances, the commando
> members and the liberated prisoners flew toward Panama and
> Venezuela, not to Cuba. Nevertheless, at the last minute, the
> Hercules plane that Carlos Andrés Pérez had sent from Venezuela
> had to return to Caracas empty. Ideology still weighed heavily, and
> Tomás Borge refused to accept support from a social-democrat
> president. To cover up the insult, [the Terceristas] sent Edén Pastora
> with the flag taken from the National Congress assembly hall to
> place in safekeeping with Carlos Andrés. It would be returned to its
> rightful place when we had a democratic parliament.[100]

While divisions still threatened the whole project, Operation Pigsty achieved its stated goal of generating popular support for the armed struggle. As soon as it succeeded, the politician-led FAO and grassroots MPU called another general strike. Five days later, young men and women in the provincial capital of Matagalpa—joined by nearby GPP fighters—rose up against the local National Guard, holding significant parts of the city for several days. Despite these setbacks, Somoza was confident and pleased that the attack was "the most serious mistake the Sandinistas had ever made." He believed that the Sandinistas, by taking the legislature hostage, had unmasked themselves as a bloodthirsty, terrorist force that would be repudiated by the populace.[101] He was wrong. In the words of guerrilla leader Hugo Torres, by the time the Terceristas called on the general population to rise up against the regime on September 7, the "insurrectional flame had been lit, and it couldn't be put out."[102]

2   Rise of the Sandinistas

· ·

By midsummer 1978, the *New York Times* could report that "the days of the dictatorship, eroded from within and assailed from without," seemed numbered. Previously off the international radar, Nicaragua was suddenly flooded by foreign correspondents eager to follow what was clearly "no ordinary political movement." Unlike other revolutions propelled solely by the working classes and radical Left, the anti-Somoza uprising was made possible by the traditional aristocracy's "betrayal" of the ruling family. In a legendary series, American photojournalist Susan Meiselas vividly portrayed both the ferocity of regime repression as well as the profound sorrow of its victims. She also captured the rebellion's idiosyncrasies. One image showed a crucifix- and beret-wearing rebel tossing a live Molotov cocktail at a National Guard outpost; another featured a well-to-do Nicaraguan couple bringing refreshments to the barricades. Meiselas's oeuvre brought to life a "national mutiny in which almost every sector of the country—left and right, rich and poor—is united against a dynastic dictatorship" sustained exclusively through force.[1]

But as correspondent Alan Riding rightly noted, it was still impossible to know exactly what would come next in Nicaragua. Despite bad portents, Anastasio Somoza Debayle insisted on retaining power. "*Ni me voy, ni me van,*" he promised, echoing one of his late father's favorite refrains. CIA analysts predicted he might hold on.[2] To some degree, Somoza's obstinacy played into the Sandinistas' hands. Faced with the regime's violent refusal to contemplate a transition, the population increasingly saw "no other way out" but its total dismantling through armed revolution.[3] At the same time, prolonged anarchy and bloodshed might narrow the Sandinista Front's path to victory. The middle and upper classes, vital to the nascent revolutionary coalition, could get spooked. To avoid a leftist conclusion detrimental to their class interests, they might feel tempted to cut a deal with the dictatorship. And while the Carter administration was unwilling to pull out all stops in defense of the Somozas, it remained determined to prevent an FSLN-dominated scenario. The threat of US intervention loomed throughout the dictatorship's terminal crisis. Furthermore, the fractured Sandinista leadership lacked the military, logistical, and financial resources to capitalize on its revolutionary appeal and mount a full-blown insurrectionary offensive. Thus, even as Somoza's exit seemed increasingly likely in 1978, the political possibilities were abundant. Armed revolution was one of many roads Nicaraguans might travel.

Though it had come a long way, the Sandinista Front still needed to further improve its position. In the first half of 1978, they had taken advantage of defecting elites and widespread popular discontent to throw the regime off balance. The sheer number of Nicaraguans risking their lives to end the dictatorship had grown beyond the Sandinistas' greatest expectations. The problem now, according to rebel commander Hugo Torres, "was not the lack of fighters but of weapons, munitions, supplies, and greater combat readiness in order to launch the next offensive."[4] Solutions would be found abroad. Convinced that US-led talks between Somoza and moderate opposition leaders were going nowhere, Torrijos and Pérez quietly scrambled to secure arms for FSLN offensives in the fall of 1978. To beat them back, government forces relied on American weaponry. But as carnage ensued, US diplomats inched toward the realization that no sustainable solution could involve Somoza remaining in power. Parallels could be drawn with the contemporaneous crisis in Iran, where another multiclass revolution was putting a sultanistic and dynastic regime against the ropes. Jimmy Carter's personal convictions made him queasy about abetting either government's human rights violations. Consequently, the Nicaraguan National Guard found it increasingly difficult to procure firepower. Much like champions of Tehran's deposed Mohammad Reza Shah Pahlavi, Somoza's defenders would later blame Carter for his downfall. Once ousted, the dictator himself put it thus: "An army without ammunition cannot fight, and so the Marxists achieved a tremendous victory in Nicaragua."[5]

Nevertheless, decisions made in Washington were only part of the story. While they may help explain the regime's collapse, changes in US foreign policy cannot account for its substitution by a radical revolutionary government led by the Sandinista Front. In fact, throughout 1978–79, Carter administration officials bent over backward to avoid such an outcome. Like Graham Greene's Quiet American in Vietnam, they searched for a moderate "third force" that might replace Somoza and box out the leftists in the process. But US embassy and State Department officials ultimately felt frustrated by their inability to shape events on the ground. They often misread local dynamics. In Somoza's Nicaragua, pro-US "moderate rebels" were, for the most part, a figment of the American imagination.

The Latin American dimensions of the Nicaraguan crisis helped put matters beyond Washington's control. Regional state and non-state actors, who typically did a better job reading the pulse of the situation, acted with greater resolve—and in closer collaboration with anti-Somoza forces—to mold their preferred outcome in Nicaragua. Global solidarity movements, enraptured by the promise of revolutionary renewal in the Third World, campaigned against negotiated settlements that might preserve elements of the dictatorship—"*somocismo* without Somoza," as many Nicaraguans called it. More importantly, armed leftist movements from Colombia, Chile, Argentina, and many other countries sent hundreds of combatants. Battered by counterinsurgent violence in their homelands, they found an outlet for their revolutionary ambitions in Nicaragua. These *internacionalistas* would play pivotal roles. Regional governments proved even more decisive. Some, such as neighboring Costa Rica, were immediately threatened by the Somoza regime and thus felt moved to assist in its undoing. Others, such as Mexico and Cuba, saw in Nicaragua an opportunity to further their own strategic interests and threw their weight behind the Sandinistas in early 1979. Along with Panama and Venezuela, these Latin American states provided the weaponry and expertise necessary to turn an unruly popular rebellion into a more conventional military campaign. They also helped broker unity between the FSLN's disparate factions. And crucially, they legitimized the Sandinistas' armed option and isolated Somoza in the diplomatic arena. By the summer of 1979, they had even helped convince the region's anti-communist military dictatorships that Somoza was more trouble than he was worth. More than most other US-aligned dictators in the Cold War era, Somoza was alone in his own neighborhood.

An unlikely fellowship of Latin American leaders operated at the nerve center of this transnational effort. Ideologically, its members—Panama's Omar Torrijos, Venezuela's Carlos Andrés Pérez, Costa Rica's Rodrigo Carazo Odio, Cuba's Fidel Castro, and Mexico's José López Portillo—were more different than they were similar. They also saw unique and sometimes contradictory state interests at stake in Nicaragua. But a shared mistrust of US meddling, which they blamed for the rise of right-wing despots like the Somozas, brought them together. Specifically, they agreed that prolonged instability in Nicaragua would inevitably serve as a pretext for another US military intervention in Latin America. Such an outcome, in their view, would inflame the tense situation in Central America and retard the entire region's development in the process. They were also bound by their personal disdain for Somoza as well as their sympathy for the young and charismatic

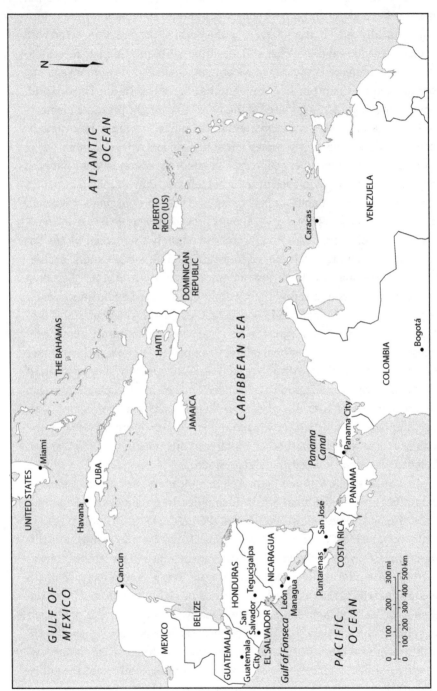

Central America and the Caribbean

Nicaraguan guerrillas. Along with other regional notables like José Figueres, they came to see those muchachos—and indeed their utopian mission—through a paternal lens.

Diplomatic archives and oral history interviews show how these foreign actors "bought stock" in the FSLN, to borrow the words of Torrijos, as a means of shaping the Sandinistas' tactics, alliances, and ultimately their revolutionary government and program. Therefore, their involvement not only helps explain how a revolution with socialist leanings entered the realm of the politically possible in Nicaragua. Multiple Cold War storylines, including superpower détente and a "global offensive" by worldwide national liberation movements, converged in the rise of the Sandinistas.[6] Above all, the Latin Americanization of their insurrection suggests the Nicaraguan Revolution had become a flashpoint in a broader hemispheric struggle to determine the region's political destiny toward the end of the twentieth century.

Giving War a Chance

Following the success of Operation Pigsty in August 1978, the Tercerista high command worked to build on the momentum. Planning was already underway for a major offensive in September. They solicited armaments from Carlos Andrés Pérez, who provided Belgian FAL battle rifles taken from the arsenal of the Venezuelan presidency.[7] The guns and other equipment were flown on a military plane sent by General Omar Torrijos and transported via Costa Rica. Nicaragua's southern neighbor served as a "strategic rear guard" for Sandinistas of various factions.[8] The democratic country was an ideal sanctuary: close to the homeland and lacking the brutal counterinsurgency apparatus developed by many Latin American governments during the Cold War era. But in 1978, Costa Rica became more than a haven. Feeling their country's core interests were at stake in the violent crisis of the Somoza regime, Costa Rican authorities chose to intervene directly in Nicaraguan politics. Costa Rica's involvement marked the increasing internationalization of the Nicaraguan situation, a fact that tended to accelerate the process by which an armed revolutionary outcome became likely.

The purpose of the Terceristas' so-called September Offensive was to channel and harness the spontaneous popular insurrections that, aided by Sandinistas of all factions, had erupted across the country in 1978. The plan was roughly similar to the previous year's October Offensive: on

September 9, when the latest FAO-led strike was coming to an end, FSLN fighters launched synchronized attacks on National Guard garrisons in Léon, Chinandega, Estelí, Masaya, and Managua. Simultaneously, Edén Pastora's Southern Front once again attempted to conquer a slice of territory for the installation of a provisional government. Because of its centrality to the greater Tercerista strategy, the Southern Front amassed the most troops and weaponry. National Guardsmen and Sandinista battalions assumed fixed positions, giving the fighting a more conventional style, unlike the door-to-door street fighting in urban areas or the guerrilla warfare along the rural periphery.[9] In September 1978, some FSLN leaders outside the Tercerista tendency still disputed the insurrectional thesis, but these differences of opinion waned, Proletarian tendency leader Jaime Wheelock recalled, "as the war moved to the cities."[10] The government's reckless response to the September Offensive, where National Guard forces racked up horrifying numbers of civilian casualties, further mobilized Nicaraguan youth against Somoza.

Predictably, Costa Rica—the staging ground for the offensive's main thrust—was irreversibly dragged into the Nicaraguan crisis. Since independence, the two countries have clashed over territorial disputes. Costa Rica annexed Nicaragua's southernmost province in the early nineteenth century and contests its northern neighbor's control over the San Juan River, which straddles most of their shared border. Additionally, Costa Ricans—who by the 1970s had built the most robust and stable representative democracy in Latin America—generally despised Somoza Debayle for his unenlightened despotism. Worse still, the elder Somoza García had previously intervened in their country's 1948 civil war. Ex-president Pepe Figueres's crusade against the Somozas therefore had a personal dimension. This history of bilateral animosity, and the increasing incidence of violent border confrontations during the late 1970s, backdropped his country's involvement in Somoza's downfall. Though anti-somocista sentiment was common among Costa Ricans, Sandinistas there did not operate without problems. Clandestine militants—who after 1976 enjoyed the support of Vanguardia Popular (the Moscow-line communist party)—were routinely persecuted by local security forces.[11] Initially, President Rodrigo Carazo Odio was disturbed by Pérez's belligerence against Nicaragua because it inevitably complicated Costa Rica's security prospects.[12] Shortly after taking office in the spring of 1978, Carazo traveled to the Nicaraguan border in order to discuss de-escalation of tensions with Somoza's foreign minister. "If you respect us," Carazo promised, "we will respect you."[13]

That concordat only lasted a few months. On September 12, Nicaraguan planes chased FSLN contingents into Costa Rican territory and bombed a group of student bystanders in the process. Costa Rica was no longer neutral. The Nicaraguan government, rather than the Sandinistas and their foreign allies, was the problem. While not yet committed to Somoza's overthrow, the Carazo administration took the first steps in what Juan José Echeverría—the minister of public security—calls an "undeclared war" on Nicaragua.[14] Carazo, a Christian Democrat elected at the head of a coalition of center-right parties, did not share the same socialist heritage as the Sandinista Front. But he sympathized with their nationalist defiance of US influence and came to believe that, with the right leadership, they could bring about a transition to electoral democracy. More importantly, he and his advisers deemed Somoza a direct threat to Costa Rican citizens and territorial integrity. After protesting the attack at the Organization of American States, Carazo called the Venezuelan ambassador in San José to coordinate next steps; within three days, the two countries had quietly signed an informal mutual defense treaty.[15] Because Costa Rica lacked a standing army, it was a one-sided deal: Carlos Andrés Pérez placed a squad of bomber planes at the international airport in San José, signaling to Somoza that he should think twice before invading Costa Rican territory. While the government in San José had previously focused on "avoiding confrontations with the Nicaraguan National Guard, as well as blocking the use of our territory to attack Nicaragua," as a result of the September 12 bombing Minister Echeverría met with Pastora and other Sandinista commanders and gave them permission to operate in Costa Rican territory, assuming they stayed within predetermined zones and so long as they promised to honor any cease-fires that emerged from upcoming negotiations between Somoza and the Frente Amplio Opositor (FAO—the broad alliance of opposition parties).[16]

Those talks were convened and mediated by the US government in reaction to the September Offensive.[17] Torrijos and Pérez, confident that Somoza would not negotiate in good faith, supported the talks but wished that Carter would simply force the dictator's resignation.[18] But the Carter White House, especially National Security Adviser Zbigniew Brzezinski and advisers from the Joint Chiefs of Staff, felt the Marxist-leaning Sandinista leadership would be worse for US interests than the unseemly Somoza family. While many career diplomats and Latin America experts shared Torrijos's and Pérez's belief that the dictator should resign as soon as possible, most US policymakers wanted to first secure a satisfactory alternative for post-Somoza Nicaragua that would minimize the influence of the Sandinistas—even the ostensibly moderate ones receiving support from Panama and Venezuela. Moreover, having promised to leave behind the overt interventionism of previous US presidents in the region, Carter was hesitant to be seen as dictating the removal of a Latin American head of state.[19]

Losing patience, Pérez warned a US diplomat on September 21 that "this will end in Cuban hands . . . the United States has not been decisive enough."[20] The following day, in a desperate attempt to sway the US president, Venezuelan and Panamanian officials told American contacts that their countries had plans to bomb Somoza's Managua bunker using planes stationed in Panama. Keeping interceptors on alert throughout the day, Carter phoned Torrijos for a tense conversation, in which he urged his Panamanian counterpart to swear off any military plans and instead support the mediation. Torrijos agreed, but told another US official that the Somoza problem "is not one for the OAS; it is a problem for a psychiatrist."[21] In a meeting the next day with Brzezinski (who was still furious at the threat), one of Torrijos's advisers reaffirmed Panama's commitment to a negotiated settlement but tried to induce US officials to include the Terceristas in their image of what a moderate Somoza replacement might look like, professing Torrijos's belief "that the extremists are isolated in Cuba and that the Sandinistas who are fighting in Nicaragua only intend to change Nicaragua into a kind of Costa Rica."[22] Brzezinski and company were unmoved. When the US government pressured Somoza into negotiating with the opposition and inviting international human rights observers, they did not bluntly demand his resignation as a precondition for talks.

The negotiations were therefore doomed by a fundamental contradiction. Somoza, who on the eve of the negotiations announced plans to double the National Guard's size, insisted on finishing his "constitutional" term through 1981. Meanwhile, the opposition FAO demanded the ruling family's immediate departure from the country. The FAO's negotiating team was led by Sergio Ramírez of the Doce (and secretly, the FSLN), Alfonso Robelo of the business sector–aligned MDN, and Rafael Córdova Rivas (Pedro Joaquín Chamorro's replacement at the helm of UDEL). A handwritten document from October 1978 reveals the different scenarios that these opposition leaders envisioned for the short and medium run.

The first scenario envisioned a "democratic-revolutionary" outcome, "not in the sense of a violent transition from a capitalist society to a socialist one," but a transition to liberal democracy. To achieve this outcome, the opposition should continue making use of private sector strikes, popular protests, and FSLN-led military operations to forcefully install a pluralistic revolutionary government that would implement a moderate, reformist agenda. This was basically the vision laid out by the Terceristas since their earliest talks with the Doce and foreign allies since 1977. A second, "constitutional" scenario imagined that Somoza might, under US pressure, resign and allow the National Congress to elect an interim president who would call for free elections. In this hypothetical scenario, the FAO would mobilize popular opinion against the caretaker government and insist on its replacement by the joint FAO-FSLN government envisioned in the previous scenario. Finally, the FAO pondered a "military" outcome. In this hypothetical scenario, the National Guard would overthrow Somoza in a palace coup and install a repressive military regime to restore order. This scenario would force the FAO to back the FSLN in ramping up the armed struggle. However, if the coup government promised to support a democratic transition, the FAO would seek participation in a joint civilian-military government so long as the Sandinista Front was included in some manner as well.[23]

The Revolution was less than a year away, but these branching prognostications highlighted the uncertainty that reigned at the time. Somoza's exit could play out in many ways. The first scenario—the closest to the Terceristas' vision—depended on the Sandinista Front making significant military advances. But the National Guard had successfully repelled the September Offensive.

Like Somoza, the FSLN backed the US-mediated talks primarily to buy time to prepare for future hostilities.[24] In order to scuttle any negotiated settlements that might frustrate the Terceristas' insurrectional plans, Sergio Ramírez backed out of the talks on October 25—just three weeks after they began. He denounced the negotiations as an imperialist maneuver to establish "somocismo without Somoza" in Nicaragua, alleging (correctly) that US officials hoped to ensure a transitional solution that preserved the National Guard and other institutions intact. While chief US negotiator William Bowdler did his best to keep the government and the FAO at the negotiating table, los Doce took up asylum at the Mexican embassy. At the same time, Sandinista commanders threatened to resume fighting if no agreement for Somoza's immediate departure was reached. Hoping to find a middle ground between Somoza and the FAO, mediating countries raised the idea of a plebiscite in late November. If Nicaraguans voted "Yes," Somoza would leave the country and a newly elected constituent assembly would form a transitional government reflecting the predominance of the FAO. If they voted "No," Somoza would see out his term in office.

While some FAO leaders expressed support for the idea in theory, the notion of a fair vote after forty-five years of rigged elections appeared ludicrous to most opposition actors. It mattered little in their eyes that Somoza lifted the latest state of martial law and restored some civil liberties in the first week of December.

In any event, the opposition was under extreme pressure from the FSLN to resist a settlement. In fact, many "moderate" FAO members were Sandinista sympathizers who would later join the party. Taking advantage of Somoza's brief political truce, the Doce left the safety of asylum to lead street protests against the plebiscite. And in a first major show of unity from its three competing factions, Sandinista Front leaders came together to warn the FAO—as well as any proponents in the international community—against the plebiscite:

> The FSLN-GPP, the FSLN-Tendencia Proletaria, and the General Staff of the Urban Resistance, FSLN-Insurreccional, have decided to unite our political and military forces in order to guarantee that the heroic struggle of our people not be stolen by the machinations of yankee imperialism and the treasonous sectors of the local bourgeoisie . . . we reject the imperialist mediation which is no more than a vulgar interventionist tactic by which yankee imperialism tries to mock the revolutionary aspirations of the Nicaraguan people by implanting a reactionary government subjected to their control: a somocismo without Somoza. We give warning that we will oppose imperialist intervention, raising revolutionary rifles against it.[25]

Pérez told Carter in a letter on December 22 that Somoza's apparent support for the plebiscite was a farce.[26] He was soon proved correct. Before the year's end, Somoza began reneging on the proposal, arguing implausibly that his cabinet had voted against the plebiscite because it violated the country's constitution and sovereignty. Having successfully pressured Somoza into talking to the opposition, the Carter administration was irritated by its inability to force him to negotiate in good faith. With the failure of the talks imminent, Bowdler paid a visit to Somoza, this time accompanied by Dennis McAuliffe, chief of the US Southern Command; they told him that they foresaw no durable peace in Nicaragua so long as he remained.[27] By February, the negotiations were declared officially dead. Carter signaled his displeasure with Somoza by suspending all military aid and recalling half of the US diplomatic staff in Managua. The National Guard would have to seek weapons from other vendors, including the governments of Argentina and Israel.

Meanwhile, tensions with Costa Rica had escalated. On November 21, Nicaraguan troops had killed two Costa Rican guardsmen near the border. The Carazo government immediately broke diplomatic relations with Nicaragua, becoming the first of several Latin American countries to do so. Echeverría, Carazo's top security official, subsequently met with Torrijos, who handed him a napkin with a written note for the Costa Rican president: "Carazo: everything that Panama has, and Costa Rica needs. Omar."[28] Torrijos and Pérez sent the Costa Rican government hundreds of FAL and M-14 rifles for the Costa Rican security forces to shore up their defenses. As Somoza became a direct threat, Nicaragua's revolutionaries essentially became a part of the Costa Rican national security apparatus; "the Southern Front of the Sandinista National Liberation Front has become our first line of defense," Echeverría declared in a public statement.[29] On December 27, Carazo called Torrijos and Pérez for further support when intelligence reports revealed Somoza was planning on invading Costa Rica to eliminate FSLN camps. The Venezuelan promised air support in the event of an attack.[30] Fidel Castro later noted that Somoza committed a fatal error by threatening Costa Rica, because even pro-US governments in the region were shocked by news of the aggression.[31] Carazo took a more active role in the fight against Somoza and the struggle to determine his replacement, believing that "as the Terceristas grew stronger there would be greater possibilities for the establishment of a pluralistic regime in Nicaragua."[32]

The mediation's failure emboldened all belligerents. Believing he had vanquished a US plot against his government, Somoza reaffirmed his intent to violently crush his opponents. The Carter administration's decision to terminate aid confirmed the dictator's suspicions; it also erased some of Washington's leverage (and information-gathering capabilities). Meanwhile, with the dictator still in power after months of US-led negotiations, the political parties grouped in the FAO lost what little trust remained in Washington and ran further into the arms of the FSLN's armed option. Panama and Venezuela took steps to accelerate Somoza's military overthrow to ensure they had a say in the formation of a transitional regime, and while Pérez was still in office (his term ended in March 1979). In December, Salamín told his boss that after months of backing the Sandinistas, "if we step back [Somoza] will kill you . . . we have no choice but to continue and topple him. It's him or us."[33] But Torrijos and Pérez had no more arms of their own to provide. In January 1979 they set about looking for additional weapons, including a harebrained scheme to enlist Gabriel García Márquez's support in acquiring guns from Colombia's leftist M-19 guerrilla movement.[34] In order to adequately arm the FSLN for its next offensive, Panama and Venezuela would have to add a more muscular state ally to their makeshift alliance.

The Latin American Fellowship of the Revolution

Torrijos and Pérez turned to Castro.[35] Cuba, despite eventually becoming revolutionary Nicaragua's most important state ally, was not the earliest sponsor of the 1979 insurrection. After the disjointed FSLN reached its nadir in 1976, Cuban officials dialed down their engagement in Nicaragua and preserved contacts exclusively with the mountain-oriented GPP faction. Thus, the Terceristas' 1977 and 1978 offensives did not enjoy significant Cuban support.[36]

It was not until the spring of 1978 that important Tercerista–Cuban contacts took place. Sergio Ramírez and Ernesto Cardenal, traveling to Cuba in March under the pretext of international literary gatherings, met with officials in Havana—albeit without much consequence.[37] More fruitful were the meetings of Cuban envoy Julián López and Humberto Ortega in San José. This particular Cuban–Nicaraguan connection was facilitated by Manuel Mora Valverde, the historic leader of the Costa Rican communist movement, and allies of the San José–based Terceristas since 1976.[38] According to a secret report Mora later submitted to the Soviet Communist Party, Ortega had been hesitant to meet with the Cubans. The Nicaraguan allegedly told Mora: "I want you to know that both Cuba and the Soviet Union have always refused to help us. That's why we've had to seek help from other sources."[39] Fortunately, López and Ortega immediately struck up a personal rapport. As a result of their March 1978 meeting, the Terceristas sent a small contingent of soldiers to Cuba for training. A high-level delegation headed by Daniel Ortega traveled to meet with Castro the next month. Meanwhile, Pérez successfully petitioned Castro to provide some weapons for the September Offensive later that year. Those friendly steps notwithstanding, the Cuban government refused to fully commit its support for the insurrection in Nicaragua.[40]

Only in January 1979 did Havana adopt a significant and sustained policy of arms transfers to the Sandinistas, once Cuban officials saw the viability and value of the Tercersitas' insurrectional strategy.[41] The decision to ship guns came partly at the behest of Pérez and Torrijos, who sent Marcel Salamín to Cuba that month to hammer out the details.[42] Perhaps, as Gerardo Sánchez Nateras has argued, Castro chose to intervene not as a favor to his Panamanian and Venezuelan allies but as a means of siphoning some of their influence over the Sandinista Front.[43] In any event, Castro agreed to provide rifles, rocket-propelled grenades, and light artillery for the conventional warfare of the Southern Front.

He did not take this decision lightly. There were major risks involved. To start, there was no way the Sandinistas could defeat the National Guard, Castro told his Panamanian guest, if the revolutionary forces remained divided into three competing tendencies.[44]

Torrijos concurred. "If [the Sandinistas] want to overthrow Somoza as much as we do," he told Salamín, "they have to unite themselves and unite the rest of the anti-somocista opposition. That's my condition for handing over all the weapons."[45] The Panamanians therefore summoned FSLN leaders from all three tendencies—including Tomás Borge and Henry "Modesto" Ruiz from the GPP, and the Ortega brothers on behalf of the Terceristas. But the hosts were unable to leverage their weapons in order to broker a solid unity agreement at this point. "The guests," Salamín recalls, "hardly looked at or greeted one another. The level of distrust and tension was very high."[46] The points of contention were well known by this point. In private, GPP leaders complained to the Torrijos camp that the Terceristas were writing blank checks to untrustworthy domestic and international allies, and that their aggressive military strategy was fraught with danger. For their part, the Terceristas felt that those political connections entitled them to a leading role within the organization (though it was recognized that the TP and GPP were better represented in grassroots movements), and argued that taking the GPP's long-term strategic approach would squander a favorable domestic and international juncture and doom the FSLN to failure.[47] Torrijos and his advisers strongly agreed that the strategy of alliances was best suited for defeating Somoza quickly without provoking the United States or alienating sympathetic voices elsewhere in the international community.

Confronted with this division, Torrijos decided to "cut his losses" and promise most of the available weapons to the Terceristas in the short run, while keeping the conditional offer open to the GPP and TP in the medium term.[48] The Tercerista faction itself, however, was also riven by divisions. To ease them, leaders of that tendency held a series of tense meetings known as the "Little Congress" at Torrijos's vacation home near the Panamanian military base of Río Hato. In the past, Pérez, Carazo, and Torrijos had pushed for Edén Pastora of the Costa Rica–based Southern Front to have a more prominent leadership role, because they saw him as a guarantor of FSLN moderation.[49] Rival commanders of the so-called Internal Front, led most notably by Óscar Pérez-Cassar, resented Pastora's leadership style and lack of ideological purity, and they disputed the wisdom of mounting a conventional military drive from the south.[50] But unity was now the priority. Once again brandishing the weapons as leverage, Torrijos's advisers pressed Tercerista commanders to set aside their differences, recognize the importance of both the Internal and Southern Fronts, and subscribe to a unified command led by the two Ortega brothers plus Victor Tirado. They also agreed to accelerate their work with the Doce, COSIP, FAO, and other anti-Somoza allies.

Tercerista divisions were healed "under Torrijos's watchful eye," but Castro was the godfather of greater Sandinista unity.[51] Castro's "mythical prestige" became crucial, according to Ramírez, "so that the commanders from the three tendencies would accept a compromise for unity."[52] The Cuban leader—along with key operator Manuel Piñeiro, who led Cuban efforts to export revolution in the region from his post as head of the Cuban Communist Party's Americas Department—warned the Terceristas that if they managed to seize power without the others' help, the exclusion of some Sandinista groups would come back to haunt them in the long run. Thus, Castro supported a proposal for a nine-person National Directorate centered on the idea of factional parity: three Terceristas (Humberto and Daniel Ortega and Victor Tirado), three GPP leaders (Tomás Borge, Bayardo Arce, and Henry Ruíz), and three Proletarians (Luis Carrión, Jaime Wheelock, and Carlos Núñez).[53]

In return for their power quota, Castro encouraged the factions to bless the Terceristas' alliance with the moderate bourgeoisie and endorse post-triumph plans for political pluralism, nonalignment, and a mixed economy.[54] As historian Piero Gleijeses has argued, Cuban efforts to assist Third World revolutionary movements were motivated by a rational strategy of "the best defense was offense"—winning international allies and therefore weakening the influence of a hostile US foreign policy apparatus in the process.[55] Communist ideology and a sense of "revolutionary mission" no doubt played a role as well, but Castro only became deeply involved in Nicaragua when regime change seemed feasible, at which point he pragmatically backed the relatively moderate Terceristas over Cuba's less flexible allies in the GPP. The

Cubans reasoned that the Terceristas possessed the winning strategy. And as Ramírez recalls, they did not necessarily think it wise for the Sandinistas to copy the Cubans' approach from 1959 and the early years of their Revolution: "[Castro] was the first to understand that the development of the Nicaraguan Revolution had to be different. He was also the first to suggest that we respect political pluralism and a mixed economy. In other words, we should respect the realities we were faced with."[56] Cuban demands for rebel unity conformed to "simple, often unwritten rules," as Jorge Castañeda described them, that Piñeiro followed when advising Latin American revolutionaries during this period. This was also the case with Cuban pressure for the Sandinistas to build broad alliances: "Castro understood full well both the true lessons of the [Cuban] Revolution itself and those of years gone by. Without the support of broad sectors of the middle classes, part of the private sector, and the international community, revolution in Latin America was impossible."[57] Regardless of what lessons Sandinista leaders had drawn from the Cuban experience in the past, this is what Castro was prescribing in 1979.

Despite Castro's support for a moderate revolutionary posture at this time, one might ask why Carazo, Pérez, and Torrijos would so willingly accept and court his help. After all, in supporting the Terceristas they made it abundantly clear that they wished to avoid the revolution's transformation into a second Cuba. However, they also held the conviction that only a swift revolutionary victory could prevent the Nicaraguan war from becoming a regional one, potentially involving a disastrous intervention by US military forces. Cuban officials shared this view and agreed on the need to move with haste. Moreover, Castro was certainly moderating, rather than radicalizing, the Sandinistas' outlook at this time. And while the others surely had different ideas of what a postrevolutionary Nicaragua should look like, Castro would later encourage the Sandinistas to make virtually all the promises and concessions asked of them by the other Latin American countries on the eve of Somoza's exit.

In the end, it was a matter of trade-offs. When later asked about their entanglement with Castro, Carazo gave a simple response: "It was more important for Somoza to fall than to keep out the Cubans."[58] The alliance's fragility suggested historical fault lines in inter-American relations. But at the same time, its surprising coherence suggested how much had changed on the regional scene since the early years of the Cold War. Castro noted how Cuban exiles and US intelligence services had previously used Costa Rican territory as a launching pad for covert operations against his revolutionary government. He saw his rapprochement with Carazo's government as something like a reverse Bay of Pigs—a poetic turn of events in the Caribbean Cold War.[59]

In another surprising twist, a substantial portion of the weapons he supplied were of North American origin. Cuba, for obvious reasons, felt it would be unwise to provide its own Soviet-made weapons.[60] The Cubans therefore secretly petitioned their allies in Hanoi's communist government to help out with armaments the Vietnamese military had recovered from US forces. In the 1960s and '70s, the nationalist war waged by the Democratic Republic of Vietnam and its allies in South Vietnam was the cause célèbre of global progressives, with socialist groups worldwide contributing military, diplomatic, and economic assistance. Vietnam historian Lien-Hang T. Nguyen notes the Sandinistas modeled themselves after Vietnamese revolutionaries, who they saw as "the leading experts in defeating the United States and its allies."[61] And in 1979, Nicaragua's revolutionaries quickly followed in the Southeast Asians' footsteps in achieving pride of place in a truly global revolutionary offensive.

These international dynamics were a shot in the arm for Nicaragua's revolutionary process. After agreeing to the "basic aspects of FSLN unity" in Havana, FSLN leaders officially put pen to paper in Panama City on March 7, 1979, finally setting the stage for a concerted insurrectionary offensive. Meanwhile in Nicaragua, the FAO—whose leaders were briefly jailed after talks with Somoza failed—reformalized its alliance with the Doce and MPU under a new "National Patriotic Front" committed to the Sandinistas' armed struggle. For his part, Somoza continued expanding his forces and made the most of an ambivalent US policy that had cut off bilateral military aid while still allowing the regime to finance itself through multilateral lending institutions.[62] The National Guard would have to confront an FSLN that had taken "a qualitative leap in its military capacity" with the injection of Cuban assistance, as Humberto Ortega put it. The insurgents had also created the "strategic bridge"—wherein arms would be flown secretly from Cuba to Panama, then transferred with Venezuelan support to Sandinista camps in Costa Rica—without which "it would have been *impossible* to introduce the [Cuban] weapons" into Nicaraguan territory.[63]

Some of the most important preparatory work for the so-called Final Offensive was done beyond Nicaragua's borders. Over a hundred solidarity committees around the world sent money to the FSLN and, more importantly, mobilized international public opinion against Somoza. Central American guerrillas launched attacks on their own governments in order to press them not to intervene in Somoza's favor (though this arguably back-fired).[64] Other sympathizers literally joined the fight. The Victoriano Lorenzo Brigade—a Panamanian battalion led by doctor and human rights activist Hugo Spadafora—had joined the FSLN's 1978 September Offensive. In early 1979, the internationalist presence in the cause grew rapidly. Socialist parties in Costa Rica and Colombia organized hundreds-strong contingents (the Carlos Luis Falla and Simón Bolívar Brigades, respectively). Battered by repression in their homelands, Chilean communists, Argentine Montoneros, and Uruguayan Tupamaros found a second revolutionary life fighting in Nicaragua and advising the revolutionary command at its Palo Alto headquarters in San José.[65] Castro also sent twelve high-level military and intelligence advisers—including Renán Montero, a veteran of Americas Department operative—along with Cuban-trained contingents of Latin American fighters who traveled with the approval of their countries' respective socialist and communist parties.[66] Castro claimed the internationalist operation played a "decisive role" in the 1979 victory; one Uruguayan guerrilla said that while Somoza's downfall was a done deal by the time they arrived on the battlefield, their "modest" contribution hastened the process and therefore saved lives.[67]

On the political side, Pérez also provided a plane for the Doce to tour the Caribbean Basin for additional support. Some countries they visited—such as Jamaica, the Dominican Republic, and Colombia—would soon do their part in isolating Somoza and frustrating the United States at the OAS. Even the anti-communist military junta in Tegucigalpa, to which the Doce made confidential appeals, began acquiescing to Nicaraguan guerrilla camps in Honduran territory.[68]

The Doce's most important destination by far, however, was José López Portillo's Mexico. After a March 1979 meeting, the López Portillo government agreed to send funds and weapons to the Sandinistas for the first time.[69] Just as importantly, the president told the Doce that he would follow the lead of Costa Rica, Panama, and Venezuela in breaking diplomatic relations with Nicaragua.[70] The move, a departure from the Estrada Doctrine preceded only by the momentous refusal to recognize Franco's Spain in 1939, was carefully coordinated with Sandinista military commanders and political leaders. The Doce asked the Mexican Foreign Ministry to only break with Somoza once the guerrillas were ready to launch the Final Offensive.[71] The Mexican government had been amenable to the Sandinistas in the past. When Gustavo Iruegas was sent to Managua as interim manager of the Mexican embassy in September 1978 (the ambassador had just been recalled), Foreign Minister Santiago Villarroel gave him clear instructions: "Go to Nicaragua and do everything possible to help that people and their revolution." From that moment on, Iruegas's embassy became a haven for clandestine Sandinista operatives and granted asylum to nearly 1,000 dissidents.[72]

Mexico, which along with Venezuela was experiencing an oil-fueled spurt of Third World activism, pursued specific national interests when it ramped up its involvement in Nicaragua in the spring of 1979.[73] According to Mexican diplomatic historians René Herrera and Mario Ojeda, López Portillo intervened more decisively at this point in order to fill the vacuum left by Pérez, who had just left office in Caracas (the defeat of Pérez's AD party in the December 1978 elections disappointed the Sandinistas and delighted the Somozas). The ultimate motive, they allege, was the same one shared by Pérez and Torrijos: the risks inherent to the Sandinista Revolution would be fewer "if Somoza's downfall was accelerated before the conflict evolved into an open international confrontation." Absent Mexican support, the Institutional Revolutionary Party (PRI) government believed, "the Sandinistas would see the need to seek more decisive support from Cuba . . . which itself implied the danger of a direct US intervention." Thus, Mexico joined the "collective security" effort against Somoza after its government "became conscious of the political-strategic importance of stability in Central America for its own security."[74] It helped that—as in Panama, Costa Rica, and Venezuela—efforts to overthrow Somoza were wildly popular. As it had done in the past, the PRI could use support for leftists abroad to bolster its revolutionary credibility at home.[75]

The Sandinistas were not the only ones clued in to Mexico's plans. Before announcing the rupture of relations with Nicaragua on May 20, López Portillo conferred with Fidel Castro, with whom he met in Cozumel on the 17th. He also consulted with Rodrigo Carazo, whom he met earlier the same day as the announcement in Cancún; the Costa Rican, following discussions with Pérez and Torrijos, had previously advocated for Mexico's diplomatic rupture.[76] On a symbolic level, those Yucatán meetings marked the completion of the Latin American fellowship born to support the Sandinista-led coalition in its path to power.

It was a "fellowship" in the sense that the fraternal bonds between these leaders—and with the very young FSLN leadership—were defined by a strong affective component that went beyond hatred for Somoza and transcended their shared strategic interests. In a meeting with the Doce, López Portillo was moved to tears when he realized that the children of Joaquín

Cuadra Chamorro and Emilio Baltodano were on the front lines leading Sandinista fighters.[77] The Mexican president later wrote that he felt "a moral commitment to a moving group of young Nicaraguans who, straight out of secondary school, had joined *la guerrilla* and aspired to build a government of national dignity."[78] Indeed, as French sociologist Gilles Bataillon has argued, the youthful "muchachos" leading the FSLN (very few guerrilla chiefs were over the age of thirty at this point) "embodied the symbolism of political renovation" promised by the Revolution.[79] Torrijos was similarly moved when Francisco "el Zorro" Rivera interrupted a high-minded, theoretical discussion of military tactics and political strategy with a raw, emotional plea: "*Lo que necesitamos, General, son tiros en puta.* If this isn't possible, we'll see how to make do, but what is certain, beyond any doubt, is that we'll topple Somoza even if it's a little slower and costlier for our people. In any event, General, we sincerely appreciate your solidarity." Torrijos, teary-eyed, promised to find the extra ammunition.[80] These leaders' sense of ownership over the insurrectionary cause derived from the paternal relationship they forged with its young leaders; Torrijos "sees the Sandinistas as his kids," Brzezinski reported to Carter.[81] In fact, it had literally become their fight: by May 1979, Torrijos and Manuel Mora Valverde both had sons fighting alongside the Sandinistas inside Nicaragua.[82]

FSLN leaders leveraged international sympathy and the simple fact that, as Jaime Wheelock observed, "the Somoza regime had become a factor of instability for the region's governments."[83] But in receiving external support, they had to conciliate their goals with the concerns of foreign backers who worried that the radicalization of the insurrection would boomerang in the form of a direct US intervention. In this way, Latin American involvement in the insurrection helped consolidate the stated goals of political pluralism, a mixed economy, and nonalignment as central pillars of the Nicaraguan Revolution.

Despite ideological differences between them, the FSLN's Latin American sponsors were bound by a shared rejection of US unilateralism. The Venezuelan ambassador to the OAS flipped US Cold War rhetoric about hemispheric security on its head; he told the regional body that Somoza, and not Nicaragua's left-wing revolutionaries, was the threat to peace in the hemisphere, citing as evidence Nicaragua's participation in the covert overthrow of Guatemala's Árbenz government in 1954 and the subsequent Bay of Pigs invasion.[84] Castro told the Soviet ambassador in Havana that regional support for the Sandinista-led government was "the latest in a series of crippling defeats suffered by American imperialism in the Western

Hemisphere."[85] Hyperbole aside, the conspiracy was an extraordinary rebuke by Latin American leaders of all political stripes who had found a rare strength in unity and purpose. When the US ambassador in San José chastised the Costa Rican president for covering for the Sandinistas, Carazo reportedly told the North American diplomat "to go to hell."[86]

As the Latin Americans strove to groom the FSLN-led revolutionary coalition to their liking, the US government desperately searched for a moderate alternative that no longer existed, if indeed it ever did. Historians of the Cold War in Latin America rightly focus on the motives and consequences of US foreign policy. But as senior Carter administration diplomat Anthony Lake later determined, events in Nicaragua had "surged far ahead of Washington's real power or even understanding."[87] "Decisions on the future government of Nicaragua were being made in Washington," Robert Pastor wrote, "but they were not being implemented anywhere. Other decisions would matter more."[88]

Race to the Finish

On June 4, two weeks after Mexico's diplomatic bombshell, the Sandinistas broadcast their long-awaited call for the final insurrection on Radio Sandino. Those two coordinated developments on the political and military fronts marked the beginning of the end for Somoza. Together, they set off a race to the finish wherein the different components of the revolutionary coalition and their foreign allies scrambled to determine exactly who would be in Managua to take power when the dust settled.

Mexico's breaking of diplomatic relations with Nicaragua further catalyzed Somoza's reversal of fortune on the Latin American scene. Just days later, the foreign ministers of the Andean Pact—the association of the Venezuelan, Colombian, Ecuadorian, Peruvian, and Bolivian governments—met to declare the Nicaraguan crisis a threat to hemispheric peace. Privately, Ecuador's and Venezuela's top diplomats met with Somoza in Managua and urged him to resign. Somoza had previously boasted to US ambassador Mauricio Solaún that the OAS would never pass a resolution condemning his government, because Nicaragua could always count on the support of the anti-communist military dictatorships of South America (Argentina, Brazil, Bolivia, Chile, Paraguay, and Uruguay) and Central America (Guatemala, Honduras, and El Salvador).[89] But by June 1979, even they had decided that Somoza must go. None of them except Alfredo Stroessner's Paraguay—where Somoza was later exiled—came to Nicaragua's defense at crucial OAS meetings that month.[90] His days now clearly numbered, Somoza traveled to Guatemala to ask the country's military government—and those of El Salvador and Honduras—to mount their own intervention in Nicaragua to stop the FSLN from taking power. His erstwhile allies shrugged off the request. Guatemalan general Romeo Lucas García thought Somoza a "dinosaur" facing certain extinction.[91]

Meanwhile, the unified and Cuban-armed FSLN was making significant inroads. The guerrillas timed the announcement of their Final Offensive with a general strike coordinated by the MPU (the federation of social and workers' movements), MDN (the business sector–aligned party), and FAO (the broad coalition of traditional anti-Somoza parties). While the insurrection's civilian leaders paralyzed the national economy with greater success than ever before, the FSLN mobilized thousands of fighters across several fronts in the northern, Pacific, South Atlantic, and central mountain chains.[92] They also instructed cadres in urban centers to lead carefully timed citizens' revolts against local National Guard positions. The political-strategic fulcrum of the Final Offensive was once again Pastora's Southern Front, which led a force of 700 troops across the Costa Rican border with the old objective of conquering a swath of southwestern Nicaragua for the establishment of a provisional government. Recognizing the political menace that such a strategy represented, and aware that Pastora's troops were equipped with the heaviest of the Cuban-provided military equipment, Somoza focused much of his armed forces against the Southern Front.[93] Indeed, by mid-June, Coronel Pablo Salazar ("Comandante Bravo")—later recognized as the most accomplished of Somoza's field marshals—successfully blocked Pastora and the internationalist brigades on the isthmus of Rivas, a narrow land bridge connecting the Pacific Ocean and Lake Nicaragua near the Costa Rican border. But the massing of National Guardsmen along the southern flank left Nicaragua's provincial capitals—such as Jinotega, León, Matagalpa, and Estelí—vulnerable to their own incensed populations. When Somoza's elite infantry battalions—stationed in Managua to protect the president, cabinet, and legislature—expelled Sandinista fighters from the capital in late June, the insurgents simply beat an organized tactical retreat and joined the provincial rebellions. By the first week of July, the regime had lost most of these towns and cities. The rebels now had the upper hand. But they could not seize Managua and achieve a total military victory without incurring massive casualties or heightening the risk of a US intervention launched under humanitarian pretenses. A negotiated settlement of some kind was therefore inevitable.

With such an agreement in mind, the revolutionary coalition's leaders in San José made plans for a provisional government. The five-person Junta of National Reconstruction announced on June 18 was the formal, living expression of the multiclass and ideologically plural alliance that would overthrow Somoza. Daniel Ortega, the only Junta leader to wear a military uniform, represented the Sandinista National Directorate; Sergio Ramírez—who was not so secretly pledged to the FSLN—represented the Grupo de los Doce; Moisés Hassan—also loyal, albeit discreetly, to the Sandinista leadership—spoke for Nicaragua's social movements and popular organizations as represented in the MPU; Alfonso Robelo served as the representative of the MDN and the traditional business class; and finally, Violeta Barrios de Chamorro—Pedro Joaquín's widow—further symbolized the inclusion of the bourgeoisie, civil society (particularly the free press), and the various democratic parties that her husband had led in the legal struggle against the dictatorship. In their first "proclamation" of June 18, the Junta unveiled their governing agenda for a "New Nicaragua." They called for the "political, economic, social, moral, and cultural" transformation of the fatherland. The platform made explicit the aforementioned three pillars of the Revolution. First, "nonalignment in international affairs," including reduced dependence on the United States; second, a "mixed economy," where the government would expropriate the Somoza estate, nationalize some key industries, implement agrarian reform, and spend heavily on social programs but otherwise privilege market forces; and third, "political pluralism," guaranteed by full civil liberties, an independent legislature, and free and regular elections.[94]

The inclusion of Chamorro and Robelo in the Junta was designed to satisfy the FSLN's main political-strategic goal at this late juncture: avoiding a US-led foreign intervention of any kind.[95] The pluralism and moderation of the incoming government helped secure the insurrection's widespread Latin American backing (or at least grudging acceptance, in the case of the region's anti-communist military regimes). The same day as the proclamation, the Andean Pact recognized the Junta as a legitimate belligerent. Ecuador—which had just transitioned to democracy in 1978—went further, breaking relations with Nicaragua. US diplomats had urged these South American countries against such actions, arguing that legitimizing the FSLN-allied Junta would diminish the possibilities of finding a more agreeable post-Somoza alternative. They ignored the advice, stunning the Carter administration, "which had not fully grasped," according to Robert Pastor, "and was not yet ready to accept, just how different the Latin American view of the Sandinistas was from its own."[96]

The Carter administration's lack of faith in the provisional Junta raised a question: Had the Sandinistas masqueraded as democrats for political expediency? Some of the FSLN's socialist allies thought so. Todor Zhivkov, the long-serving leader of communist Bulgaria, noted in an April 1979 memo after a meeting with Fidel Castro that the Cuban leader told him as much: "The Sandinista rebels are mature revolutionaries, sharing Marxist-Leninist beliefs. Cuban comrades advise them against giving publicity to their beliefs and speaking publicly about Marxism-Leninism. They should be raising other slogans for the time being—for democracy, revival of the nation, etc. So far they are heeding the advice."[97] Similarly, Costa Rican communist leader Manuel Mora reported to Soviet Communist Party officials that Humberto Ortega "definitely considered himself communist, Marxist-Leninist," though "his organization was interested in being known by the people of Nicaragua as very broad, which is to say, with a fundamentally democratic character."[98] But in any event, the insurrection's base did not necessarily share these ideological inclinations, and often pursued goals (sometimes more radical, sometimes less) that differed from those set by top leaders. Moreover, the internally divided FSLN was only one component of the anti-Somoza coalition that was poised to take power. Latin American leaders— who knew that the Sandinistas could not have gotten this far without building a very broad coalition—recognized the situation as such. In turn, the enthusiastic support of several Latin American governments, along with the quiet acquiescence of many anti-communist dictatorships, made it impossible for US diplomats to publicly depict the Junta as a Castroist front. In congressional testimony in June, the assistant secretary of state for inter-American affairs told the committee that "our democratic friends in Latin America have no intention of seeing Nicaragua turned into a second Cuba, and are determined to prevent the subversion of their anti-Somoza cause by Castro."[99] Privately, many in the Carter administration held a different view. By June, the consensus emerged that Somoza was going to fall, but some key officials—notably Brzezinski—still hoped to block the Latin American–backed, Sandinista-led provisional government.[100]

In late June, two events dealt fatal blows to those efforts. On June 20, foreign correspondent Bill Stewart was summarily executed by National Guardsmen in Managua. The murder, caught on camera by his ABC crew and repeatedly televised, turned US public opinion against Somoza. The incident was seen as having shifted Washington's policy.[101] With that said, the Carter administration had decided months before Stewart's killing that Somoza should leave the picture.[102] Of greater consequence for US policy were the OAS meetings that began the following day, which culminated on June 23 with a resolution, supported 17–2 by American foreign ministers calling for the "immediate and effective" replacement of Anastasio Somoza and the formation of a democratic interim government in Managua. Five countries abstained (most of them anti-communist military governments, although Brazil and Argentina supported the measure). While Deputy Secretary of State Warren Christopher voted for the measure and publicly celebrated its passing, in private the US delegation was left licking its wounds. Secretary of State Cyrus Vance, who called this special meeting of OAS foreign ministers, had floated an initial proposal that similarly condemned Somoza but also called for the creation of an international, OAS-sanctioned peacekeeping military force to manage the transition in Nicaragua. Hearing echoes of the United States' 1965 military intervention in the Dominican Republic, which was similarly carried out under the guise of multilateral peacekeeping, Mexico and Panama led Latin American countries in blocking Vance's plan. López Portillo hated the American proposal. "Truly," he wrote in his journal ahead of the vote, "they think they are kings of the universe."[103] The Panamanian foreign minister ceded his seat on the floor of the OAS to Doce member Miguel D'Escoto, who made the case for the Junta. As a minor concession to Washington, those countries agreed to drop any overt references to the Sandinista Front in their own, successful resolution.[104]

In the wake of the resolution's passing, Carlos Andrés Pérez urged the Junta to reaffirm its democratic intentions. Thus, they sent a letter to OAS secretary general Alejandro Orfila on July 12 in which they swore to "call Nicaraguans to the first free elections" in the country's history. They attached their "plan for achieving peace," which promised an immediate cease-fire and generous treatment for the National Guard.[105] Aside from serving as the reference by which the revolutionary government would later be judged, the letter to the OAS further cemented hemispheric support for the Junta's ambition of being the undisputed heir to the Nicaraguan state. Indeed, as Costa Rica's Echeverría saw it, the OAS resolution—which called for an interim government "composed of the principal representative groups which oppose Somoza"—"incorporated the principal aspects that had been discussed since late 1978 and during the meetings of Panama [in early 1979]."[106] Castro privately celebrated to Soviet diplomats how the OAS resolution showed that "today ever more Latin American countries are exhibiting disobedience to the demands of the United States."[107] For his part, Somoza finally accepted that the end was nigh. Like the case of the Algerian Front de Libération Nationale (FLN) in the early 1960s, the Sandinista revolutionary Junta was treated as the de facto government of Managua by key international players even before the National Guard had been defeated.[108] Proving that this was truly a "diplomatic revolution" as much as anything else, it was on the day that the OAS condemned his government that Somoza drafted his letter of resignation.[109]

The Carter administration, which ultimately supported an unsatisfactory resolution in order to preserve at least some say in the formation of post-Somoza Nicaragua, spent some time in the early summer of 1979 pursuing wildly unrealistic ideas for a caretaker government. For example, in early July, Ambassador Lawrence Pezzullo—who had been in Managua for less than a month—suggested to State Department leaders that the US might have Somoza hand over power to his long-serving foreign minister, Julio Quintana. "The transitional president," Pezzullo predicted, "would ride a wave of public joy occasioned by Somoza [sic] departure" and "sap an unknown, though perhaps considerable amount of FSLN support and thereby permit moderates to play a bigger role in forming transition government."[110] Such a scheme was fanciful, to say the least. In reality, the FAO's repeated and unequivocal statements of support for the FSLN, along with the Latin American consensus shown at the OAS, had made the Junta the only game in town.[111] By the end of June, the White House had slowly begun to accept that it should seek the moderation of the Junta itself, instead of focusing on its outright replacement.[112]

But as Torrijos had told the US ambassador to Panama in early June, it was unfortunate for the Carter administration that it had not invested in the Sandinista Front when it had the chance.[113] While Panama and several other Latin American countries had cultivated and taken advantage of its say in the composition and orientation of the revolutionary leadership, the US government had little leverage—short of threatening unilateral intervention—other than its relative control over Somoza's precise departure date. Thus, when US envoy William Bowdler returned to Central America to meet with Torrijos in Panama City on June 27, ahead of his direct talks with the FSLN and Junta in San José, he came with a much-reduced set of objectives. First, the US government wanted to dilute the Sandinistas' power in the provisional government, and therefore sought the expansion of the five-person Junta to nine members. Second, with the aim of avoiding complete FSLN control of the armed forces, Bowdler hoped to force the guerrillas to accept the inclusion of National Guard commanders somewhere at the top of the revolutionary government.[114]

Carter summoned Torrijos to a meeting in the Oval Office on July 3, hoping to convince his Panamanian friend to ask the revolutionary coalition to accept these conditions before Pezzullo, who was meeting with Somoza regularly in Managua, asked the dictator to leave the country.[115] Tellingly, Torrijos agreed to float the ideas to the Nicaraguans as if he, Pérez, and Carazo—rather than Carter—had come up with the proposal. Under pressure from these Latin American leaders, and encouraged by Castro, the Sandinistas agreed to an expanded Junta and voiced no opposition to the moderate figures proposed for inclusion.[116] Ironically, however, the Junta's moderates blocked the proposal. Naturally, Chamorro and Robelo feared that an expanded Junta would dilute their own power as much as it would weaken Ortega, Hassan, and Ramírez. They also distrusted Carter officials for having taken so long to tell Somoza to resign. Robelo saw "no reason why the US should lay down conditions on how we should run Nicaragua" and "no logic in broadening the Junta when it has been backed by COSEP and the FAO." A furious Chamorro threatened to resign, calling the scheme "an unwarranted intervention in Nicaraguan affairs." Highlighting the "us versus them" dynamic of the Nicaraguan Revolution, Torrijos swiftly reversed his support for the Junta expansion and began referring to the idea as the "American plan," giving it the kiss of death.[117]

The Nicaraguans did, however, concede the more substantial of the two demands. When Bowdler finally met with them in San José on July 10, the Junta promised that it would incorporate moderate elements of the National Guard into a hybrid military structure led by a Joint Chiefs of Staff composed of a roughly equal number of Sandinista and ex-Guard commanders.[118] Castro, who took credit for the decision, pushed this move as necessary for preventing a US intervention to deny a Sandinista victory (fear of which he shared with Pérez, Torrijos, Figueres, and the Sandinistas).[119] Now that Washington had given up on Somoza, this was the Latin Americans' chief concern.

For the other Latin American allies and the United States, the logic was simple: if the FSLN won a monopoly on military power, the non-Sandinista elements in the revolutionary government would become subordinate in practice to the National Directorate. The hybrid military plan was, in effect, a small dose of *somocismo sin Somoza*. Scholars have glossed over this contingency in the immediate origins of the Nicaraguan Revolution. Just days before triumphantly marching into Managua, the pragmatic Sandinista leadership had settled for something slightly less than—following Samuel Huntington's classic definition—the "rapid, fundamental, and violent" change to Nicaraguan society, at least when it came to the country's political institutions and government activities.[120]

The preservation of some part of the National Guard—which had not yet been defeated—was an important aspect of the final plan for post-Somoza Nicaragua, which was officially agreed upon at a meeting at Carazo's beach house in Puntarenas, Costa Rica, on July 11. That last meeting, with Bowdler present, provided a microcosmic view of the Nicaraguan Revolution and its transnational dimensions. In attendance were the broad-based Junta of National Reconstruction, Humberto Ortega and Tomás Borge, Rodrigo Carazo along with some of his cabinet members, top-level Torrijos emissary Jorge Ritter, and now-ex-president Carlos Andrés Pérez. Also present was ex-president Pepe Figueres, who delivered a letter from Manuel Mora Valverde—himself acting as a sort of de facto representative for the absent Cubans—in which the communist leader affirmed Castro's intention to refrain from turning Nicaragua into a Cuban military base and to continue respecting the pluralistic and liberal characteristics of the Revolution.[121] After Carazo and Pérez made one final, failed attempt at convincing the Nicaraguans to expand their Junta, the revolutionary coalition reiterated its commitment to a democratic process and—more importantly—to the non-destruction of the National Guard in its entirety. The next day, Bowdler assented to the plan. The US government, for the first time, had faced the reality that the Junta—due to its members' authentic leadership of the anti-Somocista cause, and because it enjoyed such wide-ranging support from Latin American countries of all political orientations—was the legitimate government of Nicaragua, and recognized it as such. In return, and as an additional display of good faith, the Junta promised Bowdler that the new government would name a defected National Guard commander—Bernardino Larios—as defense minister. Larios would join a cabinet that, other than with Borge as minister of the interior, featured relatively few out-and-out Sandinistas.

On July 13, Humberto Ortega ordered significant Sandinista forces to stand down in the first step of what became known as the Puntarenas Plan. Pezzullo would have Somoza resign, and upon his departure from the country the next day, a predesignated interim president would immediately transfer power to the Junta. The new government would subsequently decree a full cease-fire, oversee the integration of the hybrid FSLN–National

Guard armed forces, and implement the rest of the democratizing plan laid out before the OAS.

Although the FSLN and Junta made a major concession—the preservation of the National Guard in some form—to minimize the risk of US intervention, the Puntarenas Plan still represented a surprising rebuttal of North American hegemony with little precedent in the history of the hemisphere. On July 13, a despondent Brzezinski told his president that he "felt a considerable degree of unease" as he sensed "the passing of the baton of influence over the future of Central America from the US to Cuba." Given that it was too late to intervene unilaterally and because Latin American countries refused to support any multilateral intervention, the national security adviser told Carter that working with those countries to moderate the FSLN was "the best we can do."[122] The stage was meticulously set, on the other hand, for precisely the sort of outcome that the Latin Americans had hoped for. The Sandinistas, unified around the Tercerista strategy, had accelerated the downfall of the Somoza government. Better yet, they promised to co-govern with moderate sectors of Nicaraguan politics under a mixed revolutionary Junta whose agenda was, despite its promise of radical social transformation, a far cry from the Cuban-style agenda of the FSLN's earlier *Programa Histórico*.

Those plans unraveled, however, as quickly as they had been laid. Pezzullo, promising Somoza that the National Guard would not be destroyed—and suggesting that he might be able to return to Nicaraguan politics some day—persuaded the dictator to tender his resignation on July 16. Following promises that he and his family would be well received in Miami, Somoza's family left the country early on the 17th—a date unofficially celebrated as *El día de la alegría* by many Nicaraguans. Following the protocol of the Puntarenas Plan, Somoza's predesignated interim president, Francisco Urcuyo Maliaños, assumed power that morning. Meanwhile, Humberto Ortega sent a trusted FSLN representative to the Costa Rica–Nicaragua border to negotiate the cease-fire with Federico Mejía, now the highest-ranking general of the National Guard.

But Mejía never showed up. In a shocking twist, Urcuyo did not hand over power to the Junta. Instead, he gave a bizarre press conference during which he called on the FSLN to lay down its arms for the good of the country. He also announced his intention to serve out the rest of Somoza's term through 1981 as Nicaragua's "constitutional president." It is unclear why Urcuyo, whose rogue presidency would only last forty-three hours, sabotaged the Puntarenas Plan. Some say that he did so on telephoned instructions from

Somoza in a last, desperate ploy to force a US intervention to crush the FSLN. Urcuyo's memoir, in which he claims—against all other accounts—that nobody told him he was supposed to transfer power to the "communists," suggests that he may have simply suffered from delusions of grandeur.[123] Whatever the reason, the immediate consequence was that the National Guard, facing a completely disadvantaged military situation, began to disintegrate as FSLN columns marched on Managua. Carazo—cognizant that the Puntarenas Plan, and its plans for a *political* victory for the revolutionaries, was only workable if the Junta reached Managua *before* the Sandinista fighters—frantically urged Sergio Ramírez, Violeta Chamorro, and Alfonso Robelo (Daniel Ortega and Moisés Hassan had already departed) to leave Costa Rica for Nicaragua immediately. Because it was still too unsafe to land their plane in Managua, the Junta landed in León in the wee hours of the 18th; they were quietly proclaimed the official government of Nicaragua on Carazo's urging.[124] Urcuyo abandoned the country later that day. Absent its leaders, and facing annihilation, the National Guard had largely disbanded by sunrise of the 19th.

Sandinista columns soon breached Managua's outer perimeter (members of the FSLN National Directorate disagree on who among them was first to arrive) and, within hours, controlled the entire country. Much of the new government's cabinet departed from San José to Nicaragua on the *Quetzacoatl II*, a plane provided by López Portillo. The Junta's members, nominally the official government of Nicaragua, did not make it to Managua until later that day. They had lost the race to the finish.

As Ramírez explains in his memoir, the implications were as straightforward as they were seismic: "When Urcuyo Maliaños refused to relinquish his provisional command to the Government Junta, as had been agreed, this gave complete authority to the FSLN National Directorate's nine commanders."[125] Before the Junta even made its official entrance into Managua, *comandantes* from the Sandinista National Directorate met at Somoza's bunker. Overlooking the dictator's tabletop war map, they discussed plans for a transition based on their total military defeat of the regime. This picture was not the one envisioned by the revolutionary coalition's Latin American allies. But it also came as a complete surprise to the Sandinistas themselves, who had prepared for a partial, political victory. As Óscar René Vargas, an FSLN leader dating back to the organization's earliest years, explained: "The Sandinista Front thought it was going to have a piece of power and no more. . . . We thought we were going to be one factor in decision-making. . . . But when the Guard fell apart, we found ourselves in complete command. It was a better situation than we had imagined in our wildest dreams."[126]

Conclusion

The Revolution's Latin American allies could ponder the ramifications at a later date. Perhaps the Puntarenas Plan would have fallen apart anyway—would hard-line FSLN leaders and the troops they commanded seriously have accepted shared control of the military with "purged" remnants of the National Guard?[127] For now, it was time to face a grim and immediate reality: by an early estimate of the Inter-American Commission on Human Rights, the insurrectionary war killed 35,000 people, injured 100,000, orphaned 40,000, and displaced many more in a country of only 3 million people (later estimates of war-related casualties vary). The economy was in tatters, with nearly half the country facing hunger.[128] How would the new government, the leadership of which was incredibly young and had no governing experience to speak of, rule and rebuild this country, let alone achieve social transformation? Still, they had reason to celebrate. Just two years before, nobody in Nicaragua or beyond—except for one small faction of the FSLN and a few coconspirators scattered around Central America and the Caribbean—thought that Somoza's ouster was anything more than a pipe dream. And as Carlos Mejía Godoy's "Sandinista Anthem"—which identifies the "yankee" as the great "enemy of humanity"—played over loudspeakers in a city center packed with jubilant Nicaraguans and foreign sympathizers on July 20, onlookers were reminded that the Sandinista Front and its allies had pulled off an extraordinary upset.

A host of short- and long-term domestic factors explain both the crisis of the dictatorship and the emergence of a powerful, multiclass coalition against it. Outside actors did not create a mass movement against Somoza. But without their support in 1977–79, Nicaraguan revolutionaries and their supporters could not have posed a serious military threat and toppled the regime. The rise of the Nicaraguan Revolution therefore was deeply informed by tacit agreements forged with and between the FSLN's foreign allies.

The Latin American fellowship of the Revolution had agreed to provide decisive diplomatic and military backing to push the revolutionaries over the finish line. The Sandinistas, for their part, could feel free to transform Nicaraguan society into a more just one, so long as they respected the three pillars of political pluralism, a mixed economy, and nonalignment in international affairs. The policy of alliances with the bourgeoisie—which French analyst Régis Debray dubbed "radical moderation"—helped build a wide national consensus for insurrection in Nicaragua. In so many other countries, Debray noted, insufficient societal backing had killed the ambitions of otherwise formidable guerrilla movements.[129] The FSLN's relatively moderate posture was also considered the least likely to backfire in the form of a US invasion, because the fears of diplomats in Washington—and indeed, in Buenos Aires, Santiago, and other capitals of the anti-communist Americas—would be somewhat assuaged. Fidel Castro and Carlos Andrés Pérez may have had different views on what the Nicaraguan Revolution would ideally look like. But they and their other fellows agreed that a direct US invasion in the Central American powder keg would be disastrous: for Costa Rica's territorial integrity, for Mexican and Venezuelan aspirations to regional influence, for the fate of the Cuban Revolution, and more. In this way, many Latin American governments came to see the triumph of the armed Left in Nicaragua as a collective security strategy that would shield the region from superpower intervention.

It had been a "diplomatic revolution," in the sense that Nicaragua's ruler believed his fate had been sealed when Latin American countries recognized the Sandinista-led parallel government in Costa Rica, well before fighters approached his bunker in Managua. But it was also something more. The transnational intervention against Somoza was a historical rejoinder to US unilateralism by an alliance of state and non-state actors hoping to reset the agenda and parameters of regional politics on Latin American terms. As a result, the revolution that took place in July 1979 bore the strong influence and stamp of approval of a remarkable plurality of Latin American leaders who came to see this utopian project as their own. The subsequent unfolding of the revolutionary process within Nicaragua must be understood in this light.

Putting the 1979 victory in this transnational context helps account for the importance that Nicaragua acquired in the hemisphere in the subsequent decade. For the same reasons that regional actors intervened there in the 1970s, Nicaragua would become intertwined with the great political debates and conflicts of Latin America's 1980s. The dramatic seizure of state power by the Left—for the first and only time since Cuba—was only the beginning of that story.

Part II   **Consolidation, 1979–1981**

· ·

3   In the Labyrinth of Latin American History

In a speech delivered in Managua a few months after Somoza's overthrow, Mexican president José López Portillo described the Nicaraguan Revolution in epic terms:

> In the painful labyrinth of Latin American history, you [the Nicaraguans], in the final two decades of this century, represent yet another critical juncture. After so many false exits, you can build— with your revolutionary responsibility—a way out for Latin America.
>
> At the beginning of the century that critical juncture belonged to Mexico, which waged and won the first social revolution of this century. We made it a reality; through the path to liberty, we sought the path to justice. But on occasion, it has become bogged down and justice has been sacrificed in the name of liberty. . . . Halfway through this century another revolution represented the historic critical juncture in the American labyrinth: the Cuban Revolution. Through the path to justice it has sought to achieve liberty and, on occasion, it too has appeared to become bogged down.
>
> That is why you, the Nicaraguans, at the end of this century, with those two turning points in Latin America's labyrinth as precedents, represent the possibility that liberty, justice, equality, and security can be conjoined and become the hope for our future. . . .
>
> That is why the eyes of the world are upon you. You are Nicaragua today, but America tomorrow.[1]

His sympathy for the cause aside, López Portillo's words pointed to greater truths about the Sandinista Revolution. Somoza's overthrow had been a regional effort. Thus, as Nicaragua confronted the principal dilemmas of revolutionary consolidation (Who would rule? How far should they go in destroying the old order?), those processes acquired regional significance. They reverberated across the hemisphere and traversed broader debates about Latin America's history, underdevelopment, and place in the global Cold War. Western European social democrats paid attention too; they saw in Nicaragua "a kind of test case," as one German analyst put it, "for the willingness of social-revolutionary, Marxist-oriented movements to try to arrive at some kind of arrangement with the basic principles of Western pluralistic democracy and to avoid any alliance with international communism."[2]

The Nicaraguans who found themselves with greatest control over the revolutionary process were initially surprised to wield such influence. "We were not going for the whole deck," recalls Comandante Jaime Wheelock of the FSLN's expectations for the transition.[3] Playing a weak hand relative to their domestic allies and international partners, Sandinista leaders had accepted significant concessions ahead of Somoza's toppling. On paper, it appeared they had seized only a modest share of the spoils of victory. A minority of the new government's cabinet ministers were declared Sandinistas, and the FSLN lacked even a simple majority in plans for a new legislative body. Crucially, the executive leadership of the new government—the Junta of National Reconstruction—was shared with two moderate bourgeois leaders.

But in one fell swoop, with an unexpected military victory, the Sandinistas vastly improved their position. Naturally, the collapse of the National Guard killed plans for a hybrid military. Instead, the nine *comandantes* of the FSLN National Directorate took de facto control over the Interior Ministry and armed forces, even as a former National Guardsman formally held the post of defense minister.[4] While it would not become apparent for several months, the FSLN's newfound monopoly on violence had relegated the Junta of Reconstruction to a secondary plane on July 19.[5] The Puntarenas Plan, crafted in Panama and Costa Rica with the hope of a smooth and democratic transition, had been compromised.

Additionally, the revolutionary coalition's ideological heterogeneity—an asset during the insurrectionary period—was bound to become a source of unsustainable contradictions when it came time to govern. In September 1979, just three months after the mixed revolutionary junta was installed, a leaked Sandinista pamphlet known as the *Documento de las 72 horas* (after the three-day assembly of cadres that preceded its drafting) called the immediate post-Somoza moment a "phase of democratic transition" on the path toward the full "transformation of the social relations of production." The overriding need to avert a US intervention had forced a reluctant FSLN into an alliance with the bourgeoisie, the document suggested. But the National Guard's implosion left Nicaragua knowing "no power other than that represented by the FSLN."[6] In retrospect, some Sandinista leaders have argued that the document's uncompromising vision was less a serious expression of strategic policy than an attempt at cohering a zealous party base that required convincing of the National Directorate's revolutionary intentions in light of the ongoing alliance with bourgeois sectors.[7] Indeed, the Nicaraguan Revolution never came close to the implementation of the radical vision for politics, economy, and society laid out there. Still, even if the National Directorate was pragmatic in practice, the rhetorical nods to "real socialism" raised doubts about the durability of the broad revolutionary coalition.

Despite these contradictions, the first Junta succeeded in consolidating the new Nicaraguan state and reconstructing the country. Humanitarian relief and reconstruction aid flowed from across the Americas to help rebuild in the wake of the insurrectionary war. Much of the assistance was inspired by the ulterior political motive of holding the revolutionaries to their promise of liberalism and nonalignment. Having failed to block the Sandinistas' path to power, US president Jimmy Carter welcomed Junta members Daniel Ortega, Sergio Ramírez, and Alfonso Robelo to the White House in September 1979 and proposed a strengthening of ties. His administration believed that the FSLN was "wearing a moderate mask," and substantial economic relief aid might help "nail it on," a strategy many Latin American diplomats encouraged.[8] Panama helped train the new Sandinista police force to ensure, in Omar Torrijos's words, that "the coloration of the new government will be neither Castro nor Iran."[9] Mexico sent important financial assistance so that Nicaragua would not have to rely exclusively on either Soviet or US aid; excessive involvement from either superpower, its Foreign Ministry believed, might destabilize Central America.[10] With Havana's advice, the FSLN quickly organized the new Sandinista Popular Army and secured full territorial control. Following the Cuban model, they also integrated the populace into the state-building process through grassroots Sandinista Defense Committees. Significantly, the new government consolidated its takeover while abolishing the death penalty and avoiding the televised show trials or public executions of old regime officials seen in the Cuban and Iranian revolutions. Arbitrary detentions, extrajudicial killings, and violations of due process ("special courts" were created to try those accused of being old regime collaborators) were reported, especially in the early weeks when the new government had not yet asserted full control.[11] But relative restraint indicated that the Sandinistas might live up to their slogan "relentless in combat, generous in victory." In a supererogatory display of revolutionary humanism, the new government tapped the well-known poet Francisco de Asís "Chichí" Fernández to direct the prison system.

The mixed Junta also fulfilled key promises from the "Plan for Achieving Peace" presented by the revolutionary coalition to the OAS prior to taking power. First, they approved a "Fundamental Statute" that restored civil liberties and enshrined the most expansive list of human rights Nicaraguans had ever seen, including a section on economic rights. Within a month of taking power, the Junta decreed the expropriation of the vast holdings of the Somoza estate. While critics would later point to arbitrary confiscations as evidence of FSLN totalitarianism, the outgoing dictator's expropriation (and the economic policy of redistributing his wealth through a program known as Area Propiedad del Pueblo) was a key commitment of the broad-based insurrectionary coalition, and was widely popular. In the health and education realm, early social reforms to expand basic public services—best symbolized by the 1980 Literacy Campaign, which reduced illiteracy from around 50 percent to perhaps as little as 12 percent in a matter of months—were the most materially impactful policies of a decade-long revolution that generally fell short of altering the socioeconomic structure of society.[12]

All told, despite the last-minute collapse of plans for a shared military, the evolution of post-Somoza Nicaragua in the first months seemed to smoothly proceed along the lines drawn by the transnational coalition in Panama and Costa Rica. The bourgeois-FSLN alliance initially held steady as the government implemented bold reforms. After conversations with Miguel D'Escoto (a Doce member and the new government's foreign minister) and Comandante Humberto Ortega in December 1979, Cuba's deputy minister of foreign relations reported favorably on the surprising revolutionary zeal of the Junta's non-Sandinista members.[13] At the same time, Carter administration officials concluded that their worst fears for the transition had been "overdrawn."[14]

Even in the first year, however, cracks began to show. In April 1980, Violeta Chamorro and Alfonso Robelo abruptly resigned over the National Directorate's moves to bring the government further under FSLN control. On his way out, Robelo cited the Junta's July 1979 letter to the OAS, claiming its promise of democracy had been broken.[15] The first mixed Junta's collapse suggested that the moderates' presence in government was more a function of short-term alliances and negotiations with international allies than a truly constitutive element of the revolutionary project. In retrospect, many Sandinista leaders have recognized this to be the case.[16]

The drama of the first revolutionary Junta exposed the Revolution's core identity crisis. Would it be a fundamentally socialist project, responding mainly to the constituency of workers, social movements, and intellectuals, prioritizing cooperative forms of production in pursuit of a "radical" democracy? Or would liberal notions of democracy, centered on representative political institutions and reliant on the productive capacity of the private sector, take pride of place? How would FSLN leaders navigate this "double agenda," as Ileana Rodríguez termed it, balancing their ideological and strategic vision of socialist modernization with the tactical promises of moderation they made to their domestic and international partners? Scholars still differ regarding what type of revolution this had really been.[17] During the 1980s, that question repeatedly surfaced at every stage of the revolutionary process, overlapping each time with international debates over the meaning of democracy and the shifting legitimacy of different political regimes.

Though the "consolidation" phase did not produce clear answers to these questions, it did help clarify the interests and loyalties of the various players in the Nicaraguan political arena, and therefore set the tempo for the rest of the decade. The FSLN, emboldened through military victory and empowered by popular support, seized control of the state and moved the agenda toward the more radical goal of fundamentally remaking the structure of Nicaraguan society, down to the creation of a "New Man" and "New Woman" imbued with revolutionary values. The Sandinistas' moderate political allies were marginalized, and the class groups they represented saw their interests severely challenged by the government's redistributive economic policies. Notably, the Revolution's turn to the left—which owed primarily to the ideological and strategic consensus of the FSLN's nine-person National Directorate—and the concomitant collapse of the multiclass coalition were paralleled by the gradual disillusionment of some of the Latin American and Western European leaders that supported their struggle against Somoza.

The Consolidation of a "Sandinista" Revolution

In many capitals south of the Rio Grande, the July 19 Revolution augured a historic opportunity for political renewal on a continental scale. An internal memo from the Costa Rican presidency outlined the unprecedented nature of Somoza's overthrow and its international implications: "Recent events in Nicaragua have opened an enormous hope in all Latin American countries, and particularly in those ruled by dictatorial regimes. For the first time in the history of our countries' international relations, a democratic liberation movement has received the support, first of all, of the continent's democratic regimes and also, at least the neutrality of other governments which in other eras would have offered their moral and material support to the sustenance of the dictatorial system." The Revolution, the document observed, was poised to trigger the liberation of other countries ruled by dictatorships, but only if Nicaragua established a regime that respected human rights, allowed for ideological pluralism, and pursued an authentically independent and self-determined foreign policy. Its leaders must be enormously responsible in the decisions they took; "at play" were the "fates of many brother peoples of Latin America."[18] Echoing this feeling, Spanish Socialist Party leader Felipe González declared that for other democratic transitions in Central America, "Nicaragua can and should be an example, a symbol. Its leaders have no right to fail."[19]

Much of that promise rested on the fate of the mixed Junta, which was weighed down by contradictions from the beginning. Since its installation, Alfonso Robelo was caught between the revolutionary and centralizing impulses of the Sandinista Front and the conservative outlook of the Consejo Superior de la Empresa Privada (COSEP, formerly COSIP), the federation of business associations he used to preside over. In the first few weeks and months, the country's producers' associations and chambers of commerce complained that the decree to expropriate the Somoza estate could open the door to arbitrary or targeted confiscations of political opponents. Robelo privately shared many of those concerns, but for several months he brushed aside criticisms so that he might keep his seat on the Junta and therefore preserve his say in the policymaking process. As late as March 1980, he positioned himself as a democratic socialist and claimed total dedication to the Revolution.[20]

Nonetheless, the broad anti-Somoza coalition faltered as the FSLN took more direct control of Nicaragua's governing institutions. In December 1979, the National Directorate pushed through a reform that substituted many non-Sandinista cabinet ministers with FSLN guerrilla chiefs.[21] Importantly, decorated commanders from 1978–79 (either one of the nine comandantes from the National Directorate, or one of thirty-seven *comandantes guerrilleros* just below them in the FSLN political-military hierarchy) came to staff all key security posts.[22] The first revolutionary Junta collapsed after the Council of State (the new government's yet-to-be-inaugurated legislative body) was restructured to bring it under Sandinista control. According to the original government plan presented at the OAS, the FSLN would control only twelve of thirty-three seats. At a meeting at Sergio Ramírez's house on April 16, 1980, the FSLN-loyal members of the Junta proposed to expand the legislature to forty-seven seats in order to give representation to various popular organizations (for example, the Nicaraguan Women's Association, the Sandinista Youth, various FSLN-affiliated workers' unions) created after Somoza's overthrow. As Junta member Moisés Hassan recalls, this "imposition"—which in practice gave the Sandinistas an absolute majority in the legislature—was a clear violation of the spirit and letter of the agreements reached in Panama and Costa Rica in the early summer of 1979, where he was present.[23] Faced with a 3–2 Sandinista voting majority on the Junta, Robelo could not block the move; instead, he resigned in protest of "fundamental changes" to the original plans for the transition. Chamorro also resigned after citing health and personal reasons, although she too became a vehement critic of the FSLN in due course. Reporting on the Council of State's restructuring and the collapse of the first Junta, diplomats at the Mexican Foreign Ministry—a branch of a (self-styled) revolutionary, one-party regime—wondered in a memo if the Nicaraguan government had "ceased to represent a true coalition, instead becoming a regime of 'limited pluralism.'"[24]

The cabinet shuffle and the rebalancing of the legislature formed part of the Sandinista leadership's efforts to attain a degree of control over the Nicaraguan state that they believed their armed struggle and popular support had entitled them to. At the time, the remaining members of the Junta simply denounced Robelo's resignation as a counterrevolutionary provocation. Comandante Humberto Ortega later wrote that Robelo and the private sector wanted a legislature that functioned like a "bourgeois parliament under their hegemony"; the new "popular democratic" assembly, Ortega suggested, corresponded to the "real balance of forces" established by the Sandinista Front's military overthrow of the National Guard and its predominance in every area of Nicaraguan society other than private enterprise.[25] Jaime Wheelock similarly pointed to Somoza's military defeat in explaining the centralization of power in Sandinista hands:

The FSLN exercised unopposed hegemony; it made the major decisions for change. This did not seem to jibe, however, with the FSLN's declared desire to govern based on broad and effective citizen participation. But the FSLN's strength lay primarily in the fact that it had been the architect of the overthrow of Somoza. It had accumulated, if not a consensus, at least the support of the most numerous and best organized popular sectors. And, of course, the FSLN represented, in a more radical sense, the mission to bring the significant change Nicaragua demanded. The Sandinistas' right to assume a high degree of control over the state came from the overwhelming political legitimacy acquired by Sandinismo.[26]

FSLN leaders, their supporters, and their critics tend to agree that a major turning point in the Revolution was the sudden and unexpected change in the Sandinistas' position vis-à-vis their allies in 1979. Having previously depended on domestic and foreign allies in order to share power, they now enjoyed undisputed military hegemony after Somoza's ouster. This turn of events widened the National Directorate's imaginary of the politically possible. Nicaraguan analysts Silvio de Franco and José Luis Velázquez, writing from a critical perspective, put it in the following terms: "Once the Tercerista leadership became aware of the realities of power, which they had previously underestimated, they realized that sufficient political space had opened up to allow the [FSLN] to go beyond a simple social democratic experiment. This was the beginning of the attempted 'transition to socialism' project."[27]

The Junta's collapse raised questions about the Revolution's promise of "political pluralism." Comandante Luis Carrión later discussed the Sandinista elite's understanding of the concept: "We spoke of political pluralism. What did we mean by that? First, that we would not declare a one-party system. Second, that we would allow other political parties to subsist, although they would not have any possibility of real influence in the country's political life."[28] This version of political pluralism contradicted the expectations of allies at home and abroad, who specifically expected the prompt holding of a national vote in which Nicaraguans would choose their rulers and lawmakers. Robelo had resigned in April 1980, in part, over the Sandinista Front's decision to delay electoral plans. Days after the resignation, Comandante Bayardo Arce privately told Western diplomats that the triumph of the revolution was "the triumph of the FSLN" and that therefore the Sandinistas had the right to govern unilaterally. Elections, he added, would only be held once key reforms were implemented and the people had become conscious of gains made under the Revolution.[29] Continued support by non-Sandinista, middle- and upper-class leaders seemed to bolster the FSLN's claim that their armed victory represented a form of popular sovereignty. Indeed, the National Directorate briefly neutralized criticism from the private sector (and provoked divisions within it) by swiftly replacing Robelo and Chamorro with Arturo Cruz Porras—a Doce member and Inter-American Development Bank technocrat—and Rafael Córdova Rivas, a Conservative Party leader and close ally of the late Pedro Joaquín Chamorro.[30] Despite this implicit approval of Sandinista hegemony, Comandante Henry "Modesto" Ruiz recalls with regret that the government "should have held elections immediately."[31]

Rather than being sensitive to the interests of allied sectors in the bourgeoisie, Sandinista leaders felt that their mandate was to empower Nicaragua's impoverished, marginalized majority. When the Revolution toppled Somoza, Luis Carrión recalls, "it produced an explosion of popular demands and participation." This energy was channeled through groups—notably the Asociación de Trabajadores del Campo (ATC), Central Sandinista de Trabajadores (CST), and Unión Nacional de Agricultores y Ganaderos de Nicaragua (UNAG)—that organized rural and urban workers. Along with unions for civil servants, teachers, and other professions, these organizations saw the unionized workforce multiply many times over in the Revolution's first few years.[32] Popular militias and the Comités de Defensa Sandinista (Sandinista Defense Committees)—neighborhood organizations modeled after Cuba's own Revolutionary Defense Committees and designed to distribute goods and provide basic services, while also policing and surveilling communities—gave citizens new opportunities to participate in political life under the rubric of what the Sandinistas called "popular" or "direct" democracy. Highlighting the importance of this notion of democracy for the Revolution's self-image, government-affiliated social scientists obsessively worked to quantify what was, by all accounts, an exponential growth in the level of civic engagement compared to the prerevolutionary period.[33] Though the organizaciones de masas were vertically integrated into the Sandinista Front and therefore subordinate to its interests, they nonetheless demanded real "power quotas" in government and exercised some influence over administrative decisions in their respective areas.[34] Moreover, FSLN leaders sometimes had to address spontaneous seizures of land and property carried out from below.[35]

While critics raised concerns about the future of electoral democracy in Nicaragua, the Sandinista upper echelon prioritized the democratization of society along social and economic lines. For example, educational policy was one area where the FSLN articulated the goal of destroying the old regime and fostering the development of a "new person" motivated by the values—as Education Minister Fernando Cardenal enumerated them—of patriotism, collectivism, and commitment to the impoverished masses.[36] In addition to the deployment of teaching brigades that rapidly improved literacy indicators, access to schooling expanded dramatically as educational spending rose, the number of teachers grew, and new schools were built. Similarly, access to medical care expanded as health spending grew as a portion of GDP; ambitious urban reform programs sought to improve access to housing. Finally, the government sponsored cultural programs that tried to bring the arts to all levels of society. Naturally, these social programs were designed with the legitimization of Sandinista rule in mind. But they were also conceived of—along with fiscal policies designed to redistribute the gains from economic growth—as necessary steps toward the "economic democratization" revolutionary leaders believed were necessary to correct the tangled legacies of colonialism, imperialism, and uneven capitalist development. The FSLN elite were reluctant to subordinate those efforts to the whims of representative institutions; "social justice could be done at the expense of democracy," Sergio Ramírez put it, "but not democracy at the expense of social justice."[37]

This emphasis on social democracy was attributable, in part, to the National Directorate's socialist inclinations. Carrión recalls the "influence, without a doubt, of Marxist ideas" among the Sandinista Front's nine-person supreme leadership, though the group—and, to an even greater extent, intermediate-level cadres—came from a vast range of ideological backgrounds. Nor did ideological preferences override pragmatism in major decision-making scenarios. But a shared commitment to some type of socialist vision helps explain the cohesion of a collective leadership that, despite grave rivalries during the insurrectionary period, did not suffer major divisions once in power. Some "more orthodox" members "privileged models of real socialism from the Soviet orbit," Humberto Ortega explained in a memoir, while others advocated for ensuring that "in the future conditions could mature to allow for socialism, but without specifying what *type* of socialism."[38] According to Carrión, the salience of Marxism within the Sandinista Front grew after 1979 as cadres were sent to socialist countries for training and said countries sent advisers to Nicaragua.[39] At the same time, some of the FSLN's first repressive actions came against far-left, explicitly Marxist-Leninist groups encouraging labor agitation and criticizing the government's perceived alliance with the bourgeoisie.[40] Only a month after taking power, the National Directorate expelled the one-hundred-strong Simón Bolivar Brigade—a group of largely Trotskyist, mostly South

American internationalists who assisted the fight against Somoza—for allegedly radicalizing workers, committing abuses against non-Sandinistas, and causing other sorts of headaches for the new government.[41]

The National Directorate adopted a Leninist approach to politics. In the Revolution's first year, the FSLN rebuilt Nicaraguan institutions in a way that left little distinction between the state and the ruling party. This state formation contradicted the earlier promise of liberal democracy, but was legitimized—at least in the minds of FSLN supporters—by the promise of social democracy and high levels of popular support in this early period. FSLN leaders' understanding of their position in society was crucial: "The Sandinista Front was the 'enlightened vanguard,'" Carrión recalls, "that had to direct everything in Nicaragua, like a right born from the Revolution. That was the mentality that prevailed from the beginning."[42] Vanguardism explains the Sandinista Front's top-down control over civil society organizations as well as the imposition of vertical, hierarchical discipline within the party. Humberto Ortega wrote that rapid, transformative reform required "revolutionary centralism," with power concentrated among the nine comandantes ("the vanguard within the vanguard," sociologist Dennis Gilbert called it).[43]

Nationalism and anti-imperialism, arguably more lucid themes in Sandinista elite thinking than Marxism, also informed the National Directorate's perspective and action in this early period. FSLN leaders predicted—correctly, it turned out—that the government of the United States would mobilize great resources to undermine their government. Reducing the influence of the private sector and "bourgeois" political parties was a matter, in their view, of minimizing Washington's capacity to influence Nicaraguan politics through local allies. From the moment they took power, Sandinista forces faced military threats by remnants of Somoza's National Guard. This security threat justified, in the government's view, tighter control over institutions as well as the suppression of some criticism. Thus, Humberto Ortega later argued that the alliance with the traditional elite ultimately fell apart because bourgeois politicians did not comprehend the need for an "army-party-state" form of government, which the "threat of a war of aggression [from the United States] turned into an imperative."[44]

In the first year of the Revolution, however, confrontation with the United States was still inchoate. The Carter administration remained hopeful that it could leverage economic aid to moderate and contain the Sandinistas. With that same goal in mind, Carter authorized the CIA to fund opposition parties and critical civil society organizations as soon as Somoza was overthrown. From very early on, US-funded civilian opponents explored ties with former National Guardsmen plotting armed incursions against the Sandinista government.[45] Some exiles set up military training camps in the Florida Everglades. But Carter officials saw direct efforts at militarily undermining the FSLN as "out of the question, particularly given the warmth with which the revolution was greeted by its democratic neighbors."[46] And just a few months after Violeta Chamorro and Alfonso Robelos's resignations, Ambassador Lawrence Pezzullo marked the first anniversary of Somoza's removal by publicly declaring that the Nicaraguans were carrying out an "acceptable model of revolution."[47]

International Reverberations

As the business sector increasingly called for elections during the summer of 1980, the issue of Nicaragua's revolutionary consolidation resonated more loudly on the international scene. On August 22, 1980, at a ceremony held in Managua to commemorate the end of the literacy crusades, guest of honor Rodrigo Carazo took the podium to remind the FSLN of the commitment it made before the OAS to hold free and fair elections. Only the people, the Costa Rican president insisted in front of a plaza audience of Sandinista sympathizers, could choose and therefore legitimize their government. Shortly thereafter, Humberto Ortega walked on stage to offer a bitter rebuke: "For the Sandinista Front, democracy is not measured only in political terms, nor is it confined merely to participation in elections. . . . Democracy begins in the economic order, when social inequalities begin to weaken, when workers and peasants improve their standard of living. This is the beginning of true democracy—and never before." At the end of his speech, Ortega announced that elections would be held in 1985—six full years after Somoza's overthrow—but cautioned that they would be "elections to improve the power of the revolution" rather than "a raffle to see who has power, because the people have the power through their vanguard, the Sandinista Liberation Front and its National Directorate."[48]

The public dispute reminded Carazo of an early milestone in the Cuban Revolution, in which former Costa Rican president Pepe Figueres, who had supported the anti-Batista rebels, made a similar plea for liberal democracy on his visit to newly revolutionary Havana in March 1959. He was similarly reproached by Castro. Much as that incident marked a distancing between the Cuban Revolution and the non-Marxist Latin American forces that supported it, for Carazo the dispute symbolized the greater cooling of relations that was taking place between revolutionary Nicaragua and one of the foreign actors most responsible for aiding its rise.[49] It also had a divisive impact on the global social democratic forces expressed by the Socialist International (SI), the association of center-left parties led at the time by Western European politicians like Willy Brandt, Olof Palme, and Bruno Kreisky. "To equate elections with a lottery," historian Bernd Rother notes, "was a provocation of social democracy." Ortega's comments ruptured the prevailing SI consensus in favor of enthusiastic solidarity with Nicaragua, with some member parties now doubting whether the Sandinistas were still committed to the principles espoused in 1979.[50]

Humberto Ortega's speech was read by business leaders as the "FSLN stat[ing] its intention of remaining in power forever."[51] Unsurprisingly, the organized private sector became a consistent source of criticism; as political economist Rose Spalding has written, early Sandinista policies "delivered a heavy blow to the traditional bastions of economic power in Nicaragua."[52] Alejandro Martínez Cuenca, a key economic adviser who later became the FSLN's minister of foreign commerce, succinctly explained the party's policy logic in this realm: "In those [early] years, there was an extremely distributionist thesis. According to that view, a skewed distribution of resources was the prime factor in the economy's failure to meet human needs."[53] In pursuit of redistribution, the Sandinistas took control of the nation's banks and financial institutions, created state trading monopolies, massively expanded the state bureaucracy and, most importantly, expropriated the Somoza estate.[54] Without intending to "adopt the socialist system," Humberto Ortega later wrote, FSLN leaders sought to "plan" the national economy and put the state—rather than the market—at the center of plans for economic growth and social change.[55] Producers and businessowners agglomerated in COSEP saw Sandinista statism as incompatible with their notion of a "mixed economy," and they increasingly argued that the government was arbitrarily targeting political opponents—including those who had no connection to the ousted dictatorship—for confiscation, a criticism that some FSLN leaders have accepted in retrospect.[56]

Citing these grievances, COSEP pulled out of the Council of State in November 1980. Polarization reached new heights with the killing by security forces of Jorge Salazar, the young and charismatic leader of the Agricultural Producers' Union, who the FSLN accused of conspiring with ex-somocista Guardsmen to plot a coup.[57] The deterioration in government–business relations, in turn, seemed to enable the FSLN to press forward with more radical economic measures. In the summer of 1981, the FSLN announced the

Ley de los Ausentes, a controversial decree that granted authorities the power to confiscate idle lands as well as the properties of business leaders who had left the country after 1979. The subsequent Ley de Cooperativas regulated the transfer of those lands into state hands for the creation of either state-owned or collectively owned agricultural communes. They also announced in July the beginning of an agrarian reform that would eventually become decisive because it increased tensions "not just with big producers, but medium and small producers too, some of whom took up arms and joined the counterrevolution."[58] Ultimately, the mixed economy model relied on private sector production, and therefore a minimum of dialogue with business leaders was kept. A CIA estimate noted, moreover, how the Mexican government, in hopes of keeping the grand 1979 alliance intact, influenced the Sandinistas to maintain such dialogue.[59] Still, by August 1981 Sergio Ramírez was celebrating that the country's "backward" and "primitive" bourgeoisie had lost political clout.[60]

In a more ominous blow to the Sandinistas' pluralistic, social-democratic image, Comandante Guerrillero Edén Pastora—who had become vice minister of defense and chief of the Sandinistas' civilian militias—quit the government in June 1981. In a handwritten letter that echoed Che Guevara's 1965 letter of resignation to Fidel Castro, Pastora told Humberto Ortega that he felt compelled "to go after the smell of gunpowder" and lead internationalist brigades in national liberation struggles elsewhere in Latin America.[61] His true motives were unclear at the time, but in any event, his resignation was a poor marker of the evolution of the Puntarenas vision for post-Somoza Nicaragua. After all, when Panama, Venezuela, and Costa Rica began collaborating to overthrow Somoza in the fall of 1978, their strategy was, in Carazo's words, to "support Pastora 100 percent."[62] Pérez and Torrijos made efforts to coax the guerrilla leader back into Nicaragua in exchange for the government making democratic concessions.[63]

Within a year, however, Pastora was making his true feelings known to the international press: "I fought 23 years for a government that was pluralist, nationalist, democratic, revolutionary and anti-imperialist, but this government has violated all of those things. . . . In Nicaragua we won the war; we haven't won the peace. What is the point of victory if the comandantes start living like the super-bourgeoisie in Las Colinas [an upper-class neighborhood in Managua], where the somocistas used to live? We took to the hills to fight and they take to the hills to their heated swimming pools, with five Mercedes parked out front."[64] Given his popularity abroad and close ties to other Latin American governments, the Sandinista National

Directorate worried more about Pastora's defection than reports of organizing by Somoza-era National Guardsmen. "We should not forget," stated a National Directorate prognosis on Pastora's counterrevolutionary plans, "that this is the real counterrevolution, which will have international scope, serious financial support and dangerous propaganda means. The [somocista] guardsmen will go on to a secondary plane."[65] The Directorate's alarmed response to Pastora's defection evinced particular concern with threats originating from within the revolutionary coalition of 1979. Tellingly, Pastora had signed his June 1981 resignation letter "Sandinista yesterday, Sandinista today, Sandinista forever." Similarly, Doce member Arturo Cruz Porras, who quit the government a few months before Pastora, insisted in his resignation speech that "he would continue in the revolution until the end."[66]

Cruz, Pastora, Alfonso Robelo, and Violeta Chamorro had all played prominent roles in overthrowing Somoza and bringing the FSLN to power, and co-governed with the Sandinistas in the early period. These same people would become some of the most visible figures of the incipient, US-backed political and military struggles to undercut the revolutionary government. As the multiclass coalition continued to unravel in the summer of 1981, Carlos Andrés Pérez wrote to Willy Brandt—former West German chancellor and then president of the SI—that the "situation in Nicaragua is grave, delicate. . . . The ambiguity of the policies implemented by the Sandinista government" were producing serious disputes within the global social-democratic movement.[67] Torrijos, who died in a mysterious plane crash that summer, shared many of these concerns.[68]

Conclusion

Between 1979 and 1981, the revolutionary government in Nicaragua had taken a shape not quite envisioned by the transnational coalition in Panama and Costa Rica before Somoza's overthrow. The multiclass, ideologically plural revolutionary coalition had broken down, and the FSLN hegemonized the new government. However, the new system was pluralistic in significant ways: the revolutionary government had restored press freedoms (opposition daily *La Prensa*, burned down by Somoza's National Guard, with some exceptions operated free of censorship in this early period), announced amnesties for National Guardsmen during the July 19, 1979, seizure of state power, and pragmatically sought dialogue with its foes in the business elite to avoid a collapse in production. Indeed, as Pérez wrote to Willy Brandt, Nicaragua would not "necessarily end up radicalizing, in the hands of the Soviet Union and Cuba," but the outcome depended much on social democrats' "firmness and ability to pressure."[69] And given the difficult circumstances of reconstruction, and as a much more hostile Ronald Reagan replaced Carter in 1981, most SI members favored a policy of "solidarity despite doubts."[70] For the time being, the promise of a new type of revolutionary experiment in Nicaragua remained alive.

The tensions inherent to the Revolution's double agenda would vex FSLN leaders throughout the 1980s, but it was those same contradictions that made the Sandinista project so enchanting to the Latin American Left. Historian Patrick Iber has described a Latin American "Cultural Cold War," where leftist intellectuals in the region, reacting to the Cuban Revolution's evolution in the 1960s and '70s, splintered over the question of how to build a sustainable and humane socialism in their countries.[71] Much like Salvador Allende's *Vía Chilena*, the Nicaraguan Revolution seemed to offer something for those on all sides of that debate. The Cuban-aligned factions identified with the centrality that the FSLN gave—both before and after 1979—to armed struggle as the only way to bring about real change. At the same time, orthodox communists could praise the relative gradualism of the Sandinistas' approach to building socialism in the long run, which stopped well short of a hasty seizure of the principal means of production, and left a realistic role for a private sector bourgeoisie in the short and medium run. Finally, with its promise of elections, parliamentary politics, and full civil liberties, even leaders of the anti-communist Left, such as Mexican Nobel laureate Octavio Paz, could feel at home in the *Revolución Popular Sandinista*. Where some saw contradictions, others saw an exciting synthesis in the making. Argentine writer Julio Cortázar thought the Sandinistas might resolve the core dilemmas of democratic socialism by marrying state-led social transformation to political pluralism and cultural freedoms. He observed that this post-Leninist revolutionary agenda was "no more than an ideal" to Western socialists and Eurocommunists. The Nicaraguans, he gushed, "have actually put it into action since July 19, 1979."[72]

The shaping of the Nicaraguan Revolution therefore mattered very much in Latin America—more so than in Washington, perhaps. To most observers outside of the hard-line anti-communist orbit, the Sandinistas represented at least the faint possibility of reconciling the dueling emphases on "liberty" and "justice" contained in López Portillo's vision of the Cuban and Mexican revolutions before them. Both independence and the state- and nation-building projects of the late 1800s had left core dilemmas of inequality, both within countries and between Latin America and Western

Europe, untouched, and other promises unfulfilled. Twentieth-century nationalism and revolutionary movements had offered uneven correctives. But if they played their cards right, the Sandinistas might just point to the exit to the labyrinth.

The question of Nicaragua's revolutionary process was not merely symbolic. Many states had interests in Central America, which they pursued during Somoza's downfall. They understandably watched every step the new government took, paying special attention to one dynamic in particular: the emergence of direct Sandinista control over Nicaraguan foreign affairs after July 1979. New regime policies in the realm of international relations were especially consequential for inter-American politics and, eventually, for the fate of the revolutionary government in Managua.

4 Revolution without Borders?

Anastasio Somoza Debayle could potentially have lived out the rest of his days in relative comfort. Attempting to console him as his dictatorship crumbled in 1979, Carter administration officials even raised the possibility that he might one day return to Nicaraguan politics. Such hopes, however, rose and fell alongside plans for a negotiated transition. When his interim president failed to follow the script and transfer power to the FSLN-led Junta of National Reconstruction, Deputy Secretary of State Warren Christopher called Somoza and reminded him that safe asylum in the United States was part of the bargain. "Those sons-of-bitches will come after me," the now *ex*-dictator said as he hung up the phone.[1] Interpreting the call as a threat to hand him over to Sandinista justice, Somoza no longer felt secure in his Floridian exile. He and his retinue soon fled Miami on yachts toward the Bahamas, before eventually settling in Paraguay.

Arriving in Asunción, the capital city, might have felt like coming home. Paraguayan dictator Alfredo Stroessner, who had ruled the country since 1954, was the only Latin American head of state who stood by Somoza in the insurrection's final days. Though newspaper reports suggested the relationship between the two men was less than warm, *stronismo* and *somocismo* had much in common.[2] Both dictatorships had a strong personalist bent that called to mind the Trujillos of yesteryear more than the developmentalist, bureaucratic-authoritarian regimes that ruled much of South America in the 1960s and 1970s. Maybe anti-communist military governments, and the Stroessners and Somozas of the world especially, were still on the right side of history. And perhaps 1979 was only an aberration, a reversible setback like the plot that took the first Somoza's life in 1956.

Those hopes were blown away by a rocket-propelled grenade. On September 17, 1980, a group of commandos ambushed Somoza outside his home on an avenue named, incidentally, after Spanish dictator Francisco Franco. The assailants destroyed his Mercedes-Benz and lobbed a barrage of automatic gunfire before speeding away. For the next few days Paraguayan police turned Asunción upside down. The assassination of an ally on home turf shattered the veneer of invincibility hitherto enjoyed by the longest-ruling dictator on the continent.[3] Was nowhere safe? The military junta in nearby Buenos Aires was outraged to learn that Argentine guerrillas associated with the Ejército Revolucionario del Pueblo claimed responsibility for the hit.[4] The Nicaraguan government denied responsibility; citing testimony from defected Cuban intelligence officials, a former CIA officer suggested that Fidel Castro may have directed the operation as vengeance for the Somoza family's involvement in counterrevolutionary operations including the failed invasion at the Bay of Pigs.[5] Perhaps the question of authorship did not matter so much. "We *all* killed him" was the message broadcast from government radio stations in Managua, some 5,000 kilometers away.[6]

The consequences, in any event, were far-reaching. Somoza Debayle's death in Paraguay indicated that, beyond its symbolism, the rise of the Left in Nicaragua could directly touch vital state interests across the region. The Latin American intelligentsia devoted many pages to Sandinismo's implications for the prospects of revolutionary change on the continent. But the regional political establishment responded far more transparently to the ways in which events surrounding the Sandinista Revolution affected their security goals, economic plans, and in a few cases their domestic politics. Political leaders across Latin America—and in the United States and Western Europe, for that matter—therefore paid even more attention to the revolutionary government's foreign policies than they did to the Sandinistas' domestic reform agenda.

For their part, the Nicaraguans saw a new-look foreign policy, alongside promises of political and socioeconomic change, as a coequal pillar of their revolutionary agenda. For the Left, as FSLN diplomat Alejandro Bendaña wrote at the time, "a radical reorientation of Nicaragua's international posture was a logical consequence and an immediate necessity of a revolution fought to attain genuine national independence."[7] The Sandinistas were inspired by the revolutionary nationalism of both their early twentieth-century namesake and the Cuban Revolution. Its ideologues sincerely believed that Nicaraguan underdevelopment was the result of a symbiotic relationship between the Somoza regime, the country's capitalist and financier classes, and the US empire.[8] At the same time, while they did not make the same integrated economic critique of North American imperialism, much of the country's middle and upper classes similarly held Washington responsible for the installation and prolongation of the dictatorship. Thus, foreign affairs were destined to be of central importance for a revolutionary project born, to a large degree, from the belief that Nicaragua's problems were external in nature.

Indeed, while international actors played a decisive role in bringing the Revolution to power in the first place, external forces only increased in importance for the country as the FSLN consolidated power and launched its ambitious social agenda. Even before the US and its allies sought to destabilize the new government, the international sphere became the Nicaraguan Revolution's front line of defense. From the outset, international affairs occupied much of the National Directorate's time; "foreign policy was seen as fundamental," recalls Deputy Foreign Minister Victor Hugo Tinoco.[9] Shedding light on the basis of Sandinista foreign policy is similarly fundamental for understanding the outsized significance that the Nicaraguan Revolution acquired at the inter-American level throughout the decade. The same ideological tensions that drove the revolutionary process at home were at play as Sandinista leaders redefined Nicaraguan national interests and devised plans to defend them in a complex Cold War environment.

The strategies they pursued in this early revolutionary phase proved enormously consequential for both their regime and the inter-American system. Though nonaligned in meaningful ways, the revolutionary government's growing ties to Cuba and other socialist countries and—most crucially—its support for left-wing guerrillas in El Salvador provided a pretext for US aggression and therefore breached the tacit agreement among Latin American regional leaders that propelled them to power in the summer of 1979. Some right-leaning governments identified Managua as a threat and moved to undermine the Sandinista government. These were soon eclipsed by the Reagan administration, which reinvigorated Washington's habit—somewhat muted under Carter—of intervening against Third World regimes whose existence, in its view, denoted global Soviet clout. Yet other Latin American leaders, haunted by a past of North American meddling, found that the threat of US intervention exceeded any danger posed by Cuban-leaning revolutionaries in the poorest country in Central America. Thus, the consolidation of a truly Sandinista government in Nicaragua, coupled with the arrival of the hawkish Reagan administration, set the stage for an international battle that would define the final decade of the Cold War in Latin America: a contest between an East–West vision of global affairs—in which leftist radicalization in the region appeared as a foreign socialist menace—and a North–South conceptualization of Latin American history, which identified the endogenous, social roots of revolutionary agitation and therefore sought local solutions to the conflicts those upheavals had unleashed.

The Sources of Sandinista Foreign Policy

The Revolution's core ideological dilemmas—the tense balance between its liberal and socialist impulses—played out visibly in the new government's behavior in the international arena. Carter's opponents in the Republican Party, along with their anti-Sandinista Nicaraguan allies, argued that the FSLN government was determined to attempt an expansionist, destabilizing foreign policy as a result of the Revolution's fundamentally Marxist character.[10] By contrast, those opposed to intervention in Central America claimed that Nicaragua's new leaders pursued a pragmatic and defensive policy stemming not only from socialist inclinations but also from the Revolution's nationalism and commitment to democracy.[11] In reality, competing ideological strains were in constant tension with one another; rather than choosing between them, the FSLN project was itself the product of interactions and contradictions between the two. In remaking Nicaraguan foreign affairs after the fall of Somoza, the new government articulated *both* nonalignment and closer ties to the Eastern Bloc as an extension of their domestic revolutionary process. In doing so, they anticipated a counterrevolutionary offensive directed by the United States and made plans to open as much maneuvering space as possible within the confines of that tremendously asymmetric relationship.

The revolutionaries' first major step abroad came in September 1979, when Nicaragua joined the Non-Aligned Movement (NAM). In his speech at that year's NAM conference in Havana, Comandante Daniel Ortega marked a break with the past by depicting the United States as the enemy of "the people" on a global scale (by contrast, the exiled Somoza grumbled that "no president anywhere supported the policies of the United States more devoutly" than he had).[12] Ortega described how Third World states were "playing an important role and exercising a growing influence in the international sphere, in the struggle of peoples against imperialism, colonialism, neocolonialism, apartheid, racism, including Zionism and every form of oppression."[13] The speech reflected instrumental goals. By 1979, Third World decolonization had produced a tripling in the number of United Nations member states since the organization's founding in 1945. The new Nicaraguan government dramatically expanded relations with African and Asian countries—roughly doubling them, overall—because, as Deputy

Foreign Minister José León Talavera explained, such countries "were fundamental for the balance of forces in voting in international organizations."[14] Throughout the decade, Nicaragua turned the UN and satellite institutions like the International Court of Justice into forums for the denunciation of US aggression. The numerous favorable resolutions they achieved depended on consistent voting support by the newly independent nations of the Global South.

Nonalignment was a strategy for survival. Ortega pleaded for aid and debt relief; a month later, a UN General Assembly resolution recommended massive assistance "with the utmost urgency" to the war-torn country.[15] Nicaragua took help from wherever it came. Having initially refused to normalize relations with the Republic of China (it sold weapons to the Somoza regime), the Junta quickly accepted the Taiwanese ambassador's credentials once it realized that money was on the table.[16] Even the anti-communist military regimes of Guatemala and El Salvador provided emergency credit to the cash-strapped government in Managua.[17] The new foreign policy ethos was "very simple," Talavera explained: "It was a product of a revolution that had to be defended. It implied having good relations with everybody."[18]

Moreover, this friendly and nonaligned posture dovetailed in important ways with the government's internal policies. Alejandro Bendaña, ambassador to the UN and later secretary general of the Foreign Relations Ministry, stated: "the truism that a nation's foreign policy is the extension of its domestic policy applies to Nicaragua. The Sandinista commitment to political pluralism at home found its counterpart in a foreign policy seeking to maintain friendly relations with as many countries as possible."[19] Indeed, for sympathizers including the parties of the Socialist International, the belief that the Sandinistas would not embrace full Soviet alignment was proof that they would establish an inclusive political system at home, and vice versa (just as critics saw FSLN ties to the Eastern Bloc as evidence of totalitarian ambitions at home). International relations provided an opportunity for the Revolution to brand itself; when Nora Astorga—an FSLN combatant known for advocating women's rights—became deputy foreign minister, she helped heighten the humanistic appeal that the Sandinista project cultivated in contrast to other left-wing revolutions of the era.[20]

While the early revolutionary government maintained cordial relations with the United States and became an outspoken NAM member, it also showed signs of preferring especially good relations with the countries of the Soviet-led Council for Mutual Economic Assistance (COMECON). Only five days after taking power, the FSLN National Directorate traveled to Havana to celebrate their victory with Fidel Castro—a sight that disturbed some Latin American allies—and military, diplomatic, technical, and cultural ties of all sorts were rapidly developed.[21] Vietnam, Albania, North Korea, and the USSR also opened relations by the end of 1979. A Soviet embassy was not established in Managua until February 1980; the next month a high-level delegation—including Junta members Sergio Ramírez and Moisés Hassan, as well as Jaime Wheelock, Tomás Borge, and Humberto Ortega of the FSLN National Directorate—visited Moscow to establish ties between the Sandinista Front and the Communist Party of the Soviet Union (CPSU). Formal agreements amounted to little more than technical and educational cooperation and the establishment of routine consultations between party leaders. Privately, the FSLN and CPSU agreed on transfers of light arms, though these were only executed in the 1979–81 period through third parties like Algeria, Libya, Cuba, and Vietnam.[22] Financial assistance from socialist countries in this period was dramatically outmatched by that which came from Western and Latin American countries; the same gap applied to Nicaragua's volume of trade.[23] Even Arab states provided more direct aid in this period.[24]

Western money sought to both moderate the FSLN leadership and buttress non-Sandinista elements in the government at the former's expense.[25] When the Carter administration offered to train officers from the newly formed Sandinista Popular Army at US Southern Command facilities in the Panama Canal Zone, the FSLN refused.[26] They reasoned, correctly, that one purpose of US military cooperation was to surveil their inchoate security apparatus. As Robert Pastor reflected, the Nicaraguans "did not want a military relationship with the United States for the same reasons that the United States wanted one."[27] While they accepted Panamanian assistance in training their new police forces, the Sandinistas politely rejected military assistance from Latin American countries, such as Venezuela, which they perceived as being too close to Washington. As a rule, they felt more comfortable accepting military assistance from socialist countries firmly outside the Western Bloc.[28]

As the broad anti-Somoza coalition started fraying, its outgoing members denounced Nicaragua's rapprochement with the East as a betrayal of the promise of nonalignment.[29] After leaving the government, Comandante Guerrillero Edén Pastora told journalists: "Look, the Nicaraguan economy is directed by Bulgaria, its politics by the USSR, and its defense by Cuba. I respect Cuba and Fidel, but that does not mean I would put in Cuba's hands the defense of Nicaragua. That is not Sandinismo."[30] US officials were initially more measured in their assessment. In early 1980, Secretary of State Cyrus Vance reported to Carter with satisfaction that the Sandinistas were pursuing a "quite pragmatic" foreign policy despite the militant rhetoric.[31] But US analysts found more cause for concern as the months went by. In November 1980, another FSLN trip to the Eastern Bloc produced loans from Bulgaria, Hungary, and Czechoslovakia. Although the amounts still were small when compared to credit received from multilateral lending institutions like the International Monetary Fund and Inter-American Development Bank, the State Department's intelligence division saw the March and November 1980 trips to the East as marking an "immediate shift in Nicaraguan foreign policy from ostensible nonalignment to a pro-Soviet stance."[32] The CIA noted Nicaragua's abstention from votes that year on UN General Assembly resolutions condemning the recent Soviet invasion of Afghanistan.[33]

The Afghanistan vote was an early touchstone in debates over Nicaragua's true foreign policy orientation. For some, the Sandinista voting record at the United Nations was evidence of active Soviet alignment; others saw ties with the socialist camp as a response to threats by Washington.[34] These disagreements echoed earlier debates over whether the Eisenhower and Kennedy administrations had pushed Fidel Castro's Cuba into communism and alignment with the Soviet Union.[35]

Seen from Managua's perspective, it would be most appropriate to identify two somewhat distinct but complementary tracks of Sandinista foreign policy. As part of a defensive posture assumed in anticipation of US efforts to undermine the Revolution, the FSLN National Directorate sought the patronage of the Soviet Union: "we needed an 'umbrella' that would protect us from the 'monster,'" as Comandante Luis Carrión put it.[36] For both reactive and proactive reasons, "Sandinista foreign policy was inclined to seek alliances with the Soviet Union," Comandante Jaime Wheelock wrote.[37] But a Soviet-facing strategy had severe limits. Nicaragua could not, and therefore would not, attempt the sort of integration with communist countries that Cuba had achieved (even though some Sandinista leaders allegedly expressed such a desire to the KGB's Latin America chief when he visited Managua a few months after Somoza's exit).[38] Geographical proximity to the United States was a major constraining factor. Additionally, friendly governments in Latin America and Europe did not want to see Nicaragua enter the Soviet orbit. And in any event, Soviet officials were ambivalent about the

Sandinistas, wary of unnecessarily threatening the US in its sphere of influence, and therefore unwilling to commit major resources to Managua.[39]

Nonalignment was therefore necessary. Close ties with a broad range of nations made Nicaragua different from Cuba. Sergio Ramírez told an interviewer in 1983: "We are facing the same kind of divided world that Fidel confronted in the early sixties. But for us, the world is not divided as strictly into East and West. . . . At the moment, we have the support not just of the socialist countries but of Western countries, of Arab and African countries, of Latin American countries as well, despite their ideology."[40] The Sandinistas also knew what the incoming Reagan administration knew: US plans to intervene aggressively in Central America were unpopular among American allies in Western Europe and Latin America.[41]

But nonalignment had limits, as well. The collective rejection of membership in bipolar alliances—motivated by the belief that said alliances came at the expense of national autonomy—peaked in the 1960s. But its organizational expression, the Non-Aligned Movement, had faded by the 1980s.[42] Due in part to its internal contradictions (African, Asian, and Latin American member states often pursued competing economic and strategic interests), the NAM was not a coherent source of economic backing for the Revolution. Military support was certainly not a possibility. Sandinista Nicaragua pursued autonomy and independence, but like most other countries it had to "lean to one side," to paraphrase Mao Tse-tung's declaration of revolutionary China's international orientation decades earlier.

The FSLN's founding elite tended to accept a bipolar vision of international affairs, believing that the United States' capitalist model was in decay and that communism would eventually prevail globally.[43] Jaime Wheelock later said of their outlook: "We thought that there was great potential and vast resources in the socialist countries and the USSR. We underestimated the extent of the crisis of socialism."[44] From the moment they took power, Humberto Ortega wrote, the Sandinistas "set on a path different from that of the communist system" while still being "closely tied to the socialist camp, under a framework of fraternity and mutual respect."[45] In their eyes, a long history of American interventions in Nicaragua necessitated the alliance even before Washington approved plans for a multifront intervention. "We were convinced," Luis Carrión later wrote, "that the United States would always try to destroy the Revolution, that this was in its imperialist nature."[46]

Faced with the impossibility of single-mindedly pursuing either strategy, the Sandinistas pursued both in tandem. This duality was loosely reflected in the organizational structure of FSLN foreign policy. The Foreign Ministry (and related governmental institutions like the Foreign Trade and Foreign Economic Cooperation Ministries) typically handled formal relations with the United States, Western countries, and multilateral organizations like the UN and OAS. Another set of party apparatuses—most notably FSLN's Department of International Relations (DRI), modeled after the Cuban Communist Party's Departamento de América—managed relations with Latin American leftist parties and guerrilla movements, global solidarity committees, and the party-states of the socialist world. While both sets of institutions ruled over distinct spheres of influence, they were united under the coherent policy direction of a Foreign Policy Committee, which usually included Daniel Ortega (first as Junta coordinator and later as president of the republic), army chief Humberto Ortega, DRI director Julio López Campos, and the minister and deputy ministers of foreign relations. This rough division of labor in FSLN foreign policy therefore allowed for coordination between both camps at all levels.

Throughout the decade, Nicaraguan foreign policy alternated between its formal, diplomatic strategy—centered on the West and the nonaligned states—and its informal, political relations to equally important effect.[47] As subsequent chapters explore, both dimensions of Sandinista foreign policy helped the government secure two things necessary to survive US aggression: enhanced military capabilities and legitimacy in the international arena. Arguably, revolutionary leaders managed the ideological contradictions inherent to the project with greater success in foreign relations than in domestic policy.

Revolution without Borders?

The multidimensionality of Sandinista foreign policy was on display at the Revolution's one-year anniversary celebrations in July 1980.[48] In attendance were the US ambassador to the UN, senior French diplomat Claude Cheysson, and various heads of state from across Latin America. The world of national liberation movements also arrived in force. Alongside Jamaica's Michael Manley and Grenada's Maurice Bishop was Yasser Arafat of the PLO. But the guest who drew the most headlines was Fidel Castro.[49] The Cuban's attendance called to mind his November 1971 trip to Salvador Allende's Chile, a flash point in the political polarization that preceded Augusto Pinochet's coup two years later. But Castro hit moderate notes in his speech, praising the wisdom of the Sandinistas' promise of political pluralism.[50]

On all foreign policy fronts, Havana was undoubtedly the most important partner. Carter administration officials watched with trepidation as hundreds of Cuban doctors and technical advisers came to Nicaragua to help reinforce the Sandinista regime. Washington urged the Carazo administration to send Costa Rican volunteers to lead the 1980 literacy campaign, but the FSLN preferred Cuban teachers.[51] They also bemoaned the presence of Cuban advisers at senior government levels, an issue of concern for outgoing moderates as well. Along with other *internacionalistas* from the Latin American Left, Cubans staffed technical posts in the Nicaraguan state for which the Sandinistas were unable to recruit local professionals.[52]

When it came to the Revolution's social and economic policies, Cuba provided a point of reference but did not impose a model. The creation of neighborhood organizations, as well as health and literacy brigades, suggested Cuban inspiration. But the specifics of Nicaraguan political economy, as well as the nature of the 1979 coalition, imposed inevitable differences on the Sandinista Revolution compared to the Cuban model: market forces operated, people relocated freely, opposition political parties were allowed to exist to a certain extent, and critical civil society organizations functioned to a much wider degree. There is no evidence, moreover, that Cuban officials ever had the final say in decisions concerning local policies. Indeed, FSLN leaders were sometimes wary of relinquishing too much authority to foreign advisers.[53] Comandante Guerrillero Joaquín Cuadra recalls pushing back against the advice of his own adviser, the Cuban revolutionary leader Arnaldo Ochoa, who had previously led Cuban military missions to Congo, Angola, and Ethiopia. "I don't know what you think you're doing," he remembers saying, "with your experience in Africa, in Ethiopia; but this is something else entirely. Nobody made the revolution for us here. We did it ourselves, we won it. This [war] is fought by us, the dead are ours. It's not Cubans that are dying here."[54] The nature of Cuban involvement in the anti-Somoza insurrection—coming relatively late in the game, negotiated through several other international partners—no doubt shaped the post-1979 relationship in a way that favored Nicaraguan autonomy.[55]

Throughout the decade, the Castro government tended to encourage Sandinista leaders to maintain their commitment to political pluralism and private property. Comandante Humberto Ortega later explained: "Fidel told us that the Cuban experience was unrepeatable and that therefore we had to avoid certain aspects of the Cuban experience."[56] Moderation was recommended, moreover, to attract help from Western countries.[57] When Sandinista leaders promoted policies or delivered rhetoric more reminiscent of

Cuba's version of "real socialism," they often did so against Castro's advice. As Ramírez explains in his memoir, Cuban impact on Sandinista rule was not always straightforward: "Cuba was the model that held our greatest hopes. Cuba shared them as well. . . . Nevertheless, this does not mean that Fidel Castro insisted on offering up the Cuban model for imitating in Nicaragua after the Sandinistas suddenly triumphed. . . . It is not that Fidel did not want Socialism in Nicaragua, but he imagined a Socialism that differed from the Cuban type. Moreover, he saw, perhaps, a new field for experiment to avoid repeating the errors that he could neither recognize nor amend in Cuba."[58]

Cuba's influence was, however, clear-cut in the security sphere. Cuban advisers helped train the Sandinista Popular Army as well as the various agencies of the Ministry of the Interior (such as the National Police and the General Directorate for State Security), which allowed the new government to assert a monopoly on violence across the national territory very quickly despite pockets of resistance by remnants of Somoza's National Guard. Without Cuban assistance in these areas, Jorge Castañeda rightly notes, the "Sandinistas could not have survived the revolutionary decade, under extraordinarily adverse circumstances."[59] Those circumstances—US intervention and, eventually, a full-scale civil war—would become "*the* issue" of the Revolution as General (and army chief of staff) Joaquín Cuadra saw it. Cuba, thus, had a "decisive influence in the whole revolutionary process."[60]

The Cuban government was involved in one of the Sandinistas' most important defense and foreign policy decisions: supporting a left-wing guerrilla insurgency in El Salvador. Ruled by a variety of personalistic and collective military dictatorships since roughly the time of the elder Somoza's installation, the neighboring country witnessed the rise of several armed leftist groups in the 1960s and '70s. The sudden triumph of the first armed revolution in Latin America after Cuba—next door, no less— was a watershed moment for El Salvador. In October 1979, seeking to avert the utter collapse that had befallen Somoza's National Guard, moderate sectors of the Salvadoran military overthrew the long-ruling Partido de Conciliación Nacional and installed a joint civilian-military "Revolutionary Junta," which promised social reforms and dialogue with the Left. That modest reform project quickly collapsed under pressure from conservative business groups and right-wing operators inside the armed forces, who instead addressed the threat of a potential Nicaragua-style popular uprising by intensifying military repression against political opponents like the Catholic archbishop Óscar Romero, famously gunned down at the altar in

March 1980. In turn, the ratcheting up of regime repression inspired the country's disunited rebel groups to begin unity talks and hatch plans for a revolutionary war.

The example of the Sandinistas' 1979 victory was another factor that motivated the Salvadoran armed Left to coordinate new efforts.[61] The unlikely success of the Nicaraguan insurrection made victory in El Salvador—where the armed Left was larger, longer-running, and better resourced—more plausible. And the Sandinista experience, which saw a divided movement settle its personal rivalries and tactical differences ahead of a successful seizure of state power, provided an attractive blueprint.

In October 1980, fourteen months after the FSLN takeover, the leaders of the four main Salvadoran rebel groups and the national communist party unified under the single banner of the Frente Farabundo Martí para la Liberación Nacional (FMLN). Historian Andrea Oñate persuasively emphasizes the role played by Castro, whose surrogates had spent over a year mediating between the disparate factions. As he did with the Sandinistas, Castro made unity a precondition for his support. The FMLN established its base of command in Managua immediately after its founding, turning the Nicaraguan capital into the place where Salvadoran guerrilla leaders discussed strategy and, in some cases, settled internal disputes—longtime guerrilla leader Cayetano Carpio "Marcial" mysteriously committed suicide in his Managua hotel room a few days after the murder of his second in command and ideological rival, Comandante "Ana María" Montes in April 1983.[62] For their part, FSLN commanders and their Department of International Relations mediated Salvadoran relations with Havana.[63] And Nicaragua, along with Cuba, became central to the FMLN's offensive capabilities; the Sandinistas stockpiled weapons for what they hoped would be the second Central American revolution.[64]

In sponsoring the FMLN, the Sandinistas reneged on earlier promises and consciously contradicted an organizing principle of the broad transnational fellowship that propelled them to power—that they should remake Nicaraguan society as they wished, but without unjustifiably provoking a US intervention in the process. On September 24, 1979, two months after Somoza's overthrow, President Jimmy Carter received Junta members Daniel Ortega, Alfonso Robelo, and Sergio Ramírez at the White House, promising millions in reconstruction and relief aid so long as they retained their commitment to pluralism, human rights, and, above all, their promise not to export revolution abroad. Ortega explained that revolutionary upheaval in Central America was the result of preexisting social tensions and assured

Carter that Nicaragua "is not a factor in the radicalization of El Salvador; it was not in the past, nor the present, and will not be in the future, nor in Guatemala."[65]

By the following year, however, CIA analysts observed arms reaching the Salvadoran guerrillas from Nicaragua and judged there to be a "very high likelihood" that these shipments represented "official FSLN policy."[66] FSLN leaders later admitted that to be the case; as Ramírez notes, arms were sent to El Salvador just as Carter submitted the aid package to Congress.[67] However, the same CIA report cautioned that the evidence was inconclusive. Therefore, the Carter administration ignored a conservative outcry in Congress and continued the aid program to the Nicaraguan government, believing the policy had strengthened moderates and helped preserve political openness in general.

Sandinista involvement and weapons shipments ramped up substantially in the fall of 1980. Worried that the incoming administration of President-Elect Ronald Reagan would increase lethal aid for the Salvadoran military, the newly unified FMLN made Cuban-advised plans for a "Final Offensive," reminiscent of the Sandinistas' successful summer 1979 uprising. As caches of captured FMLN documents and aerial surveillance soon revealed, the Sandinista military spent the autumn months rerouting Cuban-provided arms—as well as guns Venezuela had provided to the Sandinistas during the 1979 insurrection—to El Salvador via land, air, and sea.[68] On the eve of the Final Offensive in January, believing they now had the conclusive proof they previously lacked, Carter instructed Ambassador Lawrence Pezzullo to confront the Sandinistas. FSLN leaders served up a glib response. As the US diplomat reported, Comandante Tomás Borge "could not discount that some arms were passing through Nicaragua or that some people connected with the government were assisting," but repeated that it was not official policy to get involved.[69] The following day, Radio Liberación—the clandestine FMLN radio station broadcasting from a hidden location in Nicaragua—called on all Salvadorans to rise in popular insurrection against their government.

Within two days, Salvadoran military forces had repelled the guerrilla assault. The accompanying popular uprising failed to materialize. Immediately afterward, the Carter administration suspended its aid package to the Nicaraguan government, portending an end to the period in which Washington sought to contain the Sandinistas by using aid to strengthen moderates inside and outside their government. The failure of the Final Offensive and Carter's swift response led the FSLN to hide Salvadoran rebel leaders in Managua, close Radio Liberación, and suspend the most conspicuous arms shipments.

After taking power in January 1981, shortly after the Final Offensive, the Reagan administration turned the suspension of US aid into a permanent cutoff. The new White House shared the previous administration's fear of revolutionary contagion in Central America but disagreed that the Sandinista Front could be moderated. In fact, key incoming defense and intelligence officials thought coexistence with Nicaragua was either impossible or unacceptable; where Latin American and Western European leftists saw a potential new model for developing countries to follow, Reagan administration hard-liners saw a test case for an emerging effort to roll back communism in the Third World. Some top diplomats on the new team believed pressure should be used to extract basic concessions from the Sandinistas at negotiations, namely that they cease support for rebels in El Salvador. But officials operating with a starker regime-change mentality had greater success in driving Reagan's foreign policy.[70] As political scientist William Leogrande has written: "Even if the Sandinistas seemed responsive to US demands, the Reaganites regarded such moves as merely temporary and tactical—designed to buy time while the Leninists consolidated themselves. Nothing the Sandinistas did could penetrate this seamless web of ideological certainty. The threat to US interests, in the hard-liners' view, stemmed from *the very existence of the Sandinista regime*. The only choice for the United States was to find a way to dislodge the Sandinistas from power, or acquiesce in the creation of a 'second Cuba.'"[71]

The slide toward an openly confrontational American foreign policy was delineated by the Reagan administration's first significant diplomatic overtures to the FSLN. In August 1981, Assistant Secretary of State for Inter-American Affairs Thomas Enders met with top Sandinistas in Managua. According to Nicaraguan transcripts of the talks, the envoy struck a reasonable enough tone, telling Daniel Ortega and Foreign Minister Miguel D'Escoto: "Just as you all consider your revolution to be irreversible, so do we."[72] In that meeting and in his discussions with the FSLN National Directorate, Enders raised concrete concerns over arms shipments to El Salvador and the expansion of the Sandinista Popular Army, but did not make demands related to Nicaragua's internal affairs. "We don't share the same ideology as some of you," he told the comandantes, but it was up to Nicaraguans to determine their country's political economy, "just as we decide what's best for the United States."[73] Based on this understanding, Enders floated a deal in which the US would restart aid if Nicaragua downsized its military and stopped trafficking arms abroad. By the end of 1981, however, hard-liners had moved the Reagan administration away from efforts at dialogue and normalization. They instead began insisting on Nicaragua's "democratization" as an item on the negotiating agenda, seeking to thwart such talks altogether.

Given the emphasis that the Sandinistas gave to the concept of national sovereignty, such demands were a nonstarter. Jaime Wheelock told a journalist at the time: "What guides Sandinismo is the conviction that our country, Nicaragua, has never been a country with real sovereignty or national independence; Nicaragua has been an appendage of the United States. We have been abused and humiliated. Nicaragua was kept dependent and backward, a country of illiterate farm laborers."[74] Exiting the US orbit was synonymous with FSLN leaders' notion of overcoming underdevelopment at home. Negotiating with any American administration on foreign policy matters would be difficult. To listen to Reagan officials press them on how they should run Nicaragua was inconceivable.

Fresh off the war against Somoza, and distrustful of the new administration's intentions, FSLN leaders assumed a defiant attitude. "We were still in a wartime mentality," Comandante Bayardo Arce later recalled: "I myself was still running five kilometers every morning in order to stay fit for combat."[75] Reagan's aggressive measures seemed to justify their edginess. Shortly after he entered office, CIA agents began meeting with Nicaraguan exiles plotting the overthrow of the FSLN government. While the Sandinistas negotiated with the Enders team in September, the US Navy conducted exercises with Honduras near Nicaragua's Caribbean coast. And in November, Reagan approved National Security Decision Directive 17, a policy document calling for expanded intelligence-gathering in the region and increased military aid for the Honduran and Salvadoran governments. The following month he signed a presidential finding authorizing covert actions against Nicaragua, including support for anti-Sandinista rebels.[76] In public, administration officials made the dubious promise that proxy rebels only existed to stem the flow of arms to the Salvadoran guerrillas and denied any regime change project for Nicaragua.

Even though El Salvador was the main point of contention for both Carter and Reagan, Nicaragua's revolutionary leaders continued collaborating with the FMLN throughout the decade. Even when the Sandinistas dialed down their arms shipments to El Salvador after the Final Offensive, they continued smuggling weapons across the Gulf of Fonseca. In his memoir, Ramírez humorously recalls how the smugglers—known as *cayuqueros* after the canoes they piloted—were honored at the July 1981 anniversary celebrations by being seated just one row below Venezuelan president Luis Herrera Campins.[77] Humberto Ortega, general and chief of the Nicaraguan army, stated frankly that the Sandinista government knew it was playing with fire: "The FMLN, from the beginning of the Revolution, received vital support from the Sandinistas. . . . We always assured the flow of arms through the Gulf of Fonseca, with Nicaraguan sailors in *cayucos* that defied both the tides as well as the vigilance of the US Navy, with the risk of compromising the position of the government of Nicaragua."[78]

Nicaraguan leaders continued the policy in part because they judged that Reagan's stance would not shift meaningfully if they dropped it. Comandante Guerrillero Hugo Torres, then general and director of political affairs in the Sandinista Popular Army, asked, "Who actually believed that the altitude of the US would change by the fact that we would stop sending arms to El Salvador?"[79] General Joaquín Cuadra agreed that a different policy in El Salvador may have removed a layer of complexity to the relationship with the Reagan administration, but without changing the overall reality of animosity.[80] Indeed, when the Sandinistas interrupted the flow of arms to El Salvador in the wake of the failed 1981 offensive, it had little effect on the White House's approach to Nicaragua.

Moreover, the Sandinista elite was deeply committed to the revolution in El Salvador for reasons of solidarity. Nicaraguan revolutionaries had incurred a "moral debt" to the Salvadoran armed Left, which contributed substantial money and fighters to the 1979 insurrection, and now faced an increasingly well-armed and ruthless counterinsurgency apparatus.[81] As Luis Carrión put it: "We were brothers. We were *compañeros*. We were family. We had to do something."[82] Even as Daniel Ortega promised noninterference in El Salvador to Enders, he coyly noted that among the Nicaraguan populace "there exists great sympathy to collaborate with the Salvadoran people."[83]

There were equally important strategic reasons behind the policy. In involving themselves in El Salvador's civil war, the FSLN leadership took inspiration from the Cuban strategy of creating problems abroad as a means of focusing its defense beyond its borders.[84] The strategy differed according to Nicaraguan realities; Nicaragua is squarely in the middle of an isthmus composed of several countries connected by land borders. FSLN strategists sought to turn this weakness into a strength. Shortly after taking power, they made plans with allied Central American leftist organizations to activate guerrilla cells across the region in the event of a US invasion.

The idea, as Ortega described it, was to turn the region into a "political-military powder keg."[85] Beyond the hope that a friendly revolutionary regime in El Salvador was an achievable reality, Sandinista support for the FMLN was undertaken as part of plans to regionalize a potential conflict with the United States and heighten the costs of a direct military intervention. "The political consideration was to create one or two Vietnams, to disperse the enemy," General Hugo Torres recalled. "To regionalize the focus of attention to the US so that it wasn't just Nicaragua."[86] Luis Carrión put it in very similar terms: "There was this idea that, in order to relieve some of the pressure from the United States, it was necessary to—and this is where Che's slogan comes in—create one, two, three, many Vietnams."[87] "The only defense we had," Ramírez explained, "was to have another revolution."[88]

At the Nicaraguan Revolution's second anniversary celebrations in July 1981, Tomás Borge proclaimed the transnational dimensions of the Sandinista project: "this revolution goes beyond our borders." His comments became fodder for the Reagan administration, which justified aggression toward Nicaragua in terms of a Central American domino theory wherein the consolidation of the Sandinistas would lead to like-minded, left-wing regimes elsewhere in the region. In the case of El Salvador, at least, Borge's comments were not empty sloganeering: the FSLN elite had taken the strategic decision to "support the guerrillas of Central America," as Luis Carrión later wrote, "not only for reasons of solidarity but also defensive ones."[89] Because that choice enraged their foreign adversaries and upset a number of international allies, some Sandinista leaders later looked back on it with regret; "the support we gave to the Salvadoran guerrillas brought high costs for our national security," Humberto Ortega said in retrospect.[90]

But contrary to Reagan's propaganda, the Sandinistas had not "exported" revolution to El Salvador: "revolutions are not exportable like Coca-Cola or paperbacks," diplomat Nora Astorga told the press. "Revolutions are made in a country when the conditions in that particular country are for a process of change."[91] In the context of a long-running struggle between the forces for and against social change in El Salvador, perhaps the Sandinistas' most important impact was simply their motivating example. FMLN comandante Cayetano Carpio told a journalist: "The revolutionary process of Central America is one. The triumphs of one are the triumphs of the other. . . . Guatemala will have its hour. Honduras its own. Costa Rica will live a stellar moment. The first note was heard in Nicaragua. History will sing in Central America."[92] And yet the emergence of a revolutionary, left-wing government in Managua also inspired a strong response by US-backed right-wing forces. This reaction would ultimately make it extremely difficult for another revolutionary movement to take power in Central America.

Complicating the Cold War

Sandinista foreign policies also had an impact beyond Central America. Consider a January 1981 conversation between Jaime Wheelock and US ambassador Pezzullo, in which the former challenged the latter to provide concrete evidence of Nicaraguan involvement in El Salvador:

> Wheelock threatened: "if you can't reveal to us any details of these operations, when you suspend assistance and make it public, you won't be able to prove your case, especially in Latin America. It will appear as if you took arbitrary action." [Pezzullo] replied, "the evidence would be terribly embarrassing to you." . . . [Wheelock] then said, "it would be a political act which will undercut our economy. We won't have the funds to make repayment, our credit standing will suffer, and the effects will be catastrophic." Wheelock added that it will appear as "economic aggression by the US," and Ortega added that "all Latin America will support us." [Pezzullo] said, "you will also be revealed for having supported a guerrilla movement in a neighboring country which violates the principle of self-determination that you hold dear, and would be indefensible in international terms."[93]

In effect, Pezzullo and Wheelock were both right. In the early revolutionary period, the Sandinistas' activist foreign policy evoked a bifurcated reaction in Latin America, pitting those who held East–West notions of conflict in the region versus those who saw those same upheavals as a symptom of the region's underdevelopment and unequal relations with the United States.

On the one hand, the Sandinistas' Cuban-oriented and -influenced foreign policy, its arms buildup, and assistance to regional rebel movements induced the anxiety of several Latin American governments. This even applied, to a certain degree, to some of the indispensable countries that helped overthrow Somoza: both Carazo and Torrijos refused to join the Revolution's first anniversary celebrations when they learned that Fidel Castro would be the keynote speaker.[94] Nicaragua's relations with Costa Rica, in particular, witnessed a marked cooling that took an abrupt turn for the worse when Carazo was replaced by the strongly anti-communist president Luis Alberto Monge in 1982. Though he came from Pepe Figueres's Liberationist Party (a Socialist International member), the newly inaugurated Monge immediately expelled several Nicaraguan diplomats and accused their government of supporting a leftist plot to undermine his country's democratic system.[95] The following year, Monge professed Costa Rica's neutrality in Central America's conflicts and disappointed Reagan officials by dropping the policy of outright hostility toward the Sandinistas; nonetheless, he turned a blind eye to CIA-supported Contra operations throughout his tenure.[96] Similarly, relations with the Venezuelan government of Luis Herrera Campins cooled in this period.[97] The governments of Honduras and Guatemala allowed ex-somocista Guardsmen to operate in their territory. Argentina's military dictatorship provided vital support as well.[98]

But other countries, as Wheelock had promised, seemed less concerned by the radical government in Managua than they were threatened by the Reagan administration's bellicose response to it. Therefore, when he expressed his concerns over the radicalization of the Nicaraguan Revolution to SI president Willy Brandt in the summer of 1981, Carlos Andrés Pérez added an important qualification: "However, it would not be fair to ignore the conflictive circumstances in which the Nicaraguan movement has been placed by the new North American administration—based on the a priori notion that for the United States the Sandinista Revolution is unacceptable, a position which has sowed panic or heightened the distrust of the country's private sector. And it has served also to dangerously polarize Sandinista leaders, making more radical the radicals and weakening the position of the moderates." Indeed, when the Reagan administration permanently cut off bilateral aid to the FSLN government in April 1981, millions of dollars in loans from Cuba and Libya—as well as the first major wheat shipments from the USSR—filled the void. While Western hostility seemed to be having a negative effect, Pérez cautioned that the world's democracies should not issue a blank check, either. Social-democratic solidarity, he told Brandt, should come "without conditions, but cannot be called unconditional." This nuanced policy was meant partly to keep the FSLN on the road to a pluralistic form of revolutionary renewal. It was also rooted in the belief that Western European aid should crowd out Eastern Bloc investment and therefore prevent the FSLN's drift toward the Soviet orbit.[99]

At the same time, this policy was meant to counterbalance Washington's support for anti-communist military regimes in Central America. In the Venezuelan's view, Reagan was boosting the regional "ultra-right," amplifying the threat of violence, and frustrating progress toward democracy on the isthmus; the situation "could lead to an armed international conflict, which would affect the whole region of Latin America and the Caribbean and lead to very negative changes in relations with the United States."[100] The SI's promotion of political pluralism and a mixed economy became more important than ever in this context. The organization's assessment, as Rother put it, was that "only if the Sandinistas moderated their polices . . . could the revolution in Nicaragua still be saved from US intervention."[101]

Pérez exemplifies how the Sandinista victory in Nicaragua complicated the traditional US foreign policy precept that revolutionary movements in Latin America were inherently dangerous and represented a Soviet peril. Nicaraguan and Cuban diplomats were eager to emphasize that a remarkable variety of Latin American countries supported the toppling of Somoza in 1979. Cuban vice premier Carlos Rafael Rodríguez outlined this perspective in a secret meeting with Secretary of State Haig (sponsored by Mexican diplomats) in 1981:

> It is not only we who say it would be a mistake to conceive of that
> which is happening now in Central America as a result of external
> subversive activity; even such moderate leaders as López-Portillo are
> completely open in their adherence to this view. . . . I believe that
> Carlos Andres Perez is a right-wing Social Democrat and holds the
> same assessment. . . . We helped the Sandinista Front in every way
> that we could, with all of the means that we were able to deploy. But
> we were not the only ones who helped them. You know that there
> were several governments in Latin America who helped them
> substantially more than we did. Thus, this was a situation which was
> regarded by Latin America as a fatal tumor which it was necessary
> to remove.[102]

For López Portillo's Mexico, the triumph of the armed Left in Nicaragua was a pivotal moment. Fed by their country's own revolutionary mythology, Mexican intellectuals and statesmen viewed the Sandinista process through a romantic lens. When an aide asked López Portillo what kind of formal treatment they should give the Nicaraguan delegation on the president's final visit to Managua in 1982, he replied: "Just like a Mexican state."[103] But while sympathy no doubt played a role, Jorge Castañeda wrote that Mexico's intervention in favor of the Sandinistas "was based exclusively on self-interest." Unlike US policymakers, Castañeda said, Mexican officials saw an opportunity, rather than a threat, in Central America's left-wing revolutionary movements: if these groups saw Mexico as an ally, the country could carve a sphere of influence and counterbalance US influence in the

Caribbean Basin.[104] In 1981, Mexican leaders joined the French government in declaring the Salvadoran FMLN as legitimate belligerents with a right to participate in political negotiations to end that country's civil war. For other analysts, Mexico's involvement in Nicaragua and El Salvador was less interventionist and more defensive in nature, motivated by fears that US intervention in Central America—or worse, a superpower confrontation—would have spillover effects for Mexican politics, economic growth, and security.[105]

Mexico sought to both bolster the new revolutionary regime in Managua and moderate its behavior. The PRI government sent generous loans, helped negotiate Nicaragua's debt before multilateral lending institutions, and in February 1980 assumed, alongside Venezuela, most of Nicaragua's oil needs.[106] But preserving the new ally in Managua required some sensitivity to US interests and concerns. Therefore, they used their generosity as leverage; Mexico helped maintain a minimum of business–government dialogue in the early revolutionary period and became the FSLN's main intermediary with the US government during the Reagan years.

The Sandinistas' distortion of typical Cold War international relations extended, crucially, to Western Europe. A notable example was French president François Mitterrand, who, when asked about Nicaragua, told Le Monde in 1981: "How can we not understand popular revolt? It's not about communist subversion, but of the refusal of misery and humiliation. The West would be better advised to help these peoples than to force them to live under the boot. When they call for help, I would like for Castro not to be the only one that hears them."[107] The French socialist president put his words into action: in December 1981, his government secretly negotiated an arms deal with the FSLN worth around $20 million.[108] In selling weapons to Nicaragua, France—a Western democracy and North Atlantic Treaty Organization (NATO) ally of the United States—incurred Washington's ire (though Mitterrand also warned the FSLN not to abandon the "original" goals of the Revolution).[109] Some in the Washington foreign policy establishment saw this break with US policy as an unprecedented and unacceptable violation of the Monroe Doctrine.[110] As a Rand Corporation analysis described, it was not just the Soviet Union, "but also resurgent European powers, notably France and Germany," that were challenging Washington's uncontested hegemony; "they are contributing as much to stabilizing as to destabilizing [Central America's] politics. Simultaneously, local governments and anti-government actors in the region are also soliciting support from outside the hemisphere, independent of the United States. Although

West European involvement can contribute to the region's economic and political development, this general push-pull process is fostering the internationalization of local conflicts and eroding US leverage."[111]

FSLN foreign policy reasoned that it, too, might erode US leverage by exploiting Latin American discontent with Reagan's approach to the region. Deputy Foreign Relations Minister José León Talavera notes that South American governments sometimes "would view us as a small buffer which perhaps cushioned them against some of the United States' aggressive policies, and it was of interest to them to see somebody laying into the gringos."[112] Over the course of the decade, Nicaraguan diplomats appealed to Latin American governments with a simple idea linking underdevelopment and instability in Central America: that the Reagan administration's "conceptualization, which pretends to explain the region's crisis as part of the East–West conflict, is incorrect because the peoples of Central America have rebelled against this situation throughout history, long before the existence of the Russian Revolution."[113]

Opposition to US meddling created common ground. In their August 1981 meetings with Thomas Enders, the National Directorate deflected questions about Cuban ties by emphasizing their ties to a broad range of Latin American leaders, including Costa Rica's Rodrigo Carazo. Enders shocked the comandantes with his retort; Carazo, he said, was unpopular and corrupt: "he stole millions of dollars in sending arms to you all. . . . I don't understand how you could use him as an example of 'good relations.' . . . Even you should feel repugnance because that man has sold his office for private enrichment."[114] Bayardo Arce shared a transcript with the Costa Rican president, who furiously demanded an apology from the US ambassador in San José, and eventually confronted Enders at a conference in Belize. Commenting on the incident in a letter to López Portillo, Carazo promised to not collaborate with US intervention in Nicaragua and strongly rejected the new administration's East–West characterization of Latin American politics: "If the superpowers wish to fight amongst themselves, they should do it in their own territories and not in ours."[115]

Conclusion

In February 1982, exactly two years after the speech cited at the beginning of the previous chapter, López Portillo returned to revolutionary Managua. Much had changed. The broad-front government envisioned by the transnational coalition at Puntarenas had given way to hegemonic Sandinista rule. The destruction of the old regime had unleashed long-simmering desires for rapid change, and the FSLN harnessed this popular energy to control the state and advance a radical agenda for remaking Nicaraguan society along lines different from those imagined by the original Junta of National Reconstruction. Their efforts to centralize power were a response to the immediate threat posed by remnants of Somoza's National Guard, as well as the likelihood of more aggressive intervention by the United States and other anti-communist forces abroad. Early FSLN reforms massively expanded rights and redistributed wealth in ways that favored many formerly marginalized Nicaraguans, especially in urban areas. At the same time, statist and collectivizing policies challenged many in the upper and middle classes, as well as large parts of the rural peasantry; such groups were further alienated by the revolutionary government's intolerance of dissent. Tensions also had risen among the county's Indigenous communities. By the Revolution's third year, several of the anti-Somoza coalition's leaders had become its fiercest critics.[116] For most top members of the Socialist International, an "initial phase of great hope for a democratic-socialist model for the Third World" had ended.[117]

This change over time was apparent in the speech López Portillo delivered during his second visit. Whereas his 1980 address focused on Sandinista Nicaragua's promise for the region, in the 1982 iteration the Mexican leader found himself defending the regime's continued existence. By this time, many US analysts saw in the FSLN government a Soviet foothold in Central America. Certain anti-communist regimes in the region, threatened additionally by Sandinista efforts to inspire revolution elsewhere in the region, shared this thinking and joined Washington in actions—most notably, the creation of a proxy army of Nicaraguan exiles—designed to undermine the government in Managua. In the face of this superpower threat, López Portillo told Nicaraguans to continue the revolutionary path they had chosen. Further, he warned that "an intervention in Central America and the Caribbean would represent a gigantic historical error. . . . It would provoke a continental convulsion and a resurgence of a profound anti-American sentiment among the best people of all Latin America."[118]

The triumph of the armed Left in Nicaragua struck at the heart of Latin America's Cold War–era dilemmas. By seizing state power with wide popular support, advancing a radical agenda, and supporting revolutionary movements abroad, the Sandinistas posed a vexing question: What was the nature of social upheaval in Latin America, and how legitimate were the political organizations born from those movements? CIA analysts had come to believe that the "Soviets have by and large successfully implemented a policy of encouraging unrest in various Central American states."[119] But López Portillo offered a different explanation for the roots of this agitation:

> In the same way that most of the Asian and African [anticolonial, independence] struggles could not be forcefully inserted into the East–West or capitalist–socialist dichotomies, the Central American revolutions of our times resist these Manichean classifications. . . .
>
> I can assure my good friends in the United States that what is happening in Nicaragua; what is happening in El Salvador and the winds that blow throughout the whole region; these do not represent an intolerable danger for the fundamental interests and national security of the United States; what *is* a danger is the risk of historical condemnation for violently infringing the rights of the peoples (which without a doubt the United States claims for itself) to self-determination, independence, and the exercise of their autonomy.[120]

Thus, the first two years of the Sandinista decade witnessed a setting of the stage. As a war emerged between the FSLN regime and US-backed counterrevolutionaries, an international battle between those two emergent narratives would also unfold on the international scene.

Part III   **War, 1982–1985**

· ·

5 A Kind of Civil War

When Mexican novelist Carlos Fuentes visited revolutionary Managua in 1984, the first thing that struck him was the capital's "unfinished" quality: "The heavy damages caused by the great earthquake of 1972 hadn't been repaired by either the Somoza dictatorship or the Sandinista Revolution. The Cathedral was in ruins. The streets had no names. The city had its back turned toward the lake; moreover, it dumped its sewage there. I asked various Sandinista officials about this state of abandonment. The answer was in their gaze, rather than their words. Nicaragua was at war."[1] By that point tens of thousands of Nicaraguan citizens had been mobilized to fight against the enemies of the Revolution. Anti-government rebels, led by remnants of Somoza's National Guard, called themselves *comandos*. But they quickly came to be known as *contras* (as in *contrarrevolucionarios*, or counterrevolutionaries), a designation they generally made their own. Such groups began operating in small numbers, and unsuccessfully, in the Revolution's first few months. Their prospects greatly improved in the final months of 1981, when Ronald Reagan formally directed the US national security apparatus to "support democratic forces" in Nicaragua. By March 14, 1982, when explosives took out two bridges along the country's northern border with Honduras, the insurgents leveraged training, supplies, and intelligence provided by Washington.

Those early Contra attacks accelerated the polarization of post-Somoza Nicaragua. Sandinista officials saw in them the beginning of the imperialist invasion they had long foretold. In response, they expanded emergency powers, further curtailed civil liberties, and levied new taxes on business leaders not deemed part of the "patriotic bourgeoisie." In turn, the political opposition became further convinced of the FSLN's totalitarian ambitions. A month after the attacks, Edén Pastora declared that he too would seek to dislodge the National Directorate by force, citing the government crackdown as his casus belli. Alfonso Robelo, another former ally, soon fled the country and joined Pastora's exile rebellion. To face the increased threat, Comandante Daniel Ortega made a highly publicized trip to the Eastern Bloc and concluded significant arms deals with the USSR and Bulgaria in May.[2]

This turn of events validated fears expressed by Latin America's moderate Left. Peruvian novelist (and future Nobel laureate) Mario Vargas Llosa had summed up these concerns after a visit to Managua a year prior. If the world's democracies did not oppose Washington's hostilities toward the FSLN government, he asked, "why would it be strange to expect that the Nicaraguans would turn to hear the siren song coming from the other side?"[3]

The period 1982–85 saw tremendous violence befall Nicaragua as the Sandinista Popular Army (EPS, by its Spanish acronym) mobilized to counter the growing ranks of the various Contra factions. For another Latin American literary luminary, albeit one with a stronger leftist bent, responsibility for the carnage lay exclusively in North American hands. "Once more," wrote the Argentine novelist Julio Cortázar after visiting the front lines in 1983, "David has stood up to the monumental Goliath."[4] In many ways, the biblical reference was fitting; the greatest power in history was exerting diplomatic, economic, and paramilitary pressure—both overt and covert—on an impoverished, mostly agrarian country of roughly 3 million inhabitants. Nicaraguan diplomats exploited this narrative as they denounced Washington's aggression in their country and elsewhere in the Third World.[5] Their speeches and communiqués resonated with a generation of idealistic US and European citizens who protested intervention in Central America. But for Nicaraguan writer Gioconda Belli, a student of Cortázar (and a Sandinista propagandist tasked with selling this message at home and abroad), it was precisely this "vision of good and evil, of imperialism, of David and the Goliath" that ultimately undercut the FSLN's mission to transform Nicaraguan society.[6] In the mountainous Nicaraguan interior, it blinded revolutionary leaders to the unexpected side effects of their governing style and transformational agenda. FSLN strategists were slow to recognize that, for the many thousands of peasants who felt excluded by the Sandinistas' nation-building project and opted to join the US-backed Contra, *they* were David and the Nicaraguan state was the Goliath.

The collective memory of Nicaragua's armed conflict is a battleground in and of itself. The FSLN National Directorate saw it as a war of foreign aggression, a perspective echoed in scholarship that calls it a "proxy war" and centers the Reagan administration's role in financing and training the Contra to pursue its own foreign policy objectives. A minority of academic observers have sharply diverged from such characterizations, instead downplaying evidence of US involvement and emphasizing the domestic roots of violence; "the conflict in Nicaragua," one analyst has written, "was a *civil war* caused by Sandinista policies."[7] To an extent, this binary—civil war on the one hand, and foreign intervention on the other—simply reflects polarizing debates that Reagan's interventionism animated among US citizens regarding their country's relative responsibility for violence in the Global South. At the same time, competing emphases can also be glimpsed in the way Nicaraguans remember the conflict today, although most simply call it *la guerra*. The fighting claimed, in any event, a number of lives comparable to those lost in the insurrectionary war that ended the Somoza dictatorship (perhaps more).[8] It also lasted much longer. But taxonomy is not trivial in this instance. Competing characterizations of the war in Nicaragua shaped belligerents' military strategies (with disastrous results for both sides, sociologist Orlando Núñez noted) and informed the ways foreign actors got involved.[9]

It is common—consider France, Mexico, Russia, or Iran—for revolutionary coalitions to collapse soon after the ancien régime is overthrown, plunging society into violence as a result. Comandante Humberto Ortega recently reflected that the Revolution's leadership had been "unable to sustain the great patriotic alliance it had advanced after 1977 in order to vanquish somocismo."[10] The Sandinistas' political and economic agenda was bound, if not intended, to alienate the private sector and the traditional oligarchy. But ambitious FSLN policies to restructure social relations and redistribute wealth—informed not only by revolutionary idealism but also by a confidence in scientific progress and top-down, centralized planning—also had the wholly unexpected consequence of driving significant popular sectors, especially in the countryside, into opposition. The National Directorate had difficulty assimilating criticism, even from recent allies. Sheila Fitzpatrick—a leading historian of the Russian Revolution—has written that all revolutionaries are "Manicheans, dividing the world into two camps: light and darkness, the revolution and its enemies."[11] Sandinista leaders were no exception.

Additionally, revolutionary governments often face hostile intervention by foreign forces. In the Nicaraguan case, intensive US efforts to undermine the FSLN had the effect of militarizing grievances with Sandinista rule that might otherwise have been channeled through peaceful, institutional avenues. More generally, Nicaragua became disputed terrain in the global confrontation between capitalism and communism. The Reagan administration's construction of a proxy counterrevolutionary army built upon prior training that Argentina's anti-communist military dictatorship had provided to anti-FSLN rebels. Any hopes of using the Contra to pressure or overthrow the Sandinistas depended on the participation of conservative governments in Central America, which lent their territories as staging grounds to attack Nicaragua from two land borders and two oceanic coasts. This permanent threat put the revolutionary government in a "fight to the death for its own survival," as Comandante Luis Carrión described it, further hardening its attitude toward critics. But the Sandinistas did not walk alone. They counted on generous advice, armaments, and financial assistance from the Soviet Union, Cuba, and numerous other countries and non-state actors in the socialist camp.

Nicaragua's revolutionary dynamics collided with the equally polarizing forces of the global Cold War. The result, as Carrión put it, was "a *kind* of civil war: organized, financed, and administered by the United States, but fundamentally sustained by the peasant population."[12] As witnessed during the insurrection and subsequent consolidation of a post-Somoza state, external and internal factors combined in complicated ways to shape the unfolding of the revolutionary process in the middle of the decade. The emergence of a second armed conflict all but suspended efforts to eradicate poverty and inequality. But importantly, it did not kill the Revolution itself.

Visions of War

In the early 1990s, after fighting between the Sandinistas and the Contra had ended, a Nicaraguan think tank made a bold claim about the conduct of the war. The Center for Rural Promotion, Research, and Development (CIPRES, by its Spanish acronym) argued that "by tactics or purposeful disregard of the facts, the Sandinista Front never recognized—not even partially—the existence of a civil war."[13] Indeed, Sandinista elites instead tended to see the conflict—one that claimed tens of thousands of lives between 1981 and 1989—in terms of imperialist aggression. For Sandinista leaders, fighting against the Contra was nothing less than the continuation of the fight from 1979. "The struggle is the same," Junta member Sergio Ramírez said in a 1983 interview. "Against whom were we struggling? Somoza's National Guard. Who supported, armed, financed the old National Guard? The United States! Against whom are we struggling now? The National Guard. Who arms and supports the National Guard today? The US government! The only difference I see is this: Before, we did it from underground, from the mountains. Now we do it from the Government House—now we do it from power."[14] This mentality helped the Sandinista Front maintain discipline in its ranks and attract sympathy abroad. But it also made it difficult for officials to acknowledge that their governing style and reform efforts, including an ambitious land redistribution program, were also responsible for the rise of the Contra.[15]

To acknowledge the local sources of armed opposition—to utter the term "civil war"—would have been mortally contradictory to the Sandinistas' revolutionary self-image. David Armitage, a historian of the term, explains that to call a war "civil" is to "acknowledge the familiarity of the enemies as members of the same community." By contrast, the FSLN leaders needed to prove—to themselves, even—that they were fighting "others" manipulated by a foreign imperial power.[16] Government propaganda therefore depicted the Contra as genocidal, profiteering, and beholden to the interests of the Somoza dictatorship and the US empire. Worse than mercenaries and stooges, its soldiers "metamorphosed into animals, vermin, beasts, and monsters" in the official discourse, as Nicaraguan scholar Irene Agudelo has pointed out.[17] Government propaganda outwardly reflected what was, on the inside, a real difficulty in seeing beyond the foreign dimensions of the war. Decades later, Ramírez described his and his colleagues' dismissal of local opposition to the government: "the people could not be against their revolution," the leadership believed, "because this was a *popular* revolution."[18]

It was only as the war came to an end—and the ideological fervor of the Cold War began to subside—that Sandinista leaders publicly accepted otherwise. Comandante Jaime Wheelock said after the fact: *"even without foreign aggression,* there were a series of policies, programs, and ways of projecting state power which at the political and social levels caused the population to repudiate us."[19] Even some of the Sandinista Front's most successful programs—the ones that suggested the revolution might meet its stated goal of altering the socioeconomic structure of society—generated pushback in certain sectors.

Central among such efforts was land reform. As in virtually every other modern social revolution, the promise to democratize land ownership was a central pillar of the Nicaraguan revolutionary agenda, dating back to the earliest versions of the Sandinistas' *Programa Histórico*. The FSLN's allies outside the Nicaraguan Left blessed this objective in 1979, reflecting a widespread Latin American consensus that agrarian reform was a necessary precursor to economic development; it featured prominently on the Junta of National Reconstruction's first proclamation in June 1979. Predictably, the Sandinistas and their bourgeois partners came to disagree on the type and degree of land redistribution to carry out. But significant contradictions would also emerge at the level of the rural peasantry, where Wheelock said that support for the Sandinistas had been "minimal" in 1979.[20] FSLN guerrillas spent two decades building support in Nicaragua's central highlands—*la montaña* is a key setting in Sandinista mythology—and in some parts of the country where agro-export production was relatively industrialized, the insurrectionary coalition drew strength from long-running agrarian movements agitating for reform.[21] But in national terms, the insurrection against Somoza had been primarily an urban phenomenon; "as a social segment," Comandante Guerrillero Joaquín Cuadra argued, "the peasants did not participate."[22] Both Wheelock (agrarian reform minister) and Cuadra (EPS chief of staff) hailed from upper-class Managua backgrounds. Most Sandinista bosses—at least the ones who survived the decades-long struggle against Somoza—were of middle-class, urban extraction. Some had been born into the urban proletariat, but relatively few came from *campesino* backgrounds.

These young guerrilla commanders brought about the most ambitious attempt in Nicaraguan history to modernize the country's agriculture-based economy, improve the conditions of rural workers, and reduce extreme land inequality. The stakes were tremendous: "the 1980s," sociologist José Luis Rocha wrote, "was a time of bitterness for those whose land was confiscated and of jubilation for the beneficiaries of reform."[23] So were the consequences. The agrarian reform, Humberto Ortega later wrote, "further aggravated the clash between the bourgeoisie and the Sandinistas, because the excesses and errors committed in its implementation—as well as its strongly statist orientation—generated disapproval amongst the peasantry in general (including Sandinista sympathizers), a fact that the Contra took advantage of to build its army and rural support networks."[24]

Salvador Martí and Eduardo Baumeister—an Argentine social scientist who worked in Wheelock's Agrarian Reform and Agriculture Ministry (MIDINRA, by its Spanish acronym)—explain that the 1981 Agrarian Reform Law sought to modernize agricultural production through five main thrusts. First, state planners would aggressively promote agro-industrial technologies. Second, they would massively expand farmers' access to state financing. In order to optimize gains, government agencies would control prices in both internal and foreign commerce. The law would also professionalize rural workers by organizing them into cooperatives and trade organizations. All these objectives hinged on one initial play: breaking up some of the country's *latifundios* by expropriating the holdings of the Somoza family—which alone represented a whopping 20 percent of the country's agricultural land, much of it idle—and their "known associates."[25] Agrarian reform planners had identified a central problem: larger farms were neither optimally productive nor equitable in the way they distributed the gains from growth.

Instead of splitting up the confiscated mega-estates and distributing land titles to individual farmers, the Sandinistas initially followed a collectivist land tenure scheme. Most farms were absorbed into state-owned enterprises or workers' cooperatives known as Cooperativas Agrarias Sandinistas. As two analysts of the reform note, this decision was based in the premise "that small and medium peasants could not play a role," and in the policy logic that smallholding private farmers were both less productive and less easily coerced into planting export crops such as coffee instead of other produce.[26] Cooperative forms of production, moreover, would generate solidarity at the expense of competition and exploitation, and therefore help build the values of the New Man and Woman.[27] In practice, the state-owned agricultural sector—despite the widespread adoption of new machinery, techniques, and chemical inputs—quickly reported declining productivity and persistent losses compared to the private sector. Labor shortages consistently affected agricultural production.[28]

Those problems notwithstanding, the policy quickly met the stated goal of dramatically altering the structure of land tenancy. Large farms (140 hectares or greater), which represented half of all land ownership before 1979, accounted for only a quarter by 1984. Whereas all arable land had been privately owned in 1978, state-owned enterprises and cooperatives came to account for 19 percent and 17 percent, respectively, by 1984.[29] A major social upside of this policy was that it benefited landless peasants who, working on the collectivized farms as members of the Rural Workers Association, received access to consistent wages and new social benefits.

Notably, privately owned small farms (thirty-five hectares or less) also declined in their share of the total, from 18 percent to 8 percent by 1984. This turned out to be a problem because "peasants," as Wheelock later explained, "favored a more traditional allocation of land as individual property."[30] By the middle of the decade, planners had started reforming the agrarian reform, increasing the proportion of land that was to be redistributed to individual smallholders. The shift away from collectivism was driven, Rocha argues, by pressures and demands coming from mass organizations. While the farmworkers represented by the Rural Workers Association (ATC) were primarily interested in securing high wages and therefore found little problem with the government's early preference for large farms, the campesino membership of the National Union of Farmers and Ranchers (UNAG) demanded land and challenged the official view of the collectivization process. Just as importantly, military reasoning played a role. As disaffected farmers joined or supported the Contra, planners were forced to revise their land tenure policy.[31]

An oral history of peasants turned Contra commanders, carried out by another FSLN-affiliated research center, explored the political and military consequences of the initial cooperativizing and collectivizing approach to land distribution. The study's authors concluded that, for the smallholding "middle peasantry" who faced expropriation or pressure to join collective farms, "the benefits of the Revolution were not evident; on the contrary, they felt more closely identified with the complaints and preoccupations of the large landowners and producers, with whom they maintained close and long-lasting relations."[32] In addition to the expropriation of land belonging to relatively well-off peasants, Wheelock adds that the price controls and lack of financial assistance for the private agricultural sector also generated distrust: "The adoption of these economic, trade, and price policies in the countryside created tensions with the peasantry which, along with the military draft and military abuses, fed the ranks of the counterrevolution."[33]

Well-off ranchers and coffee farmers in northern Nicaragua, many of whom developed military experience fighting against Somoza, organized early attacks against the Sandinista government and later joined forces with ex–National Guardsmen in Honduras. For example, Commander Luis "Johnson" Fley, who had fought in the Sandinista guerrilla column that liberated the northern town of Jinotega in 1979 and later worked in the revolutionary government's coffee monopoly company, became disillusioned with the Sandinistas' confiscation of small, private farms. After attending an Alfonso Robelo rally, he was locked up in the same provincial jail where he had been held by Somoza's National Guard in 1979.[34] Rural leaders like Fley did not simply take up arms; as studies by Lynn Horton and Alejandro Bendaña observed, middle peasants like him became the "strategic link" between the rural elite, CIA-sponsored ex–National Guardsmen, and the poorer peasants who eventually filled the ranks of the Contra army.[35] They also became some of the counterrevolutionary army's most capable field commanders. It took time for Sandinista chiefs to identify this connection; the agrarian reform, after all, was meant to ignite economic growth and vanquish hunger. Comandante Henry "Modesto" Ruiz revisited this initial optimism after a postwar conversation with Israel "Franklin" Galeano, another talented campesino commander who rose to become chief of staff of the largest, Honduras-based, Contra faction. When Modesto asked Franklin why a peasant would choose to fight against a revolution that promised to liberate the countryside, the latter responded matter-of-factly: "Well, you *were* going to expropriate me, weren't you?"[36]

The precursor to the major Contra forces was the Guatemala-based September 15th Legion, founded by National Guard coronels Enrique "3–80" Bermúdez and Ricardo "Chino" Lau. In return for outside support, the Legion participated in Argentine intelligence-gathering operations in Central America and assisted the Honduran military's efforts to hunt down dissidents as well as collaborators of the Salvadoran FMLN. Lau, in fact, was implicated in the 1980 murder of Salvadoran archbishop Óscar Romero, carried out by right-wing paramilitaries in that country.[37] In the summer of 1981, the September 15th Legion connected with another Nicaraguan organization funded by the Argentine government: the Miami-based Unión Democrática Nicaragüense (UDN), led mostly by middle- and upper-class civilian exiles. The result of their August 1981 merger in Guatemala City, encouraged by both Buenos Aires and Washington, was the Fuerza Democrática Nicaragüense (FDN), which soon got to work with the bridge bombings cited at the beginning of this chapter. CIA agents told FDN leaders to publicly deny that they were funded by the United States or that their goal was to overthrow the Nicaraguan government.[38]

Though founded by leftovers of Somoza's National Guard, "in percentage terms, it was the peasantry which filled the ranks of the Contra," according to General Hugo Torres, who became the Sandinista Army's director of intelligence.[39] The United States provided weapons and financing, and somocistas like Bermúdez and Lau ran the newly organized army, but recruitment of ground troops fell to gifted campesino commanders who had previously mounted their own armed operations in northern Nicaragua in 1980 with the support of coffee farmers and cattle ranchers who feared expropriation. The peasant commanders of the so-called Milicias Populares Anti-Sandinistas (MILPAS)—notably, Encarnación "Tigrillo" Valdivia and Pedro Joaquín "Dimas" González—were also former Sandinista guerrillas who fought against the National Guard in 1979.[40] Now, having crossed the border to Honduras in 1981–1982, they absorbed themselves into the US-backed, somocista-led FDN. In an inside account of the FDN, journalist Sam Dillon identified the tacit agreement that made the project click: the ex-Guardsmen would provide weapons to local leaders like Tigrillo and Dimas, which they would use to arm disaffected rural peasants in Nicaragua; in exchange, they would incorporate these fighters into the formal FDN structure and swear loyalty to its CIA-anointed leaders back in Honduras.[41] Along with the FDN and MILPAS, two other groups—the Alianza Revolucionaria Democrática (ARDE), founded by Edén Pastora and Alfonso Robelo, as well as an alliance of disaffected Black and Indigenous groups from the Caribbean region—animated the early counterrevolution. Within a year, the so-called Contra had some 10,000 fighters and eventually more than 17,000 by the end of the war.[42]

Beyond the material impact of revolutionary policies, fundamental questions of identity also drove polarization. Religion proved especially divisive. Ernesto Cardenal, the poet and Catholic priest who became the Revolution's culture minister, argued in 1983 that "as Christians, we don't think that there should be any incompatibility with Marxism."[43] Indeed, the Church hierarchy formally endorsed the FSLN in 1979, and other prominent priests joined Cardenal in assuming senior government roles, including Miguel D'Escoto as head of the Foreign Ministry.[44] Nevertheless, compatibility issues arose soon after Somoza's overthrow. The Sandinista leadership clashed with Catholic bishops when ecclesiastical authorities failed to condemn early Contra attacks that killed government officials and civilians alike. Relations with the Church hit rock bottom when the pope visited Managua in March 1983. Upon arriving at the Augusto César Sandino International Airport, John Paul II publicly chastised a genuflecting Cardenal for violating his priestly vows and taking public office as culture minister. More importantly, in his subsequent homily he made pointed remarks about Sandinista rule but remained silent about US support for armed rebels. Thousands of government sympathizers booed and heckled; the FSLN's relations with the Church hierarchy and Vatican were damaged beyond repair.[45] Miguel Obando, the Catholic cardinal, transformed into an anti-Sandinista icon.

The Revolution's complicated relationship with Christianity exemplified how broader identitarian clashes helped fuel the war. When asked why he took up arms against his former colleagues in the Sandinista armed forces, Tigrillo said he was tired of his *compañeros* trying to convince him of God's nonexistence.[46] Farmers turned Contra leaders denied the FSLN's class-based overtures to poorer, landless agricultural workers by appealing to a multiclass "peasant identity" built around historical community ties, rural culture, and religion.[47] Putting it succinctly, Irene Agudelo characterized the Contra as "the armed branch of a sector which did not feel included in the nation-building discourse of the Sandinista Revolution."[48]

The narrowness of the Sandinistas' egalitarian discourse created problems among the country's ethnic and racial minorities. These communities are especially concentrated along Nicaragua's Caribbean coast, a particularly impoverished part of the country. Whereas Nicaragua's majority mestizo population has historically been Catholic, Spanish-speaking, and concentrated on the Pacific side of the country's central mountain chains, their Atlantic-facing, Indigenous and Afro-descendant compatriots have more often subscribed to Protestant Christianity and spoken various Indigenous languages as well as English creole. From the outset, FSLN leaders promised to develop Caribbean Nicaragua and assimilate its inhabitants. But those efforts quickly went sideways, with Black, Indigenous, and Afro-Indigenous Nicaraguans mounting some of the first significant armed rebellions against the revolutionary government. The Sandinista Revolution, FSLN leaders like Ernesto Cardenal soon realized, "was a revolution of *españoles*" in the eyes of people in the Caribbean regions; it was "foreign to them and they felt it was imposed."[49] Indeed, many Indigenous leaders saw increased state presence as a threat to their autonomy, and integrationist policies—including the teaching of Spanish via the literacy campaigns—as an attempt at cultural erasure. The reason for Indigenous rebellion, Miskitu leader Brooklyn Rivera proclaimed, was "the antagonism created by the Sandinista government policy which denies the ethnic identity of our people."[50] Black creole and Indigenous Nicaraguans were also alien to most FSLN cadres, who treated their institutions and beliefs as obstacles to centralization and modernization.[51]

Ultimately, the FSLN came to terms with MISURASATA (later, MISURA), the pan-ethnic army of Miskitu, Sumo, and Rama Indians who fought alongside the Contra and in many cases received direct CIA assistance. Aside from the military threat it posed, the breakdown in relations with Black and Indigenous Nicaraguans exposed the FSLN to propaganda efforts that justified US intervention as a response to the Revolution's alleged persecution of ethnic and religious minorities. Eager to close at least one front of the war, Latin American and European governments brokered talks between Comandante Luis Carrión and Rivera in 1985.[52] The Sandinista Front eventually made peace with MISURA. Having previously viewed Indigenous demands for land and autonomy with suspicion, FSLN leaders took them into account in order to resolve the conflict.[53] In 1987, they promulgated a constitutional amendment recognizing the ethnic pluralism of the Nicaraguan nation and granting limited self-rule to the country's two Atlantic provinces.

These legal provisions represented a real innovation in Latin American constitutional law and in the Left's approach to race and ethnicity, though they were not part of the Revolution's original vision—they were the unexpected outgrowth of the contradictions it unleashed.[54]

Elsewhere, the government's intolerance of criticism grew as the war developed. Its state of emergency threatened to jail those accused of organizing strikes, intentionally removing assets from the country, or otherwise abetting the deterioration of the economy. Opposition daily *La Prensa* (which enjoyed US funding) was frequently censored and occasionally shuttered for publishing "destabilizing" information. On one occasion, Humberto Ortega famously threatened to hang business owners from lampposts in the event of a US invasion.[55] Viewing them as little more than an arm of the US foreign policy apparatus, EPS leaders swore they would never negotiate with armed insurgents. Gioconda Belli recalls the slogan being, "we will not speak with the dogs, when we can instead speak with their masters."[56] "The one we talk to has to be the one paying the bills," Foreign Minister D'Escoto declared.[57] Notably, many in the counterrevolutionary sector had participated in the 1979 insurrection and revolutionary government. For example, the main Contra faction on the southern Costa Rica border—the Alianza Revolucionaria Democrática (ARDE)—was headed by 1979 personalities like Edén Pastora and Panamanian internationalist Hugo Spadafora. Though Pastora received significant financial and military support from the US via CIA Latin America chief Dewey Clarridge, ARDE clashed with the leadership of the somocista-led FDN and claimed a "commitment to redeem our true and original Nicaraguan Revolution" and its 1979 principles.[58] This, to the Sandinistas and their supporters, was meaningless posturing.

As fighting intensified, so did disruptions to economic growth and social development programs. Several factors—US economic sanctions, the war, and unfavorable prices on the international market—conspired to hamper production. In the dominant agricultural sector, the "over-politicization" of production (Baumeister notes that expropriations increasingly targeted political goals, rather than following an economic logic), along with overzealous price controls, also hurt growth. Falling production, combined with increased government spending to fund the war, led to declining real wages, shortages, inflation, and other economic distortions, especially in the countryside.[59] The deteriorating economic picture further weakened support from the upper and middle classes, who increasingly fled the country and supported the anti-Sandinista cause from exile. It also threatened the sustainability of social reforms. Between 1979 and 1983, infant mortality had plummeted as medical consultations and caloric consumption rose; education spending had skyrocketed in tandem with school enrollment. But that was before the onset of war. By 1983, the government was already spending 37 percent of its budget on defense; the number would jump to over 50 percent by 1985.[60]

The war naturally compounded difficulties in the political sphere. In the "context of a war," wrote Luis Carrión—a powerful leader within the state security apparatus from his post as vice minister of the interior—"the repression and the abuses tend to multiply."[61] Believing that nefarious outside forces were to blame, the leadership became inflexible in its positions and policies, a fact that helped push nonaligned Nicaraguans into the arms of the US-backed Contra. Major defense policies also had political consequences. On September 13, 1983, the government decreed a "patriotic," compulsory military service (SMP by its Spanish acronym); all Nicaraguans aged eighteen to twenty-five were subject to join the EPS or face jail time. Army strategists later argued that the Servicio Militar Patriótico was necessary for maintaining the massive superiority in numbers—a ratio of at least seven Sandinista troops for every insurgent—required to prevent the Contra from holding territory.[62] But conscription further undermined the government's popular appeal and generated a significant exodus among the middle class. Thousands of young professionals, according to the government's budgeting office, fled the country between the start of the draft and the end of the war.[63]

Nicaragua in the Global Cold War

In Nicaragua as in other "hot spots" such as Afghanistan, the Reagan administration increased the tenor of US interventionism in the Third World, updating its tool kit to include the creation of proxy revolutionary armies. The domestic picture, described above, helped enable the relative success of this outside paramilitary operation. As Luis Carrión argued, "North American aggression stumbled upon the growing disaffection of the Nicaraguan peasantry, itself caused by factors of our own manufacture."[64]

Intense superpower intervention was a major fact of revolutionary life because, absent money and equipment from Washington, anti-Sandinistas would not have enjoyed the means to mount a sustained, large-scale rebellion. Having previously operated in relative poverty, exiled National Guardsmen received enormous outside funding after 1981, which allowed them to arm disaffected Nicaraguans and recruit the commanders who led them in the field. The Contra also had access to quality uniforms, communications equipment, and heavy weaponry; one analyst even called them "the best equipped insurgent force in history."[65] Further, they relied on intelligence gathered by US aircraft and even advice on when and where to strike: according to FDN chief Enrique Bermúdez, his troops executed the March 1982 bridge bombings at the behest of Pentagon strategists.[66] Bermúdez, the Contra's most visible commander, survived numerous attempts on his leadership because he enjoyed the blessing of CIA officials, who selected top Contra commanders based on their loyalty to the operation, often disregarding credentials or performance.[67] Having found that "the Americans liked to make all the crucial decisions," another civilian leader, Edgar Chamorro, abandoned the Contra in 1984. In a scathing "confession" published in the *New Republic*, he differentiated the Contra leadership from its rank and file: "The idealistic young people who have actually fought against the Sandinista army have real grievances. Their land has been confiscated or they have been persecuted for their religious views or they have resisted the Sandinista draft. But they are being used as an instrument of US foreign policy by the CIA and the Reagan administration."[68]

As Chamorro suggests, the armed conflict in Nicaragua came about as a result of the interplay between local grievances and foreign plots. Sometimes US policymakers seemed as oblivious to this dynamic as the Sandinista leadership initially was. Diplomat (and later, analyst of the Contra's origins) Timothy Brown noted that while the Reagan administration publicly referred to the FDN as "freedom fighters" and the "moral equivalent" of the American Founding Fathers, some in the White House actually shared the Left's "darker image" of the FSLN's internal opponents as little more than thuggish, somocista mercenaries. He cites the testimony of CIA officer Dewey Clarridge, who alleged that Ronald Reagan referred to the Contra as the "CIA's vandals."[69] Like Managua, Washington initially understood the armed conflict in Nicaragua as being caused by US intervention there. Alejandro Bendaña recognized this irony in 1991, shortly after the Revolution fell and he vacated his post in the Nicaraguan Foreign Ministry: "there is no evidence that the Central Intelligence Agency had thought to develop a parallel social and military force in the Nicaraguan countryside. In fact, the Contra army seems to have grown beyond the expectations of the North Americans—not because of sophisticated recruitment techniques, but primarily because of the impact on the peasantry of the policies, limitations, and errors of Sandinismo."[70] Indeed, Robert Kagan notes that the scope and ambition of US intervention grew as "the contras' apparent capabilities grew beyond anything originally planned by the Reagan officials."[71] Naturally, without North American funding, discontented Nicaraguans would not have had access to weapons, and their localized rebellions would not have approached the dimensions they acquired. In retrospect, Jaime Wheelock dismissed the binary debate surrounding the war in the 1980s: "There is the 'pure aggression by the US' thesis, and 'civil war' thesis. I don't think it's one or the other."[72]

Another crucial factor in the Contra program was the collaboration of US allies in the global Cold War. Honduras's ruling military junta resented Sandinista support for Salvadoran insurgents, who had built an extensive support network inside Honduran territory (their country, unlike Nicaragua, shares a land border with El Salvador).[73] They also decried the rapid growth of the Sandinista Popular Army, which at its zenith possessed nearly double the troop strength of either the Salvadoran or Guatemalan militaries at their respective peaks in the 1980s.[74] Even before Reagan was sworn in, and nearly a year before he authorized support for a proxy force, Honduran general Gustavo Adolfo Álvarez Martínez mounted an operation to fund, train, and house the small army of ex-somocista Guardsmen known as the September 15th Legion.[75]

The Hondurans received crucial support and financing from the military government of Argentina (where Álvarez had received military training and shaped his anti-communist worldview). The Argentines, as Ariel Armony has argued, were on an ideological crusade, but also saw a threat to their real interests in Central America: exiled Argentinian leftists had participated in the Nicaraguan insurrection, and their continued presence in the country prompted the fear that they might use Central America as a platform for operations back in South America.[76] The fact that Argentine leftists claimed responsibility for the hit on Somoza in nearby Paraguay may have reinforced the belief in Buenos Aires that revolutionary politics in Central America were part of the same "transnational communist conspiracy" supposedly fueling subversion against the military junta.[77] Though the CIA eventually took ownership of what became known as the Contra, Latin American actors—responding to their own fears and interests—pioneered its creation. Moving forward, US intelligence services would supply the Contra from bases in Honduras, El Salvador, and Costa Rica. This inter-American intervention, furthermore, had extra-hemispheric dimensions. For example, the Israeli government extended significant military assistance to US partners in Central America, in part because the Palestine Liberation

Organization provided loans and training to the FSLN (a policy motivated, in turn, by Israel's earlier, longtime support for the Somoza regime).[78]

Significant economic warfare complemented the Contra project. The Reagan administration started by permanently canceling aid packages that the outgoing Carter administration had suspended due to Nicaragua's support for FMLN guerrillas in El Salvador. US diplomats discouraged both private banks and multilateral lending institutions, such as the World Bank and Inter-American Development Bank, from providing credit to the government in Managua. Most importantly, Washington increasingly imposed trade restrictions, dramatically reducing the purchase of Nicaraguan sugar in 1983. Beyond the realm of sanctions, direct sabotage operations by Navy SEALS and CIA operatives—designed to look like they were the Contra's doing—targeted vital economic infrastructure. As William Leogrande notes, the structure of the Nicaraguan economy—low-income, agriculture-based, dependent on trade (primarily with the United States) and foreign assistance—made it especially vulnerable to Reagan's squeeze tactics.[79]

As foreign adversaries acted with greater force, the Sandinista leadership became more aggressive and transparent in its pursuit of socialist camp support. In the years immediately following Somoza's ouster, the Nicaraguan government had been wary of openly accepting substantial military aid from Warsaw Pact countries, for fear of either alienating "bourgeois democratic" countries in Latin America or providing an easy excuse for a US invasion. Early agreements with Eastern European countries were of limited scope and arranged without much fanfare; for related reasons, the Soviet Union preferred to ship weapons and military equipment through partners such as Algeria and the German Democratic Republic.[80] According to a tally by the US Department of Defense, the estimated value of all socialist bloc military aid amounted to $10 million in 1980. However, once the Reagan administration took power and began supporting anti-Sandinista military groups, Nicaraguan leaders felt less shy about seeking open assistance from communist countries.[81] The socialist camp also felt the increased threat justified a much larger investment; total military aid ballooned to $160 million in 1981 and continued to grow in subsequent years as the EPS engaged the US-backed Contra.[82]

For communist leaders like East Germany's Erich Honecker and Bulgaria's Todor Zhivkov, the Sandinistas were genuine partners who deserved support as part of the global struggle against US imperialism and capitalist encirclement. Soviet leaders' approval of support to the FSLN government somewhat fit under the policy that justified their 1979 intervention in

Afghanistan; under the doctrine established by former premier Leonid Brezhnev, socialist countries should act to shore up any allied government threated by forces hostile to their ideology. By defending the Nicaraguan Revolution from US animosity, the USSR could also help maintain its appeal to national liberation movements across the Third World (and especially in Latin America). Actual military aid generously matched the importance these countries gave to Nicaragua in their vision of the global Cold War. According to Klaus Storkmann's analysis of GDR Defense Ministry archives, Nicaragua eventually topped the list of countries receiving military aid from the East German National People's Army, which trained hundreds of EPS officials and sent trucks, clothing, basic military equipment, communications technology, and thousands of antipersonnel mines and rifles.[83] East German archives also list evidence of missiles from Czechoslovakia, rocket-propelled grenades from Bulgaria, and anti-tank guns from Algeria, among other armaments. Indeed, support came from across the global Left; according to the US Department of Defense, the Sandinistas also successfully made requests of Poland, Libya, Vietnam, Romania, the PLO, and North Korea. Most equipment and weaponry came from the Soviet Union itself. Thanks to their combined support, the Sandinista Popular Army acquired tanks, armored vehicles, and helicopters. By 1986 the estimated dollar amount of socialist camp military aid reached roughly $500 million per year.[84] That tally excluded Moscow's efforts to meet Nicaragua's emergency needs by spending well over $100 million per year on oil shipments and other forms of economic assistance.

But there were dangers, and therefore limits, to helping the Sandinistas. Moscow made clear to both FSLN leaders and Eastern European allies that the USSR would not come to Nicaragua's rescue in the case of a direct US intervention. They also privately assured US officials that they were unwilling to further worsen their relationship with Washington over a transition to socialism in Nicaragua (the prospects for which Soviet analysts doubted, in any event). Some partners, including Bulgaria, feared they might suffer American retaliation for their activities in Central America.[85] Others, such as East Germany, were willing to act more forcefully. But their assistance was motivated by a sense of duty to revolutionary comrades, rather than necessity. "By and large," Storkmann points out, "Nicaragua did not affect the security interests of the GDR."[86]

It was a different story for Cuba and Latin America's national liberation movements, who felt much more at stake in Nicaraguan war's outcome. For this reason, and because a more obvious Soviet presence was out of the question, Latin Americans played a more direct role on the ground. While the Soviet Union and Eastern European countries provided the bulk of the material assistance, their representatives were a comparatively scarce presence in the Nicaraguan bureaucracy. For example, Humberto Ortega later said that the EPS enjoyed the support of roughly 150 Cuban advisers and 12 Soviet officers at any given time; US intelligence agencies estimated at one point that there were 1,000 to 1,500 Cuban advisers across all security institutions, compared to 50 to 75 from the USSR and another 200 from the rest of the world's socialist countries.[87] Marxist movements from elsewhere in Latin America, such as exiled Chilean communists, also sent cadres to help structure the EPS in its early years, train its soldiers, and fill out the officer corps; internacionalistas were a permanent fixture of revolutionary high society. As Victor Figueroa Clark notes, this was not a one-way deal; Chilean revolutionaries gained crucial combat experience and political training in preparation for a potential insurrection in their own country against the Pinochet dictatorship.[88] Assisting the survival of Nicaragua's government also fit naturally into Havana's security doctrine of protecting Cuba by "making the world safe for revolution," redirecting the gaze of US counterrevolution away from the island.[89]

The Nicaraguan Revolution became dependent on socialist bloc assistance but, importantly, was not directed by it. Cuban officials insisted that their role was to respect Managua's decisions (by contrast, Contra commander and ex-Guardsman Luis "Mike Lima" Moreno complained in his memoir that American operatives in Honduras "considered themselves gods" and "took decisions without consulting or taking us into account").[90] At times, the Sandinistas sought greater alignment than socialist countries were comfortable with, as evidenced by their rebuffed attempt to join the Soviet-led Council for Mutual Economic Assistance as full members, rather than observers. Moreover, both Cuba and the USSR stressed that their assistance should not come at the expense of Nicaraguan relations with Latin America and Europe. While US foreign policymakers tended to worry that international peace proposals would undermine the Contra, Cuban officials supported Nicaragua's participation in the Contadora Peace Process—sponsored by several Latin American countries beginning in 1983—under the assumption that a regional settlement would strengthen the Sandinista government.[91]

Despite its limits and caveats, socialist-world help was indispensable and decisive. With that solid foundation of support, the Sandinistas resisted a multilayered, multifront, low-intensity conflict that threatened their ouster.

One significant challenge was to balance the fight against the Contra with preparations to fend off a conventional invasion by US forces. In the war's initial stages, from roughly 1981 to 1983, EPS strategists focused on the latter threat. Anticipating a direct invasion, they massed troops and resources near cities and vital infrastructure in the densely populated, economically vital Pacific regions.[92] This decision left mountainous northern regions— close to the Contras' base in Honduras, and where popular opposition to the agrarian reform was strongest—vulnerable. The EPS also spent considerable resources acquiring foreign weaponry such as Soviet tanks, which might raise the cost of a hypothetical US ground invasion, but were less useful in a war against homegrown guerrillas in mountainous terrain.[93] In 1984, Nicaragua sought Soviet MiG-21 supersonic jet fighters in order to establish air supremacy over its Central American neighbors and further heighten the costs of a direct military intervention. Moscow, for fear of provoking Washington, ultimately decided against sending the planes. The enormous Punta Huete airfield the FSLN constructed was left to decay, and the dozens of pilots they sent to Bulgaria for specialized training were left without planes to fly.[94]

The EPS successfully revised its approach after 1983, adopting a counterinsurgency strategy. During this second phase, the Sandinista army leveraged numeric superiorities created by the military draft announced that year. Conscripts were organized into counterinsurgency units called Batallones de Lucha Irregular (BLI) that operated in the areas where the Contra was most present. Essential to counterinsurgency success was the enhanced mobility and maneuverability of these retooled military units; by 1985, then, Soviet trucks and combat helicopters (which were better suited to counterinsurgency than MiGs would have been, Humberto Ortega later noted) had helped created a military balance more favorable to the government than it had been at the start of the conflict.[95]

Sometimes, direct actions against the Sandinistas backfired on US officials. For example, sabotage operations such as the mining of several ports in 1983—including the main Pacific harbor at Corinto—created serious disruptions to Nicaraguan trade but also resulted in "political disaster" for the Reagan administration in Washington.[96] To fund its Central America operations, the White House depended on the approval of the US Congress, where lawmakers—led by those wary of creeping escalation similar to what they had seen in Vietnam—had in late 1982 placed limits on the use of Americans funds for the specific purpose of "overthrowing the government of Nicaragua."[97] CIA-planted mines in Nicaraguan harbors were one of many policies that flew in the face of such restrictions and infuriated even some supporters of aid for the Contras.[98] Direct US involvement also created the legal basis for the US government's loss to Nicaragua at the International Court of Justice in 1986, a high point in Sandinista attempts to isolate Washington and its Central America policy.[99] Additionally, direct US intervention justified deeper diplomatic involvement by governments more accepting of the Sandinistas. After the Corinto attacks, France offered to sweep the Nicaraguan coast for additional mines in 1984, and that same year secretly brokered talks between the Nicaraguan and Costa Rican governments to defuse tensions.[100] And while the US sanctions program crippled the Nicaraguan economy, businessman and opposition leader Enrique Bolaños complained that "politically it was a blessing for the Sandinistas" because it rallied their base and prompted outcry from countries around the world.[101]

The FSLN also leveraged political advantages over the Contra. Because the anti-Sandinista insurgency was tied to the Reagan administration, and because US intervention in Central America was unpopular internationally, there was a ceiling to the Contra's legitimacy inside and outside Nicaragua. The Contra was unified in its military efforts—and backing by the United States—but unlike the Sandinistas lacked a coherent political agenda or identity; it was a very young, heterogenous movement constituted by a wide collection of anti-Sandinista forces (some of them, notably, formerly associated with the FSLN).[102] Former ally and opposition leader Arturo Cruz Porras lamented that US involvement "gave the Sandinistas the pretext to cry to the world that they were the victims of Yankee imperialism . . . this was their preferred scenario." Because of its relationship to Washington, Cruz notes, "the Contra's struggle lacked international legitimacy from the outset."[103] Indeed, as one historian of US solidarity networks has written, "in a paradox of history, instead of destroying the Sandinista Revolution, Reagan's Contra policy helped boost its political-ideological allure as a tiny 'David' that defied a global Goliath."[104]

For the Sandinista government, the global Cold War provided a complex set of opportunities and risks. Outside of Eastern European support enabled by socialist solidarity, it is difficult to imagine the survival of a leftist government openly defiant of US power in Central America. Unfortunately for the FSLN, such aid had clear limits. While Russian fighter jets would not have been much use against guerrillas hidden under dense forest canopy, they were a missing symbol of Soviet commitment they did not and would not ever receive. Nicaragua's revolutionary leadership, aside from dealing with foreign-backed insurgents, could therefore never feel completely safe from the risk of a direct US invasion. Even as Reagan officials assured nervous lawmakers that the United States would not commit ground troops to a Central American military adventure, they kept the threat alive through the massive Big Pine II military exercises in the fall of 1983. When the Reagan administration militarily overthrew the left-wing government of Grenada in 1983, the Sandinista government and its Cuban advisers believed that Nicaragua was the "next stop."[105]

Conclusion

Luis Carrión later reflected that the consequences of the war in the 1980s "have no equal in the history of our country." Nicaragua experienced almost too many internal armed conflicts to count in the nineteenth and early twentieth centuries, but the Sandinista commander does not think that "any of the many wars between Conservatives and Liberals produced even a tenth of what the war of the 1980s caused in terms of dead, orphaned, maimed, mentally ill, large-scale material destruction, hatreds, and resentments."[106] The conflict's special ferocity can only be explained by the encounter between two polarizing forces: the Revolution and the Cold War.

The war almost completely consumed the Sandinista Front's project to remake Nicaragua. Once the fighting began in earnest in 1982, "the main objective of the Revolution was to defeat the US war of aggression while avoiding an invasion by its regular troops," according to Humberto Ortega.[107] Resources and energies were diverted accordingly. Sergio Ramírez recalls that "everything became subordinated to military priorities, and that destroyed any possibility of change."[108] The FSLN hierarchy tightened control over grassroots organizations and social movements, limiting the possibility of autonomous popular participation in the revolutionary process.[109] By the middle of the decade, early gains in terms of health care and education had frozen and increasingly looked like they might melt away.

The war did not destroy the government itself, though. Some CIA and Contra leaders had expected an easy victory. In 1983, the armed opposition formed a short-lived parallel government led by Alfonso Robelo, Enrique Bermúdez, and members of the Nicaraguan business community; Honduran military leader Gustavo Alvarez boasted that they would be in Managua by Christmas.[110] Instead, a deadly stalemate emerged as the Contra grew but the Sandinistas revised their counterinsurgency strategy: the

Contra found itself unable to hold any urban centers it captured, and the FSLN failed to annihilate an ever-expanding rebel army. The government's survival, along with the destabilizing threat that the foreign-fueled war posed, meant that the Sandinistas and their revolution would continue to be relevant to world affairs in the middle of a decade of profound changes.

Revolutionary governments often encounter existential danger in the diplomatic arena. After emerging victorious in their war against the British Empire, America's founding elite had to build national security in a world
hostile to the very concept of republican government. When the Bolsheviks
established a socialist state in the ashes of the Russian Empire, they waited
years—over a decade, in some cases—before the world's capitalist powers
recognized the regime's existence. For Nicaragua's revolutionary elite, the
most relevant antecedent was the so-called Cuban question—hemispheric
debates about the place of Havana's Soviet-aligned communist regime in the
community of legitimate American states.[1] The United States, and most
Latin American countries, had decided that Fidel Castro's revolutionary government was a threat to their security and incompatible with the values
of the inter-American system. They voted to suspend Cuba from the
Organization of American States in 1962; most severed bilateral diplomatic
relations with Havana. The Cuban Revolution's isolation was a defining moment in inter-American affairs that resonates to this day.

Though people did not refer to it as such at the time, what might be
called the "Nicaraguan question" of the 1980s created a similar controversy: given the Marxist orientation of the FSLN National Directorate, its
ties to the socialist bloc, and the Revolution's origins in violent struggle,
could the Sandinista government be a legitimate member of the American
community of states?[2] This question formed the crux of a wider diplomatic war that emerged coextensive with the fighting in Nicaragua between the EPS and the Contra. On the one hand, the US government and
allied anti-communist regimes in Latin America, seeking to justify their
policy of militarily undermining the FSLN, argued that both the Sandinista government and leftist rebel movements in Central America were the
result of extra-hemispheric Soviet meddling and therefore lacked legitimacy. On the other hand, a bloc of Latin American states—one that enjoyed unusually firm backing from US partners in Western Europe—began
pushing back against Reagan's intervention in 1982. Their diplomacy, best
expressed in a multilateral peace initiative known as the Contadora Peace

Process, refuted Washington's answer to the Nicaraguan question. In a collective effort to manage US intervention, and in contrast to the initial Latin American response to the Cuban Revolution, they sought to legitimize and reintegrate the FSLN government. Their multilateral efforts to broker peace were inspired by the belief that the origin of Central America's revolutionary upheaval "lay in the great inequalities and economic problems the region faced," as Panamanian foreign minister Oydén Ortega put it, "not in the affairs of East and West."[3]

European and Latin American involvement highlighted the relevance of the Nicaraguan Revolution for world politics beyond the interests of Havana, Moscow, and Washington. The latter has received the most attention from scholars. But Latin American foreign ministries were just as preoccupied with the fate of Managua's revolutionary government, if not more, as Foggy Bottom was. At least twelve Latin American countries, including the five largest, became directly involved in efforts to broker peace in Nicaragua by the mid-1980s. Most regional states came to believe that militarized US policies in Central America were counterproductive (because they pushed Nicaragua further into the arms of the socialist camp) and dangerous (because they undermined stability, thereby imperiling their economic and security interests). They fretted over the risk of a direct superpower confrontation in Central America, a fear shared by Western European diplomats who longed for the relative détente of the previous decade. By way of this unusual break with the hemispheric hegemon, Latin American governments collectively evinced an interest in greater regional autonomy, especially after a disastrous run of Cold War–related interventions in their countries' affairs. Their response to the Nicaraguan Revolution marked a departure from the earlier reaction to the Cuban Revolution because the former—with its nods to ballots, the market, and nonalignment—was significantly different from the latter. But the differentiated responses can also be explained by the fact that wider Latin American politics had changed between the 1960s and 1980s. In the years after the Somoza dictatorship was toppled, anti-communist dictatorships collapsed across South America, giving way to civilian, democratically elected governments with new interests and sensibilities.

International debates on the FSLN government's legitimacy fed back into Nicaragua's war and revolution in important ways. Absent legitimacy in the eyes of the international community, Nicaragua's revolutionary leadership could not assert national sovereignty, without which the ultimate goal of social transformation became moot. Fortunately for the Sandinista Front,

Washington proved unable to convince many friends in Europe and Latin America of the righteousness of its Central American crusade. This failure was an important reason why a "second Cuba"—to the extent that it can be considered as such—was able to survive a decade surrounded by hostile actors, without receiving nearly the same level of support from the USSR that Castro's government had enjoyed. That diplomatic victory had important, unexpected consequences at home. Though sympathetic to the idea that the Sandinista Front had given voice to an impoverished majority after vanquishing Somoza, many of the Revolution's international partners wanted to see Nicaragua's rulers demonstrate the consent of the governed through representative institutions. Thus, as the Sandinistas fought for legitimacy on the global stage, they found themselves subtly altering the basis for their mandate at home.

Two Wars

US intervention via proxy, designed to contain the spread of revolution in Central America by undermining Managua's left-wing government, had two notable effects. As the previous chapter outlined, CIA weapons and training militarized sectors of Nicaraguan society disaffected by Sandinista rule, helping create and exacerbate a protracted civil war. But US rollback and containment policies also had the unintended consequence of further internationalizing the Nicaraguan Revolution, as several Latin American governments subsequently intervened to mediate a peaceful resolution to a crisis that threatened their interests. The first major Contra attacks in the spring of 1982 therefore marked not only the beginning of an armed conflict in Nicaragua but also the start of a parallel war on the international, diplomatic scene. While Reagan promised to begin rolling back Soviet communism in Central America, a group of Latin American governments found common cause in pushing back against US unilateralism in Nicaragua.

The Mexican and Venezuelan governments spearheaded the diplomatic counterattack against US intervention in Nicaragua. In response to increasing Contra attacks in the summer of 1982, their respective presidents José López Portillo and Luis Herrera Campins wrote a letter to Reagan demanding that Honduras "cease the support, organization and deployment of exsomocista Guardsmen." Another September 1982 missive to Honduran president Roberto Suazo Córdova additionally criticized his government for holding joint military exercises with US forces along the Nicaraguan border.[4] López Portillo and Herrera Campins called on both governments to negotiate de-escalation with the Sandinistas. Mexico and Venezuela had already helped reinforce Managua's fledgling revolutionary government by providing oil and credit on generously subsidized terms. This aid came with strings attached; Nicaragua's revolutionaries, Campins argued in 1981, were "morally committed with Latin America, which gave its support to their struggle, to carry out the pluralist project which they proclaimed when they took power."[5] Both governments sought to moderate the Sandinistas because they believed a "second Cuba" in Central America would provide the pretext for a direct US intervention. With civil wars already raging between right-wing governments and left-wing insurgents in El Salvador and Guatemala, militarized US policies in Nicaragua would, the argument went, only pour gasoline on the fire. Campins and López Portillo understandably felt the heat; as they emphasized in their letter to Suazo Córdova, their countries were "linked by geography to the Central American area and felt its problems as if they were their own."

While Nicaraguan foreign minister Miguel D'Escoto praised the Mexican-Venezuelan initiative as "timely and realistic," the American response was much cooler.[6] Reagan waited a month before delivering an icy retort; the solution to Central America's problems, his own letter argued, was to "achieve democratic pluralism" in each country.[7] In other words, as American diplomats told Sandinista officials in Managua, Washington's support for "democratic forces" in Honduras would persist until the FSLN held free elections and satisfied the otherwise vague criteria of "democratic pluralism" as defined, in this instance, by the US government. This premise was unacceptable to the Sandinista Front. In its view, demands to alter Nicaragua's internal system of government represented a violation of national sovereignty.[8] Unfortunately for them, the Honduran government rejected the Mexican-Venezuelan call for bilateral peace talks and, echoing the American position, called on the Nicaraguan government to first introduce hazily defined democratic reforms. Seeking to isolate FSLN diplomacy on this issue, and in direct response to the Mexican-Venezuelan position that support for anti-government insurgents should cease *before* the Sandinistas were asked to make reforms, the US organized a "Forum for Peace and Democracy" in Costa Rica.

The October 1982 conference, to which all Central American governments except Nicaragua were invited, was "organized to put Nicaragua in a box," according to the American ambassador in San José.[9] Nicaragua's Central American neighbors expressed genuine concerns about the size of the EPS and the FSLN's ties to insurgent left-wing organizations in their territories. But the conference was structured to argue that rising tensions on the isthmus were caused more broadly by Sandinista leaders' relations with the Soviet bloc, their Marxism, and their alleged efforts to build a totalitarian state. It mattered little that no Central American government, save that of Costa Rica, came to power through robust, free elections. The conference operated within the theory, developed by political scientist and US diplomat Jeane Kirkpatrick, that noncommunist "authoritarian" states had democratizing *potential*, which Marxist "totalitarian" states lacked.[10] Therefore, the October 1982 Democratic Forum cast a clear judgment on the core aspect of the Nicaraguan question: the Sandinistas' revolutionary government—a "cancer," as Reagan later dubbed it—was illegitimate and contrary to the inter-American system a priori.[11] Central American alignment with this position recalled the broader Latin American response to the Cuban question in the 1960s, when most regional governments voted to excommunicate Havana's revolutionary government from inter-American organizations.

This time, however, regional political winds blew against Washington. Two months after the Democratic Forum, Gabriel García Márquez—a Sandinista coconspirator during the 1979 insurrection—received the Nobel Prize in literature and used his global platform to call for peace in Central America.[12] Countless high-profile intellectuals, such as Julio Cortázar, fervently championed Nicaragua's revolutionary cause in the region. The Sandinista Revolution marked a new chapter in debates within the regional intelligentsia over the best way to build democratic socialism in the era of the Cuban Revolution. Some, like Mexican Nobel laureate Octavio Paz, felt that the Sandinistas too closely followed the Cuban example in restricting political liberties and seeking alignment with Moscow.[13] But virtually everyone in Latin America's cultural elite agreed that Nicaragua should be defended from North American aggression. Carlos Fuentes later explained how his cohort balanced its assessment of the Sandinistas in light of Reagan's intervention: "How could one not stand with that heroic group of men and women who changed Nicaragua's course of history—dictatorship, humiliation—with a promise of dignity? That was enough to stop one from looking too closely at sins or peccadilloes that were ultimately subordinated to two things. The revolution's internal policies; the literacy campaign, first and foremost. And its foreign policies: the affirmation of sovereignty in the face of the US"[14] Notably, regional blowback to Reagan's Contra policy transcended the Left. As Cuban vice premier Rafael Rodríguez had stressed to US secretary of state Alexander Haig in their secret 1981 meeting, the

Mexican and Venezuelan governments were hardly leftist.[15] Indeed, most of the governments that soon answered García Márquez's call to help mediate the Central American crisis were vocally anti-communist, economically dependent on the United States, and hostile to socialist bloc influence in the hemisphere.

A wider diplomatic rejection of Contra policy began taking shape in early 1983. In January of that year, in reaction to the US-sponsored Forum for Peace and Democracy, the foreign ministers of Venezuela, Mexico, Panama, and Colombia gathered on the island of Contadora in the Gulf of Panama to discuss how to build peace in Central America by sidelining US diplomacy altogether. At a July follow-up summit in Cancún, the Contadora countries' presidents—Herrera Campins, Mexico's Miguel de la Madrid, Colombia's Belisario Betancur, and Panama's Ricardo de la Espriella—called on "states with interests and ties in the region" (that is, the United States and Cuba) to support "without reservations" a diplomatic solution. A multilateral negotiated settlement between Central American countries, they argued, should be based on the principles of nonintervention and self-determination. First, each Central American country should cease their respective arms buildups and expel foreign military advisers—Cubans in the Nicaraguan case, and Americans in the case of Honduras, Costa Rica, and El Salvador. Second, and perhaps most importantly, Central American countries should desist from allowing foreign actors to use their territory to launch armed attacks against neighbor countries. This second point was aimed not only at FSLN support for the armed Left in El Salvador but also at the Honduran and Costa Rican governments' policy of allowing the US to recruit, arm, and base anti-Sandinista proxies in their territories.[16]

At the heart of the matter were competing explanations for the social upheaval that rocked Central America in the 1970s and '80s. Whereas US intelligence services pointed the blame at Moscow and Havana, Mexican foreign minister Bernardo Sepúlveda argued that "conflicts developing in Central America have their origin in the deep economic and social problems plaguing that area's countries during the last few decades."[17] As Wolf Grabbendorf wrote at the time, most European analysts similarly believed that the causes of unrest were inherent to the region rather than the result of outside communist meddling.[18] López Portillo saw the crisis in Central America as a "North–South" (rather than "East–West") problem and likened the Sandinistas and their revolutionary comrades on the isthmus to the anti-colonial nationalists of Afro-Asian decolonization, who "resisted" the "Manichaean" classifications of the Cold War.[19]

These statements strongly echoed the official Nicaraguan narrative. In bilateral discussions with North American diplomats, such as Miguel D'Escoto and Comandante Daniel Ortega's October 1983 meetings with Assistant Secretary of State Langhorne Motley, Sandinista officials invariably brought up the United States' long record of overthrowing governments in the region. Motley, who was born and raised in Brazil, acknowledged this history but told the Nicaraguans that the Reagan administration "should not be forced to pay for past sins." Still, Ortega insisted: "Why was there a revolution in Nicaragua? Not because of the USSR, nor Cuba, nor because of any other country, but because of bad North American policies, and because our people decided to defend their nation. We are the fruit of those bad policies. It's similar to the situation that we see in El Salvador and Guatemala. . . . With respect to your concern for democracy, did you have it when there were five dictators in Central America?"[20] When former secretary of state Henry Kissinger visited Managua later that year, Daniel Ortega proffered a similar history lesson before explaining: "We have no illusions about defeating a possible North American invasion. What we are pursuing is a long-term resistance, responding to the United States' strategy in the region. [Your] strategy is to push the region against Nicaragua. This logically forces Nicaragua, as well, to push the region in our favor."[21] Discursively, at least, the Sandinistas enjoyed the advantage in the hemisphere. Edgard Parrales, the FSLN's ambassador to the OAS, recalls that Nicaragua consistently enjoyed the backing of most countries at the regional body; though some voiced it discreetly, abstaining from votes to either condemn or affirm Reagan's anti-Sandinista initiatives, for fear of incurring the spite of "Big Brother."[22]

Sandinista diplomacy took note of a regional anti-imperialist current that cut across the traditional Cold War ideological divide. Nicaragua's government acted upon this somewhat remarkably when Argentina and the United Kingdom went to war over the Malvinas (Falkland) Islands in the South Atlantic Ocean in 1982. Despite the Argentine Junta's aforementioned efforts to undermine the Sandinista government, the FSLN joined Latin American countries at the OAS in rallying around its claim to be fighting an anti-colonial war. On a trip to Buenos Aires, Sandinista culture minister Ernesto Cardenal even casually offered to send Nicaraguan troops to help. "Latin America was one thing before Malvinas," he declared, "and another thing entirely afterward."[23] Argentina, burned by Reagan's support for the UK in the war, soon retired most of its military advisers from Central America.

Latin American governments also had practical reasons to resist Reagan's Central America policy. When Miguel de la Madrid assumed the presidency in 1982, Mexican diplomacy characterized the risks of US intervention in Central America in terms of "core interests." As Sepúlveda explained: "It is highly risky for Mexico . . . that just beyond its southern border there be an arms race that might force us, in a time of economic difficulties, to modify our military capabilities. Nor would a climate of civil wars and internecine conflicts help us reactivate the economic growth that we need. Migratory flows and polarization in neighboring countries would surely also affect the social peace which is indispensable for facing the challenges which await us in the coming years."[24] Colombian foreign minister Augusto Ramírez Ocampo similarly explained that Central American instability complicated his country's efforts to reorient its economic growth model toward the Caribbean coast, while Panamanian officials frequently commented that instability might jeopardize the implementation of the Torrijos-Carter treaties, which saw Panama win control of its interoceanic canal.[25]

Moreover, political elites across the continent worried that US proxy intervention might evolve into a direct military invasion. Raúl Alfonsín, Argentina's first elected president after the country's military dictatorship collapsed in 1982, told FSLN leaders that such an invasion would be a "holocaust."[26] Unlike in Cuba or the Dominican Republic, geography would not contain the spread of political violence; the interconnectedness of Central American politics was already being demonstrated by the intensification of revolution and repression in Guatemala and El Salvador after the Sandinista victory in 1979. These concerns brought together governments of different ideological backgrounds. Even center-right heads of state—such as Colombia's Betancur, a Conservative Party president who pursued peace talks with Marxist insurgents and incorporated his country into the Non-Aligned Movement—sought to distance themselves from Reagan's "East–West thesis." Herrera Campins, a Christian Democrat, warned on the 1983 anniversary of Simón Bolívar's birthday—an occasion often taken by Latin American leaders to provide a progress report on the region's bicentennial quest for independence—that the "shadow of the East–West dispute" loomed over Central America.[27]

A collective reassertion of national sovereignty came in response to the challenge posed by US policy in Central America. In the face of US unilateralism, Mexico's de la Madrid made "Latin American solutions to Latin American problems" a mantra of his administration's foreign policy. "The region," he asserted, "is capable of generating its own answers to the problems which it is affected by."[28] They understood that the US government found the Sandinista government unacceptable a priori, and felt that Washington, by attempting to topple the FSLN, was reserving for itself the long-held prerogative to decide what type of government could or could not exist in the hemisphere. Mexican negotiator Claude Heller saw Contadora as part of a historic effort to build "a new order" in inter-American affairs "that accommodates the interests of the Latin American countries with the interests of the United States." The old order, in his view, was exemplified by US pursuit of regime change in Guatemala (1954), the Dominican Republic (1965), and Chile (1973). Contadora proposed that this time should be different. "The question," he told a journalist, "comes down to the ability of the United States to coexist with Latin American experiments that are in contrast with the fundamental interests of the United States."[29]

These two basic principles—self-determination and "Latin American solutions to Latin American problems"—harkened back to García Márquez's 1982 Nobel Lecture, in which the Colombian literary giant called on Western democracies to "end the solitude of Latin America" by supporting its countries' pursuit of autonomy and local models for development. They should also eschew fears of Soviet meddling; "Latin America neither wants, nor has any reason," he assured the audience in Stockholm, "to be a pawn without a will of its own." Why, then, he asked, "is the originality granted us in literature so mistrustfully denied us in our difficult attempts at social change?"[30]

The Contadora Group's 1983 Cancún Declaration strongly rebuked the US view on the Nicaraguan question. It also marked a clear contrast with early Cold War Latin American diplomacy. In the 1954 Declaration of Caracas, OAS member states resolved that communism served "the interests of an alien despotism" and ensconced their "faith" in "representative democracy as the best means to promote their social and political progress."[31] Political actors of Marxist persuasion, in other words, were deemed contrary to the inter-American system. The Caracas Declaration thereby created the diplomatic basis in the OAS for US-led sanctions and interventions in the 1950s and '60s against leftist regimes in Guatemala (the only state to vote against the resolution), Cuba, and the Dominican Republic. The Cancún Declaration, by contrast, framed the growth of revolutionary movements in Central America as a local problem rooted in historic socioeconomic challenges, making no mention of extra-hemispheric involvement. It explicitly delegitimized unilateral interventions within the inter-American system. And crucially, it broke with the United States on the issue of the Sandinista regime's a priori legitimacy. The left-wing FSLN government, the declaration implied, was as legitimate and amenable to the inter-American system as its US-backed, anti-communist neighbors.

A Multilateral Crisis

The Nicaraguan question was more than a narrow diplomatic dispute between the United States and a handful of Latin American countries. The evolving debate on the Sandinista Revolution's legitimacy reflected changes in European foreign policies as well as major transformations in Latin American politics. Apart from UK prime minister Margaret Thatcher, most Western European heads of state—mainly from social-democratic parties—opposed Reagan's Contra policy and supported Latin American diplomatic efforts toward a negotiated solution that would defuse a potentially explosive East–West confrontation. This Latin American effort grew as anti-communist military governments—which had been sustained, in part, by Cold War ideologies and alliances—collapsed and gave way to democratic, civilian rule on the continent. Overall, European and Latin American involvement averted a scenario in which the Sandinista Revolution and subsequent civil war were exclusively framed by either the US–Nicaraguan relationship or Soviet–American competition. Specifically, it helped isolate Reagan's position in international organizations such as the United Nations. It also had a significant impact on the Nicaraguan government's position. By shoring up its legitimacy, European and Latin American diplomacy provided an additional layer of protection against US pressure. The multilateralization of the crisis eroded Washington's leverage in negotiations with Sandinista leaders and generally raised the costs of their efforts to undermine the government in Managua.

Latin American politics experienced profound changes over the course of the 1980s that helped determine the regional response to the Contra War. Having previously succumbed to military rule during waves of authoritarianism in the 1960s and '70s, most countries in South America transitioned to electoral democracy in the 1980s. The "Third Wave" of democratization in Latin America saw the Contadora consensus swell. Where civilian leaders replaced US-backed military rulers, government opposition to Washington's intervention in Central America soon followed. In July 1985, four countries that were in the midst of or had recently completed democratic transitions—Argentina (Alfonsín elected December 1983), Uruguay (José

María Sanguinetti elected November 1984), Brazil (Tancredo Neves indirectly elected January 1985), and Peru—formed the Contadora Support Group after their respective countries' foreign ministers met at the inauguration of left-leaning Alan García in Lima.

Leaders of these fledgling democratic governments, seeing both national and regional sovereignty at stake in the Nicaraguan crisis, typically affirmed the Sandinistas' responses to Washington's demands. Mexico's Miguel de la Madrid privately told Comandante Henry "Modesto" Ruíz that the Americans were at fault when bilateral negotiations collapsed.[32] Alfonsín told Sergio Ramírez that if Washington refused to let the Contadora process play out in good faith, Managua should feel no obligation to downsize its army or hold direct talks with the Contra.[33] Uruguayan foreign minister Enrique Iglesias and Colombian president Belisario Betancur echoed this strongly pro-Sandinista sentiment in private meetings.[34] Wilson Ferreira, leader of Uruguay's National Party, told Daniel Ortega that while the US was pressuring individual countries to abandon support for the FSLN, these pressures crashed against a wall of Latin American consensus on the issue.[35] Summing up the way in which Latin American governments increasingly interpreted US intervention in Central America in the 1980s, Alan García told Sandinista officials that Peru was "willing to defend the thesis of continental sovereignty which has been put to the test in Nicaragua."[36]

Notably, Western European governments—which, as Eline van Ommen has demonstrated, were a key target of Sandinista diplomacy—helped enable this challenge to US unilateralism.[37] In the first half of the decade, a wave of center-left social democrats dominated European elections. These heads of state—Austria's Bruno Kreisky (in power since 1970), Greece's Andreas Papandreou (elected 1981), Sweden's Olof Palme (1981), Spain's Felipe González (1982), France's François Mitterrand (1981), and Italy's Bettino Craxi (1983)—shared Contadora's interpretation of the Nicaraguan question and the Central American crisis more broadly. These leaders supported the Contadora process because, as Felipe González put it, Latin American countries were seeking "regional solutions to regional conflicts . . . which is a way of avoiding a local, zonal conflict becoming another scaffold in the escalating tensions between East and West."[38] West Germany's Christian Democrats were more skeptical of the FSLN than these SI stalwarts, but they similarly opposed the Reagan administration's belligerent approach. European efforts were somewhat of a holdover from the superpower détente of the 1970s; having benefited from the easing of East–West tensions in the previous decade, they were proactive in restraining an American foreign policy that might make superpower relations worse than they had already gotten after the Soviet invasion of Afghanistan. Nicaragua was central to those efforts; no country, Bernd Rother notes, occupied more of Willy Brandt's time during his tenure as Socialist International president.[39] European criticism of the Contra program also recalled earlier trans-Atlantic rifts over the Vietnam War; Olof Palme of Sweden—the Western country that most consistently criticized US policy in Southeast Asia—was particularly amicable toward the Sandinista leadership.[40]

European and Latin American involvement put limits on the Reagan administration's ability to pursue its policies and determine the Sandinistas' fate. First, it denied the United States the role of sole power broker. Historically, the United States disproportionately influenced the resolution of political crises in Central America and the Caribbean; indeed, it had acted as peace- and king-maker in several Nicaraguan civil wars, often through direct military intervention. But in the 1980s, there were many other cooks in the kitchen. Second, outside involvement left the Reagan administration with fewer local allies to work with. In the past, the United States had relied on Latin American governments to help mount interventions against adversarial governments. For example, the Somozas' Nicaragua acted as a launching pad for the failed Bay of Pigs invasion as well as the successful effort to depose Guatemala's Árbenz government; the 1965 US invasion to preempt a leftist government in the Dominican Republic took the form of a multilateral, OAS-sponsored mission. During the Sandinista episode, by contrast, collaborators were relatively hard to find, especially as hard-line anti-communist dictatorships faded from view. Finally, so long as a negotiated peace process backed by US allies existed, lawmakers on Capitol Hill had reason to refuse or put limits on economic assistance to the Contra.

The multilateralization of the crisis was frustrating to US officials who felt that the Sandinistas were as skeptical about Contadora—which centered on a deal between Nicaragua and its neighbors—as they were. Richard Stone, the US ambassador-at-large for Central America between 1983 and 1984, at one point asked Daniel Ortega if he thought Contadora was "actually useful." The Nicaraguan leader replied: "Honestly, we just want to have an agreement with the United States." Internal Foreign Ministry memoranda complained that the Contadora countries lacked the will to confront Washington head-on.[41]

Bilateral talks, however, were unproductive. In December 1983, a bipartisan presidential commission, headed by veteran diplomat Henry Kissinger,

traveled to Managua to meet with various comandantes and cabinet officials. Neither side enjoyed the visit. According to Nicaraguan transcripts and
memoranda of the meetings, FSLN officials felt that Kissinger and company
did not pay attention to detailed explanations of their social and economic
policies. In their view, the bipartisan commission only came to ratify and
legitimize the Reagan administration's program of economic sanctions and
paramilitary pressure.[42] On the opposing side, members of the Kissinger
commission complained of having been treated "shabbily" by the Nicaraguans, who, in their assessment, were more interested in lecturing their
guests on the history of US intervention than in having an open-ended
discussion.[43] In a subsequent report, the Kissinger Commission recommended economic aid programs to address the social roots of revolutionary upheaval on the isthmus, while simultaneously calling for increased
military assistance to Central America's anti-communist forces. It also dismissed the idea that US officials might simply "contain" the Sandinistas or
otherwise try to live with "a Marxist-Leninist Nicaragua" in military alliance with Cuba and the Soviet Union.[44]

Nicaraguan diplomats identified two faces of US foreign policy with
which they had to engage. On the one hand, Reagan administration hard-
liners saw the Contras as part of an effort to remove the FSLN from power
in the short run. On the other hand, pragmatists felt that the anti-Sandinista
rebels were bargaining chips that could be used to extract key concessions
from Nicaraguan leaders and were less interested in seeking the FSLN's unconditional surrender.[45] Sandinista leaders correctly associated the latter
posture with Secretary of State George Schultz, who traveled to Managua
in June 1984.[46] Schultz displayed his pragmatist bona fides by agreeing to
discuss the issue of democratization horizontally—that is, alongside security concerns—rather than placing it first in a vertical list of priorities (in
other words, demanding that the Sandinistas *first* democratize *before* the
US toned down aid to the Contra).[47] Having pleased Daniel Ortega and
Miguel D'Escoto during a brief meeting at Managua's Augusto César Sandino International Airport, the breakthrough served as the basis for a serious round of bilateral negotiations.

The two sides agreed on the Mexican port city of Manzanillo as the location. Mexico did not mediate or observe the talks, as the Nicaraguans had
requested, but the de la Madrid government was happy enough to host a
dialogue that might lead to reduced tensions. But the talks, which started
in July 1984, went nowhere. "Almost everybody in the administration was
opposed to any discussion or negotiation with Nicaragua," Schultz recalled.[48]

Hard-liners, agitated that the talks were happening to begin with, made sure that US delegates offered no real concessions and demanded unreasonable ones from their Nicaraguan counterparts. The other side came in tough, as well. According to documents outlining their negotiating strategy, the Nicaraguan Foreign Ministry instructed its representatives to keep any discussion of the country's internal affairs off the table. Specifically, they were to refuse any proposal that asked their government to hold direct talks with Contra leaders.[49] They were willing to contemplate security concessions like those floated by the Contadora countries, but not for nothing in return from Washington. In retrospect, the Manzanillo talks, which muddled along through the rest of 1984, were condemned to failure because Reagan was still committed to the Contras and the Sandinistas were not ready to give up trying to destroy them on the battlefield.

Bilateral US–Nicaraguan talks foundered in the shadow of the Contadora Peace Process, which set ground rules far more attractive to the FSLN. Unlike any agreement proposed at Manzanillo, the first multilateral draft treaty—submitted by the Contadora foreign ministers to their Central American counterparts in September 1984—would, if ratified, call on the United States to cease support for the Contra and reduce its military footprint across Central America. The memoir of FDN leader Adolfo Calero suggests that Contra chiefs saw in Contadora nothing more than an obstacle to continued congressional funding for their troops.[50] And beyond the terms of the agreement itself, the multilateral Latin American initiative took legitimacy away from Reagan's intervention in Central America and transferred it to the Nicaraguan government. But Contadora also asked much of the Sandinistas. The September 1984 draft treaty required that Nicaragua expel Cuban and socialist bloc military advisers, suspend foreign military purchases, reduce the size of the EPS, and cease support for the Salvadoran FMLN. It also included language around political pluralism and democracy that tied Nicaragua's internal affairs to the negotiations, a pill the Sandinistas said they would never swallow.

Nicaraguan diplomats signed the first draft treaty on September 21 anyway, surprising international observers by being the first party to do so. They did so under the assumption that the terms were unacceptable to Washington, which would surely oppose the agreement. In the meantime, the Nicaraguan signature burnished the Sandinistas' international profile and made it harder for the Reagan administration to justify a military intervention that did not enjoy resounding support at home and among US allies.

Therefore, and even though it had initially paid lip service to the Cancún Declaration, the Reagan administration quickly moved to undercut Contadora. The other Central American countries, which had hitherto expressed willingness to sign the agreement, suddenly walked out on the process in the wake of Nicaragua's signature and demanded amendments to extract further concessions from the Sandinista government. A National Security Council briefing paper leaked to the *Washington Post* revealed that Central American diplomats abandoned talks following pressure from the Reagan administration, which claimed victory: "We have effectively blocked Contadora group efforts," it read.[51] But celebrations were premature. By sabotaging the Contadora treaty—which the Cuban government had encouraged the FSLN to sign—the United States confirmed the multilateralists' view that American foreign policy, rather than leftists in power in Managua, was the main obstacle to peace in Central America. In reporting on the document, journalist Alma Guillermoprieto accurately predicted the consequences of American hostility to Contadora: "The administration will have difficulty implementing a workable regional strategy for its friends and allies in Latin America as long as it fails to take their legitimate national interests into account, expecting them instead to adopt the United States' national interests as their own."[52]

Joint Latin American and European diplomacy succeeded in isolating Washington's foreign policy and turning their own position into the consensus view in the international community. A slew of resolutions at the United Nations and OAS general assemblies backed the Contadora approach, and Nicaragua's temporary membership in the UN Security Council (1983–84) further legitimized Sandinista rule.[53] The international community came to adopt Contadora's argument that external involvement exacerbated violence in Central America and should be curtailed as a first step toward any peaceful outcome. Washington's position—that indirect US military involvement was in fact indispensable to said outcome—became increasingly isolated as a result. Ongoing negotiations hurt the Reagan administration's ability to secure congressional funding for the Contra because a majority of lawmakers—eager to avoid another Vietnam-style escalation of commitments in the Third World—were in favor of a peace settlement. The Reagan administration did try to use ongoing negotiations, as Kenneth Roberts explained, as a "useful cover for bullying tactics"; US diplomats could claim that sanctions and support for proxies were simply bargaining chips for achieving a better peace agreement. However, because it had been formally excluded from the negotiations, the US government could only influence Contadora indirectly through its Central American allies.

Because they successfully "constrained US policy choices," Roberts wrote, multilateral efforts to resolve the Central American crisis were "one of the most significant and concerted challenges ever posed to US hegemony in the Western hemisphere."[54] As this book's conclusion explores, that collective effort would visibly shape inter-American relations later in the decade and through the post–Cold War era, well after Contadora had faded. At the time, what mattered to the Sandinistas was that Washington's "East–West" thesis was losing the war of ideas against what Alan García called the "thesis of continental sovereignty."

Revolutionary Contradictions: The 1984 Elections

The Nicaraguan question—the debate over what made the FSLN government legitimate—was also relevant because it cut at some of the Sandinista Front's core dilemmas at home. Five years into their revolutionary project, the Sandinista leadership had not yet resolved the contradiction between their vision of power—premised upon their leadership of Somoza's military defeat and the promise of socioeconomic transformation—and the promises of representative government they made to their allies and the world in 1979. Western European and Latin American governments wanted to see more of the latter. The external war for legitimacy therefore helped push the Sandinistas to change the way they built it at home—most notably by formalizing a multiparty political system and holding presidential elections in November 1984.

Indeed, one reason the FSLN signed the Contadora treaty was to improve their regime's image ahead of those elections. A victory by the Sandinista Front's candidates—Daniel Ortega ran for president with fellow Junta member Sergio Ramírez as his running mate—would silence complaints that their government did not have a democratic mandate. In its campaign materials, the FSLN distinguished itself from the traditional Conservative and Liberal parties and promised to deepen the social transformations it claimed to have carried out since 1979. The "first free elections in Nicaraguan history," as they sold them, would also demonstrate that there was no need to discuss the country's internal affairs at international peace talks. One North American adviser at the Foreign Ministry suggested that holding elections, along with a relaxation of press censorship, might produce "a positive change in US policies."[55]

The elections put Nicaragua's civilian opposition in a tight spot. Many in the Coordinadora Democrática (Democratic Coordinating Committee), the opposition alliance of business leaders and conservative parties, believed that authorities would never allow anti-Sandinistas to win a fair contest. To participate, in their view, would gift unwarranted legitimacy to both the process and the inevitable Sandinista president-elect. At the same time, they weighed the potential benefits. Their candidate, Arturo Cruz—the former Doce leader and Junta member who had broken with the FSLN the previous year—hoped that running in the elections might grant democratic legitimacy to an opposition increasingly associated with the Contra, making participation worthwhile even in the case of defeat.

The Latin American and Western European forces behind Contadora were desperate to see the elections happen. They worried that if the FSLN did not ensure conditions for a free and fair contest, the Coordinadora would have ample reason to opt out. This, in turn, raised fears of a US military intervention, prompting visits to Managua by Willy Brandt and Belisario Betancur to promote a pre-electoral compromise between the two sides. To that same end, Carlos Andrés Pérez and one of Brandt's advisers hosted a meeting in October between Arturo Cruz and Comandante Bayardo Arce on the sidelines of an SI meeting in Rio de Janeiro in October. Reports suggested that, at least initially, Arce had agreed to most of the Coordinadora's demands: the FSLN promised to guarantee full speech and press liberties during the campaign, ensure the safety of the Cruz team, and most importantly, delay the elections until January 1985 to give the opposition sufficient time to prepare. As part of the deal, Cruz would immediately and irreversibly register the opposition's participation in the elections. Crucially, the Contra would also have to declare a cease-fire. At some point, however, the deal fell through; accounts differ on which side walked out first.[56] Satisfied that they had shown a willingness to compromise, the Sandinistas announced that the elections would go ahead as planned in November. The Coordinadora, similarly satisfied that its position had been vindicated, stayed away.

In retrospect, political and military circumstances created obstacles to a pre-electoral agreement that might have been impossible to surmount. The Coordinadora bristled at the notion of asking the Contra for a cease-fire. To do so would put the civilian opposition leaders exactly where the FSLN wanted them: in open coordination with the US-backed military insurgency. Arce almost certainly knew that Cruz and other Coordinadora leaders could never hold up that end of the bargain because civilian figures lacked authority over the Contra's military leadership. Key opposition leaders were against participation under almost all circumstances, anyway. US policy was also stacked against the 1984 elections. Some Reagan administration hard-liners pressured opposition leaders, many of whom were on CIA payroll, to "say no" to any pre-electoral agreement.[57] And in any event, indirect US actions weighed very heavily. By prioritizing military tools in Nicaragua over diplomatic strategies, the United States indirectly created conditions wherein the internal opposition could hardly have mounted a peaceful, political challenge against the Sandinista government (nonetheless, Cruz later said the opposition committed a "political error" by not running in 1984).[58]

The resulting elections were free and fair, but noncompetitive at the highest level. In elections where roughly three out of four eligible voters participated, Ortega and Ramírez won the presidential contest with 67 percent of the vote.[59] Despite the boycott by leading anti-Sandinista groups and half-hearted participation by smaller ones, opposition parties took 35 out of 96 seats in the legislature. A mission of observers from the European Economic Community found no irregularities in the vote counting. Another one dispatched by the Latin American Studies Association (LASA) reached the same conclusion; it also credited the 1984 Electoral Law with a proportional representation system that maximized opposition presence in the legislative branch. According to the LASA report, the main opposition's absence did not diminish the robustness of the Sandinistas' victory. In its view, the boycott was the choice of opposition leaders (under pressure by the US government) and would not have changed the final outcome anyway.[60] Nicaraguan diplomats tried to shift the focus away from the missing opposition and toward the fact of relatively high turnout, which they claimed as evidence of participation by lower classes previously excluded from politics.[61] In retrospect, however, many Sandinista leaders admitted that they never intended to hold elections that they might lose. Comandante Luis Carrión called them "semi-democratic," because "the votes were counted appropriately," but "the entire machinery of the State was put at the service of the Sandinista Front, which controlled all its institutions."[62] Jaime Wheelock, his colleague on the National Directorate, connected the episode to wider challenges the FSLN upper echelon faced after defeating Somoza: "We didn't really govern with the participation of our allies, who became very frustrated. This was a mistake that expressed itself most clearly by the 1984 elections in which we ran alone and broke the alliance of 1979."[63]

The decision to hold elections was, as Luis Carrión explained, "tactical: we wanted to give the Sandinista government a legitimacy that would be accepted by the West, thereby weakening Reagan's aggressive strategy."[64] The vice president-elect, Sergio Ramírez, later blamed the United States for casting a shadow over the process but recognized that "the 1984 elections were part of the mechanism of war," intended to undermine the Contra and its foreign benefactors.[65] At the time, the head of the Nicaraguan electoral authorities—Mariano Fiallos—framed it in similar terms: they would "give lie to the systematic detractors of our electoral process and will be a definite moral blow to the aggressors."[66] In making this tactical play, the benefits of risking real electoral defeat must have seemed low to the Nicaraguan leadership. Even if the opposition had run in an open contest, Deputy Foreign Relations Minister Victor Hugo Tinoco (Nicaragua's chief representative at the Manzanillo talks) noted, the Reagan administration likely would not have recognized the Sandinista winners as legitimate.[67]

The Nicaraguan government took steps to institutionalize political pluralism in the run-up to the 1984 elections, but the Sandinista Front's upper echelon did not yet see free democratic contests—specifically, the possibility of transitions of power—as compatible with their vision of revolutionary change. In February 1984, the Council of State—the president of which was Comandante Carlos Núñez Téllez, one of the nine members of the National Directorate—passed a law that built a multiparty system and created the legal basis for the National Assembly, the new legislative body that would replace the Council of State after 1984. In July, it decreed electoral reforms that set the rules for voting. But steps toward pluralism were limited by the vanguard role that Sandinista leaders attached to themselves, the fusion between party and state, and verticalism within the FSLN itself.

Luis Carrión notes that the Sandinista experience in the fight against Somoza conditioned their approach to pluralism and electoral competition after 1979:

The struggle against a dictatorship demanded an organizational style that had to be clandestine, very disciplined, compartmentalized, highly centralized, and with little debate. Once translated to the political system of an entire country, this generated non-democratic behaviors and values. . . . We operated on the basis that the Revolution was eternal, that it would be forever. Because what had been conquered through so much blood and sacrifice could not be raffled in an election. We thought that, if we had taken power by

risking our lives and leaving a great deal of blood along the way,
how could a few votes change that?

Other Sandinista cadres recall being more committed to the type of democratic system implemented in the Western European countries that generally sympathized with the Revolution. But throughout the young, inexperienced Sandinista elite, there was widespread fuzziness about the meaning of political pluralism. "After forty-five years of [Somoza's] dictatorship," Gioconda Belli said, "nobody here even knew what democracy was."[68]

Internationally, the elections did not have the full effect the Sandinistas had hoped for. Nicaragua's ambassador to Spain wrote in the country's paper of record that given high levels of turnout, and because electoral observers saw no foul play, "the political legitimacy of the revolution had been democratically renewed."[69] But Western European and Latin American democracies did not quite buy it. As Alejandro Bendaña recalls with disappointment: "in 1984, we won internally, but lost abroad." The elections as an "international strategy" faltered due to Cruz's exit, which resulted in Ortega winning virtually unopposed. When Ortega and Ramírez were sworn into office in January 1985, Fidel Castro was the only major head of state in attendance. Bendaña says the Foreign Ministry got the message: "This was the classic diplomatic signal that they didn't like how we won."[70] Carlos Andrés Pérez wrote a letter to the president-elect, reaffirming his support for the revolutionary process but declining the invitation to the inauguration due to his feeling "cheated, because sufficient guarantees were not given" to the opposition. He qualified his criticisms by making clear his opposition to violent US policies, but the letter was suffused with the belief that the FSLN was insincere about democracy.

Pérez's comments reflected the limits and conditionality of the Sandinistas' alliances with Western European and Latin American leaders. In private meetings held in the aftermath of the elections, enthusiastic allies such as Olof Palme and Felipe González—the Swedish and Spanish prime ministers, respectively—were relatively cool in their treatment of the president-elect, citing their displeasure with press censorship and the semipermanent state of emergency in Nicaragua.[71] Though Pérez was on the more critical side of the debate, most Socialist International leaders believed that the Sandinistas had not created conditions for a free and fair contest; on balance, the distance between the FSLN and SI grew after the elections.[72] The nature of Western European support for the Revolution had shifted over time. Initially, it had been motivated primarily by great hopes that the Sandinista model could inspire positive change throughout the Global South. Now Western European involvement was driven mostly by the concern that US policies in Central America, by dragging the isthmus into the East–West conflict, threatened international peace and security.

Their dissatisfaction notwithstanding, the Revolution's political system showed signs of profound change. Pérez—echoing other social democrats in the international arena—conceded in his letter that the 1984 elections were a promising "first step" toward fulfilling the 1979 promise of political pluralism.[73] There was no thought of formalizing a one-party system like the one seen in Cuba, and the electoral campaign further consolidated the place of alternative or anti-Sandinista political voices in revolutionary Nicaraguan. "With the elections," Humberto Ortega later said, "the Revolution marked its distance from the political models of real socialism" and moved toward the "liberal-democratic models" that predominated in Latin America.[74] And though the elections did not allow for the FSLN's defeat in practice, they quietly left that outcome as a conceptual possibility. At least in theory, the basis for the Revolution's legitimacy had been altered. Carrión later reflected on this quandary: "[the 1984 elections] fundamentally contradicted the logic which had prevailed until then: that the Revolution was eternal, that its legitimacy came from struggle and sacrifice, and that elections were merely 'raffling' of power. By holding elections we were admitting, without recognizing it, that the Revolution could lose. . . . With elections, the Revolution's legitimacy would no longer base itself in struggle, sacrifice, or martyrdom. It would have to base itself on popular will, in winning the votes of the majority of people."[75] The 1984 elections were therefore one instance where short- or medium-term decision making by the FSLN leadership had long-term ramifications for the way it exercised power and even conceived of its revolutionary mission.[76] Notably, the evolution toward constitutional, electoral politics took place in the context of Sandinista efforts to win life-saving legitimacy in the international arena.

Conclusion

In 1985, all sides of the conflict hardened their positions. Calling the November elections a Soviet-style farce, the Reagan administration dismissed the Sandinistas' participation in Contadora and doubled down on the argument that Nicaragua was a threat to US national security. Arturo Cruz and other civilian leaders left the country and joined the US-backed Contra groups that attempted to reunify under the banner of the Unión Nacional Opositora (UNO). The government in Managua, meanwhile, remained focused on militarily defeating the Contra and forestalling a potential invasion by the US armed forces. Finally, Latin American countries—an ever-increasing number of them—continued to see US intervention in Central America as a threat to be contained and therefore worked to keep the Contadora process afloat.

In its second term, the administration of Ronald Reagan—reelected shortly after the Nicaraguan elections—sought to enhance the Contra program. Its paramilitary operation in Nicaragua was emblematic of the so-called Reagan Doctrine—a policy of creating proxy, right-wing revolutionaries to match and defeat left-wing movements in countries such as Afghanistan. Reagan officials swore that the United States would counter the "steadily increasing risk to peace and stability posed by the Sandinistas" with "improved assistance to the Freedom Fighters" and oppose "any concessions which would permit the consolidation of the Marxist-Leninist regime." White House strategists did not harbor "any illusions that Nicaragua would agree to terms which would protect the interests of [US] friends in Central America."[77] The president himself, in the most candid admission of his administration's goals to date, publicly stated his desire to "remove" the Sandinista government "in the sense of its present structure, in which it is a Communist, totalitarian state and . . . not a government chosen by its own people." The United States would stop seeking the FSLN's overthrow if only the revolutionaries "would turn around and say 'uncle.'"[78] At the same time, the US slapped Nicaragua with an economic embargo, and a leaked CIA manual titled "Psychological Operations in Guerrilla War" showed the extent to which Langley was willing to push legal limits and international norms in its training of anti-Sandinista troops.[79] The CIA leadership internally complained that, in not acting forcefully enough to dislodge the FSLN, the US government was repeating mistakes it had committed in Cuba, Vietnam, and Angola.[80] But a renewed interventionist offensive would depend on fragile support in Congress for escalation in Central America.

President-Elect Daniel Ortega responded to American threats by traveling to Moscow. The much-publicized trip reflected the FSLN's belief that the USSR—which had steadily increased military and economic aid since the beginning of the war in 1982—would provide game-winning support. But the Sandinistas wound up disappointed. The Kremlin responded equivocally to Nicaraguan overtures. Premier Mikhail Gorbachev, who was facing the dual task of reforming his country's economic and political systems while sustaining a costly intervention in Afghanistan, made it clear to Ortega that the FSLN war effort could not rely on indefinite socialist bloc aid.[81] The Soviet Foreign Ministry, which had published a noticeably timid condemnation of Reagan's embargo, publicly commented that its aid to Nicaragua would "necessarily be limited," and in an apparent attempt to address US apprehensions of Ortega's visit to the East, underscored that "it would be pleased to see that help to Nicaragua come from other countries," such as France, Spain, and Italy.[82] Second, the trip upset key allies and undermined Contra aid opponents in the US Congress, which passed a major aid package to the anti-government insurgents almost immediately afterward.[83] In a meeting with Sergio Ramírez later that summer, Carlos Andrés Pérez blasted Ortega's trip, characterizing it as "stupidity" and "submission."[84] Had the Soviets shown signs of deepening their investment in the Sandinista government, these criticisms would have been easy to take. But those signs were nowhere to be found; FSLN strategists would have to begin wondering whether an all-out military victory over the Contra was still possible.

Meanwhile, Latin American countries—which widely rejected the US embargo on Nicaragua—desperately tried to revive Contadora. Later, in January 1986, the Contadora foreign ministers plus their counterparts from Support Group countries met in Caraballeda, Venezuela, and called for all Central American countries to sign the Contadora treaty and for bilateral talks to resume between Nicaragua and the United States. Tellingly, the missive did not urge the Nicaraguan government to hold direct talks with Contra leaders, a fact the FSLN took as vindication of its position.[85]

At the same time, the war grew fiercer and Nicaraguans paid a terrible price. The state of emergency in effect since 1982 allowed the government to arbitrarily target and detain critics; the Interior Ministry's state security apparatus led by Comandante Guerrillero Lenín Cerna, praised internally for its success in neutralizing Contra presence within major cities, was subject to much criticism from international monitors like Amnesty International.[86] Countless civilians were victims of war atrocities. While human rights observers pointed the blame at both the EPS and Contra forces, investigations in the mid-1980s by the Washington Office on Latin America (WOLA) and Americas Watch concluded that the latter was guilty of the majority of abuses.[87] The Contras' conduct in the war—along with the leaked CIA "Murder Manual"—proved a major liability for the anti-Sandinista cause because it undermined, among other things, the Reagan administration's moral justification for sending them money and armaments. Because

Nicaragua never experienced a robust truth, justice, and reconciliation process, we lack rigorous estimates of the number of civilian or combat deaths that took place. The carnage, in any event, was immense. And Contadora did little to stop it. For all the fuss it created, multilateral Latin American diplomacy did not succeed in creating negotiated settlements to end Central America's armed conflicts.

But even though the general picture appeared static, important changes had taken place in the background. For one, the neighborhood looked different. As more Latin American countries transitioned to democratic, civilian rule, the Sandinistas' global support network expanded. Without the diplomatic cover and legitimacy granted by Latin American and Western European governments, the Revolution might have succumbed to insurgency and intervention, especially as the limits of socialist camp support became more clearly defined. And though Contadora did not resolve Nicaragua's civil war, it placed limits on US foreign policy in the region and created a rough, conceptual road map to a negotiated settlement that leaders would follow in the war's later stages. These developments on the international front also backdropped crucial decisions by Sandinista Front leaders—namely, the holding of elections—that primed the Revolution for significant political transformations later in the decade.

Part IV **Peace, 1986–1989**

· ·

7 A Seat at the Table

The Central American Peace Accords

After a half decade in power, the Revolution's legacy hung in the balance. The old regime had been truly destroyed; despite the leadership of Somoza-era Guardsmen in the Contra, there was little chance of a restoration. However, by 1986 the revolutionary reform agenda had stalled and the economy was in a state of crisis. Through war and intervention, the revolutionaries still enjoyed control of government. But, increasingly, even state power looked at risk.

Four years had passed since Gabriel García Márquez lamented Latin America's solitude in his Nobel Lecture. Three had elapsed since the region's countries launched a major, multilateral peace initiative. Yet foreign-fueled civil wars raged on in Nicaragua, El Salvador, and Guatemala. The Contadora process was a significant diplomatic exercise that flexed Latin American autonomy while also constraining US intervention and legitimizing the Sandinista government. But Central Americans, meant to benefit from these efforts, saw little to celebrate. Luis Guillermo Solís—a Costa Rican diplomat who was later elected the country's president—said the multilateral peace process had devolved into "the tool used by Latin American countries to save face vis-à-vis the United States."[1] Ricardo Valero—Mexican vice foreign minister during this period—admitted that Contadora had almost become an object of mockery in Central America.[2] More focused on drawing a line against US unilateralism, the multilateral Latin American peace process struggled to build concrete mechanisms for conflict resolution in Central America.

Fittingly, a second Nobel Prize acceptance speech marked the moment when Central American elites took matters into their own hands. In November 1987, Costa Rican president Óscar Arias Sánchez addressed the world from the podium in Oslo: "Let Central Americans decide the future of Central America. . . . Support the efforts for peace instead of the forces of war in our region. Send our people ploughshares instead of swords, pruning hooks instead of spears. If they, for their own purposes, cannot refrain from amassing the weapons of war, then, in the name of God, at least they should leave us in peace."[3] The Central American Peace Accords signed earlier that year in Esquipulas, Guatemala—for which Arias was receiving the Nobel Peace Prize—ended foreign-backed civil wars in the region. As a result of the so-called Esquipulas Accords and subsequent follow-up summits, Central America's countries adopted liberal, election-based systems and rode the Third Wave of democracy in Latin America. Central America's presidents agreed to hold talks with armed insurgents (of the left- or right-wing variety, as the case may be) in their countries. In exchange, they received promises of nonintervention by neighboring countries, which collectively agreed to renounce foreign military involvement on the isthmus. The government of the United States, despite having built its intervention on the pretext that the FSLN regime should be pressured to democratize, frowned upon a deal that undermined the Contra program and further normalized the Sandinista government's place in regional politics.

The emergence of this peace settlement poses several puzzles. For one, it aimed to build democratic transitions in a Central American setting that lacked the "objective structural conditions" that social science research associates with democratization. Given the ravages of war, economic collapse, and meddling by foreign actors, political scientist John Booth rightly observed that the "prospects for democracy could hardly have been bleaker."[4] The picture was rather different from that of South and East Asia, South America, or Eastern Europe, regions that also saw widespread transitions to democracy in the 1970s, '80s, and '90s.[5] Moreover, there was shaky precedent, at best, for this form of government on the isthmus. In the past, Central American countries had often adopted forms of oligarchic republicanism but—save for Costa Rica—lacked an uninterrupted history of free elections or respect for civil liberties. Peaceful transitions of power had been relatively rare compared to other regions in the Americas. And in the specific context of the area's late–Cold War revolutionary upheavals, few of the main belligerents saw liberal democracy as a goal in and of itself. In fact, much of the leadership of the armed Left and anti-communist Right initially dismissed electoral systems as either secondary to or incompatible with their pursuit of victory in a winner-takes-all battle of ideologies and worldviews. The Sandinista Front's upper echelon, we have seen, was uninterested in subordinating its vision of social democracy to representative institutions that might cede ground to reactionary forces. For their part, the military-dominated governments of Honduras, El Salvador, and Guatemala were bent on avoiding a Nicaragua-style uprising in their own territories, and thus resorted to political suppression and acts of violent terror against their own citizens.

Washington's role deepens the puzzle. In a 1989 speech on East–West relations, US president George H. W. Bush famously told European countries that the Cold War division of Europe should be resolved through democratization: "The foundation of lasting security," he argued, "comes not from tanks, troops, or barbed wire; it is built on shared values and agreements that link free peoples." Bush (Reagan's vice president in the era of the Sandinista Revolution) linked several things: the United States' strategic victory over Soviet and Eastern European communism, the adoption of liberal democracy, and the construction of durable security architectures. But when it came to Central America at roughly the same time, US policymakers were skeptical about processes toward democratization designed to wind down armed conflicts. The Esquipulas Accords called on the Sandinistas to make virtually all the democratizing reforms that the Reagan administration had demanded over the course of the 1980s. Notably, it required them to allow all regime opponents, including demobilized Contras, to compete peacefully in politics. Yet the US sought to undercut the agreement because, in this case, democratization contradicted hardliners' anti-communist aim of removing the FSLN from power by force; Secretary of State George Schultz, a moderate by comparison with his colleagues, noted that "right-wing ideologues did not want a negotiated settlement that would end Contra aid."[6] They also doubted the Sandinistas' commitment to democracy, and many struggled to countenance a scenario in which the FSLN remained in power as a result of internationally recognized elections.

This chapter argues that three factors contributed to this outcome. First, changes at the superpower level reduced incentives for continued fighting in Nicaragua. In Washington, the Reagan administration found it increasingly difficult—especially after the Iran-Contra scandal—to sustain lethal aid to the Contra. In Moscow, Soviet leaders made it abundantly clear that they wished to reduce their Third World commitments. Backing the Sandinista war effort was not even the most important among them. As the USSR withdrew, the FSLN rekindled and deepened ties with alternative allies like the center-left parties of the Socialist International.[7] Second, political shifts at the Central American level created new space for a Contadora-style solution. Specifically, new presidents in Costa Rica and Guatemala after 1986 opposed the Contra program and worked to create a new multilateral peace framework. They helped convince the governments of El Salvador and

Honduras, which had collaborated closely with the Contra operation, that their ends would be better served if they reintegrated the Nicaraguan government even if it provoked the ire of US diplomats. As Arias's desperate plea in Oslo for nonintervention suggested, democratization and liberalization were not exactly deep-rooted, romantic aspirations. Rather, they emerged as practical tools for ending brutal wars that, inspired by the global struggle between socialism and capitalism, had ravaged their countries and left few clear winners. Third, changes at the Nicaraguan level brought the Sandinista leadership on board. The FSLN had long resisted any international negotiations that required them to reform their political system. They rejected outright any suggestion that they should hold talks with US-backed insurgents, whom they considered illegitimate. To put Nicaragua's internal affairs on the agenda would violate, they alleged, the country's sovereignty. However, by 1986 the Sandinista Popular Army was struggling to maintain its bloody stalemate with the Contra, the economy was in tatters due to US sanctions and internal policy mistakes, and popular support was nowhere near the extraordinary consensus of the Revolution's early halcyon days. The wearing down of the revolutionary project, caused by the interplay of domestic and external factors, forced FSLN leaders to reconsider their position and take the deal.

In signing, Sandinista leaders ultimately ended a war that the Revolution could not win. Though the agreements bound them to make tremendous concessions, it also dealt a serious blow to the Contra leadership. Indeed, the rewards were richer than that. Through the Esquipulas process, Nicaragua's armed Left secured a seat at the table where the region's post–Cold War order would be constructed. Having won another battle in the war for legitimacy they had waged since before taking power in 1979, the Sandinista Front prolonged the survival of its government and diminished the possibility that, in the future, their movement would be erased from the political map. The agreements also redefined the international stakes of the Nicaraguan Revolution. As the Cold War entered its final years, the Sandinista crisis became less about the possibility of socialism in the Americas and more about the generalization of liberal-democratic politics in the aftermath of superpower intervention.

Nicaragua's Reintegration in Central America

In the first half of the 1980s, Nicaragua's Central American neighbors played key roles in Washington's plans to undermine the Sandinista Revolution.

Aside from participating in diplomatic efforts to isolate Managua's government, countries such as Costa Rica and Honduras hosted the US paramilitary operation (their territories likely would have been used in the case of a direct invasion). But in the second half of the decade, political elites across the isthmus drifted away from positions amenable to the Contra program and began voicing support for a Contadora-style solution. Though the Nicaraguan war was entangled in the East–West conflict, changes in the immediate context of Central America were equally decisive in shaping the Revolution's prospects.

Evolving political conditions in Guatemala—Central America's largest country and colonial power center under the Spanish Empire—predictably set the tempo for politics on the isthmus in the late 1980s. After a US-backed coup against democratically elected leftist Jacobo Árbenz in 1954, the country alternated between façade electoral regimes and outright military dictatorships. In response, various Marxist-led guerrilla groups—the best-known being the Fuerzas Armadas Rebeldes (FAR) founded by dissident military officer Luis Turcios Lima—proliferated in rural areas. The four major organizations—FAR, ORPA, PGT, EGP—unified under the flag of the Unidad Revolucionaria Nacional Guatemalteca (URNG—Guatemalan National Revolutionary Unity) in 1982.[8] That same year, under the pretext of definitively crushing these leftist insurgencies, a coup led by General Efraín Ríos Montt dissolved the legislature, canceled basic republican institutions, and intensified repression against student movements, organized labor, and other "internal enemies." A Ríos Montt–led junta promised to pacify the countryside through a policy of "beans and bullets," where intensified military campaigns would be accompanied by rural development programs. In practice, this approach more often resembled a scorched earth policy that, in an effort to undermine guerrillas' social base of support, committed genocidal violence against Indigenous Maya communities. Though successful in routing already-fractious armed leftist groups, these costly counterinsurgency efforts exhausted the military and worsened an economic downturn that had upset the high command's relationship with the country's powerful business elite. Making matters worse, Guatemala's diplomatic isolation deepened during this period. In 1983, Indigenous activist Rigoberta Menchú, who subsequently won the Nobel Prize for her work, published a widely read autobiography that vividly portrayed the horrors of everyday life in Cold War Guatemala.[9] Local elites' disapproval of the status quo, combined with mounting international pressure, set the stage for a timid democratic opening.[10] The same year that *I, Rigoberta Menchú* hit bookstores, a new group of military officers overthrew Ríos Montt and—after decreeing a blanket amnesty for all army members—revealed plans for a constituent assembly to draft a new constitution and hold elections.[11] The Reagan administration equivocated greatly in pushing Guatemalan elites to restrain human rights abuses. But if Guatemala could be encouraged to adopt a modicum of civilian government, it might help further corner Nicaragua.

Guatemala's modest political liberalization led to significant changes in the country's foreign policy. In 1985 elections, Christian Democrat Vinicio Cerezo won a thumping 68 percent of the popular vote after promising to wind down the Guatemalan civil war, even if it meant holding talks with the rebel URNG. Shortly before his January 1986 inauguration, Cerezo surprised military leaders—who promised to lurk ominously behind any civilian government—by declaring Guatemala's "active neutrality" in the Nicaraguan conflict. A direct US invasion of Nicaragua, he told journalists, would mean the "Lebanization of Central America; we provide the bodies, and others provide the bombs. That's not good for any country."[12] Playing peacemaker in Central America was a source of international prestige for the president-elect, who needed as much as he could get in order to counterbalance the military back home (he would go on to survive numerous attempts on his life and office).[13] Once in power, he established a National Reconciliation Commission and invited Central American foreign ministers to Guatemala City to publicly reaffirm their collective support for the Contadora process.

Meanwhile, Costa Rica also held fateful elections. Since 1982, President Luis Alberto Monge had allowed the country to serve as a forward operating base for CIA-backed Contra groups. Though the Sandinistas were increasingly unpopular in Costa Rica by 1986, prolonged involvement in a vicious civil war next door was even less popular. Óscar Arias, a young political scientist and legislator from Monge's own Liberationist Party, tapped into this sentiment during his successful campaign for the presidency in 1986.[14] Compared to his opponent, Arias on the campaign trail was somewhat less hostile to the Sandinistas and slightly less friendly to the Contra. But once he took office in May 1986, the new president made more than a minor adjustment to the country's policy on the Central American conflict. Though he renewed calls on the FSLN to make democratic reforms, he also ordered Costa Rican police to raid several Contra camps near the Nicaraguan border. An outraged official running Contra resupply efforts cabled Washington: "boy needs to be straightened out by heavy weights."[15] But

Arias, who strongly felt that the Contra program was the main obstacle to a peace settlement in Central America, stood his ground.

The Cerezo and Arias elections generated momentum for a new, Central American diplomatic initiative to bring peace to the region. The same month Arias was sworn in, Cerezo invited all Central American presidents to a summit in Esquipulas, a popular destination for Catholic pilgrims in Guatemala near the meeting of the Salvadoran and Honduran borders. Arias, Cerezo, and Ortega, along with El Salvador's Napoleón Duarte and Honduras's José Azcona, gave the now-customary declarations in support of the ailing Contadora process. Fundamentally, Esquipulas I—as it came to be known—was a meeting about meetings: the five presidents agreed to institutionalize regular summits and discussed Cerezo's embryonic proposal for a Central American Parliament (PARLACEN).[16] They did not discuss concrete steps to end armed conflicts in their countries.

Still, this 1986 meeting marked a significant departure from the diplomatic status quo ante. For the first time, Sandinista president Daniel Ortega met directly, as an equal, with his counterparts from Nicaragua's neighboring countries. Thus, Alain Rouquié—a political scientist and France's ambassador to El Salvador at the time—described Esquipulas I as the "anti-Democratic Forum [1982]" (discussed in the previous chapter) "and a 180-degree reversal with respect to the policies inspired by the United States." Having previously collaborated with US-led initiatives to isolate the Sandinista government, Central American countries now evinced a political will to "reintegrate" Nicaragua.[17] Sandinista leaders certainly viewed Esquipulas in this light. Vice President Sergio Ramírez, after meeting with his own counterparts, privately gushed to Ortega that the meetings were "positive in every sense; Nicaragua was included unconditionally, as a country with a regime as democratic and freely elected as the rest."[18] The Contadora and Support Group countries, which saw Nicaragua's legitimization as primordial for defusing tensions in Central America, met in Panama a month later to formally voice support for Esquipulas I.[19]

Iran-Contra and Socialist Camp Withdrawal

A narrow focus on the superpower conflict, we have seen, cannot account for the rise of a leftist revolution in Nicaragua in 1979, nor can it explain the emergence of civil war. The same can be said about the conflict's eventual resolution. Nonetheless, changing superpower involvement in Nicaragua paved the road to a peace agreement in important ways. In the first half of the 1980s, the Soviet Union and the United States backed warring parties in Nicaragua. In the second half of the decade, these actors—willingly or not—modified their approach. USSR leaders expressed eagerness to reduce their financial commitment to the Nicaraguan government, especially as the premiership of Mikhail Gorbachev embarked on a risky process of internal transformation. Meanwhile, the Reagan administration found it increasingly difficult to fund an intervention that lacked strong support from voters; a 1986 *New York Times*/CBS poll found that only 25 percent of Americans supported continued spending on the Contra.[20] Changes in Washington and Moscow (and allied socialist regimes) created additional space for Central American leaders to move on a peace settlement.

Though the Reagan administration initially appreciated the new pressure that Arias exerted on the Nicaraguan government, it came to view Central American efforts—in particular, the Sandinistas' rehabilitation—with alarm. During the same month that Esquipulas I took place, Pentagon officials published a report arguing that it would be impossible to "contain the communist government in Nicaragua" via a "Contadora type" political agreement, because (and for this they cited US experiences in Korea, Cuba, and Vietnam) the Sandinistas were sure to violate any commitments they made.[21] The following month the opposition-controlled House of Representatives approved Reagan's request to send further military aid to the Contra.[22] The renewal of lethal aid was a blow for Nicaraguan diplomats, who saw ending congressional support for their opponents as one of their primary foreign policy objectives.[23]

Despite this setback, FSLN leaders believed that under the Democratic leadership of Speaker of the House Jim Wright, Congress could be convinced to change course (additionally, the Democrats won a majority in the Senate in November 1986 elections, thereby controlling both chambers). Soon enough, a prime opportunity fell into the Sandinistas' hands. In October 1986, a former US marine named Eugene Hasenfus was captured after EPS troops shot his C-123 cargo plane out of the sky. His testimony before Nicaraguan courts, along with documents found in his aircraft, detailed how the CIA directly flew supplies from bases in El Salvador, Honduras, and Costa Rica to the Contras in circumvention of the Boland Amendments— congressional restrictions on the use of American government funds with the purpose of overthrowing the Nicaraguan government. Hasenfus was tried, found guilty, and sentenced to thirty years in prison. After discussing the issue with anti–Contra aid congressmen including Iowa's Tom Harkin and Connecticut's Chris Dodd, FSLN leaders carefully choreographed

Eugene Hasenfus's humanitarian release, just days before Christmas, to maximize the gesture's impact on US public opinion in anticipation of future votes on Capitol Hill.[24]

The Hasenfus scandal was nothing to the Reagan administration compared with what came next. In November 1986 a Lebanese newspaper—citing leaks from Iran's Revolutionary Guard—revealed that US officials had sold weapons to Tehran's Islamic Republic, in violation of an embargo, as part of a deal to free American hostages held by Iranian surrogates in Lebanon. Further, it soon came to light that CIA and NSC officials used some of the Iranian payments to directly supply the Nicaraguan Contra, again in violation of the aforementioned limitations imposed by Congress. Lawmakers promptly set about investigating the "Iran-Contra" scandal and found that NSC staffer Oliver North and other senior officials had secured quid pro quo agreements with a remarkable range of foreign governments—from communist China to the Arab Gulf state of Bahrain—wherein the US offered diplomatic favors in exchange for military and financial assistance to the Contra. Several senior officials—including North, Defense Secretary Caspar Weinberger, National Security Adviser Robert McFarlane, Assistant Secretary of State Elliott Abrams, and CIA Central America chief Alan Fiers—were found guilty of lying to Congress about the illegal aspects of the Contra program and their role in them (all were eventually pardoned by Reagan's successor, George H. W. Bush). Facing plummeting poll numbers and potential impeachment, President Reagan survived the scandal by denying knowledge of any wrongdoing.[25] Aside from shaking US politics to the core, the Iran-Contra scandal saw the anti-Sandinista insurgency enter a "phase of irreversible cancellation," as Contra analyst Donald Castillo Rivas put it, because it ended illegal American supply flights to their forces and bedeviled legal efforts to fund their war through congressional approval. In the second half of the 1980s, when the Contra was approaching maximum troop strength, it lacked certainty of continued superpower backing; a direct US intervention to help finish their fight now seemed only a "utopian" possibility.[26] Furthermore, the governments of El Salvador and Honduras tried to distance themselves from the Contra—publicly, at least—in the wake of the scandal.[27]

Facing troubles of their own, the Sandinistas had little cause to celebrate. In early 1987, an FSLN delegation toured the socialist bloc in search of new economic aid. The trip bore little fruit. Sergio Ramírez, head of the mission, briefed Daniel Ortega upon his return: "I have perceived that, like with my previous visit to the USSR and other socialist countries, the framework for economic aid to Nicaragua is increasingly restricted; we cannot expect the volumes of foreign cooperation necessary to respond to the severe economic emergency that Nicaragua is undergoing; nor can we expect that such aid would fundamentally solve our trade deficit and shortage of foreign exchange."[28] Wherever they went, the Sandinistas received bad news. Muammar Gaddafi, contending with an economic crisis in Libya caused by the collapse of oil prices earlier in the decade, promised assistance but ultimately balked at the possibility of replacing the Soviet Union as Nicaragua's main source of petroleum.[29] Old friends in the PLO had few resources to spare.[30] Baghdad's Baathist government refused to help Nicaragua, in part because the Sandinistas tried petitioning the Islamic Republic of Iran—Iraq's sworn enemy and military adversary—for assistance at the same time.[31] Yugoslavia's collective presidency offered mostly symbolic help.[32]

These countries were not likely to invest in Nicaragua so long as it appeared that the Soviet Union was curtailing its own commitment there. When Comandante Henry "Modesto" Ruiz announced Nicaragua's oil shortage in March of that year, the Soviet government responded by quietly signaling in diplomatic channels that it would still be limiting its oil shipments to Nicaragua. Soviet military and economic aid to the Sandinista Revolution remained at high levels through the rest of the decade but reached its upper limits in 1987; at the time, newspaper reports emerged of Soviet officials reprimanding Sandinista leaders for squandering socialist camp assistance.[33] While Mexican president Miguel de la Madrid promised to make up for some of the lost crude, Mexico was no longer in a position to provide it on credit as it had done in the past (in part due to the country's own economic crisis, but also because Washington had pressured Mexican officials to stop subsidizing the FSLN government in this way). Still, his foreign policy team privately put a positive spin on the Sandinistas' declining superpower patronage: reduced dependency on the USSR would weaken the Reagan administration's pretext for aggression and give the FSLN an opportunity "to consolidate its revolutionary project in an autonomous and independent fashion."[34] Nicaraguan officials may not have viewed things as happily, but they were forced to accept the underlying reality. In March 1987, an underwhelming visit to Managua by Boris Yeltsin—then the Soviet Communist Party's top official in Moscow—left the National Directorate feeling increasingly insecure about the Soviet Union's support for their position.[35]

A changing international environment transformed the prospects for peace. The Contra found its indispensable outside support to be entirely at risk. But the FSLN's Soviet-bloc support—which CIA analysts saw as "vital in limiting the insurgent threat"—was also running dry.[36] The Sandinista leadership would have to ponder these superpower changes—one favorable, one not so favorable—as they weighed the potential opportunity being created by the Arias and Cerezo initiative.

"Desgaste"

If declining superpower patronage made the National Directorate doubt whether it could win the war, conditions inside the country confirmed the impossibility of the task. By the second half of the decade the basic stalemate between the EPS and Contra columns had not changed. However, the rebels only seemed to grow their popular support and territorial control in parts of the countryside. Making matters worse, the Nicaraguan government simply lacked the manpower and treasure to continue fighting at the same intensity. Notably, the economy had begun to collapse under the weight of war, foreign intervention, and inconsistencies in macroeconomic policy. *Desgaste*—or "wearing away"—is the word that many Sandinista leaders use to describe the state of their revolutionary process in the second half of the 1980s. As the domestic social and economic picture worsened, foreign policy became increasingly crucial, and senior officials took the idea of a diplomatic solution—rather than a military one—more seriously.

As early as 1984, some members of the National Directorate began raising concerns about the political situation in the countryside. The Interior and Agrarian Reform ministries dispatched diagnostic task forces to the mountainous, northern provinces where the Contra appeared to enjoy increasing popular support: Estelí, Nueva Segovia, Madríz, Jinotega, and Matagalpa. They found that rural peasants in these regions opted to join or support the US-backed insurgency for a host of interrelated reasons, including the government's perceived discrimination against owners of private property, its alleged hostility toward organized religion, and economic policies such as price controls on foodstuffs. "Until then," Comandante Luis Carrión recalls, "the focus was military: the Contra was a mercenary army, and so it had to be defeated militarily."[37] By contrast, the reports suggested that the Sandinistas' problem in these regions required other, political tools. Comandante Jaime Wheelock describes "rectification" measures that were subsequently adopted to "improve rural attitudes toward the revolution": in war zones they suspended new expropriations of rural property, lifted price controls, softened rationing policies, punished EPS officials guilty of abuses against civilians, and generally revised land distribution "from the cooperative model to one that favored requests for individual land."[38] But it proved difficult to repair distrust or reverse polarization in rural communities.[39] "Military thinking," moreover, continued to predominate in the Sandinista high command.[40]

Nevertheless, a lack of resources constrained military plans and turned negotiations into a necessity. By increasing troop numbers and adopting new counterinsurgency tactics after 1983, the EPS had achieved its immediate objective of preventing insurgents from taking—and, more importantly, holding—any population centers from which Contra political leaders could declare a provisional government. The United States, army chief Humberto Ortega later wrote, had "failed" to establish a "beachhead" in Nicaragua.[41] Additionally, state security and the National Police—deeply embedded in the population via a community policing model—neutralized internal threats within major cities.[42] Outside advice and resources, of course, made all this possible. But by the middle of the decade, when coffers and recruitment pools started to run dry, continued aid seemed in doubt. "According to all the analyses we made," EPS Chief of Staff Joaquín Cuadra said, "we were not going to hang on much longer. . . . Nicaraguan society was exhausted."[43]

The onset of war in 1982 had effectively reduced the government to fighting the war, suspending the march of major social reforms. A continued war now threatened to reduce the government. By most accounts, the fighting was growing more fierce; according to multiple estimates, the death toll on both sides rose in the period following the 1984 elections.[44] By 1987, the Sandinista upper echelon agreed that their military effort had reached a state of exhaustion.[45] Jaime Wheelock summed up, in three points, the reasons why the time had come to take a political settlement seriously: "First, the Nicaraguan economy was unable to resist such an intensive military campaign in the long run. Second, the reserve of conscripts for the military was drying up. Third, by 1987 we received the indication that the Soviet Union was not going to be able to continue supporting us because it lacked foreign exchange and faced obstacles in sending us aid."[46]

The first of those reasons—that the "economy was bankrupt," as army intelligence chief Hugo Torres put it—began occupying more and more of the Directorate's time in the second half of the decade.[47] After 1979, revolutionary Nicaragua appeared to rebound successfully from the economic collapse caused by the war against Somoza; until 1983 it experienced economic growth at roughly the same rate as other Central American countries. By

1986, however, gross domestic product (GDP) had shrunk for three consecutive years and real wages were only 40 percent of the level they had reached before the insurrection against Somoza had taken place.[48] Furthermore, 1986 also witnessed the intensification of an inflationary spiral that would eventually rank as the worst ever recorded in the history of the Americas.

Analysts of the Nicaraguan economy have debated the relative weight of external and internal factors in causing the collapse. US policies created enormous constraints: the Contra War pushed the government to spend enormous, distortionary sums on defense, while economic sanctions forced it to find alternative sources of financial aid and markets for exports. Some problems, such as labor and food shortages, were directly related to specific economic policies implemented by the government. At a broader level, the Sandinistas had trouble achieving the harmony between state planning and market forces implied by their "mixed economy" model. Economist Hans Peter Lankes noted that policymakers quickly ran into contradictory restraints, as they "had to provide immediately visible and lasting benefits to a core group of workers, civil servants and the armed forces by manipulating the wage and price system" (the centrally planned aspect), "and it simultaneously had to ensure sufficient incentives to keep the private sector from closing down" (the market-based aspect). The situation amounted to "planning without control," as evidenced by a booming black market after 1983.[49] Economist Alejandro Martínez Cuenca, the Sandinistas' minister of foreign commerce, similarly blames a neither-here-nor-there approach: "We failed to give sufficient importance to the wearing down of the economy—not only a product of the war. The conceptual differences around centralism versus a market economy took too long to be cleared up inside of Sandinismo."[50] Luis Carrión, who became minister of economy, industry, and commerce after 1988, later wrote: "During the Revolution we spoke of a mixed economy, but there was no coherent model of mixed economy."[51]

Regardless of the reasons for the downturn, the Sandinista leadership took drastic steps to reverse it in the middle of the decade. In the early years of the Revolution, policymakers had tended to rein in market forces through state controls and restrictions on the accumulation of private wealth and property. In the second half, they relaxed said controls, reduced social spending, suspended most infrastructure projects, and otherwise tempered state involvement in the economy. The "fall and rise of the market," as Phil Ryan aptly put it, showed the dire straits that the FSLN leadership found itself in.[52] That macroeconomic arc ran parallel to another one: the shift from military toward diplomatic thinking in Sandinista strategy.

Road to the Central American Peace Accords

It was in this context of revolutionary desgaste, and of the impossibility of an outright military victory for the Nicaraguan government, that Arias invited the presidents of El Salvador, Guatemala, and Honduras to a February 1987 conference in San José. The Costa Rican leader presented his guests with the "Arias Plan" for bringing peace to Central America. On the surface, the document appeared little different from previous Latin American proposals, and therefore failed to inspire much optimism. But subtle tweaks to the formula, combined with the changing context outlined above, helped convince the governments of Nicaragua, El Salvador, and Honduras to give peace a chance at another summit in Esquipulas.

The Arias Plan mostly borrowed Contadora's security aspects, such as mechanisms for regional arms reduction backed by international monitors. Directly citing previous Contadora agreements, it called on Central American governments to swear off new military aid from foreign powers; it also forbade them from lending their territories to third countries for the purpose of launching attacks on neighbors. The plan was unambiguous in demanding the end of US military assistance to the Contra in Nicaragua; it said, furthermore, that "irregular forces and insurgent groups" should abstain from accepting external aid.

But the Central American proposal departed from Contadora's assumptions in subtly significant ways. Specifically, Arias's team lent greater emphasis and specificity to those provisions that required changes to each country's internal political arrangements. Whereas the most recent Contadora treaty (from June 1986) generally called on each country to hold elections and respect their citizens' human rights, the Arias Plan went into much more detail: it told Central American governments to grant amnesties for political opponents, restore civil liberties, and negotiate with unarmed opposition groups. Importantly, the document required that "belligerents in each country" (that is, both governments and armed opposition groups) suspend military operations. After complying with these measures, Central American countries would hold elections supervised by the Organization of American States.[53] Luis Guillermo Solís, who helped draft the plan while working for the Arias administration's Foreign Ministry, explained that Contadora "largely bought the Sandinista argument" that nonintervention should come *before* democratization, while the US-backed Contra and opposition argued precisely the opposite. By contrast, the Central American initiative "satisfied the apparently conflicting demands for security and democracy" by making the implementation of agreements in both realms simultaneous.[54] Nicaraguan deputy foreign minister Victor Hugo Tinoco offered a pithy summary of the peace proposal: "Essentially, the Esquipulas Accords were a barter: end of armed conflict in exchange for free elections everywhere in Central America."[55]

Tinoco's government was notably absent at the peace plan's unveiling in San José. Arias feared that Nicaraguan president Daniel Ortega's presence would make it harder for his Salvadoran and Honduran counterparts to signal any openness to the proposal. But Cerezo pushed to further normalize Nicaragua's diplomatic position. In a joint statement in May 1987, Cerezo and Ortega bilaterally reaffirmed their desire for a peace settlement. Such an outcome, they declared, required "respect to the norms of conviviality among states."[56]

The Reagan administration grew increasingly alarmed. Arias's proposal would require the Sandinistas to make exactly the sort of democratizing reforms that the White House had demanded as a precondition for limiting aid to the Contra. Indeed, President Reagan had, as recently as 1986, promised to support "any negotiated settlement or Contadora treaty that will bring real democracy to Nicaragua." However, Thomas Carothers points out in his account of US democracy promotion in Latin America in this period: "'Real democracy' was of course the catch. The administration did not believe that Sandinista rule could ever be democratic and by 'real democracy' meant non-Sandinista rule. . . . For all intents and purposes, therefore, the administration was not interested in a negotiated solution."[57]

The Democrats controlling Congress, still upset over Iran-Contra, smiled on the Arias Plan.[58] Faced with a growing international and domestic consensus in favor of the initiative, the Reagan administration did little to block it. Instead, it tried to replace it. The US president coaxed Speaker Jim Wright into teaming up for an alternative "Reagan-Wright Plan," which they revealed just days before the Central American presidents were scheduled to meet again at Esquipulas on August 6 to debate Arias's proposal. Unlike the Arias Plan, the Reagan-Wright Plan focused exclusively on Nicaragua, but surprisingly included several Contadora-inspired concessions. The proposal included language to the effect that the US had no right to "influence or determine the identity of the political leaders . . . nor the social and economic system" in Nicaragua; it also recommended that the US government lift sanctions and suspend Contra aid as soon as the Sandinistas agreed to a cease-fire, national reconciliation, and free elections.[59] Hours before the draft plan was presented, however, Reagan handed Wright a memo that interpreted "national reconciliation" as meaning President Daniel Ortega's immediate resignation. The memo also stated that the United States reserved the right to take military action if it deemed the Nicaraguan government to have made inadequate progress on democratization. The Democratic speaker furiously alleged that the entire plan had been designed by the White House to drum up bipartisan support for a peace plan that the Sandinistas would certainly refuse, thereby corralling Congress into approving further Contra military aid.[60]

Internationally, US attempts to supplant the Arias Plan backfired. Arias recalls that White House animosity had the helpful effect of convincing European governments that he was not an "instrument of US foreign policy."[61] Among the United States' allies in Central America, the Reagan administration's maneuvers "had the opposite of the desired effect," Rouquié pointed out, because they convinced a growing sector of the political elite that toeing Washington's line would mean continued war.[62] On August 6, the countries' presidents gathered in Esquipulas, Guatemala, and listened to Vinicio Cerezo's opening remarks. "To those who would like to see us continue at war," the host declared, "we say that we are tired of suffering and dying and that we want to build in order to live better."[63]

Those comments notwithstanding, expectations for this second Esquipulas conference remained low. After all, Daniel Ortega criticized the Arias Plan for too deeply involving countries' internal affairs in the negotiating framework. Many doubted whether hard-liners in the FSLN upper echelon would stand for any deal, let alone one that—by contrast to Contadora— explicitly required a cease-fire in the war with the Contra. For their part, the presidents of Guatemala, El Salvador, and Honduras had to contend with military leaders who tended to see democratization as a threat to their interests, and national reconciliation as a form of surrender to international communism. Finally, the US government, upon which these presidents depended for economic aid—and in the case of El Salvador's Duarte, for survival in the face of persistent threats by the rebel FMLN—opposed the deal. Little progress had been made when Central American foreign ministers met in July ahead of the presidential summit in August.

As dusk fell over Esquipulas, Arias, fully aware of these countervailing pressures, set the rules for the presidents' all-night debate. First, his peace proposal was the only option on the table; his deal could be modified, but the Reagan-Wright Plan would be ignored altogether. There would be no breaks or excuses to leave the room.[64] The deal would surely fail, Arias worried, if Ortega received a call from his brother Humberto or Tomás Borge, or if Azcona or Duarte consulted with their generals.[65] By 3:00 A.M., the presidents had reached a verbal agreement, and after breakfast, they revealed the signing of the "Procedure for the Establishment of a Firm and Lasting Peace in Central America."[66] The road ahead was a long one, but each government made a pledge to make peace with their respective internal opponents, suspend military aid from extra-regional powers, and democratize their political systems.

The global reaction to the Esquipulas II deal, a largely unmodified version of the Arias Plan, was resoundingly positive. Within days, the USSR and Cuba—where Daniel Ortega traveled shortly after the summit to discuss the deal with Fidel Castro—gave Esquipulas their enthusiastic backing.[67] On August 22, the Contadora and Support Group foreign ministers met in Caracas and agreed to conform, alongside the UN and OAS secretary generals, a Verification Commission to supervise the progress of Esquipulas's Executive Commission, made up of the five Central American foreign ministers.[68]

Azcona and Duarte—who traveled to Washington as Ortega flew to Havana—had previously suggested to the Reagan administration that they would not sign the agreement. Cerezo, who had vociferously supported a Central American settlement, was more likely to sign. For the Guatemalan government, the stakes were not quite as high as in Honduras and El Salvador. Ahead of Esquipulas II, the leftist URNG—which by this point had little hope of toppling the government—announced a brief, unilateral cease-fire to signal its support for a political settlement in Guatemala and elsewhere in the region.[69] In the end, the Honduran and Salvadoran presidents also signed, having decided that the benefits of the agreement were worth defying their benefactors in Washington. "The essence of the Arias Plan," explained Alejandro Bendaña (secretary general of the Nicaraguan Foreign Ministry), "was there was something for everyone in it."[70]

Honduras's Azcona, who had been elected in November 1985, was perhaps the most surprising signatory. International observers had begun sarcastically referring to Honduras as a Central American "aircraft carrier" for lending its territory to US military and paramilitary operations. As part of the deal, US aid to Honduras multiplied several times over during the 1980s. But the arrangement was not without problems. The massive influx of dollars fed corruption and helped put the armed forces further beyond the reach of civilian institutions. Curiously, as Honduran analyst Victor Meza noted at the time, military leaders were not even fully committed to the Contra's military success (at least after the ouster of virulently anti-communist General Gustavo Álvarez Martínez in 1984).[71] In fact, the presence of the irregular Nicaraguan army, larger than the country's armed forces, was a latent security threat to Honduras. Civilian leaders, in particular, had to worry about a hypothetical scenario where far-right forces might enlist the Contra for an effort to violently seize power. Hence, Rouquié wondered if "perhaps [the Honduran government] did not mind receiving [Esquipulas's] help in getting rid of these pesky armed refugees which endangered its security."[72] Additionally, the risk of an undesired, direct confrontation with the Sandinista Popular Army remained high so long as anti-Sandinista insurgents remained in Honduras. At the very least, Sandinista Popular Army incursions into Honduran territory would continue. It did not help that Honduras was increasingly isolated; only El Salvador's Duarte expressed support on one such occasion in late 1986. For all these reasons, as CIA analysts acknowledged at the time, "leaders in Tegucigalpa have long considered their support for the Nicaraguan insurgents a potentially grave liability."[73]

Nationalism was decisive in helping Azcona make the tough call to sign. As Robert Pastor noted, Azcona "was squeezed between his military and the United States. US aid helped keep the military from overthrowing him—as in Guatemala, US officials demanded a veneer of civilian control— "but also prevented him from being an autonomous president."[74] Pastor's observation captured a wider dilemma: American support was generous but created problems of its own. Perceived subservience to Washington was a source of increasing domestic political pressure for Azcona, who had criticized US policy in Central America during his presidential campaign in 1985. At a certain point, even key leaders within the Honduran armed forces grew tired of "pawning" the country off to the United States, as one journalist put it in 1986.[75] The El País editorial board noted that overzealous US opposition to the Esquipulas Plan may have had the contradictory effect of swaying public opinion in its favor, therefore creating space for Central American presidents to jump on board the Arias Plan.[76] William Leogrande recounted that the other presidents tried to "shame [Azcona] into signing" by painting "him as a puppet of the United States."[77]

For Duarte the stakes were even higher. Unlike the Honduran and Guatemalan governments, his was very much at risk of being militarily toppled by left-wing insurgents. He told Arias that if he stopped receiving weapons and equipment from the United States, as Esquipulas II demanded, his government would fall to the Farabundo Martí National Liberation Front. His presidency, moreover, was consistently threatened by far-right politicians and military officials opposed to reform, political openings, or negotiations with rebels. But the Peace Accords had much to offer. The agreements called on all irregular forces—not only the Contra, but also El Salvador's leftist guerrillas—to cease hostilities and recognize the legitimacy of existing Central American governments. The fact that the agreement formally delegitimized the FMLN (and required they reject further Cuban and Nicaraguan support for their military operations) was reflected in the movement's ambivalent response to the signing in 1987. The FMLN leadership had called the Esquipulas meetings "a political victory for the Sandinista Revolution" (because it recognized the Nicaraguan Revolution's legitimacy) but complained earlier in the year that "the way in which the Arias Plan categorizes the armed struggle and Salvadoran guerrilla movement is unacceptable . . . the liberationist character of our struggle is undeniable given the United States' unprecedented military, economic, and political intervention in [El Salvador]."[78] In clarifying the nature of its insurrection, the FMLN rejected the equivalence that Esquipulas implied between them and the Contra.

For similar reasons, the Nicaraguan rebel leadership reacted negatively to the signing. "The Esquipulas document's main flaw," wrote Donald Castillo Rivas, "was its discriminatory treatment toward insurgent groups."[79] FDN leader Adolfo Calero was more blunt in his own memoir: "We concluded that some of the signatories had clear intentions to liquidate the Contra and leave Nicaragua to the wishes of the Sandinistas and their allies."[80] On the civilian side, Nicaragua's Coordinadora Democrática got much of the democratizing provisions it had sought from Esquipulas II but was denied its request for an invitation to the summit.[81] Though Esquipulas forced national governments to make dramatic concessions, they were rewarded by being legitimized over their internal opponents.

The Sandinista Signature

As top Sandinista diplomat Victor Hugo Tinoco noted, the basic Esquipulas formula was not entirely novel. The basic premise—democracy in exchange for peace and nonintervention—was roughly similar to the one offered, if disingenuously, by the Reagan administration via Thomas Enders in 1981, or the one promoted by the Contadora countries. "The solution was already there—what was missing were the conditions. . . . Exhaustion with the war, after years of military conflict and bloodshed, helped create the conditions to find a solution."[82]

For the Sandinista leadership, taking the deal was a major gamble. The Central American Peace Accords bound them to give a political foothold to opponents who wished to roll back revolutionary policies, and eventually accept the risk of being ousted in elections. Worse still, the US government vowed that it would continue supporting Contra military activities; these actually intensified in the months after the agreement was signed. Central American neighbors would be slow to implement promised changes, too. Nevertheless, the agreement was the only hope of saving a Revolution that, as its leaders often described in retrospect, had become "worn out." The Contras' own difficulties opened a window of opportunity; for the Sandinistas, the military balance of forces was unlikely to improve in the future.[83] In fact, the bellicose picture was scarcely sustainable. "If we had continued that way," Wheelock argued in retrospect, "maybe we would have lost the war. Perhaps we would have left power under far worse conditions."[84]

At a deeper level, the agreement achieved goals that the Sandinista Front had been pursuing since before they even took power. As the Somoza regime entered what turned out to be a terminal crisis in the late 1970s, the Sandinistas fought, in conjunction with international allies, for legitimacy as an alternative in the Nicaraguan political mainstream. Once they achieved leadership of the anti-Somoza cause inside their country, they sought acceptance in the international community as the rulers that would succeed the dictatorship. International legitimacy, we have seen, was a central component in the US-Nicaraguan confrontation during the civil war. Contadora may have failed as a peace architecture, but it successfully challenged US hegemony such that it paved the way for a peace settlement at the Central American level that recognized Managua as legitimate. And as this book's conclusion explores, that South–South initiative would deeply influence inter-American relations in the post–Cold War era.

The basic framework of the Esquipulas Accords showed that Managua's reintegration went together with another transformation: Central American elites' growing acceptance of democratic transitions as an acceptable outcome to conflicts that ran back decades. The Sandinista government's survival, combined with the persistence of left-wing insurgencies in other countries, was a key piece in the international pressure that drove right-wing Central American governments to liberalize. The FSLN, which seized power to redistribute wealth, had been swept up in another revolution: the generalization of liberal norms and electoral politics in Latin America. As the Sandinista period's final act suggests, the very meaning of revolution in Nicaragua would begin to change as a result.

8 The Revolution after the Central American Peace Accords

In October 1987, two months after signing the Central American Peace Accords in Guatemala, Nicaraguan president Daniel Ortega flew to Moscow to partake in celebrations for the seventieth anniversary of the October Revolution. In a private meeting with Ortega, Mikhail Gorbachev praised the Sandinistas' flexibility in coming to an agreement with their US-backed rivals. This must not have surprised the Nicaraguan leader. According to years' worth of correspondence reviewed by historian María Dolores Ferrero Blanco, Gorbachev consistently encouraged Sandinista Front leaders to respect the role of private business, provide institutional spaces for political opponents, and avoid provoking the United States. In at least one exchange, the Soviet premier warned Ortega against "skipping steps" in Nicaragua's revolutionary process. He tried his best to cushion calls for greater moderation: "this is what Lenin had taught," he wrote on another occasion, "not to copy him, but to learn from his experience."[1]

In prodding the FSLN along the path of the Esquipulas Accords, Soviet officials made clear that their government could not meet even the most basic of Nicaragua's requests for assistance. The *glasnost* and *perestroika* reforms destabilized their country's domestic politics, further depleting the capital required to maintain the same level of involvement in Central America. "We just don't have as much anymore as we would like to give," the Soviet ambassador in Managua told journalists in February 1988.[2] The decline of world communism as an alternative to liberal capitalism was therefore an important backdrop to significant changes that the Sandinista Revolution underwent in the final years of the 1980s.

Those changes were more directly tied to the terms and mechanisms of the Central American peace process. In the wake of their signing, the National Directorate accelerated reforms previously instituted to avert economic collapse and address the political foundations of the Contra War. Between 1987 and 1989 they reduced press censorship, negotiated with civilian opponents, and reached a cease-fire with the Contra. Perhaps most importantly, they took the liberal electoral logic of the 1984 elections to a new extreme: power in Nicaragua would be determined by popular vote, and the ruling FSLN could now *lose* to *anybody* in elections scheduled for 1990. The government also implemented market-based reforms that antici-pated the "neoliberal" structural adjustment policies of the post–Cold War era. In doing so, they unconsciously accepted that political goals—in this case, ending the war and ensuring the survival of their revolutionary move-ment by way of a democratic transition—came before the socioeconomic goal of structural, redistributive transformation. Slowly but surely, the Ni-caraguan leadership also walked back the idea of a revolution beyond its borders. Specifically, they progressively reduced their support for the rebel FMLN in El Salvador. As reformism proceeded apace in Nicaragua, inter-national momentum grew in favor of a negotiated settlement premised on nonintervention and political inclusion—though obstacles, of course, had to be surmounted at every turn.

Throughout this reform period, the Revolution's international support network in Latin America and Western Europe loudly encouraged the San-dinista Front to put in practice what the 1987 Nicaraguan Constitution said on paper: that Nicaragua, unlike revolutionary Cuba, was an ideologically plural, multiparty democracy. Indeed, what is striking about the 1987–89 period is that it saw the revolutionary leadership attempt a soft reboot of the alliances and governing program—nonalignment, political pluralism, and mixed economy—of 1979.[3] In doing so, Sandinista leaders consolidated significant differences with the Cuban communist paradigm of revolution, changing the terms of reference for Latin American revolutionary politics in the twilight years of the Cold War.

The Final Battle

The period between 1987 and 1990 was a distinct chapter in the history of the revolutionary government. It was "characterized," according to Coman-dante Jaime Wheelock of the National Directorate, "by liberalization aimed at strengthening the revolution's credibility and countering the policy of foreign aggressors. It was also directed at negotiating an end to the war and normalizing relations with Central American neighbors." Two main things, Wheelock adds, framed this reformist period. First, there was the signing of the August 1987 Esquipulas Agreements; immediately afterward, the Nica-raguan government loosened restrictions on press freedoms and held talks with civilian opponents. Second was the 1988 Sapoá Accords, which saw the Sandinista Popular Army strike a cease-fire with rebel leaders.[4] As the FSLN made measurable progress living up to commitments made at Esquipulas, the US Congress stopped sending lethal aid to anti-Sandinista insurgents, and Central American governments began phasing down their collaboration with the Contra program. By the time Reagan left office in January 1989, the US government had quietly accepted that it lacked the will to resist global and regional forces toward a negotiated settlement that would allow the Sandinistas to hold and potentially renew state power.

Within days of the Esquipulas II summit, the Sandinista government created a National Reconciliation Commission headed by the Catholic cardinal Miguel Obando y Bravo, a prominent critic. The Commission—which also included independent human rights organizations—paved the way for a national dialogue between the ruling FSLN and opposition parties, including those that had boycotted the 1984 elections. The government rejected many of the opposition's demands for electoral reforms and brushed aside calls to separate party and state—the fact of there being a "Sandinista Popular Army," rather than an apolitical Nicaraguan armed forces, was a recurring complaint. Nonetheless, national reconciliation bore tangible results by October, when a partial amnesty was declared.

Importantly, the FSLN allowed the vehemently anti-Sandinista daily *La Prensa*—which they had forcibly shuttered a year earlier—to recommence publishing.[5] FSLN leaders justified "temporary limitations" on press freedoms as a necessary measure to defend the Revolution against undue pressure from the US government, which funded the newspaper along with various civilian opposition groups.[6] Unfortunately for them, censorship provided US policymakers with an easy justification for aggression. It also sullied the Revolution's appeal in the eyes of foreign sympathizers like British Indian novelist Salman Rushdie, who visited the country the previous year. In his memoir of the trip, Rushdie praised the Sandinista leadership and program, but drew the line at their treatment of *La Prensa*, even though he disagreed with its anti-Sandinista and pro-Reagan editorial line. "The issue of press freedom," he wrote, "was the one on which I absolutely parted company with the Sandinistas." Unimpressed by their propaganda apparatus, he added that the FSLN daily *Barricada* was "the worst paper [he'd] seen in a long while."[7] *La Prensa's* reopening was therefore a significant marker of liberalization, though its chief executive—former Junta ally Violeta Barrios de Chamorro— remained suspicious of the government's intentions. In a handwritten missive a few months after her paper reopened, she complained to Óscar

Arias: "the Sandinistas have not wanted, nor do they want, to take advantage of the opportunity you have offered them."[8]

Though critics were as yet unsatisfied, the revolutionary government was clearly dropping many authoritarian tendencies. Before addressing the UN General Assembly on October 8, Comandante and President Daniel Ortega told reporters that if the United States stopped financing the Contra, the FSLN would accept a hypothetical electoral defeat: "If the people choose a different political party and form of government," he promised, "then there will be a different political party and form of government."[9] These assurances marked a significant departure from his brother Humberto's earlier claim that elections should only exist to "confirm" the power of the Revolution. Statements of openness, combined with liberalizing policy steps, allowed Óscar Arias to press more vociferously for the end of US aid to the Contra. In turn, as the Central American presidents made progress on that front, Sandinista leaders felt more comfortable making deeper alterations to their political system.

This dynamic deepened in October when Óscar Arias won the Nobel Peace Prize for his role in Esquipulas. Whereas Daniel Ortega expressed his "deep satisfaction" with the Nobel Committee's selection, the US government's response was mixed. In a speech before the Organization of American States, President Ronald Reagan complimented Arias's peacebuilding efforts—calling Esquipulas II "a step in the right direction"—and in the same breath criticized the agreement because it did not "address US security concerns in the region." Others were blunter. In Congress, Republican representative Newt Gingrich called the award "saddening." One State Department official scoffed that Arias "won the prize for de-funding the contras and taking an anti-American stance. It was largely a prize for defying the United States."[10] "Publicly, the Reagan administration refers to Arias in a cordial, friendly fashion," explained NSC staffer José Sorzano, "but actually, privately, they have a low opinion of him that borders on despising him."[11]

Esquipulas's global success threw another wrench in administration efforts to steer Contra aid legislation through Congress. Commenting on the future of further Contra funding, House Democratic whip Tony Coelho said, "This kills it; it's dead."[12] The Reagan administration did not give up so easily. But as Robert Pastor explains, after 1987, "Congress refused because the majority correctly believed that the Central American peace plan would fail if such aid were provided."[13] Arias, meanwhile, believed "the most important thing was to end Contra aid."[14] By the time the Costa Rican won the Nobel Prize, Speaker Jim Wright—having concluded that the White

House would ultimately oppose any agreement that gave the Sandinistas a path to remaining in power—circumvented the executive and began working directly with Central American governments. At the UN General Assembly meetings in New York in October 1987, he discussed with Daniel Ortega the steps Nicaragua might take to ensure Congress supported Esquipulas instead of renewed Contra aid. Personally insulted, Reagan jeered at the Democratic leader for abandoning the Reagan-Wright Plan in favor of a "Wright-Ortega Plan."[15]

In January 1988, the five Central American presidents met again, this time in a suburb of San José, the Costa Rican capital. At Esquipulas III, as it came to be known, Ortega reiterated his promise to step down if the FSLN lost the national elections envisioned by the 1987 agreement. He also announced an expanded amnesty, the release of additional political prisoners, and the lifting of the country's long-running state of emergency.[16] Most importantly, following a suggestion made by Jim Wright, Ortega went a step further and declared that his government would hold cease-fire talks with Contra leaders, regardless of whether the US stopped disbursing aid to the insurgents.[17] In recognition of Nicaragua's concessions, Arias made an ultimatum to Contra leaders based in Costa Rica: resign from your political posts, or leave the country. Later in January, Ortega toured Western Europe to rally international opposition against continued Contra aid ahead of a crucial vote in Washington over the matter.[18]

Having apparently received the messages coming from Costa Rica, the US House of Representatives narrowly rejected Contra aid in February 1988.[19] They did so despite bombastic allegations by Roger Miranda Bengoechea, a senior EPS official who defected to the United States, claiming that the FSLN was still intervening in El Salvador and did not plan on complying with the security commitments made at Esquipulas.[20] Within weeks of the vote in Congress, the Contra's CIA supply lines were interrupted.[21] National Security Adviser Colin Powell had traveled to San José to convince Duarte and Azcona to abandon the agreement and threatened the termination of US aid programs if they did not reverse course. According to Arias, Powell's visit was the last time that Duarte's and Azcona's will was tested. He told the Honduran and Salvadoran presidents that Powell was right to worry that their Nicaraguan counterpart might fail to honor his side of the deal. Arias also acknowledged the difficulties that Duarte and Azcona might face if they lost their generous US financial backing. "But if we do not comply," he assured them, "the war will continue and that is a luxury that nobody can afford."[22] The US government had succeeded in destabilizing the Nicaraguan government, but they could not stop it from securing its place in Central America's political mainstream.

The Sandinista Front's position in international negotiations depended, of course, on their military standing. In 1979, the FSLN's predominance inside Nicaragua reflected its total victory over Somoza's National Guard. Once consolidated in power, their political possibilities were determined by their security forces' ability to keep US-backed insurgents from seizing a major foothold. Later, the 1984 elections demonstrated that war, revolution, and diplomacy went hand in hand. Before Sandinista–Contra talks finally took place toward the end of the decade, both sides took to the battlefield to improve their positions. In December 1987, Contra commanders carried out their most ambitious maneuvers in taking the mining towns of Bonanza and Siuna in Nicaragua's North Caribbean region (Sandinista reinforcements retook these small urban centers within twenty-four hours).[23] The government, for its part, ordered the Sandinista Popular Army to execute a major strike in the spring. For two weeks in early March, Operation Danto—named after a fallen FSLN commander from the insurrectionary period—saw 3,000 soldiers mobilized for combat along the Honduran border. Ostensibly, Sandinista forces sought to destroy Contra camps and supply lines on both sides of the Coco River, which forms the border with Honduras.[24] But as Army Chief of Staff Joaquín Cuadra later put it, Danto 88 was a "military action planned for a political purpose."[25] It was to be "the final battle in the war" before peace talks, he declared, "and the final battle had to be ours."[26] Curiously, the Honduran military refused to stop Sandinista columns from entering their territory on various occasions between 1986 and 1988, all clear violations of the spirit and letter of Esquipulas. The Reagan administration deployed 3,000 marines to Honduras in response to the spring 1988 "border invasion," but Azcona coyly refused to acknowledge the incident as such, and only requested American assistance upon pressure from US officials.[27]

On March 21, as Operation Danto came to a close, the Sandinistas and Contras finally met face-to-face at Sapoá, a small fishing village on the coast of Lake Nicaragua near the Costa Rican border. Daniel Ortega and Cardinal Miguel Obando, who had been tasked with organizing the talks, exchanged feisty letters in the run-up to the encounter; in the event that the promised cease-fire fell through, each side was eager to blame the other.[28] FSLN and Contra commanders publicly boasted that their final attacks showed their respective sides were winning the war. But the truth was that both armies—deprived of their respective superpower patronage—were willing to make the concessions necessary for a suspension of hostilities. "Sapoá was our only hope," admitted Contra leader Adolfo Calero.[29]

For the Sandinistas, merely acknowledging the Contra was a significant concession. Government propaganda suggested that when it came to US-backed insurgents, the FSLN would only "speak with its rifles." To hold direct talks was a major about-face; as Alejandro Bendaña explained, "whereas before we had been saying we don't talk to the monkeys but [rather] to the zookeepers, now we were going to have to talk to the monkeys."[30] Additionally, by inviting OAS secretary general João Clemente Baena Soares, the government accepted the principle of international mediation of internal disputes.[31] Most importantly, the talks signaled a deeper recognition that Nicaragua's armed conflict was more like a civil war, with local dimensions and causes, than the Sandinistas had previously cared to admit Unlike the 1973 Peace Accords in Paris that brought an end to the first phase of the Vietnamese revolutionary wars, US officials only played a background role. Contra leader Alfredo César, formerly president of the Central Bank under the Sandinista government, resisted pressure by US officials to abort the talks. "These were real Nicaraguan negotiations," he said, noting that there was "a special nationalism" in the Sandinista–Contra talks.[32]

The Sapoá agreement saw the FSLN finally recognize the Nicaraguan Resistance (an overarching title that brought together disparate Contra columns under one label) as a legitimate political force, a fact that some insurgent leaders saw as their greatest achievement.[33] In signing the March 23 Sapoá Accords, however, the Contra—like the Central American countries the previous year—also recognized the Sandinista government as having a mandate to rule through the rest of Daniel Ortega's term, scheduled to end in 1990.[34]

Beyond the politics of legitimacy, the Sapoá Accords involved a concrete quid pro quo designed to wind down the war. The government invited demobilized Contra leaders to join the national dialogue as legitimate political actors, began drafting a general amnesty law, and promised the safe return of dissident exiles. For Alejandro Bendaña, both parties' acceptance of an amnesty signaled a mutual acknowledgment that "there were no angels on either side" of the war (it also deprived future generations of the opportunity to hold military leaders accountable for their abuses).[35] For their part, the Contra agreed to relocate their forces to mutually agreed "enclaves" from which the Sandinista Popular Army would keep a safe distance. While the Sapoá agreement immediately led to a substantial reduction in both fighting and human rights violations, it did not end the war altogether. As

Bendaña suggests, rather than a full-fledged peace agreement, Sapoá was "a sort of temporary cease-fire that kept renewing itself. The real peace agreement [as Esquipulas envisioned] was the election."[36]

Indeed, during the summer of 1988, tensions persisted. While many in Washington were ready to abandon the Contra, key officials—notably Assistant Secretary of State Elliot Abrams—sought to undermine the agreement and reinvigorate the insurgent military threat. The Sapoá talks exacerbated existing divisions within the Contra; some insurgent leaders refused to demobilize, seeing the terms of the cease-fire as an unacceptable form of surrender. The temperature was also high on the political front. In July, Nicaraguan security forces arrested dozens of anti-government protesters, including several high-profile opposition politicians, at a large rally in the town of Nandaime. The same month, authorities temporarily suspended *La Prensa* and expelled US ambassador Richard Melton (Carlos Tünnerman, the Nicaraguan ambassador to the United States, was likewise forced to leave Washington). All these parties, the Sandinistas argued, were guilty of instigating violence and making bad-faith criticisms of the government's compliance with the peace agreements.[37] Progress toward peace had been made, but the threats of war, intervention, and authoritarian regression remained present.

Globally, however, Sapoá reinforced support for a negotiated settlement. For one, the Contadora and Support Group countries praised the Sapoá settlement and agreed to participate in its International Verification Commission.[38] Meanwhile, the cease-fire helped drive a final nail in the coffin of US lethal aid to the Contra. In late March, US lawmakers approved a Contra aid package that consisted exclusively of humanitarian assistance, medicine, and financial assistance for cease-fire monitoring.[39] When the Reagan administration made another last-ditch attempt for lethal aid in August, the legislature once again declined.[40] That summer, Secretary of State George Schultz traveled to Central America but failed to persuade governments to denounce Nicaragua's alleged noncompliance with Esquipulas.[41]

As the previous chapter demonstrated, several factors beyond the Iran-Contra scandal had frustrated Reagan officials' hope of removing the Sandinista Front through military force. As the president's second term wound down in mid-1988, a pessimistic CIA analysis noted how the government in Managua had skillfully navigated its way out of a quagmire in the context of the Central American Peace Accords: "developments in recent months have considerably enhanced [the FSLN's] chances of consolidating Marxist-Leninist rule. Their improved prospects result not only from the recent denial of continued US military assistance to the antigovernment insurgents, but also from their success in skillfully pursuing more flexible policies in dealing with their domestic opposition, the leaders of the other Central American nations, and international pressures and opinions."[42] Mexican Foreign Ministry analysts, commenting on the state of the Contra at roughly the same time, reached similar conclusions and declared the defeat of Reagan's intervention: "The United States supported Nicaragua's counterrevolutionaries in a bid to establish a 'democratic' regime which is compatible—politically and ideologically—with the other Central American governments and with US hegemony. The economic assistance they provided to the counterrevolution has not achieved the desired objectives; on the contrary, the government in Managua has channeled the aggression to which it is subject toward its external and internal consolidation."[43]

Thus, when Reagan's Republican successor George H. W. Bush took office in January 1989, the incoming president did not continue the policy of all-out aggression. Instead, Bush brought his administration closer to Congress on Central America policy, putting on a more cooperative face at the OAS and appointing Bernard Aronson (a Democrat, albeit one who supported Contra aid legislation) to replace Elliot Abrams (a vociferous opponent of Esquipulas and Sapoá) as assistant secretary of state for the Western Hemisphere. The new White House retained official skepticism of FSLN intentions, maintained economic sanctions and military threats, and refused to abandon the Contra altogether. But the change in administration marked a shift in the US approach toward Esquipulas. Washington would now devote a greater share of its resources toward funding civilian opponents who could undermine the Sandinistas by competing with them through institutional channels.

Defining the Revolution's Future

In February 1989, a longtime player in revolutionary Nicaragua—Carlos Andrés Pérez—was sworn in for a second term as president of Venezuela. The Sandinistas' erstwhile fellow traveler took the occasion to press his guest, Daniel Ortega, to make deeper democratic reforms. Other FSLN allies abroad, such as the Spanish Socialist Party, still spoke of Nicaragua's revolutionaries in a sympathetic register, but warned that their "support is not unrestricted; rather, it will be maintained if and when the Sandinistas continue giving signs of a real democratic opening."[44] The FSLN's entire international support network—including, notably, Soviet officials—pushed the leadership to live up to the 1987 Constitution, the logic established by the 1984 elections, and, ultimately, the entire project of political pluralism, mixed economy, and nonalignment they championed in 1979. The Sandinista leadership viewed these reforms as risky but also necessary to save the future of the Revolution.

Later in February 1989, a fourth Central American summit was held at the beach resort town of Costa del Sol (also known as Tesoro Beach) in El Salvador. This meeting saw key pieces fall into place for the implementation of the Esquipulas Accords. Nicaragua, all parties agreed, would hold elections no later than February 1990—several months earlier than the date stipulated by the 1987 Constitution. The elections would be administered by the Nicaraguan government's own Supreme Electoral Council, which as part of the Costa del Sol accords adopted new regulations to ensure the ability of "political parties to organize and to be politically active in the broadest sense."[45] At all stages of the electoral process, international observers from the OAS, UN, and Carter Center (a nongovernmental organization founded by ex-US president Jimmy Carter devoted to democracy promotion) would verify its authenticity and fairness. This unprecedented level of monitoring was a sign of an expanding mandate for the OAS—which had deployed mostly token observation missions in the past—and other multilateral organizations to uphold democracy in the region.[46] In exchange for Nicaragua's decision to hold early elections, the Central American presidents agreed to draft a joint plan, supported by the UN, to finally demobilize Contra forces and peacefully repatriate those in Honduras back to Nicaragua. In practice, however, Central American countries could only do so much to dismantle the Contra because the Bush administration was solidly against its demobilization.

Still, the Contra increasingly found itself in a corner; for the Sandinistas, the danger of being ousted by votes slowly replaced the threat of military defeat. And given what polls were suggesting in 1989, this seemed like favorable terrain. Just four months out from the elections, one survey found the FSLN leading 36 to 18 percent. An unusual 42 percent of voters said they were undecided or abstained from answering; Sandinista strategists assumed that the government's approval ratings (50.7 percent said the FSLN had "brought improvement to the country") would translate into a sufficient share of the vote that was up for grabs.[47] The incumbent ticket of Daniel Ortega and Sergio Ramírez would go up against former Junta colleague Violeta Barrios de Chamorro, who was only nominated in August 1989 by an opposition that was bitterly divided: between those who stayed in

Nicaragua during the 1980s and those who fled, between those who previously worked with the Sandinistas and those who stood against them from the beginning, and between elite interest groups and grassroots opponents of the FSLN. By contrast, at a massive FSLN convention in September, Ortega saw his platform of continued revolutionary gains confirmed by rapturous unanimity. Therefore, though Chamorro enjoyed the sympathy of former FSLN allies abroad such as Carlos Andrés Pérez, with whom she met publicly while that convention took place, the Sandinistas had good reason to believe that their democratizing gamble had paid off.[48] In retrospect, many Sandinista leaders have commented that a key reason for holding clean elections was their belief that they would likely win them and see their rule legitimized as a result.[49] In fact, many US officials and UNO campaign leaders thought that the Sandinistas would prevail; for the latter, participation in the 1990 elections was part of a long-term strategy to oust the FSLN through parliamentary opposition and future campaigns for the presidency.[50]

Slowly but surely, both sides made further concessions to make possible the elections of February 1990. At a National Dialogue meeting in August 1989, the FSLN promised to expand amnesty for political prisoners; they also reached an agreement with opposition leaders over the logistics of vote counting. In return, the opposition UNO campaign formally promised not to boycott the elections and called on the Contra to demobilize by December. That same month, at yet another Esquipulas conference, Honduras and Nicaragua reached a bilateral agreement that saw the former agree to begin disbanding remaining Contra camps on its territory.[51] When Ortega made one last trip across the Atlantic in the summer of 1989, European countries promised to send aid after the peaceful celebration of the 1990 elections (Óscar Arias was still raising concerns about fair conditions), the outcome of which they swore to respect.[52] In November 1989, the United Nations Security Council established a mission to Central America (United Nations Observer Group in Central America [ONUCA]), designed to help verify regional governments' compliance with the security provisions of Esquipulas.

The Sandinistas' main concern was that the Bush administration would not play along. As William Robinson argued, Ronald Reagan's exit did not exactly mean an end to US intervention in Nicaragua. The US Congress and the new White House team funded the opposition through institutions such as the National Endowment for Democracy (NED) (though the extent to which this funding mattered for the final vote, Robinson conceded, "is open to question").[53] The more serious problem was that the Sandinistas could not feel certain that the Bush administration would respect the outcome of the elections in the event they won. Despite calls by both Central American countries and the opposition UNO campaign, the Contra had not demobilized and, in fact, remained largely intact through the entirety of the presidential campaign. Honduras should not fulfill its promise to dismantle the Contra camps, the White House argued, because the US-backed insurgents were the only guarantee that the Nicaraguan government would hold real elections in good faith.[54] While the opposition understandably felt disadvantaged by "the FSLN's control over the state apparatus and coercive power over the population," Comandante Humberto Ortega noted, continued US support for the Contra was like "a gun against the head" of Sandinismo.[55]

Helping matters was a tacit agreement between Washington and Moscow developed over the course of 1989. When Bush and Soviet premier Mikhail Gorbachev held a summit in Malta in December of that year, their respective camps had already come up with a simple deal regarding Central America: the USSR would promise to stop sending weapons that Nicaragua might then provide to guerrillas in El Salvador; in exchange, the Bush administration would promise to recognize a new Sandinista government if the FSLN won the February 1990 elections.[56] Having previously treated Nicaragua as a battleground in a war to roll back Soviet communism, some US officials now saw it as a tool for normalizing East–West tensions. On a trip to Moscow, Aronson found the Soviets in a cooperative mood: "What we said to them was that this was going to be the first test of Gorbachev's new thinking in foreign policy and it would make a difference to this new administration if they cooperated in support of Esquipulas."[57] As Robert Pastor notes, the US and USSR had by this point already reduced their involvement with warring factions in Nicaragua. One major takeaway from the Malta summit, then, "was that neither superpower had much direct influence on events in Nicaragua."[58] But even though Moscow–Washington talks did not determine the end of the Nicaraguan civil war, decreased superpower tensions were important for the eventual success of a negotiated settlement. "It's not by chance," Deputy Foreign Relations Minister Victor Hugo Tinoco noted, "that the dismantling of the ideological, East–West conflict toward the end of the 1980s facilitated the dismantling of the wars in Central America and Nicaragua."[59]

For example, Soviet officials worked to make sure that the FSLN continued walking the path opened by the Esquipulas Accords. The Washington–Moscow concordat was not entirely comforting to the Sandinista leadership;

as Alejandro Bendaña explained, the terms of the agreement were suboptimal for the FSLN, because the USSR assumed a concrete commitment (to send no further armaments to Nicaragua) in exchange for an intangible, "vague understanding that Washington would live with whatever government came out of the election."[60] Nonetheless, with Bush's verbal promise in hand, socialist countries were better positioned to push the Sandinistas to comply with the terms of Esquipulas by taking steps such as reducing Cuban presence in the EPS. "The Cubans," Bendaña noted, "were probably among the most moderate in terms of trying to push and induce the Sandinistas to accept, to make the compromises that were necessary, particularly with the advent of perestroika when things were going to be . . . quite different. There was solidarity, but within the context of solidarity there was always this push for caution."[61]

"The Soviets," he added, "were even pushier in this regard." In March 1989, Comandante Henry "Modesto" Ruíz met with Soviet foreign minister Eduard Shevardnadze in Moscow. Soviet news agencies reported after the encounter that "both sides expressed the conviction that the mechanism of negotiations, created by the Guatemala agreement, was at the present time the most effective means of bringing about a political settlement."[62] In October, Shevardnadze visited Managua and reiterated the Soviet policy of cutting military assistance to Nicaragua. In a public appearance, he enthusiastically endorsed the moderate posture that the revolutionary government assumed in the context of the Central American Peace Accords. "We have been greatly impressed," he said in a speech, "with your government's programs for economic stabilization; this is a realistic program," referring to market-based reforms undertaken to combat hyperinflation. "Stability in the region," he warned, "required the maintenance of a balance of forces, under which each Central American country should not keep more troops than its defense requires." Finally, the FSLN should, he insisted, respect the outcome of elections.[63] Meanwhile, Yuri Pavlov—the USSR's vice foreign minister for Latin American affairs—told the Mexican ambassador in Moscow that it was official Soviet policy, as part of its rapprochement with the United States, to support elections in Nicaragua and to urge the Sandinistas to cease assisting the FMLN's military activities in El Salvador; he repeated the same message to numerous Nicaraguan counterparts.[64] Victor Hugo Tinoco said the Sandinistas received these messages loud and clear: "when Shevardnadze came, he was clear: You have to negotiate. You have to find a negotiated exit because we will not be continuing [our involvement]."[65]

Shevardnadze's advice highlights how much revolutionary Nicaragua was changing in a very short time span. As Sergio Ramírez writes in his memoir, Esquipulas changed the revolutionary process from without. Unsurprisingly, because they entailed abandonment of core principles and concessions to sworn enemies, these changes alarmed some sectors of the Sandinista leadership. A document prepared by the Sandinista Assembly for the FSLN National Directorate, titled "The Results of Esquipulas II," evidenced the bleakest interpretation of the peace settlement held by members of the ruling party. The report recognized the good news that the Contra had lost financing from the US Congress thanks to the agreement. But the price had been too high: "Current geopolitical and internal conditions," they concluded, "do not allow for continued revolutionary conquests . . . the concessions we have made via Esquipulas II and the talks with the Contra have put us in a straitjacket." The report complained to the National Directorate that "the opening of press liberties has caused grave damage to revolutionary institutional life." Worse still, "popular sectors in Central America seem to be satisfied with the concepts of 'bourgeois democratization' contained in Arias' Plan." Summarizing their concerns, they wrote: "Esquipulas II was useful for us insofar as it allowed us to convince Óscar Arias of our desire to participate in a negotiated solution to the Central American conflict, with the intention of winning time and political space among European and Latin American democracies. Nonetheless, the situation has turned itself on us. Esquipulas II has created conditions which are contradictory to the consolidation of the revolutionary process and has set back the Central American revolutionary process by decades. . . . No US president will allow us to consolidate our historical project, nor spread it through the area."[66] Some FSLN commanders expressed concern to Soviet officials that reforms had moved too quickly and destabilized their position as a result.[67]

But there was no turning back now. Reformism was inextricably tied to domestic and international realities. It was the only way to avoid the government's collapse and allow the Revolution to live and fight another day.[68] Desperate economic reforms were a case in point. In 1988—the economy's worst year, when per capita GDP declined by 13.9 percent—state planners secretly implemented a massive currency devaluation called "Operation Bertha," further loosed exchange rate policies, slashed government spending, and lifted wage and price controls as part of a "liberalization of the economy."[69] According to top Sandinista economist Alejandro Martínez Cuenca, these polices were neither imposed by international lending institutions such as the International Monetary Fund (IMF), nor inspired by a particular economic theory or doctrine. "We had no alternative," he wrote, given the hyperinflation that the country was experiencing. The abandonment of central planning (some of which had been influenced by Eastern European models) and major redistributive projects anticipated the neoliberal fervor of the post–Cold War 1990s. They also highlighted a "recurrent theme" in the revolutionary period that sociologist Dennis Gilbert described at the time: "the tension between the Marxist ideology of the FSLN and the pragmatic compromises the party has made as it confronted Nicaraguan realities."[70] Much like political liberalization, economic liberalization was accelerated by the Central American Peace Accords. Martínez Cuenca recalled that Esquipulas "opened up a window to the possibility for peace and, with that, there were greater possibilities to manage the economic affairs of the country in a decisive way. With the Esquipulas Accords as a background, it was possible to have a more meaningful influence over the deteriorating economic situation, which, in my opinion, was as big a threat as the counterrevolution. . . . The people's goal of peace helped the leaders of the revolution become convinced that the economic crisis and inflation, in particular, were eroding the social base."[71]

By the end of their decade in power, Nicaragua's revolutionary leaders had modified their strategic goals. The substantial realignment of Nicaragua's class structure, the eradication of poverty and inequality, were no longer on the table in the short or medium term. "The intimate conscience of socialism was defeated by reality," Ramírez said looking back. Instead, the goal was to end the country's civil war and preserve Sandinismo as a political force by way of a democratic transition. "And so the tactical promises of political pluralism," Ramírez added, "ended up being honored out of a need for survival. It was necessity which led to loyalty to those principles, which are not the ones that the Revolution wanted."[72] The political and ideological arc of the Revolution must be placed in international context: whereas in 1979 most of Latin America was ruled by military dictatorships, a decade later a majority of its countries had adopted liberal electoral democracy. The decline of Soviet communism as a "credible alternative" to liberal capitalism, as well as Nicaragua's entanglement with wars and peace processes elsewhere in Central America, had also contributed.[73]

The Sandinista project formed part of a long-running revolutionary tradition in Latin America. Several decades earlier, the fall of Mexico's *porfirista* dictatorship inaugurated what historians Gilbert Joseph and Greg Grandin have called a "century of revolution," characterized by "sequential attempts to transcend what by the early twentieth century had become an

unsustainable model of exclusionary nationalism, restricted political institutions, persisting rural clientelism and dependent, export-based development."[74] The Mexican Revolution influenced a vast, ideologically diverse
range of revolutionary movements across the continent, from the populisms
of Getulio Vargas and Juán Domingo Perón in Argentina and Brazil, respectively, to the revolutionary reformism of the Arévalo and Árbenz governments in Guatemala. In the second half of the century, the Cuban Revolution
carried forward and expanded the ideal of revolutionary politics but supplanted the Mexican one as the main point of reference: henceforth, revolutionary politics in the region became more closely and uniformly tied to
the Marxist goal of permanently challenging the capitalist system. This
chapter in the regional revolutionary tradition was varied, as well. In Peru,
for example, left-wing military officers seized power and tried to make revolution from the barracks; in Chile, the election of Salvador Allende briefly
saw socialism hold power via democratic elections.

The Sandinista National Liberation Front, which was indebted to a great
variety of historical leftist experiences, wound up having an ambivalent
relationship with the Cuban Revolution. On the one hand, it was the movement that most closely resembled Castro's path to building socialism,
because it rose to power through armed struggle. In that sense, the Nicaraguan episode helped solidify Cuba's centrality to the Latin American
Left. But on the other hand, the Nicaraguan Revolution presented Cuba's
revolutionary paradigm with an "inescapable paradox," as Cuban historian
Rafael Rojas put it. Once in power, the Sandinistas promised and ended up
institutionalizing elements that were entirely foreign to Cuba's model and
1976 constitution: private property rights, political parties, ideological pluralism, and human rights philosophy, among other things.[75] These differences between the two projects were there from the beginning. But the
1987 Constitution was a turning point, nonetheless; as Humberto Ortega
put it, the new constitution saw the Revolution "clearly accept market economics and political pluralism" and re-affirm its distance from "the
political system of the communist bloc."[76] The document therefore marked
an important milestone in the transition of Latin America's Left to the politics of electoral democracy.

Conclusion

In October 1989, US president Bush referred to his Nicaraguan counterpart, Daniel Ortega, as "an unwanted animal at a garden party" after the

Sandinista leader made incendiary remarks at a summit in San José. Scholars have noted that behind this kind of derogatory zoomorphism lay a belief in Latin American inferiority that had long characterized US elites' approach to their southern counterparts.[77] The international history of the Nicaraguan Revolution invites us to flip the script and ask how Latin American leaders viewed US policymakers. In 1979, group action by a Latin American coalition undermined US policy in Central America and supported the rise of a government in Managua that was not aligned with Washington. The Contadora process, which saw most regional governments reject US aggression against the Sandinistas, was a second collective break with the regional hegemon. Finally, the Central American Peace Process unfolded in such a way that the United States was unable to dictate matters—curiously, at a time when the Soviet Union was withdrawing and the bipolar world order was on the verge of giving way to something that, on the surface, looked like unipolarity. Latin American autonomy, of course, had stark limits. Luis Guillermo Solís explained how the Central American Peace Accords managed US interests (regional elites have animal metaphors, too): "The United States was never absent [in the Esquipulas Process], and it couldn't be absent because the hegemonic power can't be absent. I have sometimes compared the presence of the United States in Central America in these times to that of an enormous elephant in your living room. You can try to put a curtain over it, you can pretend it's not there, you can walk by and not look at it—but you know that it's there."[78]

Beyond the realm of US-Nicaraguan relations, the final stage of the Revolution was backdropped by developments in the socialist camp, Western Europe, Latin America, and, most importantly, Central America. For example, the changing shape of the Revolution in 1989 depended on the development of the Salvadoran civil war, and vice versa. In the first half of the 1980s, the rebel leadership of the FMLN had set their sights on the outright defeat of El Salvador's US-backed government, with the hope of taking power and implementing a socialist-inspired reform agenda. But as the decade wore on, the *farabundista* leadership increasingly departed from Marxist positions and revised its strategic goal: it would now settle for the demilitarization of the Salvadoran government and a liberal-democratic transition through which the FMLN could legally participate in politics. Historian Joaquín Chávez notes that one reason for this programmatic and ideological shift was the movement's growing ties with the Socialist International and other social democratic groups in Western Europe and Latin America, something that paralleled the Sandinistas' own experience navigating the international arena.[79] The Esquipulas Process was relevant, too. By drawing an equivalence between the FMLN and the Contra, an irregular army that the agreement sought to delegitimize, the Esquipulas Accords complicated the original goal of violently seizing power. But it made the new goal of building a democratic transition more feasible. In the context of the accords, President Alfredo Cristiani of the right-wing ARENA (Alianza Republicana Nacionalista)—elected in March 1989 elections that saw the defeat of Duarte's Christian Democrats—promised to negotiate peace with the guerrillas. With that said, the ARENA government—closely aligned with the military and conservative economic elites—was very slow to offer tangible concessions.[80]

In November 1989, barely months away from Nicaragua's February 1990 elections, the FMLN launched one last "final offensive." While they once again failed to spark a popular insurrection, the guerrillas managed to temporarily seize significant parts of San Salvador, the capital city. The rebel offensive also forced a chaotic regime response; an indiscriminate wave of repression culminated in death squads' murder of several Catholic priests and intellectuals who helped run the Universidad Centroamericana, a prestigious Jesuit university. Though it did not succeed in toppling the government, the final offensive proved that the US-backed military was unable to rout the armed Left. Thus, the realization of strategic parity set the stage for more serious negotiations between the FMLN and the Cristiani government.[81] The Sandinista leadership had carefully weighed the risks and opportunities presented by the 1989 Final Offensive; they had come to view support for the FMLN as a "bargaining chip for finding a way out of the war in Nicaragua," as Victor Hugo Tinoco put it.[82] They could not push too hard, though, because as Humberto Ortega later wrote, Nicaraguan support in the Final Offensive (which they doubted would succeed) might give the Salvadoran government a pretext to walk out on the Esquipulas Process.[83] In fact, El Salvador broke diplomatic relations with Nicaragua in November, alleging that the Sandinistas provided the guerrillas with surface-to-air missiles.[84] But Cristiani still attended the final Esquipulas meeting the following month in San Isidro de Coronado, Costa Rica. Hoping to revive Central American plans to finish demobilizing the Contra before the 1990 elections, Daniel Ortega backed the democratic legitimacy of President Cristiani and formally announced his government's disapproval of the failed FMLN offensive at the summit.[85] In doing so, the Sandinistas once again walked back the idea of a revolution beyond their borders, and even marked distance from the ideal of violently overthrowing a reactionary government;

both the FMLN and Guatemalan URNG reacted with dismay. Left-wing revolutionary politics were entering a new era in Latin America.

While the specter of civil war flickered and faded in El Salvador, the long-feared US invasion finally happened—in Panama. The country's de facto military leader, Manuel Noriega, had previously developed a good working relationship with US security agencies after rising to power in the wake of Omar Torrijos's abrupt death in 1981. Key American officials turned a blind eye to Noriega's human rights abuses—as well as his notorious ties to regional drug traffickers—because he collaborated with US anti-communist policies in Central America. Even as the Panamanian government cosponsored the Contadora process, Noriega provided the CIA with information on Sandinista activities, supported a Contra faction's drug smuggling to help it raise funds, and even offered to sabotage Nicaraguan facilities in exchange for cash.[86] But not everybody in Washington was willing to stomach the relationship. One turning point was Panamanian security forces' 1985 assassination of Hugo Spadafora (a left-wing Noriega critic who, incidentally, had fought alongside the Sandinistas during the insurrection and later against them in Edén Pastora's column of the Contra). Noriega also became caught in the transition from the War on Communism to the War on Drugs; as the latter became more important in US domestic and foreign policy, the Panamanian leader became a liability in Washington. Perhaps more so than strategic anxieties over the fate of the Panama Canal, domestic and political considerations motivated Operation Just Cause, which saw US military forces invade Panama and quickly capture their former ally in December 1989.[87] As Greg Grandin noted, it had been justified "in the name of democracy" instead of being framed as a response to an imminent communist threat; the fall of the Berlin Wall on the eve of the invasion had allowed Washington to "go on the ideological and moral offense."[88] It had therefore been a quick, "post–Cold War invasion," albeit one that contrasted strangely with the slow, grinding, and ultimately frustrated effort to depose a left-wing, socialist camp-leaning government in nearby Nicaragua.

While Noriega was a pariah in Latin America (the Contadora Group expelled Panama in 1988), regional elites mostly repudiated the unilateral invasion. Among other things, it raised fears that it would jeopardize Central America's progress toward peace. The Mexican novelist Carlos Fuentes wrote: "What happened in Panama must be alarming for Nicaragua and its dual process toward peace and democracy. If the elections in February do not see a victory for Washington's official candidate, will Bush feel authorized to intervene in order to restore democracy? The war has not yet ended in El Salvador. Internal conflicts in Guatemala are becoming more visible and explosive by the day. Will the United States once again be the one who determines the future course of those countries?"[89] As it happens, the invasion *was* alarming to Nicaraguan leaders. They responded with a full-throated defense of Panamanian sovereignty, matching rhetoric with a decision to dispatch tanks to intimidate the US embassy in Managua. Before escalating the situation any further, reason prevailed; had they responded to the crisis by suspending the February elections, Humberto Ortega later said, the Sandinistas would have fallen into a "mortal trap."[90] Looking back, it is somewhat surprising that the FSLN was so sympathetic to Noriega's plight in the first place. When asked if the National Directorate knew about his enthusiastic collaboration with the Contra program, Jaime Wheelock replied: "The truth is that we had heard Noriega in some way could be involved in this. But we didn't believe it. And the truth is that he would give *us* information about many other things—information he had from Oliver North and military officials that were in Honduras."[91]

As 1990 dawned, the world around the Sandinistas looked very much different from the one they navigated when they first took power. So, too, had revolutionary Nicaragua changed. In some ways, the Esquipulas-era Revolution was quite a departure from the principles and goals espoused by FSLN leaders in the early revolutionary years. In other ways, it looked like a return to a vision of government they created along with their allies in the struggle against Somoza. The February 1990 elections would be a final test of the Revolution's political identity.

Conclusion

Fall of the Sandinistas and the Twilight of the Cold War

• •

The Sandinista Front was going to win. Just days before the 1990 elections, a *Washington Post*/ABC poll gave Comandante Daniel Ortega and Sergio Ramírez a sixteen-point lead over Violeta Barrios de Chamorro and her running mate, Virgilio Godoy.[1] Cabinet official and party boss Nicho Marenco recalled Sandinista military leaders gathering on election day itself—February 25, 1990—to place bets on the result; the question was not if, but by *how much* they would win.[2] The FSLN needed a big margin—and a widespread sense of fairness, sustained by full opposition participation and guaranteed by thousands of foreign journalists and electoral monitors—for the results to stick.[3] Sandinista leaders believed a clean victory would finally afford them the stability and domestic legitimacy required to govern effectively.[4] US foreign policy would continue posing a threat, but surely the elections would be a turning point in the relationship. As Nicaraguans filled polling stations, Daniel Ortega—in a gesture of good will—invited US president George H. W. Bush to attend his inauguration.[5]

As day turned to night, however, Ortega must have worried that the invitation had been premature. Comandante Henry "Modesto" Ruiz thought it strange that at 8 P.M., the celebrations had not yet begun. Soon afterward the FSLN high command was summoned to Comandante Humberto Ortega's office at the Loma de Tiscapa, the former hilltop bunker and residence of Nicaragua's previous ruler, Anastasio Somoza Debayle. Internal monitors were suggesting that Ortega and Ramírez were losing even in some Sandinista strongholds; the national picture was correspondingly bleak.[6] In light of the numbers coming in (the opposition UNO had picked up the lion's share of the undecided vote; Chamorro would go on to defeat the incumbent 55 to 41 percent), there was little or no debate among the National Directorate about recognizing the results. Given that the Sandinista Front had already signaled its inability to continue the war, refusing to accept defeat would have been "total suicide," Comandante Luis Carrión recalls. "The little we had won," he said, "we would have lost altogether."[7] Ortega privately conceded defeat in the middle of the night and made the concession public by sunrise the following day.

First, there was shock. "Laying in my hammock," Culture Minister Ernesto Cardenal recalled, "I struggled to understand God's will."[8] Next, adjustment to a new reality. US military intervention was no longer an immediate threat. George H. W. Bush, who enjoyed a good personal relationship with Chamorro, promised to ask Congress for reconstruction aid. Inside Nicaragua, a transition protocol saw Contra commanders bury their weapons in a symbolic ceremony, while the Sandinista Popular Army reorganized as a downsized Nicaraguan Armed Forces, perhaps the first nonpartisan military in the country's history. Antonio Lacayo Oyanguren—Barrios de Chamorro's campaign manager and chief of staff—described the transfer of power as involving a monumental, "triple transition": from war to peace, from a hegemonic party regime to one of liberal democracy, and from a state-centered economy to an open, market-based system along the lines of the so-called Washington Consensus.[9] But there were important continuities, too. The basic state institutions constructed during the revolutionary period, including the 1987 Constitution, were left in place. Importantly, EPS founding chief Humberto Ortega stayed on as head of the military (René Vivas, the comandante guerrillero in charge of the police, also kept his job). And even as the Chamorro administration slashed the government bureaucracy, privatized state-owned enterprises, and rolled back most social spending, the transition agreements legalized some of the redistribution of land and property that had taken place in the 1980s. These and other compromises, such as amnesties for Contra and EPS military officials, corresponded with the reality of the strategic stalemate that ended the war. They served as the foundation for a fraught, but surprisingly stable, period of free elections and peaceful changes of government in the 1990s and early 2000s.

The Revolution was over. "The great paradox," Sergio Ramírez observed, "was that in the end, Sandinismo left a legacy that it had not intended: democracy. It was not able to leave what it had proposed: an end to backwardness, poverty, and marginalization."[10] Cardenal offered a similar assessment, as did scholarly analysts of varying degrees of sympathy for the Sandinistas.[11] Notably, it had not occurred to Sandinista leaders to rig the 1990 elections in their favor.[12] "Over the years," Ramírez added, "what had been called a 'tactical project' wound up taking precedence."[13] Tactical decisions frequently bled into the strategic thinking of the Sandinista elite; this was a key feature of their time in power. For example,

Comandante Jaime Wheelock has described an evolving attitude with respect to democracy: "At the beginning of the period of revolutionary change, some Sandinista leaders assumed that the democratization of Nicaraguan politics would serve as a tactic to reduce support for, and thereby to prevent, US aggression against the Sandinista government. Later, in 1984, democratization in the political area would become a substantial part of the Sandinista project, and ultimately it would be an essential component of the revolution."[14] When they were founded, and up until the 1980s, Central American revolutionary movements had seen political and institutional reform as secondary to the achievement of social justice. Over time, the articulation of liberal democracy increasingly replaced the ideal of economic redistribution in the minds of the FSLN high command. In a recent interview, Humberto Ortega referred to the "revolutionary act" he and his comrades brought about in 1979 in the following terms: "its most important product was our having opened, despite all of the limitations, the road to democracy."[15]

This book argues that these changes—in the way FSLN leaders exercised power, and ultimately how they conceived of the Revolution—were partly a function of changes in the world around them. The emergence of a powerful revolutionary coalition (the only one of its kind to succeed in Latin America after Cuba) owed to a huge variety of short- and long-term factors. Those domestic elements overlapped with favorable international trends, including the rise of a regional alliance to topple Somoza. Once in power, forces beyond Nicaragua's borders helped determine a war that severely compromised Sandinista leaders' efforts to redistribute wealth, but others created unique opportunities for support. Notably, international opposition to US intervention—which included not only the global Left but also centrist governments in Latin America and Western Europe—helped frustrate the Contra program. It also helped determine the Revolution's final outcome in the form of a transition to democracy. From the beginning, Nicaragua's revolutionary leadership thought that political pluralism, along with the existence of private property and market forces, would separate their project from that of the Cuban and Russian revolutions. Steps toward a democratic transition—notably, the holding of elections in 1984 and the promulgation of the 1987 Constitution—were also a consequence of the Sandinista Front's alliances with a broad range of political actors during the 1979 insurrection. But the evolution and consolidation of representative democracy had an important international dimension, as well. Luis Carrión recalls: "The Sandinista Front came to power with the support of an international alliance that was very broad. An alliance that was very important to maintain after the triumph of the Revolution. We had very close relations with Mexico, with several European countries, with Venezuela . . . with Panama. And we understood that it was fundamental for our survival, and in order to somehow curb US aggression, to be able to count on that alliance. That made us sensitive to the importance of maintaining democratic spaces that would facilitate those countries' dialogue and sympathy with us."[16] This book focused mostly on political affairs close to the thinking of the Sandinista upper echelon. Future histories of the Revolution could delve into other dimensions—such as its cultural agenda, its relationship with ethnic and racial minorities, or its social and economic development programs—and similarly ask how they evolved in tandem with changing international trends.

In 1990, the Sandinistas became the first socialist movement in the world that, having taken power by armed struggle, handed it over peacefully in democratic elections. The journey toward that ending provides a unique vantage point on the end of the Cold War era. The rise and fall of the Nicaraguan Revolution marked both the intensification of the East–West conflict in Latin America *and* its decreasing relevance for the continent's mainstream political agenda. And while their Revolution witnessed the Cold War's collapse, the Sandinistas were also present at the creation of something new. Their revolutionary project informed—and was deeply shaped by—the generalization of liberal electoral democracy in Latin America, a major political shift that transformed the region but has also stagnated in the post–Cold War era. Specifically, 1979 and 1990 were major milestones in the history of the regional Left and its embrace of liberal democracy, a transformation most famously analyzed by Jorge Castañeda in *Utopia Unarmed*. The Sandinista episode also caused a crisis in inter-American relations at a time when bipolarity was giving way to multipolarity in global affairs.

In many ways, the Sandinista Revolution was a crepuscular episode that bridged the Cold War and post–Cold War eras.[17] In the early 2020s, many scholars, journalists, and policymakers began devoting much attention to the possible end of the latter. The debate has been motivated by several international trends: for example, the declining number and quality of democracies around the world, the return of interstate armed conflict in continental Europe, and the risk of a "new Cold War" between the United States and China. The need to make sense of a world in transition has brought welcome new interest in revisiting the global inflection point of the 1980s and

1990s, leading scholars to once again ask what changed, what remained the same, what was destroyed, and what was built during the expiration of the Cold War as an international system. Histories of the Global South, where most violence took place in the context of the Cold War, have much to add to that conversation. Look no further than the recent development of Nicaraguan politics, which explodes many assumptions—and reveals many contingencies and contradictions—that accompanied the Cold War's end. Four decades after Somoza's overthrow, a second dynastic dictatorship has emerged in Nicaragua. This one is led by none other than the Sandinista National Liberation Front, architects of Somoza's downfall, now hegemonized by the family of longtime leader Daniel Ortega and mostly devoid of the socialist politics and social progressivism that characterized the Nicaraguan Revolution.

The Last Revolution

What legacy of change did the FSLN government leave behind in Nicaragua?[18] After overthrowing a personalist dictatorship in 1979, the Sandinista Front built representative institutions and ultimately abided by the rule of law. When they lost the 1990 elections, they handed power to a former ally in that overthrow, rather than someone who had been associated with the old Somoza regime. And beyond institutional transformation toward electoral democracy, most scholars agree that the country's political culture changed as a result of the revolutionary government's promotion of popular participation in politics. The late conservative intellectual Emilio Alvarez Montalván noted that if the Sandinista Revolution accomplished anything it was the introduction, for the first time in Nicaraguan history, of "compassion for the poor" in national discourse.[19]

In socioeconomic terms, the Sandinistas tried to build equality through reforms in the areas of land tenure, housing, health, and education, but their effects were not as profound as had been hoped. This last point, which falls largely beyond the scope of this book's analysis, remains a matter of much debate. Nicaraguans on average left the revolutionary period poorer (measured by income) than they were before it, but many of them enjoyed access to health care (measured, for example, by infant and maternal mortality or the prevalence of infectious diseases) and education (see the literacy rate, or the number of teachers per 100,000 inhabitants) that they previously lacked. While union membership and property ownership both expanded during the 1980s, labor relations and land tenancy patterns remained extremely unequal in the 1990s and beyond. The revolutionary government also sought to empower women by enacting progressive social policies and promoting their participation in politics, but some feminist critics saw Ortega's defeat by a female candidate as a consequence, in part, of the nonfulfillment of the FSLN's agenda for women's liberation.[20] In other words, every section on the Revolution's balance sheet contains ambiguities.

Why did the revolutionary government lose popular support over the course of the 1980s? This question, like that of the Sandinista record, is difficult to answer because it cannot be separated from that of who was responsible—the government, anti-government rebels, or foreign actors (most notably, the US government)—for the violence and social misery associated with the war.[21] Analysts typically agree that unde- cided voters flocked to Chamorro because they believed her victory would pacify the country and stabilize its economy. Insofar as US policies determined the realities underlying the vote—armed conflict and eco- nomic collapse—Washington could take credit for bringing down the revolutionary government. But as we have seen, decisions taken by North Americans cannot by themselves account for what transpired; the in- tended effects of North American intervention were either enhanced or constrained by their interplay with various political forces inside Nicara- gua and across the global Cold War.

Because it brought immediate joy and relief to a traditional economic elite previously challenged by the Sandinistas' governing agenda, some FSLN supporters saw in the transition to democracy both a revolutionary conquest *and* a bitter retreat that evoked pre-1979 fears that Somoza's over- throw might simply lead to "somocismo without Somoza."[22] Adding to the outcome's ambiguity was the fact that the Sandinistas' US-backed defeater in 1990 had been an important personality in the 1979 anti-Somoza alliance and a member of the revolutionary government's first executive Junta. Nica- ragua in the 1980s experienced a political phenomenon common to many revolutions: once the old regime was defeated, the insurrectionary coalition began to fall apart. After conducting a survey of voters in the months follow- ing the electoral defeat, an FSLN-aligned think tank (Instituto para el Desar- rollo y la Democracia, IPADE) concluded that both US intervention and a long list of policy mistakes—including ineffective price controls, clashes with Christian institutions, abuses by security officials, and marginalization of popular sectors not formally integrated into the Sandinista Front— combined to reduce the revolutionary government's support to less than half of the population. That postmortem report grouped the mistakes under a broader umbrella: "The model that we began to execute, of socialist orientation, clashed in practice with the program of reconstruction and national unity that allowed for the toppling of the Somocista dictatorship."[23]

Any assessment of the Revolution's accomplishments should consider how the threshold for success or failure shifted over time. As they confronted the reality of governance in an extremely difficult context, and as the political world around Nicaragua changed, the Sandinista elite dynamically revised its tactical and strategic goals. In a 1983 interview, Sergio Ramírez hinted at this adjustment process: "In July 1979, the first time we entered [government], we thought we could do everything in a day. A year later, we thought we could do everything in five years. Now we think we can do everything but that it will be the work of several generations."[24] After the Revolution fell, Sandinista leaders acknowledged that they could not, in fact, do everything. Deputy Foreign Relations Minister (and former guerrilla) Victor Hugo Tinoco said: "In retrospect, I can tell you that one of the errors we committed was that we had a romantic vision of revolution and of societal transformation. We believed that revolution spontaneously generated a just society and a new man—all of that was jargon used in Guevarian romanticism. Looking back, we have realized that a revolution can change a government or a system, but not necessarily a society, its values, its principles, its culture, nor can it change the individual automatically."[25] By the time they were defeated in 1990, the FSLN upper echelon had settled for affirming national sovereignty in the face of US intervention, building an electoral democracy, and perhaps ending the country's historical cycles of war and dictatorship. Moving forward, those legacies, too, will be subject to constant debate and reevaluation in light of new developments in Nicaraguan politics and society.

The political evolution of the FSLN elite ran parallel to the discrediting of world communism as an alternative to liberal capitalism. The circumscribed quality of socialist bloc commitment held some Sandinista ambitions in check; at one point Mikhail Gorbachev praised the Nicaraguan revolutionaries for *not* declaring socialism in Nicaragua.[26] Globally, the Nicaraguan Revolution was arguably the last political phenomenon that approximated the strictest social scientific definitions of social revolutions: a violent transition that, beyond changing who was in power, rapidly brought about (or at least attempted) a structural change in a country's values and social order, especially its class structure. Like many contemporaneous revolutionaries around the world, the Sandinista elite mostly walked away from the idea of state-led structural transformation. To shore up their government, they had implemented liberalizing economic reforms and austerity measures that were comparable to those implemented across the Global South in the 1980s and '90s. During the Sandinistas' final years in power, the global economy entered uncharted territory: from that point on, capitalism—with variations within it, but few exceptions—has been the sole model for organizing economic production around the world.[27]

After they lost power in the 1990 elections, Sandinista leaders adapted to the primacy of markets and private property with relative ease. As part of their transition agreements, the outgoing FSLN leadership and incoming Chamorro administration found ways to lend de jure legitimacy to de facto transfers of wealth, land, and property that had taken place during the revolutionary period. This included, for example, agricultural lands and businesses that the state had ceded to workers' cooperatives, or homes and goods that the FSLN had awarded to veterans of the insurrectionary struggle and subsequent war with the Contra. The Chamorro team understood that attempting to turn back the clock on this redistribution would displace so many Nicaraguan families that the entire transition would be imperiled. As they left power, many FSLN bosses exploited the transition agreements in order to "privatize to themselves" major state-owned assets in a corruption scandal that came to be known as *la piñata*. As sociologist William Robinson observed, very quickly, "new Sandinista landlords and businessmen began to develop an affinity of class interests—and to merge with—the bourgeoisie."[28] Throughout the 1990s, FSLN supporters hit the streets to protest free trade agreements or cuts to social spending, but the party leadership increasingly assumed policy stances that favored private sector interests and integration with the global economy.

The Revolution's collapse left few clear winners and losers. Because neither had been militarily defeated, both the Contra and Sandinista Front could plausibly claim some form of victory. Yet they could also feel defeated because their true aims were not met. In this sense, Nicaragua looked like the rest of Central America. After decades of revolution and counterrevolution, Carlos Vilas noted, it was possible for everybody to feel disenchanted: left-wing forces could not hold power and build toward an imagined future of social justice, nor could those on the other side resist reform altogether and cling to the past.[29]

To the extent that the United States won, it was an ambiguous victory. In Congress, both supporters and critics of aggressive intervention managed to take credit for Nicaragua's transition to democracy. US policies undoubtedly contributed to the desgaste that led the FSLN to hold and lose elections (and, in turn, see their redistributive project rolled back), but elections were neither a Contra nor Reagan administration goal, as Cynthia Arnson explained in a study of the Nicaragua debate on Capitol Hill.[30] Contrary to the Reagan administration's view that the Sandinistas were a cancer to be excised from the hemisphere, many of the Revolution's institutions (most notably, the security apparatus) remained and the Sandinista Front continued having a voice in politics. Thus, US-style democratic institutions proliferated, and the transition was beneficial to transnational capital, but not on terms US policymakers designed or necessarily desired (Kissinger and Nixon, Greg Grandin once observed, resented the possibility of Allende *leaving* office through democratic elections as much as they fretted over his taking power in Chile in the first place).[31] Western European and Latin American social democrats may have felt vindicated in their efforts to shield the Nicaraguan Revolution from aggression and guide it toward electoral democracy. But they, too, had settled for something far less than what they had hoped for in 1979.[32]

On the night of their electoral defeat, former US president Jimmy Carter assured the National Directorate that they could remain a dominant force in Nicaraguan politics: "the FSLN can come out as heroes, having triumphed in a revolution against an oppressive dictator, survived a war against an enemy that was financed abroad, and at the end of ten years, brought democracy. . . . You are all young men. Six years may seem like a long time, but it's not. . . . Like you, I have won a presidential election, and I have lost one, but losing the election wasn't the end of the world."[33] It really was not the end of the world. As Nicaragua entered a period of rule by successive right-wing governments, Daniel Ortega promised that the FSLN would "govern from below" by mobilizing supports on the streets in defense of gains consolidated by the Revolution. They would also rule from above: through their presence in the National Assembly, and by way of power-sharing agreements with the rival Liberal Party that ensured posts in essential state institutions, the FSLN participated in all major decision-making processes. In a moment of striking candor, Jaime Wheelock admitted that the FSLN defeat had a silver lining: if the Sandinista Front "had won the election of 1990, democracy in Nicaragua would not have advanced as much as it has with us in the opposition."[34] Eventually, the Sandinista Front would retake the presidency, as well.

The FSLN's survival and transition to the electoral era, in turn, had an appreciable effect on Central American politics more generally. As they laid down arms and exchanged bullets for ballots, so did their comrades in neighboring countries through parallel peace processes connected by the Esquipulas framework. Dirk Kruijt found in a comparative study that "the disintegration of the Soviet Union and the downfall of the Eastern European satellite governments, along with the electoral defeat of the Sandinista government, together helped persuade the Salvadoran and Guatemalan guerrillas to the negotiating table."[35] Across Central America the fall of the Revolution and the collapse of world communism not only signified the death of a revolutionary ideal but also a new chapter for leftist politics.

Two years after the Sandinistas left office, the Salvadoran civil war—which claimed an estimated 75,000 lives—officially came to an end. While the Farabundo Martí National Liberation Front did not follow the Sandinistas' steps in seizing state power, their military campaigns had allowed them to achieve "strategic parity" with the US-backed Salvadoran government. Thus, they won significant concessions through the Chapultepec Accords, named after the Mexico City castle where peace was signed in January 1992.[36] As part of the UN-sponsored agreement, the FMLN promised to demobilize; in exchange, the Cristiani government agreed to reform and downsize security forces. Both sides accepted the FMLN's participation in politics as a legalized party. Mirroring their Nicaraguan counterparts, many Salvadoran guerrilla leaders modified their revolutionary outlook over time. Joaquín Villalobos, founder and leader of the Ejército Revolucionario del Pueblo (ERP), one of the FMLN's constituent factions, later reflected upon his career in the following terms: "When the continent was governed primarily by dictatorships, the dominant belief was that we guerrillas were the solution, but in reality we were just another symptom of the conflict that the dictatorships themselves were generating." In dropping the ideal of armed struggle, Villalobos found another one in the form of demilitarizing El Salvador and giving citizens the right to vote. "Before that," he explained, "the only thing that made a difference was changing points of view among the generals and colonels of the armed forces."[37] Not everybody within the FMLN shared the mixed assessment of the armed struggle or the rosy view that the insurrection ultimately succeeded because it helped build democratic institutions; the FMLN's transition created friction within the party, especially between the elite and the rank and file.[38] But the transition protocols, which came after a ferocious anti-communist crusade by US-backed conservative elites, allowed the FMLN to persist as a political force and eventually win the presidency via elections.

Guatemala's transition was shaped by the armed Left's relative weakness with respect to its government. According to Edelberto Torres Rivas, the URNG lacked the middle- and upper-class support that allowed the Sandinistas to seize power in 1979; revolutionary and counterrevolutionary dynamics in Guatemala played out more neatly along class lines. Because the military was in so much stronger a position than the guerrillas by the middle of the 1980s, the ensuing peace process was less about ending the war than it was about preventing future armed conflicts.[39] Under the Esquipulas framework, the Cerezo administration and Catholic Church headed a series of failed national reconciliation initiatives in the late 1980s. But an agreement reached between the government and the URNG in Oslo in 1991 set the basis for a substantive peace process later in the decade. By 1996, they had definitively signed the end of the armed conflict, though the transition was arguably messier than in Nicaragua or El Salvador.[40] For example, Guatemala's "agreement on a firm and lasting peace" envisioned a series of major reforms in health, education, and social security for "overcoming the root causes of the conflict," most of which went unimplemented. Political violence was more persistent than in neighboring countries. When civil society groups published ¡Nunca Más!—a fact-finding report that blamed the Guatemalan government for the bulk of human rights abuses committed during the civil war—one of its authors, the Catholic bishop Juan Gerardi, was brutally murdered by paramilitaries. Additionally, the URNG had much more difficulty than the FMLN or FSLN did in reinventing itself as a political party fit for competition in elections. Nonetheless, the transition brought significant changes. It ended a war that, according to Guatemala's Historical Clarification Commission (CEH, by its Spanish acronym), claimed 200,000 lives. Moreover, UN-sponsored truth and reconciliation initiatives like the CEH allowed Guatemalan society to document crimes against humanity that took place during the war and eventually hold some perpetrators accountable (this was unlike Nicaragua, which did not develop such truth and reconciliation measures as part of its transition). Political movements with some links to the civil war–era armed Left eventually made it to power via elections.

The consequences of Esquipulas were less obvious in Honduras, which did not experience a major leftist insurrection or civil war.[41] The country formally began a democratic transition with the creation of a constituent assembly in 1980 and the election of President Roberto Suazo Córdova in 1982. These institutional developments coincided, however, with the escalating crisis in neighboring Nicaragua. In the context of Honduras's active involvement in the Nicaraguan civil war, the country's military preserved or even expanded its control over institutions; the disproportionate influence of US diplomats and intelligence officials further undermined the prospects of civilian, representative rule. Over the course of the decade, Honduran civil society mobilized against human rights abuses and corruption scandals involving the military leadership, demanding a full democratic transition.[42] By winding down Central America's wars—something that naturally eroded the importance of the armed forces in Honduran society—the Esquipulas Process improved the conditions for civilian rule. As part of those agreements, the government in Tegucigalpa inaugurated a National Reconciliation Committee in 1987, a small first step toward a full transition to electoral politics. Eventually, left-wing politicians were elected to the presidency in Honduras, as well.

Latin America in the Era of the Sandinistas

Latin American politics experienced significant transformations as Cold War–era conflicts faded from view in the 1980s and '90s. During that period most of the region's countries implemented free market reforms, privatized vital sectors previously owned by the state, and opened up their economies to foreign investment—a bundle of policies often referred to as "neoliberalism." Across the continent, military regimes collapsed and gave way to civilian rule and democratic elections. In the process, Latin American governments made a nearly unprecedented effort at developing ties between themselves through regionalist and multilateralist initiatives.[43] The Nicaraguan Revolution, which in real terms was far more important to Latin American countries' core interests than to those of the United States or the Soviet Union, featured importantly in those shifts. In the years immediately following Somoza's overthrow, the Sandinista Front became a point of reference for the long-running Cold War struggle between the socialist Left and the anti-communist Right. The Nicaraguan Revolution also caused a crisis in hemispheric relations, one which saw Latin American countries come together in relatively novel ways to oppose US intervention in Central America. When the Sandinistas handed over power in 1990, they lent shape to the region's transition to democracy and exemplified the dilemmas that the Latin American Left would face in this new era of neoliberalism and electoral politics. The story of the Sandinistas' rise and fall therefore sheds light not only on the intra–Latin American dimensions of the late Cold War period but also on the origins and contradictions of the major political themes, norms, and institutions that defined the region's post–Cold War era.

Initially, the rise of the Sandinistas shifted the focus of revolutionary and counterrevolutionary violence to Central America. In 1979, leftist internationalists from across Latin America traveled to Nicaragua to fight alongside the FSLN. Their victory over the Somoza regime inspired other guerrilla organizations to continue their own struggles; suddenly, Fidel Castro's feat twenty years prior seemed a little less exceptional. The Sandinista Front's victory also provided regional conservatives with a stark example of what they should seek to avoid. Almost immediately, transnational right-wing forces mobilized to undermine Nicaragua's revolutionary government. They were led by the government of the United States, which sought to contain leftist revolution not only through major military and paramilitary operations, but also by reconfiguring and expanding its foreign aid programs in Central America.[44] At a time when Cold War–fueled political violence was beginning to ebb in South America, it intensified in Central America, where long-running social and political conflicts suddenly acquired global dimensions. National liberation movements and socialist governments from across Europe, Asia, and Africa briefly saw in Nicaragua the hope of striking a coup against American imperialism.

Importantly, the Nicaraguan Revolution cut against the traditional, East–West fault lines of the Cold War. In part, this owed to the fact that the Sandinista agenda—which melded revolutionary nationalism, Marxism, and liberalism—sometimes blurred the lines between the era's dominant ideological frameworks. Another reason was that the United States' closest allies in Western Europe were not sold on the necessity or wisdom of Reagan's anti-communist crusade in Central America. This book emphasized state-to-state relations, but non-state actors were extraordinarily important as well. Crucially, tens of thousands of "sandalistas" from the United States and Europe (the nickname was either affectionate or scornful depending on who used it) traveled to Nicaragua in support of the FSLN government. Many more marched at home against sanctions and the Contra program. As a burgeoning historical literature demonstrates, this engagement shaped the North American and European communities from which solidarity activists hailed.[45] It also helped shift public opinion in those countries against escalation in Central America. Hence the importance that Nicaraguan diplomat Alejandro Bendaña attributes to said movements: "Did solidarity have an impact? Its impact was that Nicaragua was not invaded and did not suffer the same fate as Grenada. That's the answer."[46]

In the second half of the 1980s, the East–West conflict began to recede, and Nicaragua's revolution was increasingly framed by another international trend: the Third Wave of democratization. When the FSLN-led insurrection started to gather steam in 1977, only three Latin American governments—Colombia, Costa Rica, and Venezuela—had competitively elected regimes. Two of the region's oldest and most stable democracies—those of Chile and Uruguay—had recently been reversed by military coups. But by the time the Sandinistas handed over power to Violeta Barrios de Chamorro in 1990, Nicaragua was one of fifteen countries to have transitioned from authoritarian to democratic or semi-democratic rule in the intervening years.

This regional transformation had a decisive effect on the Sandinista project. It becomes more difficult to imagine the survival of a "second Cuba" in a context where Latin America's political map was dominated by heavily ideological, anti-communist dictatorships; democratic governments proved far more likely to oppose US intervention and lend legitimacy to Managua's revolutionary government. Additionally, political changes inside revolutionary Nicaragua fed back into the regional democratic transition. As the FSLN institutionalized elements of liberal democracy and eventually consolidated electoral rule in 1990, neighboring Central American governments did as well, as part of a regional agreement that—to end interrelated civil wars on the isthmus—tied democratic processes in those countries together with one another. Victor Hugo Tinoco reflects in retrospect: "By the end of the 1980s we found ourselves in a situation where nearly all of Latin America's military dictatorships were disappearing. This was one of the by-products of the Nicaraguan Revolution, of the crisis it provoked and of the neo-conservative reaction to that crisis."[47]

Tinoco's comments reflect how the place of the Left in regional politics (and its vision for change) transformed in the period between Allende's armed overthrow in 1973 and the Sandinistas' electoral defeat in February 1990. With Cuba excepted, it gave up the armed struggle and began competing in elections; Colombia's M-19, for instance, demobilized in March 1990 and helped draft that country's current constitution. Self-described leftist actors became a normal feature of mainstream politics; in the twenty-first century, it became common to see retired Marxist combatants as democratically elected heads of state in the region (such as Brazil's Dilma Roussef, Uruguay's Pepe Mujica, and El Salvador's Salvador Sánchez Cerén, to name a few examples). The Sandinistas' democratic exit symbolized those transformations.[48] The FSLN also stands out because it underwent

Democratic Transitions in Latin America, 1978–1990

Classification of Latin American Political Regimes in Hagopian and Mainwaring, "The Third Wave of Democratization in Latin America," 3.

that transition while holding power. Rafael Rojas has aptly described what the Sandinista experience meant for the regional Left: "The Nicaraguan model was incontrovertible evidence that for Latin America's twentieth-century revolutionary tradition to have any continuity in the post–Cold War world, it was forced to opt for democracy. In that sense, the Sandinista experience was a precursor: all leftist movements which have come to power in recent years—from that of Hugo Chávez in Venezuela to that of Andrés Manuel López Obrador in Mexico—have done it through the electoral path."[49] The Left's adaptation to this new context took place in very different ways according to specific national contexts. The so-called Pink Tide of left-wing governments that swept the continent in the early 2000s evidenced differing approaches toward reducing inequality in the context of market economies, as well as varying levels of commitment to free elections and the rule of law. Many of the dilemmas faced by the early twenty-first century Left—such as how to balance the struggle for social justice with respect for liberal democratic institutions—were previously witnessed in the process by which Sandinista leaders, who simultaneously embraced and rebuffed the Cuban model, thought and rethought the meaning of democracy in their revolutionary project.

The way in which liberal democracy developed in Nicaragua and Central America foreshadowed challenges that this form of government would face in the post–Cold War era. Political scientists Frances Hagopian and Scott Mainwaring, synthesizing several studies on Latin America's Third Wave, found that structural factors such as class composition, level of industrialization, and economic performance cannot explain either the timing or the strength of the region's transitions to democracy in the 1970s and '80s.[50] Indeed, it would be preposterous to posit that Central America, which became a Cold War disaster zone of the highest order, adopted liberal democracy as a result of economic growth or modernization. Rather, they argue that political factors—such as decreasing polarization, changing attitudes toward democracy, and a favorable regional context—were more decisive.[51] In the Central American case, political elites brought about democratic transitions for the relatively circumstantial purpose of ending interrelated civil wars on the isthmus. At the time there was also great pressure for democratization (and against authoritarianism) from political forces outside Central America. What would happen when the circumstances—or the international consensus regarding democracy—changed? By the late 2010s, most Third-Wave transitions either stagnated or broke down entirely.[52]

The Sandinista Revolution was also consequential because of the crisis it provoked in US–Latin American relations. When the collapse of the Somoza regime began, the Organization of American States had lost some credibility among the Latin American political elite; many saw it as an instrument of US foreign policy (hence, Fidel Castro's famous denunciation of the OAS as the "Yankee Ministry of Colonies").[53] In 1979, however, Latin American countries used the OAS to isolate the Somoza regime, legitimize the FSLN-led provisional government, and complicate US plans to dictate the terms of the transition. This collective break with the regional hegemon formed part of a long-term effort by Latin American elites (including those on the Right connected to US foreign policy via shared anti-communism during the Cold War) to use existing multilateral institutions in order to limit Washington's capacity for unilateral, arbitrary action.[54] Later, in response to a US intervention in Central America that threatened their countries' autonomy and security interests, Latin American diplomats created new, multilateral organizations—the Contadora Group and Support Group—that sought to sideline Washington from certain regional discussions. This effort helped isolate and constrain the Reagan administration's Central America policy, while also laying the foundations for a negotiated settlement in the region on terms other than those preferred by US policymakers.

Several factors facilitated this South–South action. First, there was decreasing ideological polarization as the East–West conflict receded: it is no coincidence that Cuba—Nicaragua's most important state ally—normalized relations with many Latin American governments in this period.[55] Second, there was increased involvement by extra-hemispheric actors (namely, the countries that would go on to form the European Union) that backed Contadora and further limited US maneuvering space. Their relevance foreshadowed Latin American elites' pursuit of relations with China and Russia in the twenty-first century as a means of counterbalancing US unilateralism. Finally, the growing salience of global international organizations like the United Nations—and its various missions to Central America—also went hand in hand with Latin American multilateralism in this period.

While the Latin American response to the Nicaraguan Revolution did not alter the underlying reality of US hegemony, it was not without consequences. As Spanish diplomat Manuel Montobbio aptly reflected, the Reagan administration's failure to press its case in Central America resulted in the United States losing "its monopoly as the sole relevant actor on the Latin American scene (if not its quality as decisive and indispensable actor in any situation)."[56] Interestingly, this qualification of North American hegemony took place at a time when the United States achieved maximum leverage over Latin American countries as a result of their indebtedness to international financial institutions over which Washington exerted tremendous influence. Indeed, it was a moment of global predominance underpinned by the disintegration of the United States' strategic rival—the Soviet Union—and the related collapse of the bipolar world order. However, unipolarity—to the extent that it existed—soon gave way to multipolarity in international relations after the Cold War ended.

The Latin American response to the Nicaraguan Revolution helped foster new forms of collaboration and integration between Latin American elites. For example, Contadora quickly outgrew its purpose as a conflict resolution mechanism. The 1986 Declaration of Rio de Janeiro officially turned Contadora and its Support Group into a "permanent mechanism for political consultation" where Latin American governments regularly debated the debt crisis and other issues unrelated to the crisis in Central America specifically: legal frameworks for regional integration, food security, poverty reduction, and trade policy.[57] Contadora therefore helped catalyze post–Cold War processes of regional integration, multilateralism, and multipolarity in the hemisphere. The eight founding members of the so-called Rio Group were joined in the 1990s and 2000s by nearly every country south of the US-Mexico border, expanding this space of dialogue and consultation. In 2010, the Rio Group morphed into the Community of Latin American and Caribbean States (CELAC), the apex of post–Cold War Latin American regionalism that sought a muscular alternative to the OAS as a representative and multilateral body. The "regional solutions to regional problems" rubric from the Contadora era also lived on in the form of subregional blocs such as the South American Common Market (MERCOSUR) and the Central American Integration System (SICA). Latin America's enthusiasm for integration in the 1990s and 2000s—which, Alicia Frohman correctly notes, "originated with Contadora and Esquipulas"— accompanied wider optimism that the region was poised to leave behind the political instability of the Cold War, achieve strong economic growth on the back of high commodity prices, and assert itself on the global stage (especially in the case of regional leaders Brazil and Mexico).[58]

At the same time, the Contadora-era drive toward integration also faced limitations that would hamper regionalism down the line. During the 1980s, the main glue binding together Latin American countries was the shared desire to counterbalance US arbitrariness and unilateralism. They were not necessarily bound together by shared economic interests; Latin American countries in the 1990s and 2000s were more likely to trade with the United States, China, or the European Union than with their regional neighbors. To the extent that that the multilateral Latin American peace process was predicated on shared values, it was messy. Contadora (and to a greater extent, Esquipulas) articulated liberal democracy as a shared, supranational value fundamental to building peace in the region; regional governments later consecrated this idea in various resolutions including the Santiago Commitment to Democracy and the Renewal of the Inter-American System (1991), the Declaration of Quebec (2001), and the Inter-American Democratic Charter (2001). But Contadora also championed nonintervention, self-determination, and national sovereignty as core inter-American principles. In the post–Cold War era, the tension between the two sets of values—a basic feature of inter-American debates surrounding the Sandinista Revolution—increasingly polarized regional governments when debating how to respond to democratic or human rights crises in member states, notably Venezuela under the government of Nicolás Maduro. Devastation wrought by the COVID-19 pandemic further eroded optimism over Latin America's future in global affairs.[59]

Twilight of the Cold War

As Nicaragua entered a new period of electoral democracy and neoliberalism in the wake of the 1990 elections, the defeated FSLN underwent its own "transition within the transition."[60] In the first half of the new decade, passionate internal debates threatened to divide Sandinismo forever. Looking back on their decade in power, Sandinista cadres traded blame for the fall of the Revolution. Looking ahead to the Sandinista Front's future as an opposition political party, they fought over how its program and leadership should be updated for a new era of electoral competition. A significant wave of senior- and intermediate-level militants left the FSLN in this period and tried to build an alternative Sandinista party. But Comandante Daniel Ortega—who had emerged from the revolutionary decade as first among equals in the National Directorate by virtue of his presidency (and his brother's control of the armed forces in wartime)—was able to maintain the party's structural integrity, and most of its voting base, despite these elite defections. He did so by remaking the party in his own image. Over the course of the 1990s and early 2000s, he increasingly centralized resources and monopolized decision-making spaces within the party. After overcoming a major sexual abuse scandal, he silenced all criticism of his leadership within the Sandinista Front, pushing out those revolutionary leaders who challenged his role as secretary general or his perpetual candidacy in presidential elections.[61]

In 2006, Ortega took the FSLN back to power. His victory with only 38 percent of the vote was made possible by a power-sharing agreement he had previously reached with former president Arnoldo Alemán—known simply as *El Pacto*—which, among other provisions, lowered the threshold for a first-round electoral victory. As part of his comeback, Ortega presided over a stunning reconfiguration of the Sandinista Front's image and policy preferences. Though his government expanded social spending and welfare programs, it maintained and deepened the pro-business framework of his right-wing predecessors, closely aligning fiscal and monetary policy with the recommendations of the World Bank and IMF. The twenty-first-century FSLN, now fully hegemonized by Ortega, also rebranded itself as a Christian movement committed to conservative social policies like the criminalization of abortion.

The new-look Sandinismo brought new, unexpected alliances. Rather than rebuilding the coalition of workers, intellectuals, and progressive bourgeoisie that sustained the revolutionary government of the 1980s, Ortega built an intimate working relationship with his former "counterrevolutionary" foes in the business elite and Catholic Church hierarchy. These elite allies turned a blind eye as the FSLN government manipulated elections, challenged civil society, repressed labor organizing, politicized all state institutions, and paved the way to Ortega's reelection in 2011 and 2016 despite constitutional term limits.[62]

The corporatist alliance, as well as seemingly high levels of popular approval, was underpinned by consistent economic growth and social stability. In contrast to its neighbors in the so-called Northern Triangle, Nicaragua did not develop major public safety challenges related to organized crime or drug trafficking. This, in turn, facilitated surprisingly smooth relations with the government of the United States. Though the Bush and Obama administrations condemned the erosion of democracy in Nicaragua and suspended aid programs, the US armed forces came to see its government as a reliable partner in the fight to stem the flow of northbound drugs and migrants. Despite alliances with some of the most conservative sectors in Nicaraguan society, and although the FSLN was increasingly bereft of the best-known personalities from the 1980s, Ortega used revolutionary rhetoric to help maintain his hold over the symbolism and historical memory of the Revolution.

Ortega's authoritarian consolidation was put on pause in the spring of 2018, when latent popular grievances exploded in the form of massive street protests, originally led by university students. Rather than accede to popular demands for a new democratic transition, Ortega ordered police and para-military forces to violently repress dissidence. So many Nicaraguans were arbitrarily detained, displaced, tortured, or killed that the Inter-American Commission on Human Rights (IACHR) and a United Nations inquiry ac-cused the Nicaraguan government of having committed crimes against hu-manity.[63] The business and Catholic Church hierarchies quickly canceled their partnerships with the regime, and popular backing for Ortega col-lapsed back down to the FSLN's historical, core support base. As political instability plunged Nicaragua into a semipermanent state of social and eco-nomic crisis, many analysts believed that Ortega was against the ropes and facing imminent overthrow.

Nonetheless, the Sandinista Front soon regained its footing and, by 2021, was able to go on the offensive. Ahead of presidential elections scheduled for November of that year, the regime dismantled the fractious anti-Ortega opposition by arresting virtually every person who declared an interest in running. Dozens more—including leaders from civil society, farmworkers' associations, the private sector, and student movements—also joined the ranks of Nicaragua's political prisoners in this period. The crackdown's vic-tims included countless people from Sandinista backgrounds; indeed, some of the revolutionary leaders interviewed for this book were put behind bars for several months before being exiled and stripped of their Nicara-guan citizenship. Upon her release and expatriation following twenty months in prison, Comandante Guerrillera Dora María Tellez reflected: "I feel that the Sandinista Revolution's conviction in democracy was not as deep as its conviction for social justice, but I never would have imagined that it would evolve into a dictatorship in the style of the Somozas."[64] Nica-ragua's experiment with democracy—begun with Somoza's ouster and the holding of the 1984 elections, developed with the 1987 Constitution, and consolidated with the 1990 elections—is over.

The international community, including a majority of Latin American governments, condemned Daniel Ortega's repressive onslaught. Some, led by the United States and the European Union, sanctioned individual regime of-ficials. But external pressure failed to compel the Nicaraguan government to suspend the police state. As of this writing, the biggest risk to Ortega's power seems to be internal. After returning to power, he has increasingly co-governed with his wife, Rosario Murillo, who holds the office of vice president. Together, they have groomed their children for leadership roles. Given Ortega's age, and given the sultanistic and personalistic qualities of the regime, the question of succession has hung over Nicaragua in recent years. Will *orteguismo* follow somocismo in attempting—and pulling off—a dynastic transition?

The emergence of a second family dictatorship has naturally raised questions about the Sandinista Revolution's legacies. Specifically, observers have been debating whether the contemporary political situation can be understood as a direct result of the 1980s revolutionary period.[65] Some, such as Ortega himself, emphasize the continuities. The official narrative holds that the current regime is carrying on a new phase of the 1979 Revolution which, according to this mythology, Ortega and Murillo led all along. Many from hard-line anti-Sandinista backgrounds share the emphasis on continuity; despite the obvious differences in context, they draw a direct line between Ortega's violent authoritarianism and Sandinista rule in the 1980s, which they understood as tyrannical, repressive, and totalitarian. Meanwhile, other Nicaraguans see a break with the past. Dissident Sandinista leaders, for instance, have tended to portray Ortega as a traitor who usurped leadership of the revolutionary cause and betrayed its values. For them, there's little left of the Revolution, and comparisons to the earlier Somoza regime are more instructive. Over the coming years, historians will no doubt address these questions by balancing the continuities and discontinuities. It will likely be a long debate, with scholars locating the "place" of orteguismo in the history of the Nicaraguan Revolution much in the same way that they do for Bonapartism and Stalinism in the French and Russian revolutions, respectively.

In the meantime, the Sandinista Revolution's strange afterlife provides an opportunity to assess some of the changes—and widely held assumptions—that accompanied the end of the Cold War in global affairs. For example, Nicaragua in the postrevolutionary era witnessed how the terms of reference for politics could change very quickly in a country once the ideological contest between socialism and capitalism subsided. Central America's social and political conflicts in the 1970s and '80s were accompanied by major disputes over how to overcome underdevelopment. When power changed hands, new rulers often brought vastly new ideas compared to their predecessors for generating economic growth, positioning the state within the economy, addressing land inequality, and reducing dependence on foreign capital. Today, by contrast, little distinguishes Ortega's economic policy from earlier, "neoliberal" governments; the nominally left-wing FSLN government might be considered a case of the "Leninism without economic transformation" seen in other left-wing revolutionary projects in the Global South that survived the transition to the post–Cold War era.[66] Nor is there much daylight between the macroeconomic approaches of the different Central American governments. As economic debates have become less visible, social and cultural issues—such as abortion—have become far more salient in politics. This, in turn, has affected the relevance of the left–right paradigm in Nicaraguan politics. As Ortega's ideological metamorphosis and alliances suggest, that framework does not matter as much as it once did; Nicaraguans are either *orteguistas* or *anti-orteguistas*. In neighboring El Salvador, the rise of President Nayib Bukele in 2019 destroyed a two-party system that, in a continuation of the civil war, broke down along left–right lines in the 1990s and 2000s. To the extent that ideological polarization left–right lines determined or exacerbated the civil wars of the 1970s and '80s, Central Americans can be glad that it is gone. Though there are sometimes aftershocks (in Nicaragua, issues briefly arose with demobilized Sandinista and Contra soldiers [*recompas* and *recontras*, respectively]), full-scale armed conflicts have become a thing of the past in the Central America.

Some ideological frameworks may have crumbled, but "what did not change with the end of the Cold War," historian Arne Westad has written, "were the conflicts between the haves and have nots in international affairs."[67] At the root of Central America's problems were terrible, structural inequalities. The persistence of these underlying problems helps explain why, even as Cold War–related phenomena (such as ideological polarization or superpower intervention) went away, the level of violence has remained high in the region. In El Salvador during the 2010s, gang-related violence claimed a number of lives comparable to those lost during the worst years of the country's civil war. Even the cities of Honduras—which were largely spared the cycles of armed conflict experienced elsewhere in Central America during the Cold War—became global murder capitals in the twenty-first century. For the most part, the conflicts of the 1980s were not followed by successful reconstruction or reconciliation programs to address the physical and social destruction they caused. And as Gilles Bataillon notes, the peace agreements that ended the wars involved amnesties for military leaders on all sides, something that contributed to a culture of impunity that is intimately tied to the violence and corruption afflicting the isthmus today.[68] Those problems, taken together, have helped push Central Americans to emigrate on a massive scale in recent years.

Central America's transitions to democracy—"created from above," as Edelberto Torres Rivas described them—did not address challenges affecting their societies from the bottom up. Indeed, they were never intended to. As former Costa Rican president Luis Guillermo Solís put it: "You can't ask of Esquipulas more than what Esquipulas promised. And Esquipulas promised nothing more than what was in its title: 'Procedure for the Establishment of a Firm and Lasting Peace in Central America.' It was a modus operandi for achieving a specific objective: peace. Nobody ever said that Esquipulas would solve the problems of inequality and misery."[69] In those terms, the agreements were rather successful. The transition to democracy ended gruesome civil wars in the 1990s. At the beginning of this century, analysts could celebrate that Central America had never experienced such a sustained period of peaceful transitions in government where voters made their voices heard. It was also a period where, more than ever before, criticizing the party in power or organizing around a political agenda did not put one's life at risk.

But divorced from their original context—ending civil wars and interventions on the isthmus—the democratic norms and practices imagined by the Esquipulas Accords have looked increasingly irrelevant in Central America.[70] In Nicaragua, the transition to democracy allowed civil society and independent media to flourish. But poverty and inequality continued to affect most of the population. Moreover, given that the Chamorro government slashed spending and reduced state intervention in the economy, many Sandinista families experienced the arrival of democracy as the loss of employment in the public sector or the cancellation of social benefits—such as access to health care or housing—defended by the Revolution. It took years for the Nicaraguan economy to bounce back from the war-related crisis of the 1980s. Therefore, the transition's political conquests were not accompanied by a widespread sense of social or economic well-being. Corruption scandals in every government cast another shadow over the promise of respect for human rights and the rule of law.

In the 1990s, many political scientists worried that these sort of underlying, "objective" conditions would limit the consolidation of democracy in countries that abruptly adopted this form of government toward the end of the twentieth century. With little prior tradition of liberal electoral governance, and based on very fragile social and economic foundations, many countries in Eastern Europe and the Global South only got as far as becoming "pseudo-democracies," "hybrid regimes," or "illiberal democracies."[71] The power-sharing agreement reached between Alemán and Ortega in the late 1990s was an early sign that Nicaragua's constitutional order was severely vulnerable. Once elected, Ortega mirrored other post–Cold War "electoral authoritarians" like Hungary's Viktor Orbán or Turkey's Recep Tayyip Erdoğan who, having reached power through democratic means, subsequently used liberal institutions to consolidate authoritarian rule. Underlying dissatisfaction with the transition to neoliberalism and democracy in the 1990s helps explain why Ortega's authoritarian bargain was so attractive to many sectors in society. And the fragility of the institutions created in the 1980s and '90s explains the tremendous speed with which the new FSLN regime was able to co-opt all branches of government and neutralize any checks and balances.

As Nicaragua's democratic framework collapsed, the rest of Central America has gone in the same direction. In the 1980s and early 1990s, interlocking peace agreements meant that progress toward democratization in one country depended on the development of representative institutions in another. These tandem democratic transitions were animated, moreover, by key international organizations—such as missions from the United Nations and the Organization of American States—as well as a generalized, end of the Cold War international consensus on liberal democracy as the appropriate form of government. Today the isthmus is witnessing something similar, albeit in reverse. In 2009, a military coup overthrew a democratically elected government in Honduras. In El Salvador, the Bukele government launched an assault on basic civil rights and institutions, leveraging popular disgust with the corruption and crime that have afflicted society since the end of the civil war. In Guatemala, economic and racial inequality have allowed the oligarchy to exert veto power over republican institutions and pro-democracy actors, giving rise to a sort of Mafia state penetrated by transnational organized crime. Central American governments studiously avoid condemning their neighbors' human rights abuses. In fact, they appear to learn from and imitate one another. The region's contemporary authoritarians—despite coming from varied ideological backgrounds—evince a shared distrust of the sectors that won most from the democratic transition: nongovernmental organizations, human rights activists, journalists, and other components of civil society.

During the twilight of the Cold War, many—not only in the United States, but around the world—came to believe that liberal democracy was the ultimate, inevitable destination for human societies. Further, it was often assumed that democratization went hand in hand with the expansion of open, market-oriented economies (the contradictory example of the People's Republic of China notwithstanding). In Nicaragua and the rest of Central America, however, a solid consensus on market economics and openness to foreign investment has done little to restrain human rights abuses and restrictions on civil liberties. Nobody wishes to go back to the armed conflicts of the Cold War era. But it is worth noting that the post–Cold War period has started to look as conducive to authoritarianism as what came before. Across both periods, progress on the generation and more equal distribution of wealth has been achingly slow. Nicaragua, specifically, remains one of the poorest countries in the Western Hemisphere.

One departure from the Cold War period is the relative disinternationalization of Central American politics. Central American countries today are more deeply integrated in the global economy than ever before. But their politics are less salient on the international scene. In the context of the global struggle between capitalism and socialism, the slightest instance of political instability could serve as the spark for intervention by one of the superpowers or by transnational revolutionary and counterrevolutionary movements. Decisions made by Central American leaders sometimes reverberated globally. For better or worse, that is no longer the case. Today, when Central American countries appear in the headlines in the United States, they appear as part of a *domestic* problem—the source of immigrants or the cause of a so-called border crisis—rather than a foreign policy issue. Meanwhile, foreign actors—including the government of the United States, which retains overwhelmingly asymmetric influence in this hemisphere—seem surprisingly incapable of influencing Central American elites to change their policies one way or another.

The 1970s and '80s could have not been more different. Nicaragua—again, for better or worse—was in the spotlight. The Sandinistas and their opponents became household names around the world. This internationalized quality decisively shaped the drama that unfolded. And, in turn, Nicaraguans—more than they might recognize today, and despite their country's small size and limited resources—formed part of a critical juncture in world affairs where the post–Cold War order was constructed.

Acknowledgments

Like the events it describes, this book's creation was an international affair involving many institutions and individuals. My mentors from graduate school—Alejandro de la Fuente, Arne Westad, and especially Kirsten Weld, my primary adviser—have been fantastic in both supporting my scholarship and challenging me to take it to new heights. Many other faculty at Harvard University guided me during this project's early stages, including Steven Levitsky, Erez Manela, Tamar Herzog, and Mary Elise Sarotte. Prior to that, my classes at Grinnell College were what inspired me to study Latin American politics in the first place; Pablo Silva and Carlos de la Torre deserve special thanks.

My research would not have been possible absent the material support and community provided by Harvard University's Department of History, David Rockefeller Center for Latin American Studies, and Weatherhead Center for International Affairs. The Mellon-Mays Undergraduate Fellowship and Beinecke Scholarship provided additional funding. In Cuba and Mexico, Havana's Instituto de Historia and the Colegio de México, respectively, enabled archival access and interviews. Eugenia Solís Umaña, María Estelí Jarquín, and Federico Picado Gómez facilitated research in Costa Rica. I am indebted to the amazing staff, researchers, and directors of the Instituto de Historia de Nicaragua y Centroamérica (IHNCA) for providing me with an intellectual home in Managua. The Institute for Citizens and Scholars generously supported me while I wrote the manuscript, which received constructive feedback from the excellent peer reviewers contacted by The University of North Carolina Press. Last but not least, Michelle Witkowski, Hannah Bailey, Jessica Ryan, Debbie Gershenowitz, and the staff at UNC Press did a wonderful job turning the manuscript into a book.

Over the years I benefited from participating in collaborative projects on Nicaragua involving Brown University's Watson Institute for International and Public Affairs, Managua's *Confidencial* newspaper, the *Anhelos de un nuevo horizonte* volume, a special issue of *The Americas,* and "The Left and the International Arena" seminar at Sciences Po Centre for History. My excellent colleagues at Chapman University—especially Gregory Daddis, Kyle Longley, and Rafael Luévano—gave helpful feedback on the manuscript. I am also grateful that Luciana Chamorro, June Erlick, Stephen Kinzer, Salvador Martí, Eric Mosinger, and Kai Thaler were always available to chat or read portions of my work. And there were countless other scholars of Nicaragua with whom I was lucky to exchange ideas, or who provided advice and encouragement at key moments; I would like to thank Gilles Bataillon, Elvira Cuadra, Frances Kinloch, Antonio Monte, Juan Pablo Gómez, Eline van Ommen, Gerardo Sánchez Nateras, José Luis Rocha, Ileana Rodríguez, Ileana Selejan, Benjamin Waddell, and everybody else who took the time.

My thanks as well to all the librarians and archivists who enabled this work, and especially to the historical actors who sat down with me for interviews. Special thanks are in order for Alejandro Bendaña, Sergio Ramírez, and Marcel Salamín, who provided access to crucial documentation. Sergio Cabrales did excellent work transcribing most of the oral history interviews cited throughout.

On a personal note, I would like to thank my loved ones. The making of this book overlapped with a difficult period in Nicaraguan public life that affected me very deeply. But my friends, siblings, extended family, and my wife, Halima, gave me strength and allowed me to stay positive. More than anyone, my parents deserve gratitude for their commitment to justice and democracy in our country, and for believing in the importance of academic research for those ideals.

Notes

Abbreviations and Acronyms

AHGE-AHD-SRE	Archivo Histórico Genaro Estrada del Acervo Histórico Diplomático de la Secretaría de Relaciones de México
AHIHNCA	Archivo Histórico del Instituto de Historia de Nicaragua y Centroamérica
ANCR	Archivo Nacional de Costa Rica
CWIHP	Cold War International History Project
DNSA	Digital National Security Archive
FOIA	Freedom of Information Act
FRUS	Foreign Relations of the United States
MINREX	Ministerio de Relaciones Exteriores

Preface

1. Nicaragua 1979–2019: The Sandinista Revolution after 40 Years, held at Brown University, Providence, RI, May 2–4, 2019, https://watson.brown.edu/events/2019/conference-nicaragua-1979-2019-sandinista-revolution-after-40-years.

2. Stephen Kinzer, "40 Years Later, Grappling with Regime Change in Nicaragua," *Boston Globe*, May 9, 2019.

3. Missed Opportunities, Hanoi, Vietnam, June 20–23, 1997; the Cuban government and the National Security Archive—an American NGO—organized a private meeting of former US, Soviet, and Cuban leaders to revisit the Cuban Missile Crisis in 2002 ("At Cuba Conference, Old Foes Exchange Notes on 1962 Missile Crisis," *New York Times*, October 14, 2002).

4. Aguilar Camín and Meyer, *A la sombra de la Revolución Mexicana*. See also my essay "A la sombra de la Revolución Sandinista."

5. Alma Guillermoprieto, "The Revolution Eats Itself in Nicaragua," *New Yorker*, March 10, 2022.

6. Gleijeses, "The CIA's Paramilitary Operations during the Cold War," 304.

7. Walter LaFeber (*Inevitable Revolutions*), for example, showed how US policies in Central America historically contributed to the cycle of revolutions and counter-revolutions that swept the region in the 1970s and '80s; Greg Grandin (*Empire's Workshop*) argued that 1980s Central America policy provided a blueprint for the United States' twenty-first-century interventions in the Middle East.

8. Kagan, *A Twilight Struggle*.

9. Leogrande, *Our Own Backyard*, x. For rich accounts of US policy in Nicaragua, see also Kagan, *A Twilight Struggle*, and Pastor, *Not Condemned to Repetition*.

10. Some works that I found especially helpful include: Walter, *The Regime of Anastasio Somoza*; Gould, *To Lead as Equals*; Gómez, *Autoridad/Cuerpo/Nación*; Ferrero Blanco, *La Nicaragua de los Somoza*; and González-Rivera, *Before the Revolution*.

11. See, for example, Everingham, *Revolution and the Multiclass Coalition in Nicaragua*; Zimmerman, *Sandinista*; and Mónica Baltodano's Memorias de la Lucha Sandinista project.

12. See, for example, Close, Martí, and McConnell, eds., *The Sandinistas and Nicaragua since 1979*; Spalding, "Los empresarios y el estado posrevolucionario"; William I. Robinson, "Capitalist Development in Nicaragua and the Mirage of the Left," *Truthout*, May 18, 2018; and Óscar René Vargas, "Nicaragua: Democracia autoritaria o dictadura familiar," *Nueva Sociedad*, August 2016.

13. Soto, *Ventanas en la memoria*; Rodríguez, *La prosa de la contra-insurgencia*; Vannini, *Política y memoria en Nicaragua*.

14. Gobat, "Reconstrucción histórica de la Revolución Sandinista de Nicaragua." I was fortunate to count upon the prior scholarship of social scientists who studied Nicaragua during the revolutionary period. Many are cited throughout; I found the work of Jorge Castañeda, David Close, Dennis Gilbert, Salvador Martí, José Luis Rocha, and Carlos Vilas especially helpful.

15. IHNCA ceased to exist as we know it in August 2023, when the government of President Daniel Ortega seized its parent institution, Universidad Centroamericana. State authorities subsequently reopened the archive and research center under a new name: The Heroes of Nicaragua Historical Institute.

16. See, for example, works by Sánchez Nateras, van Ommen, and Avery, cited throughout.

17. Westad, *The Global Cold War*. On the Cold War in Latin America, see Joseph and Spencer, eds., *In from the Cold: Latin America's New Encounter with the Cold War*; and Bethell and Roxborough, "The Impact of the Cold War on Latin America."

18. Harmer, *Allende's Chile and the Inter-American Cold War*; Nguyen, *Hanoi's War*; Connelly, *A Diplomatic Revolution*; Chamberlin, *The Global Offensive*.

19. "A Family of Six Nicaraguan Presidents Looks to Provide a Seventh," *Economist*, March 31, 2021; "La venganza de Daniel Ortega contra la familia Chamorro en Nicaragua," *El País*, March 27, 2022.

Introduction

1. "Transcript of the President's Speech," *New York Times*, March 17, 1986.

2. Kagan, *Twilight Struggle*, xiii.

3. On Strummer's views, see Gall, *The Punk Rock Politics of Joe Strummer*, 70–121.

4. Ramírez, *Adiós Muchachos* (2012 English translation), 2.

5. Quoted in Leogrande, *Our Own Backyard*, 581.

6. For a critique, see Long, *Latin America Confronts the United States*.

7. Luis Carrión Cruz, interview with the author. For more of Carrión's views on the National Directorate's ideology, see chapter 3.

8. Ortega Saavedra, *La odisea por Nicaragua*, 117.

9. Vilas, "Sobre la estrategia económica de la Revolución Sandinista."

10. Carrión, "Luces y sombras de la revolución, 40 años después."

11. Wheelock, "Revolution and Democratic Transition in Nicaragua"; Ramírez, *Adiós Muchachos*. See also Gilbert, *Sandinistas*.

12. Rodríguez, *La prosa de la contra-insurgencia*, 39.

13. See Gleijeses, *Shattered Hope*; Harmer, *Allende's Chile and the Inter-American Cold War*; Nguyen, *Hanoi's War*.

14. Long, *Latin America Confronts the United States*, 2.

15. Skocpol, *States and Social Revolutions*.

16. Somoza Debayle and Cox, *Nicaragua Betrayed*, 397.

17. See Connelly, *A Diplomatic Revolution*.

18. Estimates of war-related deaths vary wildly for both conflicts. According to the Peace Research Institute Oslo (PRIO) Battledeaths Dataset, estimates for the insurrectionary war (1978–79) range between 10,000 and 35,000, and between 10,000 and 43,000 for the Contra War (1981–89); Lacina and Gleditsch, "Monitoring Trends in Global Combat."

19. Rojas, *El árbol de las revoluciones*, 231–45.

20. Ramírez, *Adiós Muchachos*, 4.

21. Torres Rivas, *Revoluciones sin cambios revolucionarios*.

22. Monteiro and Bartel, *Before and after the Fall*, 12.

Chapter 1

1. See Castañeda, *Utopia Unarmed*, 90–128.

2. "National Security Action Memorandum 162: Development of U.S. and Indigenous Police, Paramilitary, and Military Resources," Washington, DC, June 19, 1962, John F. Kennedy Presidential Library, www.jfklibrary.org/asset-viewer/archives /JFKNSF/337/JFKNSF-337-001.

3. US Senate, Committee on Foreign Relations, "Administration Briefing on the Current Situation in Nicaragua," September 13, 1978, Nicaragua Collection, DNSA; emphasis added.

4. Goldstone, *Revolutions*, 15–19.

5. Haiti's Duvalier family managed a dynastic succession when Jean-Claude "Baby Doc" replaced his father François "Papa Doc" in 1971. By that time, Anastasio Somoza Debayle had already succeeded his brother Luis Somoza Debayle, who had taken power after the assassination of his father, Anastasio Somoza García.

6. Hassan, interviewed by journalist Tina Rosenberg in *Children of Cain*, 279–95.

7. Leonard, *Central America and the United States*.

8. LaFeber, *Inevitable Revolutions*.

9. Ramírez, *Adiós Muchachos*, 90.

10. Gobat, *Confronting the American Dream*.

11. Walter, *The Regime of Anastasio Somoza*; Vilas, "Family Affairs," 312–13.

12. Gould, *To Lead as Equals*.

13. For a political biography, see Jarquín Calderón, *Pedro Joaquín: ¡Juega!*

14. Fonseca Amador, *Un nicaragüense en Moscú*.

15. On FSLN origins, see Zimmerman's biography of Fonseca, *Sandinista*.

16. Victor Tirado López, interview with Mónica Baltodano, accessed July 1, 2023, https://memoriasdelaluchasandinista.org/view_stories.php?id=10.

17. Hoffman, *The PLO and Israel in Central America*; Julián Navarrete, "Masácre en Múnich: La conexión Nica," *La Prensa*, April 10, 2017.

18. On his experience in Guatemala, see Carlos Fonseca Amador, interview by Ernesto González Bermejo, November 1970, from Centro de Documentación de los Movimientos Armados, accessed June 30, 2023, https://cedema.org/digital_items /2711.

19. Prevost, "Cuba and Nicaragua," 121–23.

20. Zimmerman, *Sandinista*, 79.

21. Borge, *La paciente impaciencia*, 185–86.

22. Andrew and Mitrokhin, *The World Was Going Our Way*, 49–50.

23. Andrew and Mitrokhin, *The World Was Going Our Way*, 53. Ernesto Cardenal and Humberto Ortega Saavedra both note in their memoirs that Castro never met Fonseca. See *La revolución perdida*, 70, and *La epopeya de la insurreción*, 390, respectively.

24. Bayardo Arce, interview by Mónica Baltodano, accessed July 1, 2023, https:// memoriasdelaluchasandinista.org/view_stories.php?id=25.

25. Arce, interview with Baltodano; see also Hugo Torres, interview by Baltodano, accessed July 1, 2023, https://memoriasdelaluchasandinista.org/view_stories .php?id=27.

26. Belli, *The Country under My Skin*, 40.

27. Ryan, "Structure, Agency, and the Nicaraguan Revolution," 196–97.

28. Inter-American Commission on Human Rights (IACHR), "Report on the Situation of Human Rights in the Republic of Nicaragua," June 30, 1981; see section titled "The Pre-Revolutionary Social and Economic Structure."

29. Vilas, "Family Affairs," 313.

30. Everingham, *Revolution and the Multiclass Coalition in Nicaragua*, 180.

31. Jarquín Calderón, *Pedro Joaquín: ¡Juega!*, 213–14.

32. The FSLN, according to Ramírez, was still viewed by middle- and upper-class Nicaraguans as a "terrorist force" of "embittered delinquents" who were "condemned to failure." Ramírez, interview with the author.

33. Edén Pastora, interview by Mónica Baltodano, accessed July 1, 2023, https:// memoriasdelaluchasandinista.org/view_stories.php?id=53.

34. Central Intelligence Agency (CIA), "Nicaragua: The Sandinista Guerrillas and Their International Links," September 6, 1978, DNSA.

35. Jaime Wheelock Román, interview by Mónica Baltodano, accessed July 1, 2023, https://memoriasdelaluchasandinista.org/view_stories.php?id=141.

36. Monroy-García, *Tendencias ideológico-políticas del Frente Sandinista*, 25, 53–76.

37. Monroy-García, *Tendencias ideológico-políticas del Frente Sandinista*, 79–92.

38. Wheelock, interview by Mónica Baltodano.

39. Monroy-García, *Tendencias ideológico-políticas del Frente Sandinista*, 93–113.

40. For an in-depth description of the October Offensive, see Ortega Saavedra, *La epopeya de la insurrección*, 315–31.

41. Ramírez, interview with the author.

42. Ortega Saavedra, *La epopeya de la insurrección*, 320.

43. Ramírez recalls Joaquín Cuadra Chamorro asking this question in *Adiós Muchachos*, 61.

44. Ortega Saavedra, *Epopeya de la insurrección*, 320. The five-point program called for: (1) a democratic regime with civil liberties, (2) abolition of the National Guard, (3) expropriation of the Somoza estate, (4) agrarian reform, and (5) an end to dependency on the United States.

45. Ramírez, *Adiós Muchachos*, 61–62: "Children drew their fathers into the struggle."

46. Vilas, "Family Affairs," 320–22.

47. Ramírez, interview with the author. Ramírez also describes the *Gabo* connection briefly in *Adiós Muchachos*, 81–84, as does Ernesto Cardenal in his own memoir, *La revolución perdida*.

48. Ernesto Cardenal, who introduced the Junta to Pérez, recalls the statesman's response in *La revolución perdida*, 31.

49. Tirado, interview by Mónica Baltodano.

50. Gleijeses, "Juan José Arévalo and the Caribbean Legion," 138–41.

51. Ortega Saavedra, *Epopeya de la insurrección*, 334. Figueres said he promised the Terceristas to do "everything that was possible to help the Sandinistas." Quoted by Pastor, *Not Condemned to Repetition*, 49. For historical background, see Moulton, "Building Their Own Cold War in Their Own Backyard."

52. "National Mutiny in Nicaragua," *New York Times*, July 30, 1978.

53. Wheelock, interview by Baltodano.

54. Ramírez recalls plans for rapprochement in a chapter of *Adiós Muchachos* titled "The Likely Number Thirteen," 113–26. Edmundo Jarquín, who in December 1977 met with Tercerista representatives on behalf of Chamorro to set up the February 1978 meeting, also recalls the Matagalpa incident and describes those talks in *Pedro Joaquín: ¡Juega!*, 277–79.

55. Somoza Debayle later told US ambassador Lawrence Pezzullo that the entire crisis would have been averted were it not for the Chamorro assassination; *Nicaragua Betrayed*, 370–71.

56. Cardenal, *La revolución perdida*, 65.

57. Castañeda, *Utopia Unarmed*, 106.

58. V. I. Lenin, "The Collapse of the Second International," 213–14.

59. Ferrero Blanco, *La Nicaragua de los Somoza*, 196–221; Kinzer, *Blood of Brothers*, 36–38.

60. Ortega Saavedra, *Epopeya de la insurrección*, 336.

61. CIA, "Nicaragua: The Sandinista Guerrillas and Their International Links."

62. Somoza Debayle, *Nicaragua Betrayed*, 103.

63. Wheelock (see interview by Baltodano) argues that the FSLN's development of "intermediate organizations," primarily under the leadership of the GPP and Proletarian tendencies, helped mobilize the urban uprisings. For a breakdown of

1978–79 combatants by occupation, see Salvador Martí i Puig, "La Izquierda Revolucionaria en Centroamérica," citing research conducted by Vilas for *Perfiles de la revolución sandinista*. On the essential role played by student movements, see Rueda, *Students of Revolution*.

64. Gould, *To Lead as Equals*, 17.

65. Kampwirth, *Women and Guerrilla Movements*, 21–44.

66. Sierakowski, *Sandinistas: A Moral History*.

67. "Memorandum from Robert Pastor of the National Security Council Staff to the President's Assistant for National Security Affairs (Brzezinski)," Washington, DC, June 5, 1979, in US Department of State, *FRUS 1977–1978*, vol. 29, Panama, 566.

68. Brands, *Latin America's Cold War*, 166, 175–79.

69. Pastor, *Not Condemned to Repetition*, 99.

70. Interview by Pastor quoted in *Not Condemned to Repetition*, 50.

71. Pastor, *Not Condemned to Repetition*, 52.

72. Aristides Calvani, cited in Pastor, *Not Condemned to Repetition*, 104.

73. Ramírez, *Adiós Muchachos*, 123; Pastor, *Not Condemned to Repetition*, 103.

74. Brands correctly notes that the Sandinista Revolution was a "truly regional affair" involving the key support of several countries other than Cuba; *Latin America's Cold War*, 182–83. Gerardo Sánchez Nateras, in *La última revolución*, goes further in detailing how and why each of the Latin American countries intervened against Somoza.

75. Joaquín Cuadra Lacayo, interview with the author.

76. Ortega Saavedra, *Epopeya de la insurrección*, 341–42.

77. Sánchez Nateras, *La última revolución*, 41–42.

78. "Memorandum of Conversation," Caracas, March 28, 1978, *FRUS 1977–1980*, vol. 24, South America, 995.

79. Victor Hugo Tinoco, interview with the author.

80. Cuadra recalls of Venezuelan support: "Carlos Andrés, he wanted to influence the way in which triumph of the revolution and overthrow of the dictatorship took place, and therefore wanted to have enough godfathership so as to guide us: '*do this, boys; don't do that, boys.*'" Interview with the author. With regard to efforts to promote moderate figures within the Tercerista faction, Cuadra cites the Venezuelans' "embrace of Edén Pastora."

81. "Memorandum of Conversation," Washington, DC, September 25–26, 1977, *FRUS 1977–1980*, vol. 29, 297.

82. Gandásegui, "La conjoncture centre-américaine et le canal de Panama," 108–11.

83. Salamín-Cárdenas and Millán-Salamín, *Omar Torrijos*, 66.

84. FSLN guerrilla leader (later, diplomat) Victor Hugo Tinoco recalls: "For Latin America the idea of a North American intervention in the region was terrible . . . for the Panamanians because, with a North American intervention in Central America—what future was there for a canal owned by the Panamanians?" Interview with the author. Ramírez notes that if "Torrijos wanted one thing more than anything else, it was to recover sovereignty over the canal," and writes of his knowledge that

"Torrijos . . . had a secret plan to immobilize the Panama Canal with dynamite charges if he was unable to recover it through treaties." *Adiós Muchachos*, 95.

85. Salamín-Cárdenas and Millán-Salamín, *Omar Torrijos*.

86. Fidel Castro recalled that Torrijos could hardly contain his impulse to use military force to pressure the United States to grant Panamanian sovereignty over the canal; see *La paz en Colombia*, 128.

87. Salamín-Cárdenas and Millán-Salamín, *Omar Torrijos*, 66. Torrijos also used the DC-10 metaphor in conversations with Carter and his advisers: "Memorandum of Conversation," Washington, DC, July 3, 1979, in *FRUS 1977–1980*, vol. 15, Central America, 645.

88. Salamín-Cárdenas and Millán-Salamín, *Omar Torrijos*, 290–91.

89. US Senate Foreign Relations Committee, "Briefing on Nicaragua," September 1978.

90. Torres Jiménez, *Rumbo norte*, 461.

91. See, for example, Everingham, *Revolution and the Multiclass Coalition in Nicaragua*. Other comparative accounts (Foran and Goodwin, "Revolutionary Outcomes in Iran and Nicaragua"; Parsa, *States, Ideologies, and Social Revolutions*) stress the same idea. For other analyses of the Nicaraguan coalition, see Wickham-Crowley, *Guerrillas and Revolution in Latin America*; Selbin, *Modern Latin American Revolutions*.

92. See previously cited interviews by Mónica Baltodano of Bayardo Arce, Jaime Wheelock, and Edén Pastora.

93. Wheelock, interview by Baltodano.

94. US Embassy, Nicaragua, "Meeting with President Somoza: March 9," March 13, 1978, DNSA.

95. US Embassy, Nicaragua, "Meeting with President Somoza: April 22," April 26, 1978, DNSA.

96. Somoza Debayle, *Nicaragua Betrayed*, 140. The Carter letter, which congratulated Somoza on his "steps toward respecting human rights," is reproduced in its entirety on pages 276–77.

97. Grupo de los Doce, "Minuta de acuerdos," June 26, 1978, Sergio Ramírez Papers, Box 57, Folder 15, Firestone Library, Princeton University, Princeton, NJ.

98. Ferrero Blanco, *La Nicaragua de los Somoza*, 222–47.

99. Ortega Saavedra, *Epopeya de la insurrección*, 346–51.

100. Ramírez, *Adiós Muchachos*, 146. See also Ortega Saavedra, *Epopeya de la insurrección*, 351.

101. US Embassy, Nicaragua, "Amb Meeting with President on FSLN Attack," August 24, 1978, DNSA.

102. Torres Jiménez, *Rumbo norte*, 456.

Chapter 2

1. "National Mutiny in Nicaragua," *New York Times*, July 30, 1978; Meiselas, *Nicaragua*.

2. As late as February 1979, US intelligence services rated Somoza's chances of finishing his term through 1981 as "better than even." Indeed, a subsequent internal CIA review noted that intelligence reports "vacillated on his chances up to a month before his departure." See CIA, "Intelligence Judgments Preceding the Sandinista Takeover in Nicaragua," April 12, 1984, CIA FOIA Reading Room, Document Number CIA-RDP86B00269R001100100002-6.

3. Goodwin, *No Other Way Out*, 137–216.

4. Torres, interview with the author.

5. Somoza Debayle, *Nicaragua Betrayed*, 393.

6. Paul Chamberlin used the term "global offensive" to describe the PLO's connections with revolutionary movements in China, Vietnam, Algeria, Cuba, and beyond in *The Global Offensive*.

7. Ortega Saavedra, *La epopeya de la insurrección*, 352.

8. Ortega Saavedra, *La epopeya de la insurrección*, 316.

9. Ortega Saavedra, *La epopeya de la insurrección*, 353–59.

10. Jaime Wheelock Román, interview by Mónica Baltodano, accessed July 1, 2023, https://memoriasdelaluchasandinista.org/view_stories.php?id=141.

11. PVP leaders Fernando Camacho and Manuel Mora Salas, interview with the author.

12. Sánchez Nateras, *La última revolución*, 190.

13. Carazo, *Carazo: Tiempo y marcha*, 262.

14. Echeverría, *La guerra no declarada*, 21. These decisions are also narrated in an internal Costa Rican government history, "Conflicto Costa Rica-Nicaragua," ANCR, Fondo Presidencia, 1480.

15. "Pacto del 15 de Septiembre," in Echeverría, *La guerra no declarada*, 27.

16. Echeverría, *La guerra no declarada*, 33.

17. Pastor, *Not Condemned to Repetition*, 75–81.

18. "Memorandum from Robert Pastor of the National Security Council Staff to the President's Assistant for National Security Affairs (Brzezinski)," Washington, DC, August 8, 1978, *FRUS 1977–1980*, vol. 29, 467.

19. Some Carter administration officials wanted to build up the FAO as an alternative to the Sandinistas but feared contradicting the administration's "nonintervention" principle; see Schmidli, "'The Most Sophisticated Intervention We Have Seen.'"

20. Quoted in Pastor, *Not Condemned to Repetition*, 71.

21. "Memorandum for the Record," Telephone Conversation on Nicaragua, Washington, DC, September 22, 1978, *FRUS*, vol. 29, 478.

22. "Memorandum of Conversation," Washington, DC, September 23, 1978, *FRUS*, vol. 29, 479–84.

23. "Posiciones del FAO frente a las alternativas de desenlace de la actual crisis política," Sergio Ramírez Papers, Box 58, Folder 5.

24. Ramírez, *Adiós Muchachos*, 155.

25. FSLN, "Communiqué to the Nicaraguan People," December 9, 1978. Reproduced in *Latin American Perspectives* 6, no. 1 (1979): 127–28.

26. "Carta de Carlos Andrés Pérez a Jimmy Carter," December 22, 1978, ANCR, Fondo Presidencia.

27. "Telegram from the Embassy in Nicaragua to the Department of State, the Department of Defense, and the Joint Chiefs of Staff," Managua, December 21, 1978, *FRUS 1977–1980*, vol. 15, 440.

28. Echeverría, *La guerra no declarada*, 56; Carazo, *Carazo: Tiempo y marcha*, 265.

29. Echeverría, *La guerra no declarada*, 110.

30. Carazo, *Carazo: Tiempo y marcha*, 283–87.

31. Castro, *La paz en Colombia*, 127.

32. Echeverría, *La guerra no declarada*, 129–30.

33. Salamín-Cárdenas and Millán-Salamín, *Omar Torrijos*, 61–62.

34. According to Salamín, Torrijos met with Gabriel García Márquez in the fall of 1978 to find ways of supporting the Sandinistas with arms from Colombia. García Márquez arranged a meeting between Salamín and Jaime Bateman, then chief of the M-19 guerrilla movement, but no Colombian weapons ever made it to Nicaragua. Salamín-Cárdenas and Millán-Salamín, *Omar Torrijos*, 50–59.

35. Castro, *La paz en Colombia*, 128.

36. Brands notes that Castro "backed the FSLN since its formative years." Brands, *Latin America's Cold War*, 180. However, the FSLN historically received minimal support compared to peer Latin American organizations, and the Tercerista faction rose to prominence with Venezuelan and Panamanian support, much to the chagrin of the Cuban-sponsored GPP. See Ortega Saavedra, *La epopeya de la insurrección*, 390–91: "In 1976–77, Cuba's intelligence services confirmed the failure of the Sandinista guerrilla effort in the mountains and the profound division in the FSLN; and decides to maintain relations with the GPP. . . . The Tercerista insurrectional process of 1977 does not count on support from Cuba." Henry Ruíz suggests Cuban support for the GPP amounted to little ("the relations with Cuba had been lost due to the bad behavior of us, the Nicaraguans") and that they "didn't even smell" any of the Venezuelan money; interview with the author. Cuba's role, a CIA analysis noted, "did not amount to more than ideological example, advice, training, and safe-haven until 1979"; CIA, "Intelligence Judgments Preceding the Sandinista Takeover."

37. Sánchez Nateras, *La última Revolución*, 166.

38. Report from Manuel Mora Valverde to the Central Committee of the Communist Party of the Soviet Union, Archivo Nacional, San José, Costa Rica, Fondo Manuel Mora Valverde, 18-2004-000129. Mora explains that "until advanced stages of the struggle, the Cuban Party was convinced that the line to follow was . . . the guerrilla *foco* defined by Che Guevara and explained by Régis Debray."

39. Report from Mora to the Soviet Communist Party.

40. Sánchez Nateras, *La última revolución*, 169.

41. Ortega Saavedra, *La epopeya de la insurrección*, 391.

42. Ortega Saavedra, *La epopeya de la insurrección*, 392. According to Salamín, Castro responded to the Panamanian request with skepticism because he doubted the FSLN's chances of success; Salamín-Cárdenas and Millán-Salamín, *Omar Torrijos*, 59–72.

43. Sánchez Nateras, *La última revolución*, 287–321.

44. In January 1979, Panamanian Manuel Antonio Noriega told CIA sources that the Cuban leader "is of the opinion that the FSLN has no chance of defeating Nicaraguan President Anastasio Somoza Debayle, unless the disparate factions unite." Central Intelligence Agency Intelligence Information Cable, Washington, DC, January 25, 1979, *FRUS 1977–1980*, vol. 23, Mexico, Cuba, and the Caribbean, 102–3.

45. Salamín-Cárdenas and Millán-Salamín, *Omar Torrijos*, 76.

46. Salamín-Cárdenas and Millán-Salamín, *Omar Torrijos*, 85.

47. Salamín-Cárdenas and Millán-Salamín, *Omar Torrijos*, 85–90.

48. Salamín-Cárdenas and Millán-Salamín, *Omar Torrijos*, 89.

49. Ortega Saavedra, *La epopeya de la insurrección*, 360–61.

50. Joaquín Cuadra, interview with the author; Edén Pastora, interview by Mónica Baltodano, accessed July 1, 2023, https://memoriasdelaluchasandinista.org /view_stories.php?id=53.

51. Ramírez, *Adiós Muchachos*, 173.

52. Ramírez, *Adiós Muchachos*, 119.

53. Ramírez attributes the $3 + 3 + 3 = 9$ formula to Castro. Interview with the author.

54. The document, aside from coordinating the military efforts of the different Sandinista factions, called for the organization of a provisional government that would include "all the anti-Somocista forces" and would be "broad, democratic, and nonaligned" in the international arena. "Aspectos basicos de los acuerdos de unidad FSLN," March 7, 1979, AHIHNCA, FSLN D11G20050.

55. Gleijeses, "Cuba and the Cold War," 340.

56. Ramírez, *Adiós Muchachos*, 77.

57. Castañeda, *Utopia Unarmed*, 61–62.

58. Quoted in Pastor, *Not Condemned to Repetition*, 104.

59. Castro, *La paz en Colombia*, 128.

60. Salamín-Cárdenas and Millán-Salamín, *Omar Torrijos*, 69–70, 75, 77.

61. Nguyen, "The Vietnam Decade," 159–72.

62. The US suspended all military aid on February 8, 1979. Still, the National Guard's ranks swelled from 7,500 in September 1978 to 11,000 by March 1979, arming the new troops with weapons purchased from Israel, Argentina, and Guatemala (Pastor, *Not Condemned to Repetition*, 101). The US did not block those purchases until the regime was on the brink of collapse, when the Carter administration prevented a vital Israeli arms shipment; Somoza later claimed that the "precious cargo" of antipersonnel grenade launchers and ammunition would have won him the war (Somoza Debayle, *Nicaragua Betrayed*, 238–40).

63. Ortega Saavedra, *Epopeya de la Insurrección*, 392.

64. Sánchez Nateras, *La última revolución*, 203–6.

65. See, for example, Estradet, *Memorias del negro Pedro*, 9.

66. The Costa Rican Juan Santamaría and Carlos Luis Fallas Brigades contributed at least 250 combatants; Picado Lagos, *Los amigos venían del sur*. According to Ortega, ninety Chilean fighters joined along with fifteen Argentine advisers (*Epopeya de la insurrección*, 398). The Simón Bolívar Brigade, organized by the

Trotskyist Partido Socialista de los Trabajadores, sent at least a hundred troops; see Ortega Reyna, "¿Revolución en la Revolución?"

67. Castro, *La paz en Colombia*, 129; Estradet, *Memorias del negro Pedro*, 127.

68. "Memorandum confidencial del Grupo de los Doce de Nicaragua para Honorables Miembros de la Junta Militar de Gobierno de Honduras," February 21, 1979, Sergio Ramírez Papers, Box 59, Folder 16. Henry Ruiz notes that "Costa Rica was the rearguard. But you can't forget about Honduras. Honduras opened up as well. There came a moment when the Hondurans were no longer persecuting us"; interview with the author.

69. According to Agustín Lara, a Sandinista fighter who accompanied the Doce on their Mexico trip, PRI leader Gustavo Carvajal provided the Nicaraguans with $1 million and a shipment of assault rifles. Interview with the author.

70. López Portillo, *Mis tiempos*, 859.

71. "Marco para el rompimiento de relaciones con el regimen de Anastacio [*sic*] Somoza," México, April 24, 1979, Sergio Ramírez Papers, Box 59, Folder 15.

72. Iruegas, *Diplomacia en tiempos de guerra*, 191–96.

73. Castillo, Toussaint, and Vázquez Olivera, *Historia de las relaciones internacionales de México*, 159–70.

74. Herrera and Ojeda, "La política de México en la región de Centroamérica," 432–33.

75. Keller, *Mexico's Cold War*.

76. López Portillo, *Mis tiempos*, 837. See also Iruegas, *Diplomacia en tiempos de guerra*, 208; Carazo, *Carazo: Tiempo y marcha*, 305–6.

77. Iruegas, *Diplomacia en tiempos de guerra*, 198–99.

78. López Portillo, *Mis tiempos*, 840.

79. Bataillon and Galindo, "Los 'muchachos' en la revolución Sandinista," 303.

80. Hugo Torres (quote taken from *Rumbo norte*, 462–63), Humberto Ortega (*Epopeya de la insurrección*, 388), and Salamín-Cárdenas and Millán-Salamín (*Omar Torrijos*, 104) all recall this exchange in their memoirs.

81. "Memorandum from the President's Assistant for National Security Affairs (Brzezinski) to President Carter," Washington, DC, July 2, 1979, *FRUS*, vol. 15, 639–40.

82. Martín Torrijos would later be elected president of Panama. Manuel Mora Salas, son of the Costa Rican communist leader, led the aforementioned Carlos Luis Fallas Brigade.

83. Wheelock, interview by Baltodano.

84. US Department of State, "OAS Debates Recent Incidents on Costa Rica/Nicaragua Border," January 25, 1979, DNSA.

85. "Soviet Ambassador to Cuba V. I. Vorotnikov, Memorandum of Conversation with Fidel Castro," June 25, 1979, CWIHP.

86. Echeverría, *La guerra no declarada*, 135–37.

87. Lake, *Somoza Falling*, 263.

88. Pastor, *Not Condemned to Repetition*, 135.

89. US Embassy, Nicaragua, "Conversation with Somoza," September 8, 1978, DNSA.

90. Only Nicaragua and Paraguay voted against the June 21 OAS resolution that condemned Somoza and called for his removal. The other countries mentioned either voted in favor or abstained.

91. Pezzullo and Pezzullo, *At the Fall of Somoza*, 187.

92. Estimates vary on troop sizes. Humberto Ortega writes of 5,000 fighters (*La epopeya de la insurrección*, 399). Some have given lower estimates (2,800 FSLN fighters, plus some 15,000 adolescents in spontaneously formed militias, according to Dirk Kruijt in *Guerrillas*, 35) as well as higher ones (an FSLN army of 7,000, according to Walker in "The Sandinista Victory in Nicaragua").

93. Ortega Saavedra, *La epopeya de la insurrección*, 392.

94. "Primer Proclama del Gobierno de Reconstrucción Nacional," June 18, 1979, AHIHNCA, JGRN D15G1 0007.

95. Ortega Saavedra, *Epopeya de la insurección*, 419.

96. Pastor, *Not Condemned to Repetition*, 113.

97. Bulgarian Ministry of Foreign Affairs, "Memorandum of Todor Zhivkov–Fidel Castro Conversation," Havana, April 9, 1979, CWIHP.

98. Report from Mora to the Soviet Communist Party.

99. US House of Representatives, Committee on Foreign Relations, "Statement by Viron P. Vaky, Assistant Secretary of State for Inter-American Affairs," June 26, 1979, DNSA.

100. Kagan, *A Twilight Struggle*, 94–95.

101. Barbara Koeppel, "A Reporter's Death that Shifted U.S. Policy," *New York Times*, June 12, 1984.

102. Pastor, *Not Condemned to Repetition*, 117–18.

103. López Portillo, *Mis tiempos*, 847.

104. Pastor, *Not Condemned to Repetition*, 117–18.

105. Junta de Gobierno, "Plan del Gobierno de Reconstrucción Nacional Para Alcanzar la Paz," Sergio Ramírez Papers, Box 60, Folder 11.

106. Echeverría, *La guerra no declarada*, 143.

107. "Vorotnikov, Memorandum of Conversation with Fidel Castro."

108. Connelly, *A Diplomatic Revolution*.

109. Somoza Debayle, *Nicaragua Betrayed*, 266. Somoza withheld the letter until he received assurances from the United States that it would give him safe haven in Florida, and that it would not let the Junta take power unless the National Guard was preserved in some form.

110. US Embassy, Nicaragua, "Contingency Possibilities," July 6, 1979, DNSA.

111. US policymakers sought to recruit numerous FAO leaders but found that they either distrusted the United States for sticking with Somoza for too long, supported the provisional Junta, or identified with the FSLN. See "Telegram from the Embassy in Nicaragua to the Department of State," Managua, June 29, 1979, *FRUS*, vol. 15, 618, and US Embassy, Nicaragua, "The Current Scene," June 29, 1979, DNSA. Carter officials also tried and failed to court a National Guard commander who had fallen out of favor with Somoza; "Telegram from Secretary of State Vance in Tokyo to the Department of State and the White House," Tokyo, June 24, 1979, *FRUS*, vol. 15, 567–68.

112. "State basically believes that the Sandinistas are likely to gain control and that we should work to increase the relative strength of the moderate forces in the Junta. . . . Defense and I believe that some aspect of the guard must be preserved or the moderate political forces will simply be overrun by the Sandinistas once Somoza leaves, since they will be the only ones with the guns." See "Message from the President's Deputy Assistant for National Security Affairs (Aaron) to the President's Assistant for National Security Affairs (Brzezinski)," Washington, DC, June 28, 1979, *FRUS*, vol. 15, 600–601.

113. "Memorandum from Robert Pastor of the National Security Council Staff to the President's Assistant for National Security Affairs (Brzezinski)," Washington, DC, June 5, 1979, *FRUS*, vol. 29, 563.

114. "Telegram from the Embassy in Panama to the Department of State and the Embassies in Venezuela, Nicaragua, and Costa Rica," Panama City, June 27, 1979, *FRUS*, vol. 15, 588–89.

115. "Memorandum from the President's Assistant for National Security Affairs (Brzezinski) to President Carter," Washington, DC, July 2, 1979, *FRUS*, vol. 15, 639–40.

116. Worried that US participation would taint the Junta expansion plan, the White House had Torrijos's advisers present it to the Junta as if it were their idea. "Telegram from the Embassy in Nicaragua to the Department of State," Managua, June 29, 1979, *FRUS*, vol. 15, 616–17; "Esquema de transicíon," July 3, 1979, Sergio Ramírez Papers, Box 60, Folder 11. From an FBI informant in Havana: "CASTRO claimed that Cuba was/is responsible for influencing the Sandinista ruling junta to 'moderate' the revolution, i.e., setting a moderate course in carrying out the final stages of the revolution and in implementing the policies of the new (Sandinista) Nicaraguan Revolutionary Government. CASTRO told Source that had he wanted to, he could have really 'screwed up' the Nicaraguan situation in terms of violence before and after the downfall of the Somoza Government" (and perhaps with respect to the membership and policies of the ruling Sandinista junta that emerged following Somoza's downfall). "Report Prepared in the Federal Bureau of Investigation," Miami, November 30, 1979, *FRUS 1977–1980*, vol. 23, 184–85.

117. Pezzullo and Pezzullo, *At the Fall of Somoza*, 171.

118. Humberto Ortega describes a "plan for the military transition and to organize the joint command" (*La epopeya de la insurrección*, 427). Ramírez writes that "we agreed that there would be a Joint Chiefs of Staff made up of 'untarnished' officers from the National Guard and an equal number of guerrilla commanders" (*Adiós Muchachos*, 181). Somoza only agreed to leave the country once assured that the Guardia Nacional would be "fused with the Sandinistas" and "be kept intact"; *Nicaragua Betrayed*, 266–67. Nicho Marenco adds that, on top of the hybrid military structure, plans were made to temporarily divide Managua into two zones: one controlled by the National Guard, another by the FSLN; see Marenco, interview by *Envío*, no. 318, September 2008.

119. Raúl Castro later claimed before Soviet officials that "[Fidel] Castro had advised the Sandinistas to appoint one of the former Somoza officers who went over to the revolutionary side as minister of defense"; "Soviet Ambassador to Cuba

Vorotnikov, Memorandum of Conversation with Raúl Castro," September 1, 1979, CWIHP. According to Salamín, Castro lectured the Ortega brothers on the history of the Cuban Revolution and showed them letters he received during that struggle from sympathetic officers in Batista's National Guard in order to "show them that reaching an understanding with the Nicaraguan army was not necessarily anti-revolutionary and, that, contrary to what is commonly believed, that was an experience that practically all the world's revolutions had gone through." Salamín-Cárdenas and Millán-Salamín, *Omar Torrijos*, 169.

120. Huntington, *Political Order in Changing Societies*, 264.

121. Report from Mora to the Soviet Communist Party.

122. "Memorandum From the President's Assistant for National Security Affairs (Brzezinski) to President Carter," Washington, DC, July 13, 1979, *FRUS 1977–1980*, vol. 15, 672–73.

123. Urcuyo Maliaños, *Solos*.

124. Carazo "made a strong point to watch the timing of the [Puntarenas Plan], doing everything possible to insure [*sic*] that Somoza does not leave before a provisional government takes over in Managua and the FSLN/GP is brought to agreement on essential commitments." "Telegram from the Embassy in Costa Rica to the Department of State (from Bowdler)," San José, June 29, 1979, *FRUS 1977–1980*, vol. 15, 608.

125. Ramírez, *Adiós Muchachos*, 70.

126. Quoted in Kinzer, *Blood of Brothers*, 73.

127. GPP leader Henry Ruíz suggests that his forces may have resisted the implementation of the Puntarenas Plan: "I was in favor of total victory, that was my position. . . . I would have found it difficult, with troops behind me. I was no longer a *guerrillero* in the mountain, I now had troops. What would have happened if they resisted? I don't know; many times I've stopped to think . . . if the forces we had would have accepted the cease-fire. Who knows, those of us on the ground maybe would have continued forward. Because [the regime] was weak. And after so many murders, so many cruelties by the National Guard. And with the momentum we had, there was no place in the imaginary of the struggle for the idea that we would go and negotiate a piece of power to share with somocismo. It's fortunate that the historic result was the disintegration of the Guard, a mass fleeing. And we filled that vacuum. That was the total victory." Interview with the author.

128. Inter-American Commission on Human Rights, "Report on Human Rights in Nicaragua," June 1981.

129. Debray, "Nicaragua: Radical Moderation," 16–17.

Chapter 3

1. López Portillo, speech in Managua, January 24, 1980, in Ojeda, ed., *Las relaciones de México con los países de América Central*, 11–42.

2. Heinrich Krumwiede, adviser to the Friedrich Ebert Foundation (FES), quoted by Bernd Rother in *Global Social Democracy*, 156.

3. Jaime Wheelock, interview with the author.

4. Tomás Borge headed the Interior Ministry (responsible for intelligence, counterintelligence, and state security) and Humberto Ortega was named general and chief of the Sandinista Army.

5. Ramírez, *Adiós Muchachos*, 70.

6. Portions of the "Seventy-Two Hours" are found in Leiken and Rubin, eds., *The Central American Crisis Reader*, 218.

7. "The *Documento de las 72 horas* was an internal Front document, by a Directorate which took power before it thought would. . . . It was necessary to have a rough idea of what the future might look like. Of what direction to go in . . . it was important that we as a Directorate could show to the Nicaraguan public, which had struggled for the Revolution, that we sincerely wanted to make changes." Wheelock, interview with the author. "Modesto" calls the document "an attempt to reconcile the [ideological] contradictions we had between us." Ruíz, interview with the author. See also Ortega Saavedra, *La odisea por Nicaragua*, 111.

8. A senior State Department official quoted in Leogrande, *Our Own Backyard*, 30. The US sent somewhere between $18.5 and $23 million in relief aid in the immediate wake of the insurrection; Congress approved a package of $75 million in February 1980. Colombian president Julio César Turbay told Assistant Secretary of State Vaky, "the best bet to counter the Cuban-Soviet strategy is to copy it and support the moderates. . . . US assistance must be substantial enough to be visibly the most important and larger than that provided by Cuba or the Soviet Union." "Paper Prepared in the White House," Washington, DC, July 30, 1979, *FRUS 1977–1980*, vol. 15, 724.

9. Quoted in Pastor, *Not Condemned to Repetition*, 168.

10. Secretaría de Relaciones Exteriores (SRE), "Notas de Nicaragua," Mexico City, September 11, 1979, and "Memorandum de Mauricio Toussaint a Raul Valdes Aguilar," Mexico City, September 17, 1979, AHGE-AHD-SRE, III-3379-1.

11. Inter-American Commission on Human Rights, "Report on Human Rights in Nicaragua," June 1981.

12. Hanemann, "Nicaragua's Literacy Campaign."

13. "Memorandum: Conversación con el Ministro de Relaciones Exteriores de Nicaragua Miguel D'Escoto," Havana, December 18, 1979, Cuba MINREX, Nicaragua, Box 2.

14. The ambassador in Managua reported: "We face in Nicaragua today what six months ago had been the worst case situation: complete victory and domination by the Sandinista forces, the elimination of the National Guard and, with it, the loss of counter-balancing military forces to assure moderates an opportunity to play a political role. Yet the Sandinistas have been restrained and we are able to maintain a position of influence despite our long and close association with the Somoza dynasty." "Telegram from the Embassy in Nicaragua to the Department of State," Managua, November 5, 1979, *FRUS 1977–1980*, vol. 15, 747.

15. Christian, *Nicaragua: Revolution in the Family*, 174.

16. The *Documento de las 72 horas* called the Government of National Reconstruction "the political alternative designed to neutralize yankee interventionism." Luis Carrión later wrote that the document "defined the number one objective as

'isolating the sellout bourgeoisie,' 'organizing the driving forces of the Revolution,' which were the workers and peasants, and 'placing all forces under the direction of the FSLN.' . . . The first result of that decision was the rupture of the national consensus. The Junta's program reflected that consensus, but from that point on everything was different: it was 'here, we call the shots and can do what we like and do not need to make concessions to anybody else.'" Carrión Cruz, "Luces y sombras de la revolución."

17. See Gilbert, *Sandinistas*, and Nolan, *The Ideology of the Sandinistas and the Nicaraguan Revolution*. For a retrospective analysis, see Rodríguez, *La prosa de la contra-insurgencia*, 36–57.

18. "Memorandum sobre la situación de Nicaragua y su incidencia en América Latina," ANCR, Fondo Presidencia, Signatura 261.

19. "Ejemplo para otros países centroamericanos," *El País*, August 2, 1979. Willy Brandt said: "The liberalization of Nicaragua will become key to the democratization of Central America." Quoted by Rother in *Global Social Democracy*, 160.

20. See "Partidos y Movimientos Políticos en Nicaragua," *Envío* no. 39, September 1984; Christian, *Revolution in the Family*, 154; Kagan, *Twilight Struggle*, 131.

21. Ramírez, *Adiós Muchachos*, 41. As part of the shuffle, army chief Comandante Humberto Ortega formally took the post of defense minister. Other key ministries included Planning (Comandante Henry Ruiz) and Agricultural Development and Agrarian Reform (Comandante Jaime Wheelock).

22. Comandantes Guerrilleros Joaquín Cuadra and Hugo Torres were the army's chief of staff and director of political affairs, respectively. In Comandante Tomás Borge's Interior Ministry, Comandantes Guerrilleros Lenín Cerna and René Vivas were heads of state security and the national police, respectively.

23. Moisés Hassan, interview in *El Nuevo Diario*, "Interioridades de la primera gran disidencia," July 12, 2008.

24. SRE, "Memorandum sobre Nicaragua," Mexico City (Tlatelolco), May 28, 1980, AHGE-AHD-SRE III-3432-1.

25. Ortega Saavedra, *La odisea por Nicaragua*, 117.

26. Wheelock, "Revolution and Democratic Transition in Nicaragua," 74. See also Kruijt, *Guerrillas*, 103–4.

27. De Franco and Velázquez, "Democratic Transitions in Nicaragua," 88.

28. Carrión ("Luces y sombras de la revolución") added: "In practice, we imposed a one-party logic. And even though other parties subsisted—weakened, controlled, approved—the logic was that of a one-party system. Following that logic we began the construction not of a national state, but of a Sandinista state . . . all institutions were under the aegis, influence, and control of the Sandinista Front."

29. Mexican Embassy, Nicaragua, "Telegrama 265," Managua, May 9, 1980, AGE III-3433-1; Humberto Ortega justified the delay: "Objectively, we required a longer period of time before going to general elections, because this was not a crisis of a government in previously established democratic system"; *La odisea por Nicaragua*, 114.

30. Borge told a journalist: "We believe in pluralism and practice it," and pointed to Córdova Rivas's presence in the government as proof; "Sandinistas: The Playboy Interview," *Playboy*, September 1983.

31. Ruíz, interview with the author.

32. Dirk Kruijt cites figures suggesting that the number of unionized workers grew from 27,000 in 1979 to 150,000 by 1982 (*Guerrillas*, 106); Carrión says there were 20,000 union-affiliated workers in 1978 and 90,000 by 1982 ("Luces y sombras de la revolución").

33. Vilas, *Mercado, estados y revoluciones*, 235.

34. Carrión, "Luces y sombras de la revolución."

35. Wheelock, interview with the author.

36. Cardenal, *Sacerdote en la revolución*, vol. 2, 150; Arnove, "Education as Contested Terrain in Nicaragua," 28–53.

37 Ramírez, interview with the author. Similarly, Carlos Vilas described a "sequenced" concept of democracy: "First, socioeconomic affairs and the development of structural transformations; then politics"; *Mercado, estado y revoluciones*, 226–29.

38. "Some of us Sandinista leaders argued that the revolutionary character of our process for historical change should be 'nationalist-democratic-popular,' within the greater framework of national liberation. . . . Others, more orthodox, believed that we were in the phase of 'national and social liberation,' and therefore privileged the models of 'real socialism' from the Soviet orbit, particularly that of Cuba." Ortega Saavedra, *La odisea por Nicaragua*, 110.

39. Luis Carrión, interview with the author.

40. The Movimiento de Acción Popular Marxista Leninista consistently criticized concessions to the "exploiting classes." On several occasions, the FSLN government censored its publications and imprisoned its leaders. See, for example, Centro de Acción y Unidad Social, "Apuntes sobre la grave crisis económica del país y del viraje de la revolución," October 6, 1981, AIHNCA, CAUS-0016.

41. Ortega Reyna, "¿Revolución en la Revolución?," 160–61, 170–71.

42. Carrión, "Luces y sombras de la revolución."

43. Ortega Saavedra, *La odisea por Nicaragua*, 116. The Directorate, he adds, "imposed itself clearly as the central generator of the country, and everything must be subordinated to this power which only gives space to certain *consultation* with the different forces of the national context." Gilbert, *Sandinistas*, 178.

44. Ortega Saavedra, *La odisea por Nicaragua*, 113.

45. Kagan, *Twilight Struggle*, 150–51; "Paper Prepared in the Central Intelligence Agency," Washington, DC, undated, *FRUS 1977–1980*, vol. 15, 737.

46. Pastor, *Not Condemned to Repetition*, 159.

47. "An Unfinished Revolution," *Newsweek*, July 28, 1980.

48. Ortega, "Statement on the Electoral Process," August 23, 1980, reproduced in Leiken and Rubin, eds., *The Central American Crisis Reader*, 227; "En Nicaragua no habrá elecciones hasta 1985," *El País*, August 25, 1980.

49. Rodrigo Carazo, interview in *La Prensa*, July 14, 2009; Carazo, *Carazo: Tiempo y marcha*, 398–99.

50. Rother, *Global Social Democracy*, 163–64.

51. COSEP, "Analysis of the Government's Performance," November 1980, reproduced in Leiken and Rubin, eds., *Central American Crisis Reader*, 236.

52. Spalding, *Capitalists and Revolution in Nicaragua*, 67.

53. Martínez Cuenca, *Sandinista Economics in Practice*, 49.

54. According to De Franco and Velázquez, the government grew from 35,000 employees in 1979 to 187,929 by the end of the Revolution; "Democratic Transitions in Nicaragua," 92.

55. Ortega Saavedra, *La odisea por Nicaragua*, 112.

56. COSEP, "Analysis of the Government's Performance." Wheelock blames the decree that expropriated the Somoza estate as being too capacious: "indicating that not only were they the properties of Somoza, but of those associated with Somocismo. And that opened up a whole series of problems." Interview with the author.

57. Carter administration officials had learned of a coup plot, decided it was not in American interests to support it, and warned Salazar against participating because they believed it was an elaborate trap laid by FSLN state security; see "Memorandum from the President's Deputy Assistant for National Security Affairs to President Carter," Washington, DC, November 15, 1980, *FRUS 1977–1980*, vol. 15, 783; "Memorandum from Robert Pastor of the NSC Staff to the President's Assistant for National Security Affairs (Brzezinski)," Washington, DC, October 21, 1980, *FRUS 1977–1980*, vol. 15, 769. FSLN cadre and human rights activist Vilma Núñez cited "the assassination in cold blood" of Salazar as an "emblematic case" of the Sandinista Front's human rights abuses, a "crime that had high political costs for the Revolution." Vilma Núñez, interview by *Envío* no. 387, June 2014.

58. Martínez Cuenca, *Sandinista Economics in Practice*, 50.

59. Department of State Bureau of Intelligence and Research, "Mexican-Nicaraguan Relations: Can Mexico Moderate the Sandinistas?" August 12, 1981, DNSA; SRE, "Memorandum de Conversación." Mexico City, March 9, 1981, AHGE-AHD-SRE III-3490-1.

60. Ramirez, "Los sobrevivientes del naufragio," in Leiken and Rubin, eds., *Central American Crisis Reader*, 239.

61. "Letter from Edén Pastora to Humberto Ortega," June 26, 1981, Sergio Ramírez Papers, Box 61, Folder 9.

62. Quoted in Pastor, *Not Condemned to Repetition*, 102.

63. In a letter to Willy Brandt dated July 13, 1981, Pérez wrote: "We continue carrying out efforts to avoid the twisting of the course of the pluralistic project. With respect to the resignation of Commander Edén Pastora (Comandante Cero), we believe that we can use it to provoke some favorable reactions among the Sandinista commanders. In Panama we are taking measures in that respect, which involve his return." "Letter from Carlos Andrés Pérez to Willy Brandt," Caracas, July 13, 1981, Sergio Ramírez Papers, Box 61, Folder 11.

64. "Edén Pastora: Fidel no debería mandarnos asesores militares, sino asesores morales," *El País*, June 5, 1982.

65. "Pronóstico sobre la contrarrevolución que encabeza Pastora," Undated, 1981, Sergio Ramírez Papers, Box 61, Folder 9.

66. Quoted in "Partidos y Movimientos Políticos en Nicaragua," *Envío* no. 39, September 1984.

67. Pérez, letter to Brandt, July 1981.

68. Marcel Salamín, interview with the author.

69. Pérez, letter to Brandt, July 1981.

70. Rother, *Global Social Democracy*, 166–67.

71. Iber, *Neither Peace nor Freedom*.

72. Julio Cortázar, "De diferentes maneras de matar," February 1984, in *Nicaragua tan violentamente dulce*, 123.

Chapter 4

1. Pezzullo and Pezzullo, *At the Fall of Somoza*, 217–18.

2. "Exeunt Somoza, Nicaraguan Era," *Christian Science Monitor*, September 18, 1980.

3. Aldo Benítez, "Somoza: El atentado que hirió el orgullo estronista," *La Nación* (Paraguay), September 22, 2019.

4. "Hace cuarenta años en Paraguay: El día que un comando del ERP mató al ex dictador nicaragüense Anastasio Somoza," *Clarín*, September 16, 2020.

5. Latell, *Castro's Secrets*, 124–25.

6. "Somoza, asesinado en su exilio de Paraguay," *El País*, September 17, 1980. Sergio Ramírez told a journalist: "If the people of Nicaragua could have killed Somoza, they would have done it. Whoever did it had the support of the Nicaraguan people." "Sandinistas: The Playboy Interview," *Playboy*, September 1983.

7. Bendaña, "The Foreign Policy of the Sandinista Revolution," 320.

8. Wheelock, *Imperialismo y dictadura*.

9. Victor Hugo Tinoco, interview with the author. Tinoco also served as ambassador to the United Nations. Carrión adds that, along with domestic political questions, international issues occupied the bulk of the National Directorate's time; interview with the author.

10. See, for instance, Cruz Sequeira, "The Origins of Sandinista Foreign Policy," 95–110.

11. Vanden and Prevost, *Democracy and Socialism in Sandinista Nicaragua*.

12. Somoza, *Nicaragua Betrayed*, 77–78.

13. Daniel Ortega's speech before the nonaligned conference in Havana, September 3–9, 1979, in Leiken and Rubin, eds., *The Central American Crisis Reader*, 208.

14. José León Talavera, interview with the author. Talavera also served as ambassador to Honduras and in the FSLN's Department of International Relations.

15. UN General Assembly Resolution 34/8, "International Assistance for the Rehabilitation, Reconstruction, and Development of Nicaragua," October 25, 1979, UN Digital Library.

16. Ramírez, *Adiós Muchachos*, 43.

17. Department of State Bureau of Inter-American Affairs, "Nicaraguan Emergency Relief Assistance," October 19, 1979, DNSA.

18. Talavera, interview with the author.

19. Bendaña, "The Foreign Policy of the Sandinista Revolution," 326. Spalding adds: "The inclusion of private elites in the new model was also a response to geopolitical objectives; charges of Marxist-Leninism and communism could be held at bay and the Cold War rhetoric more successfully challenged if a substantial private sector was retained"; *Capitalists and Revolution in Nicaragua*, 95.

20. Astorga's obituary in the *Washington Post* noted of her presence at the United Nations: "Diplomats told how she disarmed people, serving as living proof that her people were not Russian-speaking communist monsters." February 15, 1988.

21. Marcel Salamín recalls: "This was a serious blow to those forces which had faced the enormous risk of putting their skin—and that of our countries—in the game in a gamble for democratization in Central America and Nicaragua. We thought this behavior was irresponsible and put us all in danger." Interview with the author.

22. Ortega recalls: "In 1981, I met in Moscow with Defense Minister Dimitri Ustinov, who approved—for free—the first shipment of military supplies, which we brought to Nicaragua via third countries, due to the caution of the USSR which did not want to tense its relations with the United States"; *La odisea por Nicaragua*, 128–29. An internal history of the Vietnamese military suggests a special plan of arms shipments from that country in 1980; "Excerpts from 'Ordnance: Chronology of Historical Events, Volume 2,'" 1999, CWIHP.

23. US Embassy, Nicaragua, "Donations and Financial Assistance to Nicaragua in 1980," December 23, 1980, DNSA.

24. "Arab States Help Nicaragua Avoid Ties to Superpowers," *Washington Post*, July 19, 1981.

25. The Carter administration, and many Latin American governments, believed that "moderate tendencies in the GRN can be strengthened by effective cooperation from a wide range of European and hemispheric governments"; US Department of State, "U.S. Cooperation with Costa Rica and Panama on Nicaraguan Assistance," August 25, 1979, DNSA.

26. "Editorial Note," *FRUS 1977–1980*, vol. 15, 740.

27. Pastor, *Not Condemned to Repetition*, 169.

28. Sergio Ramírez (interview with the author) explains the ideological and logistical reasons for preferring Eastern Bloc military assistance: "The Front's Directorate had decided that this was a fight to the death against imperialism. This fate was already written and could not be avoided. And therefore, if we were going to arm ourselves against imperialism it could not be with weapons for which they could later refuse repairs and munitions, and therefore it could not be Western weaponry. It had to be Soviet weaponry because that way supplies would always be assured."

29. "Robelo denuncia una possible intervención de la URSS en Nicaragua," *El País*, May 13, 1980.

30. Pastora, interview in *El País*, June 1982.

31. In January 1980, Secretary of State Cyrus Vance remained optimistic on Nicaragua's nonalignment: "In foreign affairs," he wrote to Carter, "Nicaragua's orientation and rhetoric are militantly Third World, but its actual behavior is quite pragmatic." "Memorandum from Secretary of State Vance to President Carter—

Nicaragua: A Status Report," Washington, DC, January 7, 1980, *FRUS 1977–1980*, vol. 15, 752.

32. Department of State Bureau of Intelligence and Research, "Developing Soviet-Nicaraguan Relations," June 24, 1981, DNSA.

33. CIA, "Worldwide Reaction to the Soviet Invasion of Afghanistan," CIA FOIA Reading Room, CIA-RDP81B00401R000600190013-5.

34. Kagan, rejecting the notion that the Sandinistas "were pushed into the arms of the Soviets and Cubans by American policy," cites the early Afghanistan vote as evidence to the contrary; *Twilight Struggle*, 130. De Franco and Velázquez also cite the Sandinista voting record as evidence of alignment with the Soviet Union ("Democratic Transitions in Nicaragua," 96). By contrast, Vanden and Prevost argued that "problems with the United States, the contra war, the developing economic crisis . . . combined to necessitate a cautious policy of engagement with the socialist countries"; *Democracy and Socialism in Sandinista Nicaragua*, 105.

35. See, for instance, Farber, *The Origins of the Cuban Revolution Reconsidered*, 69–111.

36. Carrión Cruz, "Luces y sombras de la revolución."

37. Wheelock, "Revolution and Democratic Transition in Nicaragua," 74–75.

38. The KGB's chief for Latin America, Nikolai Leonov, traveled to Managua in the fall of 1979 and reported that Junta leader Daniel Ortega "regarded the USSR as a class and strategic ally, and saw the Soviet experience in building the Party and state as a model to be studied and used for practical actions in Nicaragua." According to Leonov's notes, Ortega told him that the FSLN would differ from Castro in being cautious with the US, but that its "strategy is to tear Nicaragua from the capitalist orbit and, in time, become a member of the CMEA." Andrew and Mitrohkin, *The World Was Going Our Way*, 119–21.

39. "The Soviet attitude towards the prospects for revolution in Central America was ambivalent. The invasion of Afghanistan in December 1979 made Moscow both wary of further military commitments and anxious to repair the damage to its international reputation by successes elsewhere. Its desire to exploit the Sandinista revolution was balanced by nervousness at the likely retaliation of the United States." Andrew and Mitrohkin, *The World Was Going Our Way*, 122.

40. "Sandinistas: The Playboy Interview."

41. Kagan, *Twilight Struggle*, 198.

42. Atwood Lawrence, "The Rise and Fall of Non-Alignment."

43. Bendaña, interview with the author: "The generation of Carlos Fonseca . . . saw the world, communism versus capitalism. And eventually [they believed], communism would impose itself. Because there was a favorable balance of forces globally. That was their strategic analysis."

44. Quoted in Castañeda, *Utopia Unarmed*, 109.

45. Ortega Saavedra, *La odisea por Nicaragua*, 178.

46. Carrión Cruz, "Luces y sombras de la revolución."

47. José León Talavera, interview with the author: "We thought that relations should be handled on two planes: the formal, diplomatic plane and the political plane, where the gamma of relations was more varied."

48. "Nicaragua conmemora hoy el primer aniversario de la revolución sandinista," *El País*, July 18, 1980.

49. "Nicaragua conmemora hoy el primer aniversario de la revolución."

50. Christian, *Nicaragua: Revolution in the Family*, 193.

51. US Embassy, Costa Rica, "Costa Rican Teachers for Nicaragua," August 14, 1979, DNSA.

52. Castañeda, *Utopia Unarmed*, 32.

53. Sergio Ramírez, on Nicaraguan officials being assigned a Cuban adviser: "It was seen as a symbol of prestige. . . . But I wouldn't tell you that they came here to direct it. . . . I always felt that sort of caution." Interview with the author. Cuban vice premier Carlos Rafael Rodríguez told US secretary of state Alexander Haig that "it would be a serious mistake to believe that the Sandinistas rely on the advice that we give them. On the contrary, they have a very clear concept of that which they are required to do," "Transcript of Meeting between U.S. Secretary of State Alexander M. Haig Jr. and Cuban Vice Premier Carlos Rafael Rodriguez," Mexico City, November 23, 1981, CWIHP.

54. Cuadra, interview with the author.

55. Jorge Castañeda cites a "senior official of the Cuban Communist Party" commenting to that effect: "Without Cuban support, the Sandinistas would not have won in the same way, but they would have won anyway." *Utopia Unarmed*, 111.

56. Humberto Ortega, interview by Andrés Oppenheimer, *Oppenheimer Presenta*, CNN en Español, July 20, 2021.

57. Kagan, *Twilight Struggle*, 129.

58. Ramírez, *Adiós Muchachos*, 77.

59. Castañeda, *Utopia Unarmed*, 111.

60. Cuadra, interview with the author.

61. Oñate, "The Red Affair," 138. See also Chávez, *Poets and Prophets of the Resistance*, 198.

62. For more on the Marcial and Ana María incident, see James LeMoyne, "The Guerrilla Network," *New York Times Magazine*, April 6, 1986.

63. The analysis of the Mitrohkin Archive shows that "at a secret meeting in Havana attended by Castro and Humberto Ortega, [Salvadoran communist] Schafik Handal and the leaders of El Salvador's four other Marxist factions united as the Dirección Revolucionaria Unida (DRU). . . . The DRU was given a secure base in Nicaragua and, in consultation with Ortega, agreed to imitate the Sandinistas' strategy against the Somoza regime by seeking to create a military machine powerful enough to defeat the army of the state. Thousands of Salvadoran revolutionaries were given rapid military training in Cuba; several hundred more were trained in Nicaragua." Andrew and Mitrohkin, *The World Was Going Our Way*, 123.

64. Oñate, "The Red Affair," 143; Castañeda, *Utopia Unarmed*, 98.

65. "Memorandum of Conversation—Summary of the President's Meeting with Members of the Nicaraguan Junta," Washington, DC, September 24, 1979, *FRUS 1977–1980*, vol. 15, 743–44.

66. "Memorandum Prepared in the Central Intelligence Agency—Nicaragua: Aid to Salvadoran Revolutionaries," Washington, DC, August 27, 1980, *FRUS 1977–1980*, vol. 15, 763.

67. Ramírez, interview with the author. Once he assumed the presidency after the 1984 elections, Daniel Ortega publicly admitted that Nicaragua had sent weapons to the FMLN in 1980 and 1981; "Salvador Rebels: Where Do They Get the Arms," *New York Times*, November 24, 1988.

68. Kagan, *Twilight Struggle*, 156.

69. US Embassy, Nicaragua, "Meeting with Borge," January 9, 1981, DNSA.

70. See the memoir of Reagan's secretary of state George Schultz, *Turmoil and Triumph*, 961.

71. Leogrande, *Our Own Backyard*, 108–11; emphasis added.

72. MINREX Nicaragua, "Reporte de la reunión entre Thomas Enders y el Comandante de la Revolución Daniel Ortega Saveedra," Managua, August 12, 1981, Archivo Bendaña, Box 3.

73. "Conversación de la Dirección Nacional con el Secretario Adjunto Thomas Enders," August 12, 1981, Archivo Bendaña, Box 3.

74. Kinzer, *Blood of Brothers*, 114.

75. Kinzer, *Blood of Brothers*, 96.

76. See Leogrande, *Our Own Backyard*, 110–23, 140–46; Kagan, *Twilight Struggle*, 200–207.

77. Ramírez, *Adiós Muchachos*, 99.

78. Ortega Saavedra, *La odisea por Nicaragua*, 170.

79. Torres, interview with the author.

80. Cuadra, interview with the author.

81. Wheelock, interview with the author: "First, we had a moral commitment with the FMLN, which had helped us greatly during the [insurrectionary] war." Torres, interview with the author: "The *compañeros* of the FMLN had shown solidarity with us. Despite their limitations, they had given us weapons . . . and they sent a few members to fight in Nicaragua and to get killed, more than anything."

82. Carrión, interview with the author.

83. MINREX Nicaragua, "Reunión entre Enders y Ortega."

84. Cuadra, interview with the author: "I think there you have some part of the Cuban influence. Cuba has always had its defense beyond its borders—creating problems or conflicts, or exporting their revolution."

85. Ortega Saavedra, *La odisea por Nicaragua*, 150.

86. Torres, interview with the author. He explains support for the FMLN in terms of "two considerations: solidarity—the act of proving that we were a movement fighting for the same cause as them—and the factor of opening up several focos."

87. Carrión, interview with the author.

88. "It was better to have a war next door, than to be isolated"; Ramírez, interview with the author. Cuadra elaborates: "In fact, in our National Defense Plan, in the face of a US invasion we had two areas: the fight against the [US-backed] Contra . . . and there was another which was the preparation of the country for a

direct US invasion. In the preparation of the country for that war, there were units ready so that in the case of an invasion, they would go off to fight in Costa Rica and Honduras. . . . A bit of that was the Cuban influence. Unlike them, however, we had somewhere to flee, on the continent"; interview with the author.

89. Carrión Cruz, "Luces y sombras de la revolución."

90. Ortega Saavedra, *La odisea por Nicaragua*, 183.

91. Quoted in "Sandinista Denies Exporting Revolt," *New York Times*, March 12, 1986.

92. Salvador Cayetano Carpio, interview by *Proceso*, September 1980, from Centro de Documentación de los Movimientos Armados, accessed June 30, 2022, https://cedema.org/digital_items/3474.

93. "Telegram from the Embassy in Nicaragua to the Department of State," Managua, January 15, 1981, *FRUS 1977–1980*, vol. 15, 806.

94. SRE, "Memorandum para Información Superior," Mexico City, September 10, 1980, AHGE-AHD-SRE III-3433-1. See also Christian, *Nicaragua: Revolution in the Family*, 189–91.

95. "El presidente de Costa Rica denuncia un complót izquierdista," *El País*, August 7, 1982.

96. See Gudmundson, "El conflicto entre estabilidad y neutralidad en Costa Rica." An internal Costa Rican history traces the change in policy between the Carazo and Monge administrations; "Síntesis del Informe sobre la labor del Ministerio de Relaciones Exteriores y Culto durante los primeros seis meses de la administración del señor presidente don Luis Alberto Monge," San José, ANCR, Fondo Presidencia 10309.

97. Mexican Embassy, Nicaragua, "Las relaciones actuales Nicaragua-Venezuela," Managua, December 19, 1980, AHGE-AHD-SRE III-3433-1.

98. See Armony, "Transnationalizing the Dirty War"; Avery, "Connecting Central America to the Southern Cone."

99. Rother, *Global Social Democracy*, 159–63.

100. "Letter from Carlos Andrés Pérez to Willy Brandt," Caracas, July 13, 1981, Sergio Ramírez Papers, Box 61, Folder 11.

101. Rother, *Global Social Democracy*, 171.

102. "Meeting between Alexander M. Haig Jr. and Carlos Rafael Rodríguez," CWIHP.

103. Ramírez, *Adiós Muchachos*, 46.

104. Jorge G. Castañeda, "Don't Corner Mexico!" *Foreign Policy*, July 19, 1985.

105. Herrera and Ojeda, "Mexican Foreign Policy and Central America."

106. Toussaint, "La política exterior de México hacia Centroamérica," 118.

107. "Un entretien avec M. François Mitterrand," *Le Monde*, July 2, 1981. Willy Brandt wrote to Spanish Socialist Felipe González that the SI was obligated "to defend developments in Nicaragua from external infringements and influences." "Letter by the President of the Socialist International, Brandt, to the Chairman of the Committee of the SI for Defence of the Revolution in Nicaragua, González," June 2, 1981, CWIHP.

108. "Armas francesas a Nicaragua," *Barricada*, January 8, 1982.

109. "Paris Defends Plan to Sell Arms to Nicaragua," *New York Times*, January 9, 1982; Rother, *Global Social Democracy*, 182.

110. Van Ommen, "'Challenging the Monroe Doctrine.'"

111. Ronfeldt, *Geopolitics, Security, and U.S. Strategy in the Caribbean Basin*, 29.

112. Talavera, interview with the author.

113. MINREX Nicaragua, "Posición de Nicaragua ante la crisis centroamericana—Documento de base," undated, Archivo Bendaña, Box 1.

114. "Ayuda Memoria y documentos: Coincidencia entre Rodrigo Carazo y Thomas Enders," ANCR, Fondo Presidencia, Signatura 9278.

115. Carazo, *Tiempo y marcha*, 404.

116. Wheelock later attested to this change over time: "We began to govern in 1979 with a broad consensus and a great deal of legitimacy. This and other factors led to a certain authoritarian behavior, which made the alliances we forged in 1979 somewhat formal. We didn't really govern with the participation of our allies, who became very frustrated." Quoted in Castañeda, *Utopia Unarmed*, 108.

117. Rother, *Global Social Democracy*, 153.

118. "Discurso del presidente mexicano José López Portillo en la Plaza de la Revolución de la ciudad de Managua, Nicaragua," in Córdova and Benites Manaut, eds., *La paz en Centroamérica*, 245–51.

119. CIA, "Soviet Policies and Activities in Latin America and the Caribbean," June 25, 1982, CIA FOIA Reading Room, RDP84B00049R000701830026-0.

120. "Discurso del presidente mexicano José López Portillo."

Chapter 5

1. Carlos Fuentes, "Sergio Ramírez y la revolución sandinista," *El País*, August 31, 2004.

2. Ortega, *La odisea por Nicaragua*, 130.

3. Vargas Llosa, "Nicaragua: Año dos," 436.

4. Julio Cortázar, "Vigilia en Bismuna," February 1983, in *Nicaragua tan violentamente dulce*, 70.

5. Nicaraguan diplomats actively cultivated this biblical metaphor; Alejandro Bendaña, "David resistió a Goliat: 10 años de política exterior," *Envío* no. 95, July 1989.

6. Gioconda Belli, interview with the author.

7. Hager, "The Origins of the 'Contra War' in Nicaragua"; Hager and Snyder, "The United States and Nicaragua."

8. Like estimates of the insurrectionary war in 1978–79, calculations for the Contra war's death toll vary immensely. Dirk Kruijt, citing "official sources," suggests that the national death toll between 1981 and 1989 was 61,825, with deaths spread roughly evenly between EPS personnel (and civilians living in government-controlled areas) and Contra (and civilians living near their bases); *Guerrillas*, 126. But third-party estimates of battle-related deaths range anywhere between 10,000 and 43,000 for the 1981–89 period (Lacina and Gleditsch, "Monitoring Trends in Global Combat).

9. Núñez, *La guerra en Nicaragua*, 21.

10. Humberto Ortega Saavedra, "Ayer y hoy," *La Prensa*, December 11, 2019.

11. Fitzpatrick, *The Russian Revolution*, 9.

12. Carrión Cruz, "Luces y sombras de la revolución," emphasis added; Humberto Ortega wrote: "Our society quickly became polarized and then came the devastating, unjust war of foreign aggression—because it was directed by US President Ronald Reagan—but also civil war, because we Nicaraguans were the belligerents" ("Ayer y hoy").

13. Núñez, *La guerra en Nicaragua*, 21.

14. "Sandinistas: The Playboy Interview," *Playboy*, September 1983.

15. See Martí i Puig, "The FSLN and Sandinismo."

16. Armitage, *Civil Wars*, 12.

17. Agudelo, *Contramemorias*, 10.

18. Ramírez, interview with the author.

19. Wheelock, interview with the author; emphasis added.

20. Wheelock, interview with the author.

21. Gould, *To Lead as Equals*.

22. Cuadra, interview with the author.

23. Rocha, "Agrarian Reform in Nicaragua in the 1980s," 103.

24. Ortega Saavedra, *La odisea por Nicaragua*, 127.

25. Baumeister and Martí i Puig, "Nicaragua," 289–90.

26. Saravia-Matus and Saravia-Matus, "Agrarian Reform." See also Rocha, "Agrarian Reform in Nicaragua in the 1980s," 105.

27. Rocha, "Agrarian Reform in Nicaragua in the 1980s," 110.

28. Laura Enríquez attributes labor shortages to the success of the agrarian reform program: "Nicaragua's agro-export base development has been dependent on the cheap labor of its campesino population. Yet the agrarian reform was specifically intended to better the lives of the rural poor, thereby lessening their willingness to provide cheap labor to the agro-export sector." *Harvesting Change*, 147.

29. Baumeister and Martí i Puig, "Nicaragua," 290–91. Carlos Vilas cites the same numbers from MIDINRA sources in *Mercado, estado y revoluciones*, 212.

30. Wheelock, "Revolution and Democratic Transition in Nicaragua," 76–77. See also Baumeister and Martí i Puig, "Nicaragua," 293.

31. Rocha, "Agrarian Reform in Nicaragua in the 1980s," 107–15.

32. Bendaña Rodríguez, ed., *Una tragedia campesina*, 16–17.

33. Wheelock, "Revolution and Democratic Transition in Nicaragua," 76–77.

34. On Fley, see Dillon, *Comandos*, 45–51.

35. Bendaña Rodríguez, ed., *Una tragedia campesina*, 17; Lynn Horton, *Peasants in Arms*, 15.

36. Ruiz, interview with the author.

37. "Confiesa uno de los que asesinó a Mons. Romero," *El Nuevo Diario*, March 22, 2010.

38. Kinzer, *Blood of Brothers*, 145; Leogrande, *Our Own Backyard*, 307.

39. Torres, interview with the author. EPS chief Humberto Ortega wrote: "The FDN in its majority were peasants that rejected revolutionary change due to their

conservative values and the abuses civilian and military authorities committed."
La odisea por Nicaragua, 123.

40. Rocha, "Agrarian Reform in Nicaragua in the 1980s," 113.

41. Dillon, *Comandos*, 66–67. See also Horton, *Peasants at Arms*.

42. Close, "Responding to Low-Intensity Conflict," 12.

43. "Sandinistas: The Playboy Interview."

44. On the controversy this caused, see the memoir of his brother Fernando Cardenal (also a priest) in *Sacerdote en la revolución*, vol. 2, 180.

45. See Kirk, "John Paul II and the Exorcism of Liberation Theology."

46. Tigrillo, interview by *El Nuevo Diario*, August 12, 2006.

47. Horton, *Peasants at Arms*, 15.

48. Agudelo, *Contramemorias*, 14. On this point Wheelock wrote: "One major problem was the government's coercive style of political and administrative management, widely resented by most rural classes. The mandate that they organize themselves politically, economically, and socially severely disrupted the peasants' traditional rural social structure, further fanning disagreement and distrust toward the revolution." Wheelock, "Revolution and Democratic Transition in Nicaragua," 77.

49. "Sandinistas committed many mistakes on the Coast due to cultural misunderstanding. The main cause was that at the time of the revolutionary triumph, anthropologists didn't go to the Caribbean—young soldiers went instead. What's worse: they came with racist prejudices." Cardenal, *La revolución perdida*, 569.

50. Brooklyn Rivera, "Statement on Indian Rights," in Leiken and Rubin, eds., *Central America Crisis Reader*, 256.

51. Ramírez wrote in his memoir: "We expected to integrate them overnight into the revolution, its values, modern life, well-being. It was an ideological paternalism, different from Somoza's, which had never created well-intentioned programs, but we knew nothing of their culture or their languages, to the point of communicating with them via interpreters, and we had no knowledge of their religious beliefs or their forms of social organization. Likewise, we knew very little about the black population, also situated on the Caribbean coast." *Adiós Muchachos*, 163.

52. Mexican Embassy, Nicaragua, "Negociaciones Gobierno Nicaragüense-líder Miskito Brooklyn Rivera," Managua, April 9, 1985, AHGE-AHD-SRE III-3962-1; SRE, "Boletín Informativo: Reunión entre Luis Carrión y Brooklyn Rivera," Mexico City, April 22, 1985, AHGE-AHD-SRE III-3963-1.

53. On the origins of the conflict and problems with its resolution, see Hale, *Resistance and Contradiction*.

54. On the regional impact of the Law on Autonomous Regions of the Atlantic Coast, see Wade, *Race and Ethnicity in Latin America*, 105.

55. Kinloch Tijerino, *Historia de Nicaragua*, 329.

56. Gioconda Belli, interview with the author.

57. Quoted in Kinzer, *Blood of Brothers*, 358.

58. Edén Pastora, "Proclamation to the People of Nicaragua," April 15, 1983, in Leiken and Rubin, eds., *Central American Crisis Reader*, 263. Eventually, Pastora broke with longtime partner Alfonso Robelo and founded the Bloque Opositor Sur

(BOS). The BOS attempted to style itself as a social-democratic alternative to the Honduras-based Contra, though even the FDN claimed to stand "for the nationalistic and patriotic principles of the historic figure, Augusto César Sandino"; "FDN Statement of Principles," February 1983, in Leiken and Rubin, eds., *Central American Crisis Reader*, 261.

59. De Franco and Velásquez, "Democratic Transitions in Nicaragua," 88–93, 97–101.

60. See these and other related statistics in Spalding, "Poverty Politics," 216–19.

61. Carrión Cruz, "Luces y sombras de la revolución."

62. Ortega Saavedra, *La odisea por Nicaragua*, 137.

63. "El servicio militar de los ochenta y las redadas de la Muerte," *La Prensa Magazine*, August 10, 2019.

64. Carrión Cruz, "Luces y sombras de la revolución."

65. Close, "Responding to Low-Intensity Conflict," 8.

66. Gutman, *Banana Diplomacy*, 104.

67. Donald Castillo Rivas, a member of the Contra's BOS faction, writes: "Support from the CIA and other North American agencies was given to a group of Nicaraguans based on previously established relationships and on the understanding that these would be loyal and obedient employees that could be trusted. In order to consolidate these relationships, Contra leaders had to be submissive and dependent; if not, the empire could replace them"; *Gringos, contras y sandinistas*, 186.

68. Edgar Chamorro and Jefferson Morley, "Confessions of a 'Contra,'" *New Republic*, August 4, 1985.

69. Brown, *The Real Contra War*, 5.

70. Bendaña Rodríguez, *Una tragedia campesina*, 13.

71. Kagan, *Twilight Struggle*, 219.

72. Wheelock, interview with the author. The CIPRES study led by Orlando Nuñez disrupted this binary as early as 1991; see "Guerra de agresión o guerra civil," in Núñez, ed., *La guerra en Nicaragua*, 18–21.

73. Mexican Embassy, Honduras, "Estado que guardan las relaciones entre Nicaragua y este país," Tegucigalpa, October 1, 1980, AHGE-AHD-SRE III-3433-1.

74. Ruhl, "Curbing Central America's Militaries," 138. According to Kai Thaler, the Sandinista Popular Army in 1983 had 20,000 troops; by 1986, the EPS had 134,000 troops under arms; "From Insurgent to Incumbent: State Building and Service Provision after Rebel Victory in Civil Wars," 94.

75. Jarquín, "Red Christmases," 103–4.

76. Armony, "Transnationalizing the Dirty War," 155.

77. Avery, "Connecting Central America to the Southern Cone."

78. Hoffman, *The PLO and Israel in Central America*.

79. See Leogrande, "Making the Economy Scream"; Close, "Responding to Low-Intensity Conflict," 8–9.

80. Storkmann, "East German Military Aid to the Sandinista Government of Nicaragua," 64.

81. Daniel Ortega wrote to Todor Zhivkov, historic communist leader of Bulgaria: "North American imperialism, historic enemy of our people, is carrying out a whole

plan of aggressions. . . . In the context of this highly dangerous situation, we view with great satisfaction the fact that we have made very significant strides in the strengthening of our relationships with the fraternal republics of the socialist camp, in particular with the People's Republic of Bulgaria. The economic and scientific-technical collaboration and financial assistance provided to our country by the Party and government which you lead, is highly valuable for the stabilization of our battered economy." "Letter from Daniel Ortega Saavedra of the FSLN to Todor Zhivkov," November 12, 1982, CWIHP.

82. "Soviet Bloc Military Equipment Supplied to Nicaragua (Jul 1979–Dec 1988)," 3; unclassified report, February 1989, National Security Archive/Understanding the Iran Contra Affair Project, accessed July 3, 2023, www.brown.edu/Research /Understanding_the_Iran_Contra_Affair/documents.php.

83. Storkmann, "East German Military Aid to the Sandinista Government of Nicaragua," 73.

84. "Soviet Bloc Military Equipment Supplied to Nicaragua (Jul 1979–Dec 1988) "

85. Yordanov, "Outfoxing the Eagle," 867.

86. Storkmann, "East German Military Aid to the Sandinista Government of Nicaragua," 75.

87. Ortega Saavedra, *La odisea por Nicaragua*, 144. "Soviet Bloc Military Equipment Supplied to Nicaragua (Jul 1979–Dec 1988)." According to Yordanov, in 1980, "the Cuban government acknowledged the presence of 4,000 Cubans in Nicaragua, including 200 military advisers, while GDR's Stasi reported that more than 5,000 Cuban citizens were present in Nicaragua, providing assistance in various fields, including the military arena" ("Outfoxing the Eagle," 878). Cuban presence was directly related to the need for a small Soviet footprint: "The KGB sought to develop such forms of cooperation that would both be efficient and capable of preventing the CIA from encountering a very obvious Soviet presence in Nicaragua. Considering Nicaragua's size, hiding Soviet officers was deemed near impossible and Moscow considered it appropriate to be represented in Managua by only a few officers, concentrating instead on providing material and technical and operational-technical assistance. The work of the advisors in the security agencies was to be done first and foremost by the Cubans" ("Outfoxing the Eagle," 884).

88. Figueroa Clark, "Nicaragua, Chile, and the end of the Cold War in Latin America," 202.

89. See Domínguez, *To Make a World Safe for Revolution*.

90. Moreno, *Principio y fin de la guerra de los contras*, 179.

91. Domínguez, *To Make a World Safe for Revolution*, 239–40.

92. See Close, "Responding to Low-Intensity Conflict," 11–13.

93. Thaler, "Ideology, Perception, and Strategic Decision-Making in a Revolutionary State."

94. Vickers, "Intelligence and Punta Huete Airfield," 13–24.

95. Thaler, "From Insurgent to Incumbent," 97; Close, "Responding to Low-Intensity Conflict"; Ortega Saavedra, *La odisea por Nicaragua*, 130.

96. Schultz, *Turmoil and Triumph*, 406.

97. The so-called Boland Amendment left room for Reagan to argue that his actions "did not envision the overthrow of the Sandinista government," but the legislation nonetheless "established as a legal norm that US policy was not to oust the Sandinistas from power"; see Arnson, *Crossroads*, 82–112.

98. Leogrande, *Our Own Backyard*, 336.

99. International Court of Justice, "Case Concerning Military and Paramilitary Activities in and Against Nicaragua" (*Nicaragua v. United States of America*, Judgment of June 27, 1986, accessed July 3, 2023, www.icj-cij.org/en/case/70/judgments).

100. These secret talks were recounted in internal Nicaraguan Foreign Ministry memoranda and transcripts: "Información Especial: Sobre reunion de las comisiones nicaragüenses-costarricenses, con presencia de Francia, el compañero José León Talavera," July 20, 1984, Archivo Bendaña, Box 1; "Confidencial: Reuniónes con Cancillera Francesa," July 18, 1984, Paris; "Transcripción de segunda reunion," July 19, 1984; "Transcripción de tercera reunion," July 19, 1984.

101. Quoted in Gutman, *Banana Diplomacy*, 287.

102. Close, "Responding to Low-Intensity Conflict," 10–11.

103. Arturo Cruz Porras, interview by Donald Castillo Rivas in *Gringos, contras y sandinistas,* 164.

104. Perla, *Sandinista Nicaragua's Resistance to U.S. Coercion*, 222.

105. Bendaña, interview with the author. In the wake of the Grenada invasion, the Sandinista leadership forced the FMLN command in Managua into hiding in order to remove a likely pretext for a potential US invasion. Bendaña notes the FSLN took the threat so seriously that they burned large portions of its internal archives or sent them to Havana.

106. Carrión Cruz, "Luces y sombras de la revolución."

107. Ortega Saavedra, *La odisea por Nicaragua*, 122.

108. Wheelock, interview with the author: "Our reaction was to always seek, as the central objective, a military defeat of the enemy. And we disposed the entire country to that purpose." On the cost, Ramírez says: "Everything became subordinated to military priorities, and that destroyed any possibility of change. That's what produced the inflation and the shortages, and that's what produced our political weakness; to have to continue, moreover, with the obligatory military service completed is what destroyed the credibility of the Revolution"; interview with the author.

109. Vilas, *Mercado, estado y revoluciones*, 230.

110. Álvarez, quoted in Gutman, *Banana Diplomacy*, 153, reportedly said this to Democratic senator Patrick Leahy.

Chapter 6

1. Harmer, "The 'Cuban Question' and the Cold War in Latin America."

2. Portions of this chapter were adapted from my article "The Nicaraguan Question: Contadora and the Latin American Response to US Intervention Against the Sandinistas." I thank the editors of *The Americas* for publishing my work and allowing it to appear in modified form here.

3. Oydén Ortega, interview with the author. See also his book, *Contadora y su verdad.*

4. "Carta de los presidentes Luis Herrera Campins de Venezuela y José López Portillo de México al presidente de Estados Unidos, Ronald Reagan," September 7, 1982; "Carta de los presidentes Luis Herrera Campins de Venezuela y José López Portillo de México al presidente de Honduras, Roberto Suázo Córdova," in Córdova and Benites Manaut, eds., *La paz en Centroamérica,* 253–56.

5. Mexican Embassy, Nicaragua, "Comentario sobre las declaraciones del Presidente de Venezuela Relativas a la Política Interna de Nicaragua," Managua, September 24, 1982, AHGE-AHD-SRE III-3490-1. Herrera Campins and López Portillo emphasized this point in a letter to Daniel Ortega on September 7, 1982; Córdova and Benites Manaut, eds., *La paz en Centroamérica,* 251–53. See also Herrera and Ojeda, "La política de México en la región de Centroamérica," 432–33.

6. Mexican Embassy, Nicaragua, "EMBAMEX para RELMEX," Managua, October 25, 1982, AHGE-AHD-SRE III-3490-1.

7. "Letter from President Reagan to Mexican President José López Portillo and Venezuelan President Luis Herrera Campins," October 1982, in *American Foreign Policy Current Documents,* 1464.

8. MINREX Nicaragua, "Propuesta norteamericana de ocho puntos presentados por el embajador Anthony Quainton a los Cros. Victor Tinoco y Julio López," April 8, 1982; "Propuesta nicaragüense de trece puntos presentados por el Embajador Fiallos a Thomas Enders el 14 de abril de 1982," Archivo Bendaña, Box 4.

9. US ambassador Francis McNeil, quoted in Gutman, *Banana Diplomacy,* 114.

10. Jeane Kirkpatrick, "Dictatorships and Double Standards," *Commentary,* November 1, 1979.

11. "Reagan Condemns Nicaragua in Plea for Aid to Rebels," *New York Times,* March 17, 1986.

12. Gabriel García Márquez, Nobel Lecture, Stockholm, December 8, 1982, accessed July 3, 2023, www.nobelprize.org/prizes/literature/1982/marquez/lecture/.

13. Iber, *Neither Peace nor Freedom,* 231–32.

14. Carlos Fuentes, "Sergio Ramírez y la revolución sandinista," *Biblioteca Virtual Miguel de Cervantes,* www.cervantesvirtual.com/obra-visor/sergio-ramirez-y-la-revolucion-sandinista/html/f8dca79e-02cb-484a-98ea-1c03b6d27ce2_2.html.

15. "Meeting between Alexander M. Haig Jr. and Carlos Rafael Rodríguez," CWIHP.

16. "Declaración de Cancún para la paz en Centroamérica," July 17, 1983, in Ortiz and Flores, eds., *Relación de Contadora,* 361.

17. CIA, "Soviet Policies and Activities in Latin America and the Caribbean," June 25, 1982, CIA FOIA Reading Room, RDP84B00049R000701830026-0.

18. Grabendorff, "Western European Perceptions of the Central American Turmoil."

19. López Portillo, *Mis tiempos,* vol. 2, 1195; "Discurso del presidente José López Portillo en la Plaza de la Revolución de la ciudad de Managua, Nicaragua," in Córdova and Benites Manaut, eds., *La paz en Centroamérica,* 245–51.

20. MINREX Nicaragua, "Reunión entre el Comandante Daniel Ortega S. y Lang-horne A. Motley," October 13, 1983, Archivo Bendaña, Box 3.

21. MINREX Nicaragua, "Transcripción de la Reunión del Comandante Daniel Ortega con la Comisión Kissinger," October 15, 1983, Archivo Bendaña, Box 4.

22. Edgard Parrales, interview by *Envío* no. 464, November 2020.

23. "Nicaragua ofrece ayuda militar a Argentina," *El País*, June 6, 1982.

24. Sepúlveda, foreword to Ortiz and Flores, eds., *Relación de Contadora*, 11.

25. Ortega, *Contadora y su verdad*, 11–25.

26. "Entrevista del Cro. Sergio Ramírez Mercado con el Presidente de Argentina Raúl Alfonsín y el Canciller Dante Caputo," July 28, 1985, Sergio Ramírez Papers, Box 62, Folder 8b.

27. SRE, "Memorándum: Resúmen de Acontecimientos en Centroamérica y Re-acciones Latinoamericanas," Mexico City, July 23–25, 1983, AHGE-AHD-SRE III-3643-1.

28. Quoted in Sepúlveda's foreword to Ortiz and Flores, eds., *Relación de Conta-dora*, 7.

29. Quoted in Gutman, *Banana Diplomacy*, 226.

30. García Márquez, Nobel Lecture.

31. "Caracas Declaration," March 28, 1954, Yale University Law Library, accessed July 3, 2023, https://avalon.law.yale.edu/20th_century/intam10.asp.

32. Nicaraguan Embassy, Cuba, "Conversación sostenida por el Cdte. HRH con Miguel de la Madrid," March 5, 1983, Cuba MINREX Archive, Nicaragua, Box 3.

33. "Entrevista del Cro. Sergio Ramirez Mercado con el Presidente de Argentina Raul Alfonsin y el Canciller Dante Caputo," July 28, 1985, Sergio Ramírez Papers, Box 62, Folder 8b.

34. "Reunión Dr. Sergio Ramírez Mercado con Canciller Enrique Iglesias," Octo-ber 10, 1985; Sergio Ramírez Mercado to Daniel Ortega, Presidente de la Republica, "Asunto: Misión a Argentina, Uruguay, y Peru," October 11, 1985; and "Entrevista Dr. Sergio Ramirez Mercado y Belisario Betancur," October 4, 1985, Sergio Ramírez Papers, Box 62, Folder 8b.

35. "Reunión Cdte. Daniel Ortega—Wilson Ferreira," March 2, 1985, Cuba MIN-REX Archive, Nicaragua, Box 3.

36. De Sergio Ramírez M. a Cmte. De la Rev. Daniel Ortega Saavedra, Presidente de la República, "Asunto: Misión a México y países sudamericanos," July 15, 1985, Sergio Ramírez Papers, Box 62, Folder 8b.

37. Van Ommen, "'Challenging the Monroe Doctrine.'"

38. SRE Dirección General para Europa Occidental, "Memorándum: Entrevista Presidente González con señores Brandt y Kreisky," Mexico City, April 9, 1984, AHGE-AHD-SRE III-3783-1.

39. Rother, *Global Social Democracy*, 153.

40. For an analysis of Sweden's (and Palme's) opposition to US policy in Viet-nam, see Logevall, "The Swedish-American Conflict over Vietnam."

41. MINREX Nicaragua, "Acta de la Reunión Ortega-Stone," November 9, 1983, Archivo Bendaña, Box 3.

42. MINREX Nicaragua, "Plan de trabajo para manejo del informe Kissinger," October 1983; and "Transcripción de la Reunión del Comandante Daniel Ortega con la Comisión Kissinger," October 15, 1983, Archivo Bendaña, Box 4.

43. "Commission Decides to Drop Nicaragua from Aid Package," *Washington Post,* December 22, 1983.

44. "Extracto del Informe Kissinger," January 1984, Córdova and Benites Manaut, eds., *La paz en Centroamérica,* 258–76.

45. Leogrande, *Our Own Backyard,* 111.

46. Schultz, *Turmoil and Triumph,* 410–11.

47. MINREX Nicaragua, "Reunión entre el Comandante de la Revolución Daniel Ortega S. y el Secretario de Estado George Schultz," June 3, 1984, Archivo Bendaña, Box 4.

48. Schultz, *Turmoil and Triumph,* 414–17.

49. Correspondence between D'Escoto and lawyer Paul Reichler: "Tactica para los asuntos de procedimientos," "Consideraciones políticas sobre nuestra agenda de negociación," and "Marco global y de principios," July 26, 1984, Cuba MINREX Archive, Nicaragua, Box 5.

50. Calero Portocarrero, *Crónicas de un contra,* 102.

51. Alma Guillermoprieto and David Hoffman, "Document Describes How U.S. 'Blocked' a Contadora Treaty," *Washington Post,* November 6, 1984.

52. Alma Guillermoprieto, "Torpedoing Latin Interests," *Washington Post,* November 11, 1984.

53. UN Security Council Resolution 562, May 10, 1985, accessed July 3, 2023, http://unscr.com/en/resolutions/562. Previously, Resolution 702 at the OAS General Assembly urged Central American countries to sign Contadora. Additionally, Contadora won prizes from UNESCO (May 1985) and the Spanish government's Prince of Asturias Prize (October 1984).

54. Roberts, "Bullying and Bargaining," 81.

55. Letter from Reichler to Miguel D'Escoto, "Analysis of Present Situation in the United States," July 16, 1984, Cuba MINREX Archive, Nicaragua, Box 5.

56. Mexican Embassy, Federal Republic of Germany, "Memorándum de Conversación para el Embajador César Sepúlveda," and "Asunto: Entrevista entre Bayardo Arce del FSLN y el señor Will Brandt en Rio de Janeiro," Bonn, December 3, 1984, AHGE-AHD-SRE III-3961-1. Versions were also reported in the *New York Times:* "World Socialists Pressing Sandinistas on Election," October 4, 1984, and "Brandt Visits Managua but Fails to Settle Vote Dispute," October 15, 1984. See also Kagan, *Twilight Struggle,* 330–36; Rother, *Global Social Democracy,* 203.

57. Kagan, *Twilight Struggle,* 331–32.

58. Arturo Cruz Porras, interview by Donald Castillo Rivas in *Gringos, contras y sandinistas,* 168.

59. Close, *Nicaragua: Navigating the Politics of Democracy,* 89–90.

60. "The Report of the Latin American Studies Association Delegation to Observe the Nicaraguan General Election of November 4, 1984," accessed July 3, 2023, https://lasaweb.org/uploads/reports/electoralprocessnicaragua.pdf.

61. Orlando Castillo, "Elecciones y legitimad política de la revolución Sandinista," *El País*, November 9, 1984.

62. Carrión Cruz, "Luces y sombras de la revolución."

63. Quoted in Castañeda, *Utopia Unarmed*, 108.

64. Carrión Cruz, "Luces y sombras de la revolución."

65. Ramírez, *Adiós Muchachos*, 101.

66. Quoted in "Sandinistas Hold Their First Elections," *New York Times*, November 5, 1984.

67. The 1984 elections, Tinoco added, "were not ones of open democratic competition—they were managed." Interview with the author. According to him, there was a lack of clarity among the Sandinista elite regarding what democracy looked like in practice: "During the struggle against Somoza we never developed a conceptual understanding of the type of society we wanted . . . there was only a debate over the method of struggle we would employ. So we had not defined a priori a concept of democracy, and we were not about to do that at the height of a war." Interview with the author.

68. Belli, interview with the author. On the diplomatic snub, see "Fresh Start for Nicaraguan Government," *New York Times*, January 13, 1985.

69. Castillo, "Elecciones y legitimad política de la revolución Sandinista."

70. Bendaña, interview with the author.

71. Mexican Embassy, Sweden, "EMBAMEX to RELMEX," October 23, 1985, reporting on meeting between Ortega and Palme, AHGE SRE III-3966-2; "Reunión Cdte. Daniel Ortega—Felipe González," March 1, 1985, Cuba MINREX Archive, Box 3.

72. Rother, *Global Social Democracy*, 207–10.

73. Letter from Carlos Andrés Pérez to President-Elect Daniel Ortega, January 1985, in Leiken and Rubin, eds., *The Central America Crisis Reader*, 300–302.

74. Ortega Saavedra, *La odisea por Nicaragua*, 139.

75. Carrión Cruz, "Luces y sombras de la revolución."

76. Gilbert wrote presciently about this in 1988: "Inaugurating a constitutional system may be a tactic in the minds of some Sandinistas, but it risks changing the character of national politics. It is now doubtful that Sandinistas agree about what is and what is not temporary and tactical." *Sandinistas*, 179.

77. US National Security Council, "Central America Strategy for the Second Term," and "Options for Funding the Nicaraguan Resistance," January 31, 1985, DNSA.

78. "Say Uncle, Says Reagan," *Time*, March 4, 1985.

79. CIA, "Psychological Operations in Guerrilla Warfare," October 18, 1984, CIA FOIA Reading Room, CIA-RDP86M00886R001300010029-9; "CIA Said to Produce Manual for Anti-Sandinistas," *New York Times*, October 15, 1984.

80. "Memorandum for Director of Central Intelligence from Deputy Director for Intelligence," December 14, 1984, National Security Archive/Understanding the Iran Contra Affair Project, accessed July 3, 2023, www.brown.edu/Research/Understanding_the_Iran_Contra_Affair/documents.php.

81. FSLN director of international relations Julio López Campos participated in Ortega's 1985 meeting with Gorbachev and recalled the experience in a published article: "Nicaragua y Afganistán: Intereses globales y efectos colaterales," *Confidencial*, August 30, 2021.

82. Mexican Embassy, USSR, "Para Secretario de Relaciones Exteriores, Dirección General para Europa Occidental y la URSS," Moscow, May 17, 1985, AHGE-AHD-SRE III-3963-1. Mexican Embassy, Soviet Union, "Memorándum de Conversación," Moscow, April 23, 1985, AHGE-AHD-SRE III-3962-1.

83. SRE Dirección General para América del Norte, "Memorándum para Información Superior: Evolución reciente de las relaciones entre Washington y Managua," Mexico City, AHGE-AHD-SRE III-3964-1.

84. "Reunión del Cro. Sergio Ramirez y Carlos Andrés Pérez con la presencia de Manuel Ulloa," July 29, 1985, Sergio Ramírez Papers, Box 62, Folder 8b.

85. "Mensaje de Caraballeda para la paz, seguridad, y la democracia," Caraballeda, Venezuela, January 12, 1986.

86. Amnesty International, "Annual Report 1986," January 1, 1986, 179–80, accessed October 13, 2023, https://www.amnesty.org/en/documents/pol10/0003/1986/en/. On Sandinista state security, see Kruijt, *Guerrillas*, 109.

87. "Rights Report on Nicaragua Cites Recent Rebel Activities," *New York Times*, March 6, 1985; Washington Office on Latin America, "Abuses against Civilians by Counterrevolutionaries in Nicaragua," 1985, accessed July 3, 2023, www.wola.org/abuses-against-civilians-by-counterrevolutionaries-in-nicaragua-1985/.

Chapter 7

1. Luis Guillermo Solís, interview with the author.

2. Ricardo Valero, interview with the author.

3. Óscar Arias Sánchez, Nobel Acceptance Speech, Oslo, December 10, 1987, accessed July 3, 2023, www.nobelprize.org/prizes/peace/1987/arias/acceptance-speech/.

4. Booth, "Vote of Confidence," 12–15.

5. Domínguez, "Democratic Transitions in Central America and Panama," 11.

6. Schultz, *Turmoil and Triumph*, 961.

7. Rother, *Global Social Democracy*, 226–28.

8. The constituent factions were the Fuerzas Armadas Revolucionarias (FAR, founded in the early 1960s), Organización Revolucionaria del Pueblo en Armas (ORPA, founded 1979), Partido Guatemalteco del Trabajo (PGT, the Moscow-line communist party founded in 1949), and the Ejercito Guerrillero de los Pobres (EGP, founded 1972).

9. Menchú, *Me llamo Rigoberta Menchú*.

10. See Torres Rivas, *Revoluciones sin cambios revolucionarios*, 426–70.

11. Former defense minister Hector Alejandro Gramajo Morales provides the military's perspective in "Political Transition in Guatemala, 1980–1990."

12. Quoted in "La difícil herencia de Vincio Cerezo," *El País*, December 10, 1985.

13. See Rouquié, *Guerras y paz en América Central*, 281.

14. "My campaign flag was peace in Central America, to struggle for a negotiated solution to the Central American conflicts." Óscar Arias Sánchez, interview with the author.

15. Leogrande, *Our Own Backyard*, 507.

16. "Declaración de Esquipulas," in Córdova and Benites Manaut, eds., *La Paz en Centroamérica*, 279–80.

17. Rouquié, *Guerras y paz en América Central*, 283.

18. "Memorandum from Vice-President Sergio Ramírez to President Daniel Ortega S." ("Asunto: Reunión de Vice Presidentes en Guatemala), May 3, 1986, Sergio Ramírez Papers, Box 62, Folder 13.

19. "Declaration of Panama," June 1986, DNSA.

20. "Poll Shows Confusion on Aid to Contras," *New York Times*, April 15, 1986. The poll also found widespread confusion: "only 38 percent knew that Washington was supporting the guerrillas and not the Government."

21. US Department of Defense, "Prospects for Containment of Nicaragua's Communist Government," May 1986, DNSA.

22. "House Votes, 221–209, to Aid Rebel Forces in Nicaragua; Major Victory for Reagan," *New York Times*, June 26, 1986.

23. MINREX Nicaragua, "Algunos elementos que deben ser considerados sobre las recientes medidas economics adoptadas por la administración Reagan contra Nicaragua," Managua, April 29, 1985, and "Memorandum from Paul Reichler and Judy Applebaum to Ernesto Castillo re: the legality of the US restrictions on trade with Nicaragua and the possibility for a successful legal challenge to these measures," May 2, 1985, Archivo Bendaña, Box 1.

24. "Reunión con Senador Tom Harkin," undated, 1986, Sergio Ramírez Papers, Box 62, Folder 13.

25. For related documents, see Kornbluh and Byrne, eds., *The Iran-Contra Scandal*.

26. Castillo, *Gringos, contras y sandinistas*, 149.

27. Kagan, *Twilight Struggle*, 522.

28. "Carta de Sergio Ramírez Mercado a Presidente Daniel Ortega S." July 27, 1987, Sergio Ramírez Papers, Box 62(a), Folder 7.

29. "Ayuda de Memoria: Entrevista del Dr. Sergio Ramírez Mercado con Mohamed Al Kadhafi, Jefe Revolución Libia," July 1987, Sergio Ramírez Papers, Box 62(a), Folder 6.

30. "Reunión con Líderes palestinos," undated, 1987, Sergio Ramírez Papers, Box 62(a), Folder 6.

31. "Carta de Sergio Ramírez Mercado a Presidente Daniel Ortega S." July 27, 1987, Sergio Ramírez Papers, Box 62(a), Folder 7.

32. "Reunión con el Presidente de la República Federativa de Yugoslavia, Lazar Mosjov," July 10, 1987, Sergio Ramírez Papers, Box 62(a), Folder 7.

33. According to CIA analysts, Soviet military aid reached a record high of $550 million in 1986—nonmilitary aid roughly equaled that sum; CIA, "Communist Military Assistance to Nicaragua: Trends and Implications," Washington, DC, December 1, 1987, CIA FOIA Reading Room, CIA-RDP97R00694R000800340001-5.

Military assistance from the USSR stayed at similar levels in 1987 and 1988 as Soviet officials warned FSLN leaders that no further increases were on the table; "Soviets Raise Profile, But Not Aid, in Managua," *Washington Post*, November 6, 1988.

34. Nicaraguan Embassy, Mexico, "Ayuda-Memoria: Reunión del Cro. Sergio Ramírez con el Presidente de la Madrid," Mexico City, May 13, 1987, Sergio Ramírez Papers, Box 62(1), Folder 5; SRE Dirección General para Europa Oriental y la URSS, "Memorandum para información superior," Mexico City, June 18, 1987, AHGE-AHD-SRE III-4202-2.

35. Ferrero Blanco, "Daniel Ortega y Mijail Gorbachov," 38; Eduardo Cruz, "Boris Yeltsin y la 'Perestroika' de Nicaragua," *La Prensa*, November 10, 2019.

36. CIA, "Communist Military Assistance to Nicaragua."

37 Carrión, interview with the author.

38. Wheelock, "Revolution and Democratic Transition in Nicaragua," 77–78.

39. Horton, *Peasants at Arms*, 228–56.

40. Carrión, interview with the author.

41. Ortega Saavedra, *La odisea por Nicaragua*, 151.

42. Thaler, "From Insurgent to Incumbent," 93–97.

43. Cuadra, interview with the author.

44. Lacina and Gleditsch, "Monitoring Trends in Global Combat."

45. See, for instance, Ortega Saavedra, *La odisea por Nicaragua*, 152. Ramírez writes: "Under the circumstances, with the level of exhaustion we had reached, and with warnings from the Soviet camp regarding future prospects for economic aid, the 1990 elections were again the key element in hastening negotiations to end the war"; *Adiós Muchachos*, 193.

46. Wheelock, interview with the author.

47. Torres, interview with the author.

48. By 1988, the average real wage was 20 percent of what it had been ten years earlier; De Franco and Velázquez, "Democratic Transitions in Nicaragua," 98–99.

49. Lankes, "Nicaragua's Hyperinflation," 20–21.

50. Martínez Cuenca, *Sandinista Economics in Practice*, 11.

51. Carrión ("Luces y sombras de la revolución") expands on this analysis: "Basically, we took mixed economy to mean the coexistence of different types of property within the country, which is what happens everywhere in the world, because everywhere there is public property, cooperatively owned property, and private property. To say 'mixed economy' did not define anything. There was no model that explained how those sectors would relate to one another, although it was said that state property would form the heart of the national economy. That was the only thing that was clear: that resources would be prioritized and concentrated in the state-led sector."

52. Ryan, *Fall and Rise of the Market in Sandinista Nicaragua*.

53. "Propuesta de paz de San José (Plan Arias)," February 15, 1987, in Córdova and Benites Manaut, eds., *La paz en Centroamérica*, 317–20; "Acta de Contadora para la paz y cooperación en Centroamérica," June 7, 1986, in *La paz en Centroamérica*, 281–314.

54. Interview with the author; see also Solís, "The Peace Equation," 26–28.

55. Victor Hugo Tinoco, interview by *Envío* no. 413, August 2016.

56. Mexican Embassy, Guatemala, "Comunicado Conjunto emitido por Presidente de la República de Guatemala y el Presidente de la República de Nicaragua," Guatemala City, March 30, 1987, AGHE-SRE III 4202–2.

57. Carothers, *In the Name of Democracy*, 98.

58. "Issue Preview: Congress and the Arias Peace Plan," US Congress, Arms Control and Foreign Policy Caucus, April 27, 1987, DNSA collection: Nicaragua, ProQuest Document ID: 1679092106.

59. "Propuesta de Paz Reagan-Wright," in Córdova and Benites Manaut, eds., *La paz en Centroamérica*, 334.

60. On the Reagan-Wright controversy, see Leogrande, *Our Own Backyard*, 510–14.

61. Arias, interview with the author.

62. Rouquié, *Guerras y paz en América Central*, 286.

63. "Palabras pronunciadas por el presidente de Guatemala, Vinicio Cerezo, al inaugurar la cumbre de Esquipulas II," August 6, 1987, in Córdova and Benites Manaut, eds., *La paz en Centroamérica*, 340.

64. Guido Fernandez, Arias's ambassador to the United States and close adviser, narrates how the signatures were achieved "against all predictions" in *El desafío de la paz en Centroamérica*.

65. Arias, interview with the author. Leogrande, *Our Own Backyard*, 515–16.

66. "Procedure for the Establishment of a Firm and Lasting Peace in Central America (Esquipulas II)," August 7, 1987, UN Peace Agreements Database.

67. Castro's camp "expressed Cuba's full support for [Nicaragua's] policy of pursuing peace in the region as well as the agreements adopted by the five Central American presidents in Guatemala City." Mexican Embassy, Nicaragua, "Presentación: Relaciones Nicaragua-Centroamérica," Managua, August 19, 1987, AHGE-AHD-SRE III-4283-1.

68. "Comunicado Conjunto y Acta de Instalación de la Primera Reunión de la Comisión Ejecutiva," San Salvador, El Salvador, August 20, 1987, in Córdova and Benites Manaut, eds., *La paz en Centroamérica*, 364–66; "Acta de instalación de la Comisión Internacional de Verificación (CIVS)," Caracas, Venezuela, August 22, 1987, in Córdova and Benites Manaut, eds., *La paz en Centroamérica*, 366–67.

69. "Carta abierta de la comandancia general de la URNG a los presidentes de Centroamérica," Guatemala, August 6, 1987, in Córdova and Benites Manaut, eds., *La paz en Centroamérica*, 337–39.

70. Alejandro Bendaña, interview by James S. Sutterlin, July 29, 1997, United Nations Oral History Project, UN Digital Library, ST/DPI/ORAL HISTORY(02)/B458.

71. Victor Meza, "The Military: Willing to Deal," *NACLA Report on the Americas* 22 (1988): 14–21.

72. Rouquié, *Guerras y paz en América Central*, 285.

73. CIA, "Nicaragua: Domestic and Foreign Policy Trends," February 1, 1988, CIA FOIA Reading Room, CIA-RDPT93T01222R00030014001-6.

74. Pastor, *Not Condemned to Repetition*, 218.

75. "Honduras quiere que la 'contra' se vaya," *El País*, December 12, 1986.

76. "Esquipulas 2 vive," *El País*, August 9, 1987.

77. "Leogrande, *Our Own Backyard*, 516.

78. "Posición del FDR-FMLN sobre el Plan Arias," May 11, 1987, in Córdova and Benites Manaut, eds., *La paz en Centroamérica*, 321.

79. Castillo Rivas, *Gringos, contras y sandinistas*, 263.

80. Calero, *Crónicas de un contra*, 262.

81. "Demandas de la Coordinadora Democrática Nicaragüense ante la próxima reunion de presidentes de Centroamérica en Guatemala, Julio de 1987," in Córdova and Benites Manaut, eds., *La paz en Centroamérica*, 323.

82. Tinoco, interview with the author.

83. Cuadra, interview with the author.

84. Wheelock, interview with the author.

Chapter 8

1. Ferrero Blanco, "Daniel Ortega y Mijail Gorbachov," 31, 41. DRI director Julio López Campos recalls similar advice in "Nicaragua y Afganistán: Intereses Globales y Efectos Colaterales," *Confidencial*, August 30, 2021.

2. "Soviets Raise Profile, But Not Aid, in Managua," *Washington Post*, November 6, 1988.

3. Vilas wrote that Sandinismo "tried to reconstruct the broad anti-somocista alliance from ten years earlier"; *Mercado, estados y revoluciones*, 253; Kagan described the Sandinistas moving back to the strategy of *tercerismo*; *Twilight Struggle*, 623.

4. Wheelock, "Revolution and Democratic Transition in Nicaragua," 79.

5. The Nicaraguan government had ordered the indefinite closure of *La Prensa* on June 26, 1986. See the memoir of executive director Violeta Barrios de Chamorro, *Dreams of the Heart*.

6. Sergio Ramírez justified press censorship in the 1983 *Playboy* interview: "We think freedom of the press is a fundamental right. The problem with La Prensa is that it is not a newspaper that publishes healthy criticism of the revolution. Rather, it is a newspaper identified with interests trying to overthrow this revolutionary government. La Prensa doesn't want to improve our form of government but to replace it with something we consider worse, much worse." "Sandinistas: The Playboy Interview," *Playboy*, September 1983.

7. Rushdie, *The Jaguar Smile*, 48.

8. Letter from Violeta Barrios de Chamorro to Óscar Arias, January 10, 1988, ANCR, Fondo Presidencia, Signatura 4086.

9. "Daniel Ortega asegura que los sandinistas cederán el poder si pierden las próximas elecciones," *El País*, October 9, 1987.

10. "Officials Assert U.S. Is Trying to Weaken Costa Rica Chief," *New York Times*, August 7, 1988.

11. "Officials Assert U.S. Is Trying to Weaken Costa Rica Chief."

12. "Costa Rican President Wins Nobel Peace Prize," *Washington Post*, October 14, 1987.

13. Pastor, *Not Condemned to Repetition*, 217.

14. Arias, interview with the author.

15. Leogrande, *Our Own Backyard*, 522.

16. "Declaración de la Presidencia de la República de Nicaragua," in Córdova and Benites Manaut, eds., *La Paz en Centroamérica*, 440.

17. "Wright, in Shift, Denounces Reagan over Sandinistas," *New York Times*, October 6, 1987.

18. SRE Dirección General para América Latina, "Memorandum para Información Superior," Mexico City, February 15, 1988, AGHE-SRE III-4283-1.

19. "House, by 8 Votes, Defeats Rebel Aid; a Loss for Reagan," *New York Times*, February 4, 1988.

20. See Miranda and Ratliff's book, *The Civil War in Nicaragua*.

21. Kagan, *Twilight Struggle*, 577.

22. Arias, interview with the author.

23. Moreno, *Principio y fin de la guerra de los contras*, 195. US Congressional Research Service, "The Military Situation in Nicaragua," February 4, 1988, DNSA.

24. Mexican Embassy, Nicaragua, "Presentación," March 23, 1988, AGHE-SRE III-4282-1.

25. Cuadra, interview with the author.

26. Quoted in "Danto 88: La Batalla Final," *La Prensa Magazine*, July 4, 2004.

27. "Ortega Denies that His Troops Crossed into Honduras," *New York Times*, March 17, 1988; Kagan, *Twilight Struggle*, 589.

28. Letter from Daniel Ortega Saavedra to Cardinal Miguel Obando y Bravo, Managua, February 23, 1988; Letter from Cardinal Miguel Obando y Bravo to Daniel Ortega Saavedra, February 25, 1988; and Letter from Cardinal Miguel Obando y Bravo to Daniel Ortega Saavedra, March 2, 1988, Archivo Bendaña, Box 2.

29. Quoted by Kagan in *Twilight Struggle*, 591. See also Calero's memoir, *Crónicas de un contra*, 239, 262–65.

30. Alejandro Bendaña, interview by James S. Sutterlin, July 29, 1997, United Nations Oral History Project, UN Digital Library, ST/DPI/ORAL HISTORY(02)/B458, 7.

31. João Clemente Baena Soares, interview by Jean Krasno, November 11, 1997, UN Oral History Project, ST/DPI/ORAL HISTORY(02/S67), 9.

32. Quoted by Kagan in *Twilight Struggle*, 584.

33. Donald Castillo writes: "One of the Resistance's greatest victories, however, was the fact that the proper government of Nicaragua recognized us as a belligerent force and at the same time we achieved, for the first time, the tacit recognition of the Organization of American States, through its Secretary General Joao Clemente Baena Soares . . . something which we had fruitlessly sought over the course of over six years of war"; *Gringos, contras y sandinistas*, 279.

34. "Acuerdo de Sapoá," March 23, 1988, UN Peace Agreements Database. As analysts from the Mexican Foreign Ministry noted, "The mere fact that the March 23 Sapoá meeting took place was a victory for the Nicaraguan government, because in it the counterrevolutionary leadership accepted the current regime as the counterpart with which it should negotiate, and therefore recognized it as a consolidated

and legitimated power." SRE, "Informe: Panorama Political Actual/Negociaciones Para la Paz," Mexico City, September 1988, AGHE-SRE III-4283-1.

35. Bendaña, interview with the author.

36. Bendaña, interview by Sutterlin, 15.

37. SRE, "Presentación: La labor de presión y provocación de la oposición política nicaragüense . . . ," July 1988, AGHE-SRE III-4283-1.

38. In the following months, the Nicaraguan government would make persistent appeals to Contadora to help ensure their neighbors' good-faith implementation of the various peace agreements; Nicaraguan Embassy, Mexico, "Carta de Daniel Ortega Saavedra a los Presidentes de Canadá, España, República Federal de Alemania y los integrantes del Grupo de Contadora y el Grupo de Apoyo," August 22, 1988, AGHE-SRE III-4283-1.

39. "Aid for the Contras Clears Congress," *New York Times*, April 1, 1988.

40. "Aid to the Contras: Same Debate, Another Vote," *New York Times*, August 14, 1988.

41. SRE, "Memorandum para Información Superior," Asunto: Consecuencias de la gira del Secretario Schultz, Mexico City, July 13, 1988, AGHE-SRE III-4283-1.

42. CIA, "Nicaragua: Domestic and Foreign Policy Trends," February 1, 1988, CIA FOIA Reading Room, CIA-RDPT93T01222R00030014001-6.

43. SRE, "Presentación: La labor de presión y provocación de la oposición política nicaragüense," July 1988, AGHE-SRE III-4283-1.

44. The Spanish Socialist Party's director for international relations, César Mogo, told the Mexican ambassador in Madrid that Spain's support for the FSLN was "not unrestricted; rather, it will be maintained if and when the Sandinistas continue giving signs of a real democratic opening." SRE Dirección General para Europa Occidental, "Memorandum para Información Superior," Mexico City, AGHE-SRE III-4283-1.

45. "Costa del Sol Declaration," February 14, 1989, UN Peace Agreements Database.

46. Baena Soares, interview by Krasno, 15.

47. Estudios y Consultas de Opinion (ECO) poll commissioned by Universidad Centroamericana, carried out October 2–7, 1989, cited in "Nicaragua's Poll Wars," *Envío* no. 103, February 1990.

48. Mexican Embassy, Venezuela, EMBAMEX Caracas to RELMEX, September 21, 1989, AGHE-SRE III-4389-1.

49. See, for instance, Ortega Saavedra, *La odisea por Nicaragua*, 175.

50. In anticipation of an FSLN victory, Assistant Secretary Aronson began negotiating post-transition normalization with Nicaragua's Deputy Foreign Minister Tinoco ahead of the elections; Leogrande, *Our Own Backyard*, 562; Tinoco, interview with the author. On Bush administration and UNO views of the elections, see Kagan, *Twilight Struggle*, 660.

51. "Tela Declaration" and "Joint Plan for the voluntary demobilization, repatriation or relocation in Nicaragua or third countries of the members of the Nicaraguan resistance and their families," August 9, 1989, and "Agreement between Honduras and Nicaragua," August 9, 1989, UN Peace Agreements Database.

52. SRE Dirección General para América Latina, "Resultados de la Gira del Presidente Daniel Ortega por 10 países europeos occidentales," Mexico City, May 26, 1989, AHGE-AHD-SRE III-4388-1; US Embassy, Costa Rica, "Arias on Central America," July 13, 1989, DNSA.

53. Robinson argues these policies undermined the quality of the 1990 elections, and Robert Pastor offers a retort, in *A Faustian Bargain*.

54. "Pact in Nicaragua: U.S. Resists Too," *New York Times*, November 3, 1989.

55. Ortega Saavedra, *La odisea por Nicaragua*, 174.

56. See Leogrande, *Our Own Backyard*, 558–59. Pastor comments on the Malta summit in *Not Condemned to Repetition*, 235.

57. Bernard Aronson, interview by Jean Krasno, October 9, 1997, UN Oral History Project, ST/DPI/ORAL HISTORY(02)/A76, 6–7.

58. Pastor, *Not Condemned to Repetition*, 235.

59. Tinoco, interview by *Envío*, 2016.

60. Bendaña, interview by Sutterlin, 7.

61. Bendaña, interview by Sutterlin, 24. See also Ortega Saavedra, *La odisea por Nicaragua*, 166.

62. Mexican Embassy, USSR, "Entrevista Shevardnadze y Ruiz," Moscow, March 30, 1989, AGHE-SRE III-4388-1.

63. Mexican Embassy, Nicaragua, "Visita Shevardnadze," Managua, October 5, 1989, AGHE-SRE III-4389.

64. Mexican Embassy, USSR, "Posición soviética en Centroamérica," December 11, 1989, AHGE-AHD-SRE III-4514-1.

65. Tinoco, interview with the author.

66. Presidencia de la República, Dirección Nacional—FSLN, "Resúmen de conclusiones de la coyuntura externa: Los resultados de Esquipulas II," Managua, July 29, 1988, ANCR, Fondo Manuel Mora Valverde.

67. Ferrero Blanco, "Daniel Ortega y Mijail Gorbachov," 44–45.

68. Carrión, interview with the author: "We saw [the agreement to hold elections] as a way of surviving. A mechanism for the survival of the Revolution, which in the conditions we found ourselves in—although we never said it explicitly—we all knew that if things continued that way we were headed for disaster."

69. Martínez Cuenca, *Sandinista Economics in Practice*, 74. GDP per capita figures cited by Vilas in *Mercado, estado y revoluciones*, 211.

70. Gilbert, *Sandinistas*, viii.

71. Martínez Cuenca, *Sandinista Economics in Practice*, 69.

72. Sergio Ramírez, interview with the author.

73. On the rise and fall of the communist alternative, see Pons, "The History of Communism and the Global History of the Twentieth Century," 20–23.

74. Grandin and Joseph, eds., *A Century of Revolution*, 28.

75. Rojas, *El árbol de las revoluciones*, 231–44.

76. Ortega Saavedra, *La odisea por Nicaragua*, 149.

77. See, for instance, Schoultz, *Beneath the United States*.

78. Solís, interview with the author.

79. Chávez, "How Did the Civil War in El Salvador End?," 1785–89.

80. Zamora, "Democratic Transition or Modernization?," 165–79.

81. Chávez, "How Did the Civil War in El Salvador End?," 1796–97.

82. Tinoco, interview with the author. Ramírez recalls in his memoir that "Daniel [Ortega] admitted to President Duarte that there was arms trafficking to the FMLN from Nicaragua; and precisely because that support existed, he said, it should be considered a factor in the negotiations"; *Adiós Muchachos*, 273.

83. "At Coronado, the FMLN pressured the Sandinistas to keep using our territory, and asked for further armaments because they were allegedly 60 days away from achieving victory. But we knew they were wrong and that we should not risk our nation any further by taking such a desperate step. Therefore, we decided with President Daniel Ortega, at San Isidro de Coronado, to find the only way out for the FSLN: negotiations with President Alfredo Cristiani to neutralize the Salvadoran far right and Salvadoran military, which were trying to sabotage the negotiated solution to the conflict"; Ortega Saavedra, *La odisea por Nicaragua*, 170.

84. "El Salvador rompe con Managua tras estallarse avioneta con SAM-7 para la guerrilla," *El País*, November 26, 1989.

85. "Declaración de San Isidro de Coronado," December 12, 1989, DNSA.

86. According to a National Security Archive review of correspondence between Oliver North and Deputy National Security Adviser John Poindexter, Noriega offered to destroy Nicaraguan economic installations in exchange for money raised from US arms sales to Iran. "Pattern of Deception, Personal Corruption, Deals with Narco-Traffickers Bueso and Noriega Highlighted in Declassified Documents," National Security Archive, May 16, 2018, https://nsarchive.gwu.edu/briefing-book /iran/2018-05-16/oliver-norths-checkered-iran-contra-record.

87. Grant, *Operation Just Cause and the U.S. Policy Process*.

88. Greg Grandin, "How Our 1989 Invasion of Panama Explains the Current U.S. Foreign Policy," *Mother Jones*, December 23, 2014.

89. Carlos Fuentes, "Las lecciones de Panamá," *El País*, December 24, 1989.

90. Ortega Saavedra, *La odisea por Nicaragua*, 171–72.

91. Q&A following Plenary Session at Nicaragua 1979–2019: the Sandinista Revolution after 40 Years, Brown University, May 2019, accessed July 3, 2023, https:// youtu.be/UPFJJMyUyEc; see 1:00:00–1:04:00.

Conclusion

1. "Pre-Election Poll Shows Ortega Leads," *Washington Post*, February 21, 1990.

2. Marenco, interview by *Envío*, 2008.

3. "Ofensiva final Sandinista para ganar los comicios," *El País*, February 21, 1990.

4. Ramírez, *Adiós Muchachos*, 193–94. Luis Carrión, interview with the author: "We thought that we were going to win. And that if we won in elections in which the Contra participated, the legitimacy would be indisputable, and we would have defeated the military strategy of the overthrow of the Sandinista Revolution. And that after that point we might be able to rule positively."

5. "Ortega Concedes Defeat in Nicaraguan Vote," *Washington Post*, February 27, 1990.

6. "El día después de las elecciones de 1990: La derrota del FSLN," *La Prensa,* September 25, 2016.

7. Carrión, interview with the author.

8. Cardenal, *La revolución perdida,* 581.

9. Lacayo, *La difícil transición nicaragüense.*

10. Ramírez, *Adiós Muchachos,* 76–77.

11. Cardenal, *La revolución perdida,* 95: "The Revolution's principal accomplishment was democracy. Although that was not what the revolution, of socialist inclination, had proposed first of all." See also Vilas, *Mercado, estados y revoluciones,* 279; Rouquié, *Guerras y paz en América Central,* 305–11; Castañeda, *Utopia Unarmed.*

12. "The consensus was to accept defeat and to immediately begin preparing the transition in an orderly manner. The tactical game turned into a fair game." Ramírez, *Adiós Muchachos,* 199.

13. Ramírez, *Adiós Muchachos,* 76.

14. Wheelock added: "In accepting the election results, not only did the FSLN take a step toward achieving peace, but it reaffirmed its long standing (pre-1979) goal of creating an opportunity for democratic development with social equality in Nicaragua in the wake of the Somoza dictatorship. Sandinismo lost the battle over the election, but nonetheless it won the real war—the achievement of peace"; "Revolution and Democratic Transition in Nicaragua," 74, 83.

15. Humberto Ortega, interview by Andrés Oppenheimer, *Oppenheimer Presenta,* CNN en Español, July 20, 2021. See also his book, *La odisea por Nicaragua,* where he frames the revolutionary period as part of a cyclical, historical struggle toward liberal democracy.

16. Carrión, interview with the author.

17. My thanks to Daniel Kent Carrasco and Gerardo Sánchez Nateras for helping me arrive at the word "crepuscular" to describe the Nicaraguan Revolution's place in history.

18. For a balanced assessment, see Close, "The Sandinistas and Nicaragua since 1979," 7.

19. Paraphrased by Sergio Ramírez in *Adiós Muchachos,* 159.

20. The FSLN's campaign song "El gallo ennavajado" likened Ortega to a fighting gamecock strapped with razorblades. Historian Margarita Vannini called the fighting gamecock "a concentrated expression of *machista* violence" ("Las conflictivas memorias de la Revolución Sandinista"). Gioconda Belli recalls that "[In the insurrection] participation by women was widely accepted. Once the revolution triumphed, as it happened in Algeria and in many other revolutions, they tried to marginalize women." Gioconda Belli, interview with the author. Belli added: "I see machismo and arrogance in the way in which we confronted the United States— that defiant stance, which was also very attractive to the outside world. Of course, it was such a small country, thumbing its nose at the United States; I'm sure many people enjoyed that. . . . And the Nicaraguan people themselves enjoyed it, but at the same time, it was a very costly thrill."

21. For a history of how this debate played out in international leftist circles (and a thoughtful contribution in its own right), see La Botz, *What Went Wrong?*

22. Vilas, *Mercado, estados y revoluciones*, 257.

23. IPADE, "Por qué perdió el FSLN las elecciones?" Managua, August 21, 1990, Archivo Bendaña, Box 2. Castañeda echoes this analysis in *Utopia Unarmed*, 112.

24. "Sandinistas: The Playboy Interview," *Playboy*, September 1983.

25. Tinoco, interview with the author.

26. Ferrero Blanco, "Daniel Ortega y Mijail Gorbachov," 31.

27. See Milanovic, *Capitalism, Alone.*

28. William Robinson, "Capitalist Development in Nicaragua and the Mirage of the Left," *Truthout*, May 18, 2018.

29. Vilas, *Mercado, estados y revoluciones*, 3.

30. Arnson, *Crossroads*, 279.

31. Grandin, *Empire's Workshop*, 60.

32. Rother, *Global Social Democracy*, 153.

33. Quoted in Pastor, *Not Condemned to Repetition*, 262.

34. Quoted in Castañeda, *Utopia Unarmed*, 4.

35. Joaquín Chávez similarly argues that "the collapse of the Soviet Union and to a lesser extent the 1990 Sandinista electoral defeat" informed the metamorphosis of left intellectuals in El Salvador; *Poets and Prophets*, 239.

36. Chávez, "How Did the Civil War in El Salvador End?"

37. Joaquín Villalobos, "De la frustración al fracaso," *Nexos*, December 1, 2018.

38. See Sprenkels, *After Insurgency.*

39. Torres Rivas, *Revoluciones sin cambios revolucionarios*, 426–70.

40. Torres Rivas, *Revoluciones sin cambios revolucionarios*, 479.

41. Boussard, "Crafting Democracy," 154–80; Edelberto Torres Rivas, "Las democracias malas de centroamérica. Para entender lo de Honduras, una introducción a Centroamérica," *Nueva Sociedad*, March–April 2010.

42. Torres Calderón, *Honduras*, 16.

43. On these transitions, see Sunkel, "Development and Regional Integration in Latin America."

44. Lee, *The Ends of Modernization.*

45. See, for example, Helm, "Booming Solidarity"; van Ommen, "The Sandinista Revolution in the Netherlands"; Perla, "Heirs of Sandino."

46. Bendaña, interview with the author.

47. Tinoco, interview by *Envío*, 2016.

48. Castañeda notes that the Sandinistas' participation in the 1990 elections "opened up two cans of worms for the Cubans: the possibility of losing power at the ballot box, a heresy for any true revolutionary, and the prospect of giving credence and moral authority to the principle of elections if they won, increasing the pressure on Cuba to do the same"; *Utopia Unarmed*, 63.

49. Rojas, *El árbol de las revoluciones*, 244–45.

50. Hagopian and Mainwaring, "The Third Wave of Democratization in Latin America."

51. Mainwaring and Pérez-Liñan, "Latin American Democratization since 1978."

52. Bizzarro and Mainwaring, "The Fates of Third-Wave Democracies."

53. Stella Krepp, "Cuba and the OAS," Wilson Center Sources and Methods blog, December 18, 2017, www.wilsoncenter.org/blog-post/cuba-and-the-oas-story-dramatic-fallout-and-reconciliation.

54. Grandin, "What Was Containment?"; Westad, "The Third World in Latin America"; Juan Gabriel Tokatlian, "El descalabro del sistema interamericano," *Nueva Sociedad*, September 2020.

55. On Cuba's shifting diplomatic relations in Latin America, see Harmer, "Two, Three, Many Revolutions?" and Domínguez, *To Make a World Safe for Revolution*, 225–33.

56. Montobbio, "La crisis centroamericana y la construcción de un nuevo orden internacional en América Latina," 137.

57. "Segunda Reunión del Mecanismo Permanente de Consulta y Concertación Política, constituido por los ministros de relaciones exteriores de los países integrantes de los grupos de Contadora y de apoyo," Campos de Jordão, Brazil, in Ortiz Taboada and Flores Olea, eds., *Relación de Contadora*, 261–62.

58. Frohman, "The New Regionalism and Collective Diplomacy in Latin America," 75–76.

59. Andrés Malamud, "Geopolítica de la pandemia," *El País*, June 29, 2020.

60. Described as such by Sofía Montenegro; interview with the author.

61. Martí i Puig, "The Adaptation of the FSLN."

62. Thaler, "Nicaragua: A Return to Caudillismo."

63. "Los expertos de la OEA denuncian 'crímenes de lesa humanidad' en Nicaragua," *El País,* December 21, 2018; "Nicaragua's govt committed crimes against humanity: U.N. experts," *Reuters*, March 2, 2023.

64. BBC, "Entrevista con la mítica guerrillera nicaragüense Dora María Tellez," February 10, 2023.

65. Jeffrey Gould, "Nicaragua: Una Reflexión Histórica," *Agenda Pública*, June 10, 2019.

66. Friedman, *Ripe for Revolution*, 269–73.

67. Westad, *The Cold War*, 628.

68. Gilles Bataillon, "América Central: Violencia y pseudemocracias, 1987–2022," *Nueva Sociedad* no. 300, July/August 2022.

69. Solís, interview with the author.

70. Pedro Caldentey del Pozo, "América Central: Fin de Ciclo, ¿nuevos consensos?" *Nueva Sociedad*, no. 300, July/August 2022.

71. Levitsky and Way, "Elections without Democracy."

Bibliography

Primary Sources

Archives and Interviews

Costa Rica
    Archivo Nacional de Costa Rica, San José
        Fondo Manuel Mora Valverde
        Fondo Presidencia
    Oral History Interviews
        Luis Guillermo Solís Rivera, San José, February 23, 2017
        Óscar Arias Sánchez, San José, February 24, 2017
        Juan José Echeverría, San José, February 28, 2017
        Fernando Camacho, San José, March 1, 2017
        Manuel Mora Salas, San José, March 1, 2017
Cuba
    Centro de Documentación, Ministerio de Relaciones Exteriores, Havana
        Nicaragua, 1966–1994
Mexico
    Archivo Genaro Estrada del Acervo Histórico Diplomático, Secretaría de
        Relaciones Exteriores, Mexico City
        Nicaragua, 1978–1990
    Oral History Interviews
        Ricardo Valero, Mexico City, September 13, 2016
        Bernardo Sepúlveda Amor, Mexico City, October 10, 2016
Nicaragua
    Archivo Histórico, Instituto de Historia de Nicaragua y Centroamérica
        (IHNCA), Universidad Centroaméricana (UCA), Managua
        Fondo Frente Sandinista de Liberación Nacional
        Fondo Junta de Gobernación y Reconstrucción Nacional
    Oral History Interviews
        Joaquín Cuadra Lacayo, Managua, August 15, 2016
        Victor Hugo Tinoco, Managua, August 23, 2016
        José León Talavera, Managua, August 23, 2016
        Alejandro Bendaña, Managua, August 24, 2016
        Óscar René Vargas, Managua, August 25, 2016
        Gioconda Belli, Managua, January 19, 2017
        Sergio Ramírez Mercado, Managua, February 2, 2017
        Hugo Torres Jiménez, Managua, February 3, 2017

Jaime Wheelock Román, Managua, February 15, 2017
Sofía Montenegro, Managua, March 29, 2017
Dora María Tellez, Ticuantepe, April 5, 2017
Henry Ruiz, Managua, April 26, 2017
Agustín Lara, Managua, July 10, 2017
Luis Carrión, Virtual, July 8, 2022
Personal Archive of Alejandro Bendaña (containing documents from
    Nicaragua's Ministry of Foreign Affairs, 1981–90—cited throughout as
    Archivo Bendaña), Managua
Panama
  Oral History Interviews
    Oydén Ortega, Panama City, January 24, 2017
    Marcel Salamín, Panama City, January 27, 2017
United States
  Firestone Library, Princeton University, Princeton, NJ
    Sergio Ramírez Papers

Online Documents

Digital National Security Archive
  Nicaragua Collection
Inter-American Commission on Human Rights
  Nicaragua, Annual Reports
Memorias de la Lucha Sandinista
  Oral history interviews by Mónica Baltodano
United Nations Department of Political and Peacebuilding Affairs
  Peace Agreements Database
United Nations Digital Library
  Documents and Publications
  UN Oral History Project
US Central Intelligence Agency
  Digital Archive, Cold War International History Project
  Freedom of Information Act Electronic Reading Room
  Woodrow Wilson International Center for Scholars

Memoirs, Published Testimonies, and Journalistic Accounts

Barrios de Chamorro, Violeta. *Dreams of the Heart*. New York: Simon and
    Schuster, 1996.
Belli, Gioconda. *The Country under My Skin: A Memoir of Love and War*. London:
    Bloomsbury, 2003.
Bendaña Rodríguez, Alejandro, ed. *Una tragedia campesina: Testimonios de la
    Resistencia*. Managua: Editora de Arte y Centro de Estudios Internacionales,
    1991.
Borge, Tomás. *La paciente impaciencia*. Managua: Editorial Vanguardia, 1989.
Calero Portocarrero, Adolfo. *Crónicas de un contra*. Managua: Esquipulas Zona
    Editorial, 2010.

Carazo Odio, Rodrigo. *Carazo: Tiempo y marcha.* San José: EUNED, 1989.

Cardenal, Ernesto. *La revolución perdida.* Managua: Anamá, 2013.

Cardenal, Fernando. *Sacerdote en la revolución, tomo II.* Managua: Anamá, 2008.

Carrión Cruz, Luis. "Luces y sombras de la revolución, 40 años después." *Confidencial,* July 19, 2019.

Castillo Rivas, Donald. *Gringos, contras y sandinistas: Testimonio de la guerra civil en Nicaragua.* Bogotá: Tercer Mundo Editores, 1993.

Castro Ruz, Fidel. *La paz en Colombia.* Havana: Editora Política, 2008.

Christian, Shirley. *Nicaragua: Revolution in the Family.* New York: Vintage, 1986.

Cortázar, Julio. *Nicaragua tan violentamente dulce.* Buenos Aires: Muchnik Editores, 1984

Dillon, Sam. *Commandos: The CIA and Nicaragua's Contra Rebels.* New York: Henry Holt, 1991.

Echeverría Brealey, Juán José. *La guerra no declarada.* San José: EUNED, 2006.

Estradet, Victor. *Memorias del negro Pedro: Tupamaros en la revolución sandinista.* Montevideo: Editorial Fin de Siglo, 2013.

Fernández, Guido. *El desafío de la paz en Centroamérica.* San José: Editorial Costa Rica, 1989.

Fonseca Amador, Carlos. *Un nicaragüense en Moscú.* Managua: Departamento de Propaganda y Educación Política del FSLN, 1981.

Gramajo Morales, Hector Alejandro. "Political Transition in Guatemala, 1980–1990: A Perspective from Inside Guatemala's Army." In *Democratic Transitions in Central America,* edited by Jorge Domínguez and Marc Lindenberg, 111–38. Gainesville: University of Florida Press, 1997.

Gutman, Roy. *Banana Diplomacy: The Making of American Policy in Nicaragua, 1981–87.* New York: Simon and Schuster, 1988.

Iruegas, Gustavo. *Diplomacia en tiempos de guerra: Memorias del embajador Gustavo Iruegas.* Mexico City: UNAM, 2013.

Kagan, Robert. *A Twilight Struggle: American Power and Nicaragua, 1977–1990.* New York: Free Press, 1996.

Kinzer, Stephen. *Blood of Brothers: Life and War in Nicaragua.* Cambridge, MA: Harvard University Press, 2007.

Lacayo Oyanguren, Antonio. *La difícil transición nicaragüense: En el gobierno con doña Violeta.* Managua: Fundación UNO, 2005.

López Portillo, José. *Mis tiempos: Biografía y testimonio político.* Mexico City: Fernández Editores, 1988.

Martínez Cuenca, Alejandro. *Sandinista Economics in Practice: An Insider's Critical Reflections.* Boston: South End Press, 1992.

Menchú, Rigoberta. *Me llamo Rigoberta Menchú y así me nació la conciencia.* Havana: Casa de las Américas, 1983.

Miranda, Roger, and William Ratliff. *The Civil War in Nicaragua: Inside the Sandinistas.* New Brunswick, NJ: Transaction Publishers, 1993.

Moreno, Luis. *Principio y fin de la guerra de los contras: La guerra civil en Nicaragua y la última batalla de la guerra fría*. Self-published, 2016.

Ortega, Oydén. *Contadora y su verdad*. Madrid: Rufino García Blanco, 1985.

Ortega Saavedra, Humberto. *La epopeya de la insurrección*. Managua: Lea Grupo Editorial, 2004.

——. *La odisea por Nicaragua*. Managua: Lea Grupo Editorial, 2013.

Pastor, Robert. *Not Condemned to Repetition: The United States and Nicaragua*. Boulder, CO: Westview Press, 2002.

Pezzullo, Lawrence, and Ralph Pezzullo. *At the Fall of Somoza*. Pittsburgh: University of Pittsburgh Press, 1994.

Picado Lagos, José, ed. *Los amigos venían del sur*. San José: EUNED, 2014.

Ramírez, Sergio. *Adiós Muchachos: A Memoir of the Sandinista Revolution*. Translated by Stacey Alba Sklar. Durham, NC: Duke University Press, 2012.

Rosenberg, Tina. *Children of Cain: Violence and the Violent in Latin America*. New York: Penguin, 1991.

Rouquié, Alain. *Guerras y paz en América Central*. Mexico City: Fondo de Cultura Económica, 1992.

Rushdie, Salman. *The Jaguar Smile: A Nicaraguan Journey*. New York: Viking, 1987.

Salamín-Cárdenas, Marcel, and Judith Millán-Salamín. *Omar Torrijos, Cuaderno I: Nicaragua*. Panama City: Self-published, 2021.

Schultz, George P. *Turmoil and Triumph: My Years as Secretary of State*. New York: Scribner, 1993.

Somoza Debayle, Anastasio, and Jack Cox. *Nicaragua Betrayed*. Boston: Western Islands, 1981.

Torres Jiménez, Hugo. *Rumbo norte: Historia de un sobreviviente*. Managua: Hispamer, 2005.

Urcuyo Maliaños, Francisco. *Solos: Las últimas 43 horas en el bunker de Somoza*. Guatemala City: Editorial Académica Centroamericana, 1979.

Wheelock Román, Jaime. "Revolution and Democratic Transition in Nicaragua." In *Democratic Transitions in Central America*, edited by Jorge Domínguez and Marc Lindenberg, 67–84. Gainesville: University of Florida Press, 1997.

Vargas Llosa, Mario. *Contra viento y marea*. Barcelona: Seix y Barral, 1983.

Zamora, Rubén. "Democratic Transition or Modernization? The Case of El Salvador since 1979." In *Democratic Transitions in Central America*, edited by Jorge Domínguez and Marc Lindenberg, 165–79. Gainesville: University of Florida Press, 1997.

Documentary Collections

American Foreign Policy: Current Documents, 1982. Washington, DC: Department of State, 1985.

Andrew, Christopher, and Vasili Mitrokhin, eds. *The World Was Going Our Way: The KGB and the Battle for the Third World*. New York: Basic Books, 2005.

Córdova, Ricardo, and Raúl Benites Manaut, eds. *La paz en Centroamérica: Expediente de documentos fundamentales, 1979–1989.* Mexico City: Centro de Investigaciones Interdisciplinarias en Humanidades, 1989.

Foreign Relations of the United States, 1977–1980, vol. 15: *Central America.* Washington, DC: United States Government Publishing Office, 2016.

Foreign Relations of the United States, 1977–1980, vol. 23: *Mexico, Cuba, and the Caribbean.* Washington, DC: United States Government Publishing Office, 2016.

Foreign Relations of the United States, 1977–1980, vol. 24: *South America.* Washington, DC: United States Government Publishing Office, 2018.

Foreign Relations of the United States, 1977–1978, vol. 29: *Panama.* Washington, DC: United States Government Publishing Office, 2016.

Kornbluh, Peter, and Malcolm Byrne. *The Iran-Contra Scandal: The Declassified History.* New York: Norton, 1993.

Leiken, Robert, and Barry Rubin, eds. *The Central American Crisis Reader.* New York: Summit Books, 1987.

Ortiz Taboada, Mónica, and Victor Flores Olea, eds. *Relación de Contadora.* Mexico City: Fondo de Cultura Económica, 1988.

Newspapers and Periodicals

Agenda Pública
Barricada
BBC
Clarín
Commentary
Confidencial
The Economist
Envío
Foreign Policy
Le Monde
Mother Jones
La Nación (Paraguay)
The New Republic

New York Times
New York Times Magazine
Newsweek
Nexos
Nueva Sociedad
El Nuevo Diario
El País
La Prensa
Reuters
Time
Truthout
Washington Post

Secondary Sources

Agudelo, Irene. *Contramemorias: Discursos e imágenes sobre/desde la Contra, Nicaragua 1979–1989.* Managua: Instituto de Historia de Nicaragua y Centroamérica, 2017.

Aguilar Camín, Hector, and Lorenzo Meyer. *A la sombra de la Revolución Mexicana.* Mexico City: Cal y Arena, 1989.

Armitage, David. *Civil Wars: A History in Ideas.* New Haven, CT: Yale University Press, 2017.

Armony, Ariel. "Transnationalizing the Dirty War: Argentina in Central America." In *In from the Cold: Latin America's New Encounter with the Cold War*, edited by

Gilbert M. Joseph and Daniela Spenser, 134–70. Durham, NC: Duke University Press, 2008.

Arnove, Robert F. "Education as Contested Terrain in Nicaragua." *Comparative Education Review* 39, no. 1 (1995): 28–53.

Arnson, Cynthia. *Crossroads: Congress, the President, and Central America.* University Park: Pennsylvania State University Press, 1993.

Atwood Lawrence, Mark. "The Rise and Fall of Non-Alignment." In *The Cold War in the Third World*, edited by Robert J. McMahon, 139–55. Oxford: Oxford University Press, 2013.

Avery, Molly. "Connecting Central America to the Southern Cone: The Chilean and Argentine Response to the Nicaraguan Revolution of 1979." *The Americas* 78, no. 4 (2021): 553–79.

Bataillon, Gilles. *Crónica sobre una guerrilla: Nicaragua, 1982–2007.* Mexico City: CIDE, 2015.

Bataillon, Gilles, and Vania Galindo Juárez. "'Los muchachos' en la revolución sandinista (Nicaragua, 1978–1980)." *Estudios sociológicos* 31 (2013): 303–43.

Baumeister, Eduardo, and Salvador Martí i Puig. "Nicaragua: De la revolución estatista a la profundización agroexportadora." In *La cuestión agrarian y los gobiernos de izquierda en América Latina*, edited by Cristóbal Kay and Leandro Vergara-Camus, 287–313. Buenos Aires: CLACSO, 2018.

Bendaña, Alejandro. "The Foreign Policy of the Sandinista Revolution." In *Nicaragua in Revolution*, edited by Thomas W. Walker, 319–27. New York: Praeger, 1982.

Bethell, Leslie, and Ian Roxborough. "The Impact of the Cold War on Latin America." In *The Origins of the Cold War: An International History*, edited by Melvyn Leffler and David Painter, 299–316. London: Routledge, 2005.

Bizzarro, Fernando, and Scott Mainwaring. "The Fates of Third-Wave Democracies." *Journal of Democracy* 30, no. 1 (2019): 99–113.

Booth, John A. "Vote of Confidence: Electoral Democracy in Central America." *Harvard International Review* 17, no. 2 (1995): 12–58.

Boussard, Caroline. "Crafting Democracy: Civil Society in Post-Transition Honduras." PhD dissertation, Lund University, 2003.

Brands, Hal. *Latin America's Cold War.* Cambridge, MA: Harvard University Press, 2010.

Brown, Timothy. *The Real Contra War: Highlander Peasant Resistance in Nicaragua.* Norman: University of Oklahoma Press, 2001.

Carothers, Thomas. *In the Name of Democracy: U.S. Policy toward Latin America in the Reagan Years.* Oakland: University of California Press, 1991.

Castañeda, Jorge G. *Utopia Unarmed: The Latin American Left after the Cold War.* New York: Vintage, 1993.

Castillo, Manuel Angel, Mónica Toussaint, and Mario Vázquez Olivera. *Historia de las relaciones internacionales de México, 1821–2000*, vol. 2: *Centroamérica, 1821–2010.* Mexico City: Secretaría de Relaciones Exteriores, 2011.

Chamberlin, Paul. *The Global Offensive: The United States, the Palestine Liberation Organization, and the Making of the Post–Cold War Order.* Oxford: Oxford University Press, 2012.

Chávez, Joaquín M. "How Did the Civil War in El Salvador End?" *American Historical Review* 120, no. 5 (2015): 1785–89.

———. *Poets and Prophets of the Resistance: Intellectuals and the Origins of El Salvador's Civil War.* Oxford: Oxford University Press, 2017.

Close, David. *Nicaragua: Navigating the Politics of Democracy.* Boulder, CO: Lynne Rienner, 2016.

———. "Responding to Low-Intensity Conflict: Counterinsurgency in Sandinista Nicaragua." *New Political Science* 9, no. 1 (1990): 5–19.

———. "The Sandinistas and Nicaragua since 1979." In *The Sandinistas and Nicaragua since 1979,* edited by David Close, Salvador Martí i Puig, and Shelley A. McConnell, 1–20. Boulder, CO: Lynne Rienner, 2012.

Close, David, Salvador Martí i Puig, and Shelley A. McConnell, eds. *The Sandinistas and Nicaragua since 1979.* Boulder, CO: Lynne Rienner, 2012.

Connelly, Matthew. *A Diplomatic Revolution: Algeria's Fight for Independence and the Origins of the Post–Cold War Era.* Oxford: Oxford University Press, 2002.

Cruz Sequeira, Arturo. "The Origins of Sandinista Foreign Policy." In *Central America: Anatomy of Conflict,* edited by Robert Leiken, 95–110. New York: Pergamon Press, 1984.

De Franco, Silvio, and José Luis Velazquez. "Democratic Transitions in Nicaragua." In *Democratic Transitions in Central America,* edited by Jorge Domínguez and Marc Lindenberg, 85–110. Gainesville: University of Florida Press, 1997.

Debray, Régis. "Nicaragua: Radical Moderation." *Contemporary Marxism* 1 (1980): 10–18.

Domínguez, Jorge. "Democratic Transitions in Central America and Panama." In *Democratic Transitions in Central America,* edited by Jorge Domínguez and Marc Lindenberg, 1–31. Gainesville: University of Florida Press, 1997.

———. *To Make a World Safe for Revolution: Cuba's Foreign Policy.* Cambridge, MA: Harvard University Press, 2009.

Domínguez, Jorge, and Marc Lindenberg, eds. *Democratic Transitions in Central America.* Gainesville: University of Florida Press, 1997.

Enríquez, Laura. *Harvesting Change: Labor and Agrarian Reform in Nicaragua, 1979–1990.* Chapel Hill: University of North Carolina Press, 1991.

Everingham, Mark. *Revolution and the Multiclass Coalition in Nicaragua.* Pittsburgh: University of Pittsburgh Press, 1996.

Farber, Samuel. *The Origins of the Cuban Revolution Reconsidered.* Chapel Hill: University of North Carolina Press, 2006.

Feinberg, Richard, ed. *Central America: International Dimensions of the Crisis.* New York: Holmes & Meier, 1982.

Ferrero Blanco, María Dolores. "Daniel Ortega y Mijaíl Gorbachov: Nicaragua y la URSS en los últimos años de la guerra fría (1985–1990)." *Hispania Nova* 13 (2015): 26–53.

———. *La Nicaragua de los Somoza*. Huelva, Spain: Universidad de Huelva, 2010.

Figueroa Clark, Victor. "Nicaragua, Chile, and the End of the Cold War in Latin America." In *The End of the Cold War in the Third World*, edited by Artemy Kalinovsky and Sergey Radchenko, 192–207. London: Routledge, 2011.

Fitzpatrick, Sheila. *The Russian Revolution*. Oxford: Oxford University Press, 1994.

Foran, John, and Jeff Goodwin. "Revolutionary Outcomes in Iran and Nicaragua: Coalition Fragmentation, War, and the Limits of Social Transformation." *Theory and Society* 22, no. 2 (1993): 209–47.

Friedman, Jeremy. *Ripe for Revolution: Building Socialism in the Third World*. Cambridge, MA: Harvard University Press, 2021.

Frohman, Alicia. "The New Regionalism and Collective Diplomacy in Latin America." In *The New Regionalism and the Future of Security and Development*, edited by Björn Hettne, Andréas Inotai, and Osvaldo Sunkel, 75–92. London: Palgrave Macmillan, 2000.

Gall, Gregor. *The Punk Rock Politics of Joe Strummer*. Manchester, UK: Manchester University Press, 2002.

Gandásegui, Marco A. "La conjoncture centre-américaine et le canal de Panama." *North-South Canadian Journal of Latin American Studies* 8, no. 15 (1983): 101–28.

Gilbert, Dennis. *Sandinistas: The Party and the Revolution*. New York: Basil Blackwell, 1988.

Gleijeses, Piero. "The CIA's Paramilitary Operations during the Cold War: An Assessment." *Cold War History* 16, no. 3 (2016): 291–306.

———. "Cuba and the Cold War." In *The Cambridge History of the Cold War*, vol. 2, edited by Melvyn P. Leffler and Odd Arne Westad, 327–48. Cambridge: Cambridge University Press, 2010.

———. "Juan José Arévalo and the Caribbean Legion." *Journal of Latin American Studies* 21, nos. 1–2 (1989): 133–45.

———. *Shattered Hope: The Guatemalan Revolution and the United States, 1944–1954*. Princeton, NJ: Princeton University Press, 1991.

Gobat, Michel. *Confronting the American Dream: Nicaragua under U.S. Imperial Rule*. Durham, NC: Duke University Press, 2005.

———. "Reconstrucción histórica de la Revolución Sandinista de Nicaragua." *Mesoamérica* 33, no. 54 (2012): 142–47.

Goldstone, Jack A. *Revolutions: A Very Short Introduction*. Oxford: Oxford University Press, 2014.

Gómez, Juán Pablo. *Autoridad/Cuerpo/Nación: Batallas culturales en Nicaragua, 1930–1943*. Managua: Instituto de Historia de Nicaragua y Centroamérica, 2015.

González-Rivera, Victoria. *Before the Revolution: Women's Rights and Right-Wing Politics in Nicaragua, 1821–1979*. University Park: Pennsylvania State University Press, 2011.

Goodwin, Jeff. *No Other Way Out: States and Revolutionary Movements, 1945–1991*. Cambridge: Cambridge University Press, 2001.

Gould, Jeffrey. *To Lead as Equals: Rural Protest and Political Consciousness in Chinandega, 1912–1979*. Chapel Hill: University of North Carolina Press, 1990.

Grabendorff, Wolf. "Western European Perceptions of the Central American Turmoil." In *Central America: International Dimensions of the Crisis*, edited by Richard Feinberg, 201–12. New York: Holmes & Meier, 1982.

Grandin, Greg. *Empire's Workshop: Latin America, the United States, and the Rise of the New Imperialism*. New York: Holt, 2006.

———. "What Was Containment? Short and Long Answers from the Americas." In *The Cold War in the Third World*, edited by Robert J. McMahon, 27–47. Oxford: Oxford University Press, 2013.

Grandin, Greg, and Gilbert M. Joseph, eds. *A Century of Revolution: Insurgent and Counterinsurgent Violence during Latin America's Long Cold War*. Durham, NC: Duke University Press, 2010.

Grant, Rebecca L. *Operation Just Cause and the U.S. Policy Process*. Santa Monica, CA: Rand Corporation, 1991.

Gudmundson, Lowell. "El conflicto entre estabilidad y neutralidad en Costa Rica." *Foro Internacional* 26, no. 1 (1985): 37–54.

Hager, Robert P., Jr. "The Origins of the 'Contra War' in Nicaragua: The Results of a Failed Development Model." *Terrorism and Political Violence* 10, no. 1 (1998): 133–64.

Hager, Robert P., Jr., and Robert S. Snyder. "The United States and Nicaragua: Understanding the Breakdown in Relations." *Journal of Cold War Studies* 17, no. 2 (2015): 3–35.

Hagopian, Frances, and Scott Mainwaring. "The Third Wave of Democratization in Latin America." In *The Third Wave of Democratization in Latin America: Advances and Setbacks*, edited by Frances Hagopian and Scott Mainwaring, 1–13. Cambridge: Cambridge University Press, 2005.

Hale, Charles R. *Resistance and Contradiction: Miskitu Indians and the Nicaraguan State, 1894–1987*. Palo Alto, CA: Stanford University Press, 1994.

Hanemann, Ulrike. "Nicaragua's Literacy Campaign." Paper commissioned for the *UNESCO-EFA Global Monitoring Report*, 2006.

Harmer, Tanya. *Allende's Chile and the Inter-American Cold War*. Chapel Hill: University of North Carolina Press, 2011.

———. "The 'Cuban Question' and the Cold War in Latin America, 1959–1964." *Journal of Cold War Studies* 21, no. 3 (2019): 114–51.

———. "Two, Three, Many Revolutions? Cuba and the Prospects for Revolutionary Change in Latin America, 1967–1975." *Journal of Latin American Studies* 45, no. 1 (2013): 61–89.

Helm, Christian. "Booming Solidarity: Sandinista Nicaragua and the West German Solidarity Movement in the 1980s." *European Review of History* 21, no. 4 (2014): 597–615.

Herrera, René, and Mario Ojeda. "La política de México en la región de Centroamérica." *Foro Internacional* 23, no. 4 (1983): 423–40.

Herrera, René, and Mario Ojeda. "Mexican Foreign Policy and Central America." In *Central America: International Dimensions of the Crisis*, edited by Richard Feinberg, 160–86. New York: Holmes & Meier, 1982.

Hettne, Björn, Andréas Inotai, and Osvaldo Sunkel, eds. *The New Regionalism and the Future of Security and Development.* London: Palgrave Macmillan, 2000.

Hoffman, Bruce. *The PLO and Israel in Central America: The Geopolitical Dimension.* Santa Monica, CA: Rand Corporation, 1988.

Horton, Lynn. *Peasants in Arms: War and Peace in the Mountains of Nicaragua, 1979-1994.* Athens: Ohio University Press, 1998.

Huntington, Samuel P. *Political Order in Changing Societies.* New Haven, CT: Yale University Press, 1968.

Iber, Patrick. *Neither Peace nor Freedom: The Cultural Cold War in Latin America.* Cambridge, MA: Harvard University Press, 2015.

Jarquín, Mateo Cayetano. "A la sombra de la Revolución Sandinista, 1979-2019." In *Anhelos de un nuevo horizonte: Aportes para la construcción de una Nicaragua democrática,* edited by Alberto Cortés Ramos, Umanzor López Baltodano, and Ludwing Moncada Bellorín, 55-78. San José, Costa Rica: FLACSO, 2020.

——. "The Nicaraguan Question: Contadora and the Latin American Response to U.S. Intervention against the Sandinistas." *The Americas* 78, no. 4 (2021): 581-608.

——. "Red Christmases: The Sandinistas, Indigenous Rebellions, and the Origins of the Nicaraguan Civil War, 1981-82." *Cold War History* 18, no. 1 (2017): 91-107.

Jarquín Calderón, Edmundo. *Pedro Joaquín, ¡juega!* Managua: Anamá, 1998.

Joseph, Gilbert M., and Daniela Spenser, eds. *In from the Cold: Latin America's New Encounter with the Cold War.* Durham, NC: Duke University Press, 2008.

Kampwirth, Karen. *Women and Guerrilla Movements: Nicaragua, El Salvador, Chiapas, Cuba.* University Park: Pennsylvania State University Press, 2006.

Keller, Renata. *Mexico's Cold War: Cuba, the United States, and the Legacy of the Mexican Revolution.* Cambridge: Cambridge University Press, 2015.

Kinloch Tijerino, Frances. *Historia de Nicaragua.* Managua: Instituto de Historia de Nicaragua y Centroamérica, 2008.

Kirk, John. "John Paul II and the Exorcism of Liberation Theology: A Retrospective Look at the Pope in Nicaragua." *Bulletin of Latin American Research* 4, no. 1 (1985): 33-47.

Kruijt, Dirk. *Guerrillas: War and Peace in Central America.* London: Zed Books, 2008.

La Botz, Dan. *What Went Wrong? The Nicaraguan Revolution: A Marxist Analysis.* Boston: Brill, 2016.

Lacina, Bethany, and Nils Petter Gleditsch. "Monitoring Trends in Global Combat: A New Dataset of Battle Deaths." *European Journal of Population* 21, no. 3 (2005): 145-66.

LaFeber, Walter. *Inevitable Revolutions: The United States in Central America.* New York: Norton, 1993.

Lake, Anthony. *Somoza Falling: A Case Study at Washington at Work.* Amherst: University of Massachusetts Press, 1990.

Lankes, Hans. "Nicaragua's Hyperinflation: A Political Economy Approach to Loss of Control." PhD dissertation, Harvard University, 1993.

Latell, Brian. *Castro's Secrets: The CIA and Cuba's Intelligence Machine*. London: Palgrave Macmillan, 2012.

Lee, David. *The Ends of Modernization: Nicaragua and the United States in the Cold War Era*. Ithaca, NY: Cornell University Press, 2021.

Lenin, V. I. "The Collapse of the Second International." In *Collected Works*, vol. 21, edited by Julius Katzer, 205–59. Moscow: Progress Publishers, 1974.

Leogrande, William M. "Making the Economy Scream: U.S. Economic Sanctions against Sandinista Nicaragua." *Third World Quarterly* 17, no. 2 (1996): 329–48.

———. *Our Own Backyard: The United States in Central America, 1977–1992*. Chapel Hill: University of North Carolina Press, 1998.

Leonard, Thomas. *Central America and the United States: The Search for Stability*. Athens: University of Georgia Press, 1991.

Levitsky, Steven, and Lucan A. Way. "Elections without Democracy: The Rise of Competitive Authoritarianism." *Journal of Democracy* 13, no. 2 (2002): 51–65.

Logevall, Fredrik. "The Swedish-American Conflict over Vietnam." *Diplomatic History* 17, no. 3 (1993): 421–46.

Long, Tom. *Latin America Confronts the United States: Asymmetry and Influence*. Cambridge: Cambridge University Press, 2017.

Mainwaring, Scott, and Aníbal Pérez-Liñán. "Latin American Democratization since 1978: Democratic Transitions, Breakdowns, and Erosions." In *The Third Wave of Democratization in Latin America: Advances and Setbacks*, edited by Frances Hagopian and Scott Mainwaring, 14–59. Cambridge: Cambridge University Press, 2005.

Martí i Puig, Salvador. "The Adaptation of the FSLN: Daniel Ortega's Leadership and Democracy in Nicaragua." *Latin American Politics and Society* 52, no. 4 (2010): 79–106.

———. "The FSLN and Sandinismo." In *The Sandinistas and Nicaragua since 1979*, edited by David Close, Salvador Martí i Puig, and Shelley A. McConnell, 21–44. Boulder, CO: Lynne Rienner, 2012.

———. "La Izquierda Revolucionaria en Centroamérica: El FSLN desde su fundación a la insurrección popular." Working Paper 203, Institut de Ciencies Polítiques I Sociales, 2002.

Meiselas, Susan. *Nicaragua*. New York: Aperture, 2016.

Meza, Victor. "The Military: Willing to Deal." *NACLA Report on the Americas* 22, no. 1 (1988): 14–39.

Milanovic, Branko. *Capitalism, Alone*. Cambridge, MA: Harvard University Press, 2019.

Monroy-García, Juan José. *Tendencias ideológico-políticas del Frente Sandinista de Liberación Nacional (FSLN), 1975–1990*. Toluca: Universidad Autónoma del Estado de México, 2005. Originally published 1997.

Monteiro, Nuno, and Fritz Bartel, eds. *Before and after the Fall: World Politics and the End of the Cold War*. Cambridge: Cambridge University Press, 2021.

Montobbio, Manuel. "La crisis centroamericana y la construcción de un nuevo orden internacional en América Latina." *Revista CIDOB d'Afers Internacionals* 37 (1997): 131–49.

Moulton, Aaron Coy. "Building Their Own Cold War in Their Own Backyard: The Transnational, International Conflicts in the Greater Caribbean Basin, 1944–1954." *Cold War History* 15, no. 2 (2015): 135–54.

Nguyen, Lieng-Hang. *Hanoi's War: An International History of the War for Peace in Vietnam.* Chapel Hill: University of North Carolina Press, 2012.

——. "The Vietnam Decade: The Global Shock of the War." In *The Shock of the Global: The 1970s in Perspective,* edited by Niall Ferguson, Charles Maier, Erez Manela, and Daniel Sargent, 158–73. Cambridge, MA: Harvard University Press, 2011.

Nolan, David. *The Ideology of the Sandinistas and the Nicaraguan Revolution.* Coral Gables, FL: Institute of Interamerican Studies, University of Miami, 1984.

Núñez, Orlando, ed. *La guerra en Nicaragua.* Managua: CIPRES, 1991.

Ojeda, Mario, ed. *Las relaciones de México con los países de América Central.* Mexico City: Colegio de México, 1985.

Oñate, Andrea. "The Red Affair: FMLN-Cuban Relations during the Salvadoran Civil War, 1981–92." *Cold War History* 11 no. 2 (2011): 133–54.

Ortega Reyna, Jaime. "¿Revolución en la Revolución? La Brigada Simón Bolívar en la Revolución Nicaragüense." *Tzintzun Revista de Estudios Históricos* 71 (2020): 149–71.

Parsa, Misagh. *States, Ideologies, and Social Revolutions: A Comparative Analysis of Iran, Nicaraguan, and the Philippines.* Cambridge: Cambridge University Press, 2000.

Perla, Hector. "Heirs of Sandino: The Nicaraguan Revolution and the U.S.-Nicaragua Solidarity Movement." *Latin American Perspectives* 26, no. 6 (2009): 80–100.

——. *Sandinista Nicaragua's Resistance to U.S. Coercion: Revolutionary Deterrence in Asymmetric Conflict.* Cambridge: Cambridge University Press, 2017.

Pons, Silvio. "The History of Communism and the Global History of the Twentieth Century." In *The Cambridge History of Communism,* edited by Silvio Pons and Stephen A. Smith, 1–27. Cambridge: Cambridge University Press, 2017.

Prevost, Gary. "Cuba and Nicaragua: A Special Relationship?" *Latin American Perspectives* 17, no. 3 (1990): 120–37.

Roberts, Kenneth. "Bullying and Bargaining: The United States, Nicaragua, and Conflict Resolution in Central America." *International Security* 15, no. 2 (1990): 67–102.

Robinson, William I. *A Faustian Bargain: U.S. Intervention in the Nicaraguan Elections and American Foreign Policy in the Post–Cold War Era.* Boulder, CO: Westview Press, 1992.

Rocha, José Luis. "Agrarian Reform in Nicaragua in the 1980s: Lights and Shadows of Its Legacy." In *A Nicaraguan Exceptionalism? Debating the Legacy of the Sandinista Revolution,* edited by Hilary Francis, 103–26. London: University of London, 2020.

Rodríguez, Ileana. *La prosa de la contra-insurgencia: "Lo politico" durante la restauración neoliberal en Nicaragua*. Raleigh, NC: Editorial A Contracorriente, 2019.

Rojas, Rafael. *El árbol de las revoluciones: El poder y las ideas en América Latina*. Madrid: Turner, 2021.

Ronfeldt, David. *Geopolitics, Security, and U.S. Strategy in the Caribbean Basin*. Santa Monica, CA: Rand Corporation, 1983.

Rother, Bernd. *Global Social Democracy: Willy Brandt and the Socialist International in Latin America*. New York: Lexington Books, 2022.

Rueda, Claudia. *Students of Revolution: Youth, Protest, and Coalition Building in Somoza-Era Nicaragua*. Austin: University of Texas Press, 2019.

Ruhl, J. Mark. "Curbing Central America's Militaries." *Journal of Democracy* 15, no. 3 (2004): 137–51.

Ryan, Phil. *Fall and Rise of the Market in Sandinista Nicaragua*. Montreal: McGill-Queen's Press, 1995.

———. "Structure, Agency, and the Nicaraguan Revolution." *Theory and Society* 29, no. 2 (2000): 187–213.

Sánchez Nateras, Gerardo. *La última revolución: La insurrección sandinsita y la guerra fría interamericana*. Mexico City: Secretaría de Relaciones Exteriores, 2022.

———. "The Sandinista Revolution and the Limits of the Cold War in Latin America: The Dilemma of Non-Intervention during the Nicaraguan Crisis, 1977–78." *Cold War History* 18, no. 2 (2018): 111–29.

Saravia-Matus, Silvia, and Jimmy Saravia-Matus. "Agrarian Reform: Theory and Practice. The Nicaraguan Experience." *Encuentro: Revista Académica de la Universidad Centroamericana* 84 (2009): 21–43.

Schmidli, William Michael. "'The Most Sophisticated Intervention We Have Seen': The Carter Administration and the Nicaraguan Crisis, 1978–1979." *Diplomacy & Statecraft* 23, no. 1 (2012): 66–86.

Schoultz, Lars. *Beneath the United States: A History of U.S. Policy toward Latin America*. Cambridge, MA: Harvard University Press, 1998.

Selbin, Eric. *Modern Latin American Revolutions*. Boulder, CO: Westview Press, 1999.

Sierakowski, Robert. *Sandinistas: A Moral History*. South Bend, IN: University of Notre Dame Press, 2020.

Skocpol, Theda. *States and Social Revolutions: A Comparative Analysis of France, Russia, and China*. Cambridge: Cambridge University Press, 1979.

Solís, Luis Guillermo. "The Peace Equation: The Need for Further Regional Cooperation." *Harvard International Review* 17, no. 2 (1995): 26–62.

Soto, Fernanda. *Ventanas en la memoria: Recuerdos de la Revolución en la frontera agrícola*. Managua: Universidad Centroamericana, 2011.

Spalding, Rose. *Capitalists and Revolution in Nicaragua*. Chapel Hill: University of North Carolina Press, 1994.

———. "Los empresarios y el estado posrevolucionario: El reordenamiento de las élites y la nueva estrategia de colaboración en Nicaragua." *Anuario de Estudios Centroamericanos* 43 (2017): 149–88.

——. "Poverty Politics." In *The Sandinistas and Nicaragua since 1979*, edited by David Close, Salvador Martí i Puig, and Shelley A. McConnell, 215–44. Boulder, CO: Lynne Rienner, 2012.

Sprenkels, Ralph. *After Insurgency: Revolution and Electoral Politics in El Salvador.* South Bend, IN: University of Notre Dame Press, 2018.

Storkmann, Klaus. "East German Military Aid to the Sandinista Government of Nicaragua, 1979–1990." *Journal of Cold War Studies* 16, no. 2 (2014): 56–76.

Sunkel, Osvaldo. "Development and Regional Integration in Latin America: Another Chance for an Unfulfilled Promise." In *The New Regionalism and the Future of Security and Development*, edited by Björn Hettne, Andréas Inotai, and Osvaldo Sunkel, 50–74. London: Palgrave Macmillan, 2000.

Thaler, Kai M. "Ideology, Perception, and Strategic Decision-Making in a Revolutionary State: Mistakes and Adjustment in FSLN Security Policy in Nicaragua." Paper prepared for the 2018 Latin American Studies Association Annual Meeting, May 23, 2018, Barcelona.

——. "From Insurgent to Incumbent: State Building and Service Provision after Rebel Victory in Civil Wars." PhD dissertation, Harvard University, 2018.

——. "Nicaragua: A Return to Caudillismo." *Journal of Democracy* 28, no. 2 (2017): 157–69.

Torres Calderón, Manuel. *Honduras: La transición inconclusa hacia la democracia, 1981–2009.* Tegucigalpa: Ediciones Subirana, 2011.

Torres Rivas, Edelberto. *Revoluciones sin cambios revolucionarios: Ensayos sobre la crisis en Centroamérica.* Guatemala City: F&G Editores, 2013.

Toussaint Ribot, Mónica. "La política exterior de México hacia Centroamérica en la década de los ochenta: Un balance ex-post-facto." *Revista Mexicana de Ciencias Políticas y Sociales* 40, no. 161 (1995): 109–34.

van Ommen, Eline. "'Challenging the Monroe Doctrine': The Sandinista Revolution and Western Europe." Paper delivered at the conference on International, Transnational, and Global Histories of the Nicaraguan Revolution, 1977–1990, May 15, 2019, hosted by the Latin America and Caribbean Centre, London.

——. "The Nicaraguan Revolution's Challenge to the Monroe Doctrine: Sandinistas and Western Europe, 1979–1990." *The Americas* 78, no. 4 (2021): 639–66.

——. "The Sandinista Revolution in the Netherlands: The Dutch Solidarity Committees and Nicaragua." *Naveg@merica* 17 (2016).

Vanden, Harry, and Gary Prevost. *Democracy and Socialism in Sandinista Nicaragua.* Boulder, CO: Lynne Rienner, 1996.

Vannini, Margarita. "Las conflictivas memorias de la revolución sandinista." *CLACSO-Megafón* 16, no. 5 (2017).

——. *Política y memoria en Nicaragua: Resignificaciones y borraduras en el espacio público.* Guatemala City: F&G Editores, 2020.

Vickers, Robert. "Intelligence and Punta Huete Airfield: A Symbol of Past Soviet/ Russian Strategic Interest in Central America." *Studies in Intelligence* 60, no. 2 (2016): 13–24.

Vilas, Carlos M. "Family Affairs: Class, Lineage and Politics in Contemporary Nicaragua." *Journal of Latin American Studies* 24, no. 2 (1992): 309–41.

———. *Mercado, estados y revoluciones: Centroamérica, 1950–1990*. Mexico City: Centro de Investigaciones Interdisciplinarias en Humanidades, 1994.

———. *Perfiles de la revolución sandinista*. Havana: Casa de las Américas, 1984.

———. "Sobre la estrategia económica de la Revolución Sandinista." *Desarrollo Económico* 26, no. 101 (1986): 121–42.

Wade, Peter. *Race and Ethnicity in Latin America*. London: Pluto Press, 1997.

Walker, Thomas W. "The Sandinista Victory in Nicaragua." *Current History* 78, no. 454 (1980): 57–61.

Walter, Knut. *The Regime of Anastasio Somoza, 1936–1956*. Chapel Hill: University of North Carolina Press, 1993.

Westad, Odd Arne. *The Cold War: A World History*. New York: Basic Books, 2017.

———, *The Global Cold War: Third World Interventions and the Making of Our Times*. Cambridge: Cambridge University Press, 2005.

———. "The Third World in Latin America." In *Latin America and the Global Cold War*, edited by Thomas C. Field Jr., Stella Krepp, and Vanni Pettina, 394–402. Chapel Hill: University of North Carolina Press, 2020.

Wheelock Román, Jaime. *Imperialismo y dictadura: Crisis de una formación social*. Mexico City: Siglo XXI, 1975.

Wickham-Crowley, Timothy. *Guerrillas and Revolution in Latin America: A Comparative Study of Insurgents and Regimes since 1956*. Princeton, NJ: Princeton University Press, 1993.

Yordanov, Radoslav. "Outfoxing the Eagle: Soviet, East European and Cuban Involvement in Nicaragua in the 1980s." *Journal of Contemporary History* 55, no. 4 (2020): 871–92.

Zimmerman, Matilde. *Sandinista: Carlos Fonseca and the Nicaraguan Revolution*. Durham, NC: Duke University Press, 2000.

Index

Abrams, Elliott, 179, 198–99

Acción Democrática (AD) party, 37, 62

Afghanistan, xiii, 102, 135, 139, 156, 166–67, 259n34, 259n39

Africa: Angola in, xii, 105, 166; decolonization in, 2–3, 9, 99, 119, 150; Ethiopia in, 105; and Nicaraguan revolution, xiv–xv, 6, 38, 103, 105, 133, 223

agriculture: agrarian reforms, 8, 39, 66, 92, 243n44, 264n28; Agrarian Reform and Agriculture Ministry (MIDINRA), 128, 181, 254n21; agricultural communes, 92, 129, 218; agro-export sector, 23, 128, 264n28; cotton production, 27, 35; export crops, 27, 129; and Marxism, 29; and Nicaraguan economy, 4, 27, 124, 127–30, 134, 138, 141; ranchers, 130–31; workers in, 35, 87, 91, 110, 128–32, 231

Alemán, Arnoldo, 230, 235

Alfonsín, Raúl, 152, 154–55

Alianza Revolucionaria Democrática (ARDE), 132, 134

Allende, Salvador, xv, 2, 94, 206, 219, 224

Álvarez Martínez, Gustavo Adolfo, 137, 188

Andean Pact, 64, 66

Angola, xii, 105, 166

Arab states, 38, 101, 103, 179

Árbenz, Jacobo, 63, 156, 175, 206

Arce, Bayardo, 26, 58, 86, 110, 117, 161

Arévalo, Juan José, 32, 206

Argentina: and Contras, 131; democratic transition in, 154; and the Falkland Islands, 151; leftist movements in, 47, 61, 68, 97, 137, 206; right-wing

movements in, 9, 64, 114, 125, 152; and support for Somoza, 55, 248n62

Arias Sánchez, Óscar, 171–72, 176–78, 181, 194–95, 201; Arias Plan, 184–89, 204

Aronson, Bernard, 199, 202, 279n50

Asia: China, 29, 100, 179, 214, 227, 229, 236; decolonization in, xv, 2–3, 9, 99, 119, 150, 172, 223; Non-Aligned Movement in, 103; North Korea, 25, 101, 139; Southeast, 60, 156. *See also* Vietnam

Asociación de Trabajadores del Campo (ATC), 87, 129

Astorga, Nora, 100, 112, 258n20

authoritarianism: in Cuba, 24; in Latin America, 37, 149, 154, 224–25, 235–36; in Nicaragua, 18, 23, 28, 193, 198, 224, 231–32, 235; in Paraguay, 96

Azcona, José, 177, 187–88, 195–96

Baltodano, Emilio, 31, 63

Barrios de Chamorro, Violeta, xvi, 66, 193, 200, 211–12, 224

Batallones de Lucha Irregular (BLI), 141

Batista, Fulgencio, 22, 24–25, 32, 38, 252n119; anti-Batista rebels, 90

Belli, Gioconda, 124, 134, 164, 282n20

Bendaña, Alejandro, 97, 100, 130, 136, 164, 187, 197–98, 203, 223, 268n105

Bermúdez, Enrique "3-80," 131, 136, 143

Betancourt, Rómulo, 37–38

Betancourt Doctrine, 37

Betancur, Belisario, 150, 152, 155, 161

Bolivia, 64, 225

Borge, Tomás, 24–26, 43, 71, 101, 108, 112, 253n4, 254n22, 255n30; and GPP, 29, 58 bourgeoisie, the, 27, 54, 92, 94, 123, 127–28, 218, 230; alliances with, 19, 30, 32–33, 41, 58, 66, 75, 77, 80–82, 87–89; bourgeois democratic countries, 138, 204; Chamorro assassination and, 34; Jimmy Carter and, 38; Terceristas and, 32–33, 38, 58

Bowdler, William, 53–54, 69–71

Brandt, Willy, 91, 93, 114, 156, 161, 254n19, 256n63

Brazil, 17, 64, 68, 151, 155, 206, 224–25, 228

Brzezinski, Zbigniew, 7, 36, 51–52, 63, 67, 72,

Bukele, Nayib, 233, 235

Bush, George H. W., 12, 173, 179, 199–203, 206, 209, 211–12, 230

business: conservatives and, 106; corporatist alliances, 27, 230; FSLN administration and, 123, 134, 143, 161, 191, 230–31; FSLN rise to power and, 31, 84, 90–93, 116; in Guatemala, 175; MDN and, 41, 52, 65–66; after Nicaraguan independence, 20; Somoza Regime and, 28, 34

Calero, Adolfo, 158, 189, 197

campesinos. *See* peasantry

capitalism: Bolshevik Revolution and, 145; FSLN and, 88, 97, 103, 191, 205–6, 217–18, 259n38; Sandinistas and, 2, 7, 30, 46, 52; Somoza Regime and, 18, 46; US–Latin American relations and, xv, 7, 9, 103, 119, 125, 138, 174, 232, 236, 259n43

Carazo Odio, Rodrigo, 47; and Castro, 58–60; and Sandinistas, 62, 64, 73, 90, 105, 113; and Somoza Regime, 50–51, 55, 92, 252n124; and the US, 70–71, 117

Cardenal, Ernesto, 31–32, 34, 56, 132–33, 151, 212

Cardenal, Fernando, 30–31, 88

Caribbean, the, 19, 21, 48, 74, 115, 118, 132, 156, 265n49; Caribbean Basin, 7,

19, 37, 61, 116; Caribbean Cold War, 32, 60; Caribbean Legion, 32; Community of Latin American and Caribbean States (CELAC), 228

Carrión, Luis, 4, 58; and the 1984 election, 162–63, 165; and the 1990 election, 211; and the Cold War, 126, 135; and Nicaraguan Revolution, 86–89, 133, 135, 143, 181, 183, 213, 253n16; and Salvadoran revolution, 111–12; and Sandinista foreign policy, 102–3

Carter, Jimmy: Carter Center, 200; and FSLN defeat, 219; and human rights, 7–8, 30, 35, 38, 46; and the rise of the Sandinistas, 45, 51–52, 54–55, 63–64, 66–70, 72–73, 81; and Sandinista foreign policy, 99, 101–2, 105, 107–8, 110; and the Somoza regime, 5, 36, 42, 45, 54–55, 96, 250n111; Torrijos-Carter treaties, 152; and US foreign policy, 7–8, 36, 38–40, 46, 82, 89–90, 98, 138, 246n19, 248n62, 256n57, 258n31

Castillo Rivas, Donald, 179, 189, 266n67, 278n33

Castro, Fidel: 1970s politics of, 105–6; and 1984 Nicaraguan election, 164; and the Cold War, 113, 116; and international affairs, 145, 147, 227; and Latin American politics, 38, 90, 92, 97, 104, 107, 187, 245n86, 247n42, 259n38, 260n63; rise to power, 9, 17, 24–26, 206, 223; and Sandinista foreign policy, 101–2, 276n67; and Sandinista rise to power, 57–59, 61–63, 67–68, 70–71, 75, 247n36, 251n116, 251n119; and Somoza regime, 8, 40, 47, 55

Catholic Church; and Esquipulas II summit, 177, 193, 221; and Liberation Theology, 3, 26, 31, 106; Pope John Paul II, 132; priests, 26, 31, 33, 132, 208; Sandinistas and, 132–33, 208, 230–31; Somoza Regime and, 42–43; the Vatican, 132

Carpio, Cayetano "Marcial," 107, 112

Central America: Central American Common Market, 27; Central American Parliament (PARLACEN), 177; Central American Integration System (SICA), 228; civil wars in, 152, 171–72, 176, 224, 226, 234–35; Cold War in, xii, xiv, 19, 113–17; Contra insurgency and, 124, 126, 131, 137, 139, 141–43; left-wing movements in, 29, 39–40, 47, 62, 64, 213; and Nicaragua in international affairs, 145–60, 165–68; post–Cold War, 218–20, 222–28, 232–36; and Sandinista foreign policy, 98–100, 103, 107, 109, 111–13, 118–19; US foreign policy in, xiii, 3, 11, 20, 22, 75, 81, 152, 199, 227, 239n7; warfare in, 9–11, 13. *See also* Central American Peace Accords

Central American Peace Accords, 11–12, 172–74, 177–78, 184–90, 220–22, 228; after, 191–205, 207–8, 210; Boland Amendments, 178, 268n97; Costa del Sol accords, 200; Costa Rica and, 171–73, 175–76, 178, 184, 194–96; Cuba and, 186–89, 192, 203; El Salvador and, 171–73, 177–79, 184–89; Honduras and, 171–72; 174–75, 177, 179, 184–88, 195–96, 200–202, 210, 221–22; Esquipulas II, 187–89, 193–95, 204; and Frente Farabundo Martí para de Liberación Nacional (FMLN), 186, 189, 192, 203, 207–9; Mexico and, 171, 180

Central Intelligence Agency (CIA): and Contras, 114, 130, 132–38, 141, 143, 147, 162, 166–67, 176, 178–79, 195, 209; and the FDN, 131; and FSLN, 35, 89, 92, 102, 108, 110, 119, 188; and Somoza Regime, 35, 45, 97

Central Sandinista de Trabajadores (CST), 87

Cerezo, Vinicio, 176–77, 181, 185–87, 221

César, Alfredo, 22, 197

Chamorro, Pedro Joaquín, 23–24, 28, 63; assassination of, xvi, 32–36, 243n55;

Chamorro-Bryan Treaty, 20; children of, 31; and UDEL, 28, 30, 41, 52

Chamorro, Violeta Barrios de, xvi; and 1990 election, 200–201, 211–12, 216, 218, 224, 234; and collapse of junta, 82, 85, 87, 90; and the junta, 66, 70, 73, 93; and press freedom, 193

Chávez, Hugo, 13, 226

Chile: Allende government, xv, 2, 94, 104, 206, 219; Chilean communists in Nicaragua, 61, 140; democratic rule in, 224–25; revolution in, 5; US and, 153

Christopher, Warren, 68, 96

Clarridge, Dewey, 134, 136

class, 7, 18, 205, 217–18, 226; financier, 23, 97; lower, 162; middle, 7, 23–24, 29, 35, 59, 86, 97, 118, 128, 131, 134–35, 221, 242n32; multiclass coalitions, 41–42, 46, 66, 74, 83, 93, 132; Sandinistas and, 4, 9, 26–27, 29–30, 34–35, 41, 45–46, 83; Somoza Regime and, 18–19; upper, 23, 26–27, 29, 34, 45, 86, 97, 118, 128, 131, 134, 221, 242n32; wealth, 13, 30–31, 33, 38, 183; wealth redistribution, 1, 4, 82, 118, 125, 190, 213, 218, 236; working, 7, 18, 23, 35, 45. *See also* bourgeoisie, the; peasantry

Cold War, xii, 1–3, 14, 7, 40, 209, 220, 227; Caribbean, 32, 60; Central American Peace Accords and, 172–75, 190; Contra insurgency and, 135, 137, 139, 142–43; Cultural, 94; global, 2, 10, 79, 126, 135–43, 216; in Latin America, 36, 47, 49, 59, 64, 67–68, 98, 145–46, 150, 153–54, 160, 224, 227; new, 214; Nicaragua and, xiv–xv, 5, 7–10, 14, 17–18, 100, 113, 118, 173, 222–23; post–Cold War era, 190, 192, 205, 209, 211, 214–15, 223–29, 232–33, 235–36; Sandinista foreign policy and, 113–18, 151; Sandinistas and, xvi, 38, 49, 63, 79, 98, 126–27, 216, 222–23; Somoza and, 18, 36, 47; superpower confrontations, 7, 10–12, 14, 19, 38, 49, 75, 116, 135, 146, 155–56, 177, 181, 202

Colombia: and Contras, 150, 152, 155; democratization in, 224; Gabriel García Márquez from, 7, 28, 31, 153; and Latin American diplomacy, 64, 253n7; leftist groups in, 47, 56, 61, 224, 247n34; M-19 in, 56, 224, 247n34

colonialism, 20, 88, 150, 175; anti-colonialism, 39, 151; decolonization, 2–3, 39, 99, 150

communism, xii, xv, 7, 109, 114, 259n43; and Central American Peace Accords, 172–73, 178, 186, 188, 192, 206, 209; in China, 179; Contra insurgency and, 125, 137–38, 140; in Cuba, 23–25, 56, 58, 60–61, 71, 94, 113–14, 140, 145, 156–57, 166; and FSLN evolution, 217; in Latin America, 9, 11, 56, 61, 64, 67, 94, 96, 100, 220, 222–24; and Nicaragua in international affairs, 145, 149–50, 153; and Nicaraguan junta, 6, 17–18, 24–25, 31, 36–41; Orthodox, 29, 88, 94, 255n38; and Sandinista Foreign Policy, 97, 100–104, 107, 109, 116, 118; Sandinista rise to power and, 47, 58, 66–68, 71, 73, 75; Soviet, 2, 17, 56, 101, 147, 180, 202, 205, 258n20. *See* Marxism

Consejo Superior de la Iniciativa/Empresa Privada (COSIP/COSEP), 28, 34, 58, 70, 84, 91

conservatives: Christianity and, 14, 230; in Latin America, 126, 152; Nicaraguan Conservative Party, 22–23, 27–28, 87, 106; neoconservatives, 3, 224; Somoza Regime and, 33–34, 42; in the United States, 1, 18, 37, 39, 108

Contadora Peace Process, 10–11, 140, 145, 150, 153–56, 158–61, 165–68; Cancún Declaration, and, 153, 159; and Central American Peace Accords, 171, 173, 175–78, 184–87, 189–90, 207, 209; Contadora Group, 227–29; Support Group countries, 155, 167, 177, 187, 198, 227–28

Contra insurgency, 123–35, 143–44; cease-fire during, 161, 185–87, 191, 193, 195–96,

198, 252n127; CIA and, 114, 130, 132–38, 141, 143, 147, 162, 166–67, 176, 178–79, 195, 209; complexities of, xvi; and end of Sandinista Revolution, 212–13, 218–19, 223, 233; Iran-Contra scandal, 1, 173, 177, 179–80, 185, 198; and global Cold War, 135–42; Manzanillo talks, 157–58, 163; and Nicaragua in international affairs, 12, 145, 147, 149–50, 154–61, 163, 165–67; and September 15th Legion, 131, 137; US Contra aid legislation, 194, 199; US support for, xii–xiii, 10, 13, 118, 124–25, 135, 137, 147, 152, 166. *See also* Central American Peace Accords

Córdova Rivas, Rafael, 52, 87

Cortázar, Julio, 94, 124, 149

Costa Rica, 8; civil war in, 32; and Cold War Latin America, 80, 82–83, 85, 90, 92–93; and Contra war, 134, 137, 142, 176; elections, 11; and Nicaraguan foreign policy, 105, 112–14, 117; and Nicaragua in international affairs, 147–50; Liberationist Party in, 113, 176; and rise of Sandinistas, 42, 47–52, 55, 58, 60–65, 67, 69, 71–73, 75; San José in, 30, 32, 51, 56, 66, 69–70, 184–85, 195, 207; Somoza Regime and, 24, 30, 32, 37, 42; and transitions to democracy, 224–25, 234. *See also* Central American Peace Accords

Council for Mutual Economic Assistance (COMECON), 101, 140

Cristiani, Alfredo, 208, 220, 281n83

Cruz Porras, Arturo, 87, 93, 142, 161–62, 164–65

Cuadra Chamorro, Joaquín, 31, 63

Cuadra Lacayo, Joaquín, 37, 105–6, 111, 128, 182, 196, 261n88

Cuba: 26th of July Movement in, 24; Bay of Pigs invasion, 60, 63, 97, 156; and Contra insurgency, 139–40, 143; Departamento de América in, 104; Havana in, 24, 26, 56, 60, 63, 81, 90, 99, 101, 105, 107, 140, 145–46, 187;

independence of, 20; and Nicaragua in international affairs, 145, 149–53, 157–58, 165–66; Nicaragua as second Cuba, 11, 17, 38, 59, 67, 109, 147–48; and post-Somoza Nicaragua, 82, 87, 92, 94; Revolution of, xii, xiv, 2, 6, 9, 12, 23–24, 75, 79, 81, 97, 146; and Sandinista foreign policy, 97–98, 101–9, 111, 113–17; and Sandinista revolution, 4, 9, 25–26, 37, 39, 47, 52, 56–62, 65, 67, 71–72, 206, 213, 224, 226–27; Sierra Maestra campaign, 25; and Somoza regime, 19, 39, 47; US intervention in, 22

D'Escoto, Miguel, 68, 82, 109, 132, 134, 148, 151, 157

de la Madrid, Miguel, 150, 152, 155, 157, 180

democracy: Democratic Forum, 149; democratic institutions, 219–20, 226; democratic liberation movement, 84; democratic pluralism, 148; democratic regimes, 11, 84, 225; democratic revolutions, 52; democratic system, 114, 164; democratic transitions, 13, 53, 80, 84, 154, 172, 190, 205, 207–8, 213, 221–26, 231, 235; democratization, 4, 6, 87–88, 110, 154, 157, 172–74, 186, 213, 224–26, 235; electoral, 6, 51, 87, 154, 204, 206, 214, 217, 219, 229; illiberal, 235; real, 185; representative, 50, 153, 213; Sandinistas as semi-democratic, 162, 224–25; Third Wave of Democratization, 6, 154, 172, 224–26

Democratic Party, 67; Christian Democrats, 51, 152, 155, 176, 208; Coordinadora Democrática, 161, 189; democratic socialism, 31, 43, 79, 84, 94, 115, 149, 155, 165, 219; in the US, 178, 185, 199

Department of International Relations (DRI), 9, 104, 107

dictatorships: anti-communist, 6, 11, 64, 67, 146, 156; Argentinian, 114, 152; Chilean, 140; Costa Rican, 32; despotism, 47;

50, 153; family, xv, 7, 232; Guatemalan, 175; Latin American, 6, 9, 13, 84, 151, 205, 224; military, 6, 13, 36, 47, 64, 106, 114, 175, 205, 224; personalist, 14, 96, 106, 215, 232, Sandinistas as, 14, 215, 217, 219–20, 231–32; Somoza, xi, xiii, xv–xvi, 4, 7, 18–42, 45–47, 51, 55, 66, 72–74, 96–98, 123, 125, 146, 163–64, 282n14; Venezuelan, 33; Salvadoran, 106

Dominican Republic, 17, 22, 32, 61, 68, 152–53, 156

Duarte, Napoleón, 177, 186–88, 195, 208, 281n82

Eastern Bloc, 24, 99–100, 102, 114, 123, 258n28

Eastern Europe, 172–73, 204, 220, 235; alliances with, 10, 138–40, 142; Bulgaria, 67, 101–2, 123, 138–39, 141, 266–67n81; communism in, 29, 173; East Germany, 138–39; Warsaw Pact, 4, 9–10, 138; Yugoslavia, 180

Echeverría, Juan José, 51, 55, 68

economy, the: commodity prices, 38, 228; economic aid, 60, 81, 89, 101, 130, 136, 139, 156–57, 166, 179–80, 186, 198–99, 275n45; economic collapse, 11, 172, 182, 191, 216; economic crises, 27, 180, 205, 231, 259n34; economic democratization, 88; economic development, 17–18, 127, 214; economic growth, 10, 27, 88, 91, 130, 134, 152, 182, 226, 228, 230, 232; economic reforms, 204, 218; financial institutions, 91, 228; GDP, 17, 27, 88, 183, 204; global, 218, 236; inflation, 183, 203, 205, 268n108; informal, 35; lending institutions, 60, 102, 116, 138, 204; loans, 102, 114, 116, 138; macroeconomic policy, 181, 183, 233; market, 14, 66, 91, 105, 134, 183, 192, 203, 206, 212–13, 218, 222, 226, 236; mixed, 8, 12, 31, 58–59, 63, 66, 74, 91–92, 115, 183, 192, 200, 275n51; price controls, 130, 134, 181, 204, 216; private sector,

economy, the (cont.)
28, 34, 41–42, 59, 83, 85, 89, 91–92, 94, 114, 125, 183, 218, 231; privatization, 12, 212, 218, 222; producers, 84, 91–92, 130; production, 27, 29, 83, 92–94, 128–29, 134, 218; sanctions, xiii, 134, 138, 142, 153, 157, 159, 174, 183, 185, 199, 223; trade policies, 23, 101, 128, 130, 138, 141, 180, 218, 228–29

Ecuador, 64, 66, 225

Ejército Revolucionario del Pueblo (ERP), 97, 220

El Salvador: Chapultepec Accords, 220; civil war in, 111, 116, 148, 207, 209, 220–21, 233; Contra insurgency and, 137–38; democratic elections in, 224–25, 233, 235; and Nicaragua in international affairs, 148, 150–52, 158; Revolution of, 4, 19, 94; Sandinista foreign policy and, 98, 100, 104, 106–13, 116, 119; Somoza and, 65. *See also* Central American Peace Accords; Frente Farabundo Martí para de Liberación Nacional (FMLN)

elections: 1984 Nicaraguan, 160–66, 168, 182, 192–93; 1990 Nicaraguan, xvi, 5, 12–13, 200–203, 208–10, 211–20, 224, 229; 2006 Nicaraguan, 14; Central American Peace Accords and, 190, 192–94, 198; electoral democracy, 6, 51, 87, 154, 204, 206, 214, 217, 219, 229; free, 13, 53, 68, 148, 149, 160, 172, 185, 212, 226; in Latin America, 11, 22, 37–39, 51, 62, 146, 148–49, 152, 154–55, 171–77, 184–85, 187, 206, 221–22, 224; post-Sandinista revolution, 230; Sandinista Revolution and, 66, 68, 86–87, 90–91, 94, 190, 234–35; Somoza regime and, 22–23, 28, 36, 53–54; Third Wave of democratization and, 6; in the US, 108, 178, 226

empire: British, 145; Russian, 145; Spanish, 175; United States, 20, 97, 127, 266n67

Enders, Thomas, 109–11, 117, 189

Esquipulas Accords. *See* Central American Peace Accords

Estrada Doctrine, 37, 61

Europe: British Empire, 145; East Germany, 138–39; Eurocommunists, 94; Hungary, 26, 102, 235; European Union, 227, 229, 231; France, 116, 125, 142, 155, 167, 177, 232; and Latin America, 11, 150; social democracy in, 79, 154–55, 207, 219, 266n58; West Germany, 93, 116, 155; Western, 2, 4, 9–12, 79, 91, 103, 109, 114, 116, 145–47, 154–56, 159–65, 195, 201, 207, 213, 219, 223; Sweden, 155–56, 164; United Kingdom, 151, 154. *See also* Eastern Europe

Figueres, José "Pepe," 7, 32, 49–50, 70–71, 90, 113, 243n51

foco theory, 21, 29, 261n86

Fonseca, Carlos Amador, 24–26, 29, 35

Foreign Ministry, Nicaraguan, 2, 104, 132, 136, 156, 158, 160, 164, 184, 268n100

Forum for Peace and Democracy, 148, 150

France, 116, 125, 142, 155, 167, 177, 232

Franco, Francisco, 61, 96

Frente Amplio Opositor (FAO), 41–43, 50–55, 58, 60, 65, 69–70, 246n19

Frente Estudiantil Revolucionario (FER), 26

Frente Farabundo Martí para la Liberación Nacional (FMLN), 12, 220–21; and Central American Peace Accords, and Contra insurgency, 131, 138; and Nicaragua in international affairs, 158, 188, 220; and Sandinista foreign policy, 107–8, 110–12, 116

Front de Libération Nationale (FLN), 69

Fuentes, Carlos, 123, 149, 209

Fuerza Democrática Nicaragüense (FDN), 131–32, 134, 136, 158, 189, 264n39, 266n58

Fuerzas Armadas Rebeldes (FAR), 27, 175, 273n8

M-19 guerrilla movement, 56, 224, 247n34
Marenco, Nicho, 211, 251n118
Márquez, Gabriel García, 7, 28, 31, 37, 56, 149–50, 153, 171, 247n34
Martínez Cuenca, Alejandro, 91, 183, 204–5
Marxism: Catholic Church and, 132; FSLN and, 2, 24, 46, 51, 88–90, 99, 145, 205, 223; in Latin America, 43, 140, 152, 153, 175, 206–7, 224, 260n63; Marxist-Leninist groups, 1, 4, 67, 157, 166, 198, 260n19; Somoza Regime and, 24, 42; Tendencia Proletaria and, 29; the US and, 8, 10
Mexico: democratic transitions in, 225–26; Cancún; and Estrada Doctrine, 37, 61; Foreign Ministry of, 61, 81, 85, 199, 278n34; Manzanillo talks in, 157–58, 163; a Mexican embassy in Nicaragua, 53, 61; Mexican Revolution, 6, 9, 13, 94, 205–6; Mexican-Venezuelan initiative, 148; and Nicaragua in international affairs, 147–50, 152, 157; Partido Revolucionario Institucional (PRI), 62, 116, 249n69; and Rigoberto López Portillo, 47, 61–62, 68, 73, 79, 94, 115, 117–19, 147–48, 150; and Sandinista foreign policy, 115–16; and Sandinista Revolution, 31, 33, 47, 62–64, 68, 75, 79, 81, 92, 214; US-Mexico Border, 228
Milicias Populares Anti-Sandinistas (MILPAS), 131–32
military aid: Contra insurgency and, 138–39, 142, 148, 157, 167, 173, 178–80, 182–88, 193–99, 201; to El Salvador, 108; to Latin America, 110, 137, 184; militias, 87, 92, 250n92; to Nicaragua, 54–55, 60, 101, 138–39, 187, 199, 203, 248n62
Mitterrand, François, 116, 155
moderates: FSLN and, 8–9, 32, 38, 52, 54, 58–59, 69–70, 72, 80–83, 108, 114–16; in Latin America, 106, 108,

124, 203 251n116, 253n14; "radical moderation," 75; Somoza Regime and, 46, 52; the US and, 64, 69
Monge, Luis Alberto, 113–14, 176, 262n96
Mora Valverde, Manuel, 56, 63, 67, 71
Movimiento Democrático Nicaragüense (MDN), 41, 52, 65–66
Movimiento Pueblo Unido (MPU), 41, 43, 60, 65–66
Murillo, Rosario, 14, 232

National Directorate, FSLN, xiv, 2–3, 9, 58, 66, 70, 73, 80–84, 86–90, 93, 210–11, 219, 229; and Central American Peace Accords, 181, 191–92, 204; and Contra insurgency, 123–25; and FSLN foreign policy, 98 101–2, 109, 117; and FSLN in international affairs, 145, 162–63
National Guard, Nicaraguan: collapse of, 80, 85, 89, 106, 196, 253n14; Contras and, 123, 126, 130–31, 135; former members of, 90, 93; remnants of, 106, 118, 250n109; and Sandinistas, 25–26, 28–30, 32, 34, 43–44, 45–46, 50–54, 57, 60, 65, 67–74, 243n44, 151n118, 252n127; under Somoza, xvi, 5, 19, 22–23, 248n62, 250n111
Nationalist Republican Alliance (ARENA), 208
Nicaragua: Constitution of, 176, 235, 272n76; legislature of, 43–44, 65–66, 80, 84–85, 162–63; Liberal Party in, 23, 42, 219; National Assembly of, 163, 219; National Congress of, 43, 53; National Police of, 106, 182, 254n22; "New Nicaragua," 66; Nicaraguan Armed Forces, 193, 212; Nicaraguan question, 10, 145–46, 149, 153–55, 160; 1987, 12, 133–34, 192, 200, 206, 212–13, 231; post-Somoza, 24, 52, 66, 69, 71, 80, 82, 92, 123, 126; provisional government of, 8, 10, 30–33, 50, 65–67, 69, 182, 227, 248, 252n124n54; as second Cuba, 11, 38, 59, 67, 109,

Nicaragua (cont.)
147–48; sovereignty of, 7, 11, 20, 22, 54, 110, 146, 148–49, 152, 155, 174, 217, 229; state institutions in, 25, 212, 219, 230; state power of, xiv, 6, 75, 93, 107, 118, 127, 171, 193, 220; state security in, 135, 167, 182; Unión Democrática Nicaragüense (UDN), 131. *See also* National Guard, Nicaraguan

Non-Aligned Movement (NAM), 99–100, 103, 152

Noriega, Manuel, 209–10, 248n44, 281n86

North America: and Cold War, xv; imperialism of, 72, 97, 135, 228, 266n81; and Latin America, 98, 124, 244n84; Nicaragua and, 20, 114 136–37, 149, 151, 216, 223, 266n67; North American Congress, 39; North Atlantic Treaty Organization (NATO), 116; Sandinistas and, 64

Núñez Téllez, Carlos, 58, 163

Obando y Bravo, Miguel, 43, 132, 193, 196

Organization of American States (OAS), 38, 52, 61, 227–28; and Central American Peace Accords, 187, 197, 199–200; and FSLN, 63–64, 68–69, 72, 82, 85, 90, 151, 153, 156, 159

Ortega brothers, 30, 57–58, 252n119

Ortega, Camilo, 30, 34

Ortega, Daniel, xv, 3, 13–14, 32–33, 56, 66, 81, 206; and 1985 election, 160, 162, 164, 166–68; and 1990 election, 200–201, 211, 216, 219; and 2006 election, 230–33, 235; after the Revolution, 229; and Central American Peace Accords, 177, 179, 185–87, 191, 194–96; and Contra insurgency, 123; and foreign policy, 99–100, 104, 107, 111–12; and international affairs, 151, 155–57

Ortega, Humberto, 30, 38, 56, 60, 67, 71–72, 165, 202, 206, 208, 210; after the Revolution, 212–13; and Central American Peace Accords, 182; and Contra insurgency, 125, 128, 134,

140–41, 143; and foreign policy, 101, 103, 105, 109, 111–13; and Latin American history, 82, 85, 88–92

Pahlavi, Mohammad Reza Shah, 7, 46

Palestine Liberation Organization (PLO), xv, 25, 104, 137, 139, 180

Palme, Olof, 91, 155–56, 164, 272n71

Panama: Contra insurgency and, 150, 152; democratic transitions in, 225; Panama Canal, 20, 23, 101; Panama Canal zone, 25, 39, 101, 209, 245n84; Panama City in, 60, 69; and Sandinista Revolution, 37–41, 43, 47, 52, 55–58, 69–61, 68–69, 81–82, 85, 93; US invasion of, 209–10

Paraguay, 64, 96–97, 133, 250n90

Pastor, Robert, 36, 64, 67, 101, 188, 194, 202

Pastora, Edén, 29–30, 43, 50–51, 58, 65; rebellion of, 123, 132, 134, 209; resignation of, 92–93, 101

Paz, Octavio, 94, 149

peasantry: in Contra insurgency, 124, 126, 128–32, 135–36, 181, 264n39, 265n48; FSLN and, 29, 31, 35, 90, 118, 254n16, 265n28; middle, 130

Pérez Jiménez, Marcos, 33, 37

Pérez, Carlos Andrés, 8, 31–32, 36–38, 92–93, 199, 201; and international affairs, 161, 164–65, 167; and the rise of the Sandinistas, 42–43, 46–47, 49–52, 54–59, 61–63, 68, 70–71, 75; and Sandinista foreign policy, 114–15

Peru, 3, 64, 124, 155, 206

Pezzullo, Lawrence, 69–72, 90, 108, 113, 243n55

Piñeiro, Manuel, 58–59

Pink Tide, 15, 226

Pinochet, Augusto, 35, 104, 140

poverty: in Latin America, 19, 98, 228; in Nicaragua, xi–xii, xvi, 3–4, 13, 27, 87–88, 126, 130, 132–33, 135, 205, 212, 215, 234, 236, 264n28

Printed in the USA
CPSIA information can be obtained
at www.ICGtesting.com
CBHW032149280324
6039CB00002B/117